VIETNAM WIVES

VIETNAM WIVES

Second Edition

◆

Facing the Challenges of Life
with Veterans Suffering
Post-Traumatic Stress

Aphrodite Matsakis, Ph.D.

International Standard Book Number   1-886968-00-4
Library of Congress Catalog Card Number   96-67798
Printed in the United States of America

Library of Congress Cataloging-in-Publication Data

Matsakis, Aphrodite.
   Vietnam wives : facing the challenges of life with veterans suffering post-traumatic stress / Aphrodite Matsakis. — 2nd ed.
      p.   cm.
   Includes bibliographical references and index.
   ISBN 1-886968-00-4 (pbk. : alk. paper)
      1. Post-traumatic stress disorder—Patients—Family relationships.
2. Veterans—United States—Mental health.   3. Military dependents—United States.   4. Vietnamese Conflict, 1961–1975—United States.   5. Vietnamese Conflict, 1961–1975—Psychological aspects.
I. Title.
RC552.P67M37   1996
616.85'21—dc20
                                                        96-15876

Dedication

From the beginning of time, men have fought each other and have suffered greatly as a result. Their women, children, and other family members have also suffered. To the "forgotten warriors"—Vietnam veterans afflicted with Post-Traumatic Stress Disorder—and to the other unsung heroes and heroines of our country—the wives and children of these men—this book is sincerely dedicated. This author also wishes to acknowledge the sacrifices and struggles of the many women who served during the Vietnam era as nurses or in other capacities.

Goodbye: To My Vietnam Veteran Lover
> I am powerless over you
> Not all my love
> Nor all my sweetness.
> Nor all my desire
> To kiss your wounds
> And give you
> More and more
> Of me
>
> Can pierce your fears
> Your basic mistrust
> Of everyone
> (Especially women)
>
> I know
> You've been hurt
> But is that a reason to
> Act like such a jerk?
> I wait and I wait
> But how long can I wait
> Until you see
> I wait and I wait
> And while I wait
> All I feel is blue
>
> Missing you
> Missing you
>
> "Come in! I need you!"
> You sometimes say
>
> But mainly
> You wall me out
> So you can go shout
>
> About Nam
> General P.
> And your stinking job
>
> You yell at me
> Call it PTSD
> And won't make love to me anymore

from "Goodbye: To My Viet Nam Veteran Lover,"
pp. 129–130, *Anti-War Poems Anthology, Vol. II*,
edited by Stephen Gill, Vesta Publications Limited,
P.O. Box 1641, Cornwall, Ontario K6H 5V6, Canada, 1986

Table of Contents

Acknowledgments

Most of all I want to thank the Vietnam veterans and Vietnam wives who trusted me with their pain and who have often served as a personal source of inspiration.

I also wish to thank Ms. Terry Lord for her interest in the plight of Vietnam wives and for her careful and creative editing of the first edition of this book, as well as the other staff members of Woodbine House who published the first edition of this book. In addition, I wish to thank Ms. Esther Giller and the staff of the Sidran Foundation for making the second edition of this book possible.

I also want to acknowledge many of my colleagues for their professional contributions and their emotional support: Brenda A. Sigall, Ph.D.; Carole Rayburn, Ph.D.; Sherwin Little, Ph.D.; Peter Valerio; William Washington, M.S.W.; and Eileen Stevens, Ph.D.

Introduction

To write about the Vietnam veteran who suffers from Post-Traumatic Stress Disorder (PTSD) is to write about pain, rage, and brokenness, aspects of the human experience which our Hollywood-infected culture is loath to acknowledge. To write about you—his wife—is to write about another kind of pain, rage, and brokenness.

Like your Vietnam veteran, you too have often gone unrecognized, unappreciated, and unacknowledged.

All too often your husband's agonies have been mistakenly seen as signs of masculine failure. Similarly, your dilemmas and sufferings have all too often been misinterpreted as feminine failure. Keep in mind that the same culture which assaults your husband (and other men) with unrealistic images of masculine heroes who can bear unbearable burdens without so much as a crack in their armor, assaults you, a real woman, with images of bikini-clad nymphs who never age and never weep.

This book is about the Vietnam veteran suffering from Post-Traumatic Stress Disorder and you, his wife—people who have had the courage to bear the many scars which life can deal to people who have been deeply affected by traumatic events or by prolonged and severe life stresses.

To all of you Vietnam wives who think that your suffering is unique, I wish to reassure you. You are not alone.

Your suffering is real. And there is help. This book is my small contribution to helping you understand why your family is in such pain and to helping you see what you can do about it. Since Post-Traumatic Stress Disorder, more commonly known as combat stress or shell shock, was officially recognized in 1980, our knowledge of the effects of the Vietnam war has grown. But we still have much to learn. However, it is well known by now that trauma of war can affect not only the warriors, but their wives and children as well.

As one wife explains:

Living with a veteran who suffers the effects of Post-Vietnam Stress is like running blindfolded with weights on. Nothing is easy; the smallest tasks become monumental. Nothing is reliable; the rules change the minute you understand them.[1]

At least 58,000 American men died in Vietnam, but many more are dying emotional and spiritual deaths here at home. In many cases the troubled vet is being held together, emotionally or financially, by a woman—usually his wife. Until recently, the Vietnam veteran was shunned by society. Since he represented a painful episode in our history, he was often rejected. During the war he received bad press and after the war, he was victimized not only by a negative public attitude, but by job discrimination and few government benefits. Many mental health professionals, historians, and social commentators view the ways Vietnam veterans were treated after the war as a "national tragedy."

In an effort to avert the psychological damage and family discord which society's rejection of the Vietnam veteran created, many efforts were made to show support to Persian Gulf troops during and after their return from that war. Many Vietnam veterans rejoiced that these fellow veterans received widespread social support and splendid "Welcome-Home" parades, at least in some areas. However, the tribute given to returning Persian Gulf soldiers also heightened the awareness of some Vietnam veterans of the meagerness of their own homecoming, which often ranged from no recognition at all to outright hostility.

Our nation, on the whole, was more supportive of the Persian Gulf venture than of the Vietnam conflict, which divided the country. While our troops waded through swamps and maneuvered through jungles, the "hawks" and the "doves" fought viciously at home.

The Vietnam veteran became caught in the crossfire between these opposing camps and in many ways has borne the burden of our national shame, guilt, and confusion regarding the Vietnam war. You, as his wife, however, have borne society's burden for him. More often than not, it is you and no one else who has nursed your husband through his flashbacks and nightmares, through his depressions and suicidal episodes, and through his mourning, as well as his rage reactions. Usually it is you and you alone who have maintained your husband's will to live and have served as a buffer between him and the world. At times, you have even served as the scapegoat for his anger: his anger toward himself, his anger toward the government, and his anger toward society.

As one wife states:

Women did not go to Vietnam in great numbers, but great numbers have been scarred by the war. One by one, without the awareness of danger that strikes those who put on uniforms, we met and fell in love with men whose combat experience would change our lives . . . The men of our generation were called to Vietnam: some went off to war, some of them came home. We thanked God it was over. And wearing frilly nightgown smiles, we slept snuggled next to walking time bombs.[2]

Often the veteran repressed his anger and grief and experienced it as depression. In some cases, he tried to make it disappear by drowning it in alcohol or drugs, or becoming a workaholic. In other instances, the vet vented his fury on you by inflicting verbal or physical abuse or both. Yet even when abused by your husband, you often remained by his side, not only from fear, but from compassion, realizing that your husband's rejections of you or his explosions were not solely due to his individual temperament, but due to the frustrations and stigmas imposed upon him by others and by a variety of societal institutions. Intuitively you may have sensed that underneath your husband's abuse lay enormous amounts of self-hate and confusion.

You have sacrificed much. Yet, despite your many sacrifices, you have been treated like a footnote. To date, outside of Vet Center women's support groups, you have received practically no acknowledgment of your pain, anger, or anguish. In many cases, you have been as misunderstood and unsupported by your family and community as your PTSD-afflicted husband. To the extent that he has been perceived as "crazy," you have sometimes been perceived as crazy too—for staying with him, for loving him, and for helping him through his PTSD attacks.

We don't know how many PTSD-afflicted veterans there are still untreated, wandering in our society, haunted by a war that everyone wants to forget. Recent evidence indicates that as many as 30 to 35% of Vietnam veterans have, or had, PTSD or significant elements of PTSD or other war stress reactions.[3]

Since by definition, PTSD is a delayed response to the war, some Vet Centers and Department of Veterans Affairs Medical Centers are experiencing an increase, rather than a decrease, in their case load. Because of the many books and films about the Vietnam war, the return of Vietnamese-American children to this country, increased negotiations regarding American MIAs and POWs, and the resumption of diplomatic relations, more and more troubled vets are beginning to acknowledge being psychologically scarred by their war experiences.

Experts disagree about exactly how prevalent PTSD is; however, several reputable authorities estimate that the number of vets eventually in need of psychiatric help may reach as many as 1.5 million.[4] Based on this figure, an estimated 900,000 Vietnam wives and partners and approximately 1.1 million children may also be affected, not to mention the approximately 4.7 million members of the vet's extended family. Already school and emotional problems among children of PTSD-afflicted Vietnam veterans are coming to the attention of school counselors and mental health professionals, suggesting that the negative psychological effects of the war extend not only to the veteran, but, in some instances, to his wife and children as well.

The numbers are staggering. It is my belief, and one held by many of my fellow counselors, that society is partly responsible for your husband's suffering and yours as well. The unwelcome and in some cases overtly hostile homecoming given your husband and the subsequent discounting of his readjustment difficulties helped to create and solidify his disorder. His problems and yours are compounded by the fact that we live in a culture with an inadequate understanding of human suffering. Our cultural ideal is often that of emotional coolness. In other societies it is, and has been, perfectly permissible for warriors to openly grieve about having been in a war. However, in our society, and in our military system especially, to be emotional is considered a sign of weakness or mental instability. If one is "too happy," "too sad," or "too angry," he may be judged by others, even by some mental health professionals, as being "neurotic" or "abnormal." Yet in other cultures, emotional intensity is the norm.

In such cultures there is no such thing as loving "too much," grieving "too long" or suffering "too deeply." Depth of emotion is not only expected but applauded. Individuals are allowed to suffer without being accused of self-pity or of dwelling in the past. In the face of death or loss, they are permitted to rant and rave and wail loudly for as long as they need to. In contrast, in our society, the appropriate response to loss is often a form of stoicism. One is expected to "get over it" as soon as possible. "Don't cry, don't feel, don't suffer, or, if you do, don't show it," is the message. Yet what here is disparagingly viewed as falling apart or going crazy may elsewhere be considered a normal emotional reaction.

As a result, your husband may have felt that he had to stifle his emotions. Similarly, you may have felt that you have had to keep your feelings to yourself lest you be judged as weak or crazy. Your husband's responses to the trauma and horrors of war and your responses to your husband's PTSD are often entirely appropriate, even when judged by uninformed outsiders to be otherwise. In this sense, both of you can be seen as victims of our society's tendency to look down upon those who are in emotional pain.

Upon coming home from the war, your husband was probably faced with a society that did not want to hear about his pain or his losses. He was blamed for his own plight. If only he was "stronger," he would not be having such readjustment difficulties. Similarly, you were often blamed for your own pain. The notion that both of you were abnormal undercut your self-esteem and probably strained your relationships with your extended family, your neighbors, and other natural support systems. Although you may not be as socially isolated as your husband, you too can suffer from profound feelings of loneliness and alienation.

The construction of the Vietnam Veterans Memorial (more commonly known as "The Wall") gave recognition to Vietnam veterans and helped to legitimize their pain. Following the example of The Wall in Washington, D.C., many localities erected similar memorials. Some veterans feel that these efforts were too little, too late. Yet for many veterans, The Wall offered solace and helped to heal not only the wounds of war, but of the social rejection which followed.

Coinciding with the construction of The Wall were a series of movies and books about Vietnam. All have helped validate the Vietnam veteran, yet many of these films and books simply glorified the action of combat or showed the horrors of war. A few, however, portrayed the veteran's torment in a sensitive manner. Some have even addressed the struggles of veterans in forming and maintaining relationships.

Societal understanding of combat stress has also increased as the result of media references to Post-Traumatic Stress Disorder in relation to the Persian Gulf conflict and to airline crashes, criminal assault, natural catastrophes, and other non-combat traumas.

Yet the image of the "crazy" Vietnam veteran persists, supported by those few cases where veterans have expressed their anger and frustrations in violent episodes widely publicized by the media. More typically, however, the vet with untreated PTSD internalizes his anger and frustrations and suffers alone. Or he may express his dissatisfactions in the context of his family. Yet when his wife seeks understanding and help from others, she, like her husband, often receives an unsympathetic response. Just as few people want to listen to her husband, few want to listen to her. In many cases she is made to feel inadequate and like a failure as a woman because she cannot wave a magic wand and produce a home life as happy as that of Donna Reed or Ozzie and Harriet.

While this book describes some of the harmful effects of your husband's PTSD on you and your children, it is not intended to be yet another betrayal of the Vietnam veteran. Nor does it intend to support any of the many unfair negative stereotypes about Vietnam veterans or otherwise portray the vet in a negative fashion. Throughout the book, the vet's pain and social predicament are emphasized.

Society failed your husband in sending him to fight an unofficial and confusing war and then in denying him the psychological and economic support necessary for adequate readjustment. While today increased recognition and services are being given to him, in many cases, significant damage to his self-esteem, psychological health, and economic opportunities already exists. His PTSD may have already resulted in low self-esteem, anger, and other psychological problems in you and your children.

This does not mean that your PTSD-afflicted husband wants you or your children to suffer because of his war experience, but rather that your family is an integrated, interdependent system. One part of your family cannot suffer without that suffering affecting the entire unit.

This book is based on my clinical experience and research with Vietnam veterans and their wives or partners, who, like you, were looking for help, or were incarcerated or in special treatment programs. The book is also based on a nationwide survey of Vet Center counselors who work with individuals who are in sufficient emotional pain or who are having coping problems of such magnitude that they have sought professional help. There is reason to believe that the majority of women seeking help for relationship problems due to their partner's war experiences are involved with veterans who experience more severe symptoms of PTSD than the average Vietnam veteran. It is my belief that there are many thousands of Vietnam veterans and their wives who are suffering as those in this book have suffered.

While I believe that the numbers of untreated vets is in the tens of thousands, it is important to point out that numerous Vietnam veterans and their families have made adequate psychological adjustments following the war. This book is written for those whose suffering is not yet over and who wish to start the healing.

The book contains my opinions, observations, and suggestions. These do not necessarily reflect the opinions or policies of the Department of Veterans Affairs Program, the Vietnam Veteran's Readjustment Counseling Program, or the educational and correctional facilities in which I functioned as a psychologist.

I have written primarily from the women's point of view. However, there are no "good guys" and "bad guys" in this book, but rather two suffering people who after being wounded severely by external forces and stressed by life's demands have, for a multitude of reasons, had difficulties connecting and at times wounded one another.

In many cases, I have also heard the male partner's side of the story and incorporated that into the book. In cases of physical battering, however, I view the woman as the victim.

In writing this book, I reviewed the literature on PTSD and the effects of PTSD on family life. In addition, prior to the first edition of this book, which was printed in 1988, I polled counselors at all the then-existing Vietnam Veteran Outreach Centers regarding the impact of the Vietnam experience on marital, emotional, and sexual intimacy, on the Vietnam wife's emotional and physical health, and on the veteran's relationship to his children. Only those problems and issues which apply to family members of Vietnam veterans nationwide are presented in this book. In general, the results from the Vet Centers which responded confirm my clinical observations of the effect of PTSD on family life. Since the Vet Center study is general and preliminary in nature, any conclusions must be considered tentative.

Furthermore, the survey was conducted in 1987, many years ago. Some of the results may be outdated, yet only one other study has been completed recently which would provide an updated picture of the veteran's family. This more recent study confirms the fact that PTSD negatively affects the veteran's wife and family.[5] The major inadequacy of both studies, however, is that they do not cover midlife issues or the impact of counseling experiences, the Persian Gulf War, and subsequent wars, such as the Somalian conflict, on the Vietnam veteran and his family.

Clearly more research is needed to obtain more precise answers to the many questions surrounding how PTSD affects wives and children. I hope that in the future other investigators with more refined research instruments will provide us with comprehensive information.

In this book I have attempted to describe the problems and issues facing you in a manner helpful to you. Just as your Vietnam vet husband may feel painfully different and apart from others because of his wartime experiences, you may feel different too. You may think you are the only woman in the world who is undergoing such struggles. Being in a Vietnam wives group, where the effects of PTSD on marital intimacy and family life are discussed, often helps dispel this burden of isolation. I hope this book will serve the same purpose.

◆ ◆ ◆

What it's Like to be a Vietnam Wife

Laura's Story

I was eight months pregnant and sick with the flu when my husband shot the phones, barricaded the house, and threatened to kill the first person in uniform who tried to enter the door. When the postman ran screaming down the block about the "weirdo" acting up again, my eight-year-old hid under the bed crying. That "weirdo" was his Daddy, not his real father, but the only father he had ever known.

Meanwhile, my thirteen-year-old (also from my former marriage) started calling Dave a "baby-killer" and yelled at me for marrying a "crazy Vietnam veteran" and ruining the family. "Divorce him, divorce him," she shouted.

As the wife of a Vietnam combat vet, I have lived through many crises. My husband has suffered from the usual symptoms—the flash-backs, the nightmares, the emotional numbing, and the rage reactions.

Every Fourth of July, Veteran's Day, or anniversary date of the death of certain buddies, I could expect smashed records, broken windows, or another hole in the wall. I could also expect that sooner or later, I would be up all night holding him. For Dave, as for a lot of Vietnam combat vets, anger and sorrow go hand in hand.

In the past 15 years, Dave has held over 20 different jobs.

If it weren't for my working, our family could not eat. In between his "Vietnam attacks," as I call them, however, he is a loving man. But he is scarred, emotionally and physically, and I blame the war for this and society for this also. If it weren't for me, he would have no one.

After 'Nam, he broke off most of his friendships and his family had no understanding of what he was going through. In fact, his father, a military man, only looked down on Dave for falling apart over a war that we didn't win. My family rejected me too. They want to know why, after one bad marriage, I went and married a vet, a vet from "that war."

Over the years I've lost touch with my parents and brothers. I've also lost myself. I don't even know how I feel anymore. Maybe I'm depressed, maybe I'm not. All I know is that I must keep on functioning. My family depends on me. I'm constantly running, from one job to the next, one chore to the next. There's always some child who needs something and of course, I never know when Dave is going to act up again. I wish he would go get help, but he won't hear of it.

So I guess I'm Dave's therapist and most of my life is organized around arranging his life to be as comfortable and stressfree as possible. He simply can't handle pressures and if he goes off, I'll have yet another problem. I am the buffer between him and the world, and at times, his only link to sanity.

I watch how I phrase my every sentence, for if I use even the wrong preposition, Dave might see this as insulting to him. I've also had to limit my friends and outside interests. Sometimes even the children have to take second place to his intense need for peace and quiet and for my attention—when he wants it, that is. At times, he walls me out entirely. We can coexist for days, barely talking, never touching.

In the early years, I did my best to pierce his wall and enter his world. But he wouldn't let me in—because I was a woman, because I hadn't been in 'Nam and therefore could not understand. Now, after 10 years of marriage, I have given up. Now when Dave withdraws, as long as he withdraws quietly, I don't care. It's a relief. It gives me time to get other things done.

Don't ask me what it means to be a woman anymore. My life is too hard, and I'm too bitter, and too afraid of the anger and the pain inside me. I'm also afraid that someday my husband's depression will engulf him—that I will lose him entirely to that sad far-away look in his eyes, to that "other woman"—Vietnam.

—Laura, wife of a Vietnam combat veteran

Anna Marie's Story

My husband was a POW During his nine months of captivity, he saw every horror imaginable and later inflicted those same horrors on as many V.C. as he could find. He has a special hatred for the South Vietnamese, who he felt had abandoned him and allowed him to be captured.

When Bob came home with two b.k. (below knee) amputations, he proceeded to fry his brains with every kind of drug imaginable. For seven years, there wasn't a T.V. set in the family. He was so heavily into drugs, he'd steal from anyone, until, on the verge of insanity, he committed himself to a VA hospital. There he experienced a religious conversion and received the help which got him drug-free.

But some of the drugs he took had half lives. Even today, residues from these drugs trickle down from his brain into his system. At such times, he leaves home to avoid possibly hurting me or the kids. Sometimes he's gone for three or four days at a time. I never know where he is or when he's coming home. Frankly, after several years of this, I'm tired of making excuses for him and of shouldering the load alone.

He needs to do something—take some responsibility for what goes on in our lives.

What Bob was like before 'Nam, I don't know. I met him afterward, while he was recuperating in an army hospital. He seemed kind and generous, and was making jokes about winning dance contests with his new prostheses. I felt sorry for him because he had lost his legs, but mainly because his family wasn't talking to him.

The whole family had marched against the war. Bob's father felt his son got what he deserved in 'Nam. In his view, God had punished Bob for killing people in Vietnam by taking away his legs. One of Bob's cousins had fled to Canada and another had preferred to cut off either a hand or a foot to avoid the draft.

The only person who forgives Bob is his mother. Whenever I talk about leaving Bob, she begs me not to leave her crippled baby, the high school athlete who won every dance contest but who can dance no more.

My mother feels the same way—that I should stick it out because Bob is a good husband and a religious man who works hard for his family and is not cruel in any way. But they don't know the hell of living with a man who is half-dead and who has lost all passion.

Mainly, Bob just goes to work, comes home, watches T.V., then goes to sleep. There's no conversation other than about the house or the children. I can go anywhere I want, see my friends as often as I please, but Bob goes nowhere with me, or with the kids. He can't take crowds or noise. Sometimes he makes it to church, but that's it.

I almost enjoy it when Bob explodes. At least I know he's there. But his rage reactions are few.

A part of Bob is a stranger to us. His war medals sit in the middle of the living room and pictures of Vietnam decorate every wall. But neither I, nor my ten-year-old son and seven-year-old daughter, can mention the word "Vietnam." Newspapers, news magazines, and rice are forbidden, too, as are most feelings. Bob just can't take anger or tears.

They give him headaches and make his legs hurt.

My son is learning to repress his emotions, too—just like his father.

It's like pulling teeth to get him to talk about how he feels. For example, last night Bob was going up to his room to watch T.V. "Can I watch with you, Dad?" my son asked. Bob said no and walked up the stairs. For a brief moment, there were tears in my son's eyes, but he quickly pushed them back. Boys don't cry. That much his father had taught him.

When I tried to comfort my son, he shoved me away. He felt it was my fault Dad was too tired to be with him. If I didn't nag Dad so much, Dad would be okay.

The worse part is that I have to be both father and mother to our son, who wants Dad, not Mom, to be at his games, take him places, and help him with his homework. He interprets his father's not wanting to do things with him as meaning that his father doesn't love him, which is not the case. However, as a result of my husband's distancing, I'm afraid my son is developing an inferiority complex. He's achieving below his potential at school and doesn't socialize much with other children. Most weekends he stays around the house, hoping his father will take him out, which hardly ever happens. I don't know whether to tell my son to give up hope or not.

Discussing these problems with Bob gets me nowhere. If I bring up a family problem, other than a mechanical one, Bob just listens and says nothing. The more I talk, the more he retreats into himself. "You handle it. I just can't take the pressure," he says.

No matter how much I do for the children, I can't be their father, too. I do everything I can for them, yet I always feel guilty for not doing enough. This guilt paralyzes me and prevents me from doing things for myself. I've repeatedly urged Bob to seek help, but he's afraid that going for help would open up feelings and memories that would destroy him.

I'm wondering if things are going to stay the way they are or whether Bob is going to crack up some day. Meanwhile, there are times I feel like a vegetable, emotionally numb, just like my husband. My sexual feelings have lessened also. I guess I just got tired of being the only person who could feel.

When I'm honest, I realize my life is being wasted. But I see no way out. Financially, I cannot afford to leave my husband, and emotionally, I don't have the strength to start all over again. Morally, I feel I must continue to plug it out one day at a time for the sake of my children. They love their Daddy and breaking up the family would devastate them. My leaving would also devastate Bob. After all he lost in Vietnam—his friends and his legs, too—I don't think he could handle yet another loss. The kids and I are his whole life.

—Anna Marie, wife of a Vietnam ex-P.O.W.

Elizabeth's Story

All I want is even one day without the pain, without the hurt. Maybe I wasn't in the Army, but after being married to a Vietnam veteran for 16 years, I have paid my price.

I met my husband two years out of 'Nam. Basically, Big Al is a kind and giving person, but there's another side to him, the angry side. But I didn't see this side until after we were married. Big Al had lots of anger, which was directed at everything and everybody, including me. Just a few weeks after the honeymoon, he would go out and not come home, and he started drinking. He cared about me very deeply, yet he continually ran away from that caring.

I didn't understand what was going on—how he could switch from the good and kind Big Al to the angry one. When he put holes in the wall and had car accidents, I thought it was just the alcohol. But once when he ran into a pole, then went on to hit two or three more objects in the road, I realized that he had a death wish. Yet I never traced it to Vietnam because he never talked about it. We had many problems: sexual problems, economic problems, depression, and loneliness. My husband was a loner. He tended to lose friends easily because he'd refuse to forgive. He withdrew from his parents and began to do poorly at work. At this point, I was starting to become depressed and withdrawn, too. I got sick with migraines and was angry a lot. Yet not being able to count on my husband for very much gave me a drive to succeed at work. Even though I started out a GS-5 secretary in the government without a college degree, I've worked myself up to a supervisory mid-level position and have enjoyed one professional success after another.

I had to succeed at work because I had to pay all the bills. My husband had trouble keeping jobs and there were always lawyer bills, fines, car wrecks, and other expenses. When Big Al would be out all night, I used to wonder if he was dead or in jail. I hate to admit it, but a part of me used to wish he was dead because we couldn't afford any more lawyer bills and court costs.

Even when he didn't come home at night, the next morning I'd go to work and function as if nothing had happened. I couldn't break, because if I did, where would I be? And what would happen to our three children?

I couldn't break, but I did internalize everything and began to withdraw even more. Besides, most of my friends couldn't cope with my problems. If I'd start talking about Big Al, they'd just tell me to leave him, not understanding that with three children, this is not easy. Also, I am a committed family woman. If Big Al had cancer, I wouldn't have left him. In my view, Big Al had a mental disease, not a physical one, and I was not going to abandon him.

Even when he would verbally abuse me, I knew a part of him didn't mean it—that it was somebody else being so nasty, not my Big Al. Besides, leaving Big Al would have felt like defeat and I was a fighter, just like he was. Deep inside, I knew Big Al was a good man and that the only reason he couldn't feel for me was because he couldn't feel for himself. Even when he'd get locked up in jail, he'd be as kind and good to me as could be.

All the while, neither of us suspected Vietnam. I was so naive to it that 11 years into the marriage I didn't even know he had been in the jungles. At that time, society didn't recognize, much less realize, what it was like to be a grunt in Vietnam. When we went to our family doctor and to two or three therapists for help; they listened, but they didn't know about PTSD either.

My children have not been deeply scarred by my husband's behavior because 99% of the time, he is a wonderful father. Also, I protected them from most of their father's depressions. Whenever Big Al would start lying around the house, smoking pot or drinking, I'd take the children out. I didn't want them to see their father unwashed and unshaven. I didn't know why he was acting like this and I'd just scream and yell.

Now when I see my husband not taking care of himself, I know that he has reached the point of depression, and I beg him to go for help. PTSD therapy has helped my husband a great deal, but we still have problems. I have problems too: mainly pent-up anger from years of always having to be strong and responsible. I'm afraid that if someone would put their arms around me, I would start crying and never stop.

—Elizabeth, wife of Big Al, a Vietnam Army hero

Lorraine's Story

My husband slit his wrists in the shower, with one of the knives from Vietnam that he had sometimes used on me. I almost left him after he used me for target practice one night. But I blame Vietnam for this, not him.

Len had been a medic in Vietnam, where he was forced to choose who would live and who would die. He talked about Vietnam night and day, but not to me. He read every book on the subject, but I was not allowed to do the same. Not until the day of his funeral did I find out any details about what he had experienced or why he finally decided to end his life.

At the funeral, his war buddies told me that the week before, Len had made some mistakes on the job. They weren't life-and-death mistakes, but his errors in reading certain lab results had messed up some patient's treatment plan. Len was a dedicated lab technician. He simply could not handle the guilt, not on top of all the survivor guilt he felt about the guys he had had to let die in 'Nam. Len used to hear their voices in the night.

I also found out that Len had gone to great lengths to save a certain Vietnamese family. The family was massacred anyway. Len blamed himself.

Is that why he made my life miserable? When Len was angry, nothing was safe. Furniture flew, curtains were ripped, toys were smashed. The name calling was vicious and PTA meetings, visits to the grandparents, and all shopping trips for the children were cancelled. I could hardly ever take the kids to the movies and we never invited anyone over for dinner.

If I felt a beating coming on, I'd lock the children in their bedrooms, or, if there was time, drive them to my mother's. Eventually, however, Len would wear out and everything would be peaceful. Sincerely repentant, he would shower us with love and many gifts.

I'm sorry Len is dead, but a part of me feels released. I was tired of walking on eggshells and having one anxiety attack after another. My thinking had become distorted, too, as I was always trying to find answers to problems over which I had no control. I was always irritable and depressed and when he'd be gone for hours, wandering aimlessly in the streets, I didn't know who was closer to suicide, him or me.

Not knowing how I could change my life, I started taking valium and then alcohol. When I realized that my drinking was making me neglect my children, however, I went to A.A. and I have been a sober and good mother ever since. But Len remembered my drinking days and my mothering mistakes and sometimes used them as excuses to physically abuse me.

Vietnam was another excuse. Why I had to take the beating for something some lieutenant or Viet Cong did 20 years ago is a mystery to me. But when Len was banging my head against the toilet bowl or smashing my back against the refrigerator, the idea made perfect sense to him. Intellectually, I knew I was not to blame for the beatings, but emotionally I felt I deserved them. It didn't help that Len pointed out everything wrong with me all the time.

Usually around patriotic holidays, or even other holidays, like Labor Day, Len would get into one of his moods and not allow me to see or talk to anybody for two or three days. Sometimes he'd abuse me, but mainly he just wanted me around. He was paranoid about me leaving him. He was also afraid that if I went outside, somebody might hurt me. I'd get so lonely that sometimes I would call the operator just to hear a human voice.

Over time, I became increasingly passive and numb to my own emotions, as well as psychologically depleted from dealing with my husband's Dr. Jekyll/Mr. Hyde personality. He would be the brute one day and Mr. Wonderful the next, leaving me in a constant state of confusion about whether to stay with him or leave him.

Now that Len is gone, I miss him. I think he was basically a good man, but a misguided one. There were times he was so loving, so giving, so charming that he melted my heart. Yet I have trouble reconciling my affection for him with his abuse of me. I can't blame Vietnam for all his problems, but I am certain that if he hadn't been in that war, he would have been a different man.

I have never set foot in Vietnam. Yet I consider myself a veteran also. Most Vietnam vets only served for 13 months. I lived, breathed, slept, and fought with that war for 13 years.

—Lorraine, formerly battered wife of a Vietnam combat vet

Angela's Story

I'm 55 now—finished, drained, and dry. Finished doing my duty—finished with Zak and his PTSD.

The kids are gone. Now it's my turn to live. Right? I'm not too old to start a new life, even if my face is falling. Right?

To go or not to go?—that is the question. Seems like every five years I agonize over what to do. I should have left Zak 20 years ago, when I was still pretty. On my 30th birthday I remember looking at myself in the mirror and wondering if I could put up with one more mood swing, one more outburst at the kids, or one more ruined night out.

But Zak was just starting therapy and I didn't want to set him back by leaving. The kids were young then too, and I knew he loved them dearly, even if he was so irritable with them most of the time.

"He can't help it. It's the war. I'll give him two more years, until he finishes group therapy," I thought. But then I sobbed for two hours.

The two years became three years, then four and five. Counseling helped Zak a great deal, but now he had depressive episodes instead of drinking binges. Instead of yelling at the kids, he'd cry in front of them. Instead of us worrying about him punching a hole in the wall, we started worrying about him shooting a hole in his head.

Therapy had taught him how to stop hurting us, his family, but we still didn't have him.

When I turned 40, I thought about leaving Zak again. His depressions were draining me of all my life energy. But the kids and he were getting along better and I didn't have the heart to break up this new kind of relationship they were having with their father, something they had hungered for for so long. Zak was treating me better too, but it still didn't feel like a marriage.

"You want too much. No marriage is perfect," I told myself. Yet in my gut, I knew these were excuses.

Slowly I became immobilized and stayed with him yet another 10 years. The older the children grew, the more my feelings for my husband shrank, the romantic feelings that is. Although Zak and I were more like friends than husband and wife, we became exceptionally close friends after my mother died and my father took sick.

Zak was like an angel to me. For three years, he drove me to the hospital, argued with the doctors, and held me in his arms as my father shriveled away before my eyes.

After dad died, Zak began to retreat again. But he was never again abusive to me. I felt loyal and grateful to him, but I still don't love him the way a woman should love a man. And even though, at 55, I should be all grown-up by now, I still don't know what to do. To go or not to go, that is the question and I still don't have the answer.

—Angela, wife of a Vietnam vet

Gwen's Story

This is my second New Year's Eve without my vet. I miss him tonight, even though we rarely spent New Year's Eve together. He was always drunk and it was the alcohol that killed him.

I felt sad at his funeral. But I didn't feel guilty. I stood by him through all his ups and downs and took him to almost every alcohol rehabilitation center in town. I tried everything, but there was no controlling his love affair with the bottle.

My husband dragged me down and made my life miserable, but I don't regret what I did for him, not one minute of it. I wasn't raised to be a quitter and my religious upbringing frowned on divorce. My only regret was that I didn't have more time and money for myself.

I loved computers, but we never had enough money to buy me one because the money went to alcohol. I couldn't even take a computer course because I was scared to leave him alone in the house in case he had a PTSD attack or a drinking binge and someone would need to be there to help him.

I could pretty much forget about going to work during his anniversary times. I'd pretend I was sick just to be home in case he fell down during a flashback or in case he wanted to kill himself.

My vet is gone now, but his anniversaries are my anniversaries, just like when he was alive. Like a combat soldier, I was always "on guard" during his anniversary times—not against him, but for him. I "walked the point," not in a jungle, but in our bedroom. The enemy wasn't people, but the feelings he considered his enemies—his rage, grief, and confusion.

My husband is gone now. I can go to as many computer classes as I want. I can even come back home without wondering what state he'll be in. You'd think I'd be relieved not to have to worry about him anymore. But I don't. I feel sad.

The last few years with him were pure sacrifice on my part. People kept telling me to leave him. But I knew he was going to die soon. Why leave a dying man? I thought.

It was only a matter of time until the drinking would cause another car accident or another fall. And that's exactly how he died—driving into a tree while intoxicated.

He might have made it if he had gotten help early on. But by the time help was available, alcohol had taken over his body, mind, and soul.

I grieve for the good parts of the man I knew, but also for the parts of him that were lost to me, and to him. If I could, I'd place his name on the Vietnam Wall. I believe he is truly another casualty of the war. Why else would a handsome, strong, intelligent man be dead at 45?

—Gwen, widow of a Vietnam vet

Terry's Story

Eight years of group counseling and two inpatient PTSD programs later, and Bic is still obsessed with Vietnam. After 10 years of playing second fiddle to his needs, his war buddies, and his war memories, I left.

Frankly, I don't know how I finally decided. For so many years, I flip-flopped between wanting to stay and planning to leave so many times I drove myself crazy.

Maybe if Bic and I had had children, I'd still be with him. But we decided not to have any children together because I had three from a previous marriage and Bic had been exposed to Agent Orange.

I married Bic with full knowledge of his PTSD. He had just been diagnosed and was in group therapy when he popped the question. I felt I could deal with it, but I wasn't prepared for the emotional rollercoaster which Bic called marriage.

His ups and downs became the focus of my life and I didn't like that. I didn't think a relationship should be that demanding, but this one was.

Because of Bic's needs, I dropped out of evening courses and eventually stopped going to see my friends or to church. I gave him my whole life, but it wasn't enough.

One day I decided life with Bic was a dead-end street. The counseling had helped him with his self-esteem and he no longer lashed out at me, but he was still more demanding of me than my three children and job put together.

One day a single girlfriend of mine was describing how much she was enjoying a night art course she was taking and something in me snapped. I knew that if I didn't leave immediately, I would never leave, and I would stagnate.

I packed up as soon as possible, knowing that if I hung around, my love feelings for Bic would overtake me and I'd never leave.

I loved and still love Bic very much. I miss his smile and the sex and his honesty, the kind of honesty a lot of vets have. I haven't found a new man yet. But I have found myself.

I hope the price of finding myself won't be a loveless, sexless life. But that's what it seems to be, at least for now.

Three months ago he asked me to come and see him. But I knew that if I ever slept with him again, it would be hard not to go back to him. Last week he called again, not for me to visit, but for me to go with him to the funeral of one of his buddies who had committed suicide.

I knew the buddy, and his wife, but I mainly went for Bic, because I knew he couldn't handle it alone.

At the funeral, I felt a deep solidarity with Bic. I know he and other vets have been wronged. But that doesn't mean I'll go back to him. I'm still not over him and might never be. But that doesn't mean I was wrong to leave. Without him, I have a chance for a future. With him, I'd have been stuck in his Vietnam rut all my life.

Even though his rut kept getting better and better due to his being in counseling, it was still a rut and he was in it; there wasn't enough room for me.

—Terry, former wife of a Vietnam vet

1

What Is Post-Traumatic Stress Disorder (PTSD)?

"I hate Vietnam!" Jessica sobbed. "Ed went over there a warm, out-going person. He came back angry, withdrawn, taking out all his anger on me and the kids. Why he has to turn on us—the ones he loves the most—I just don't understand. The yelling, being called every name in the book; it hurts deep, very deep, even more than the physical abuse.

"He's angry at me, his own wife, almost all the time. It's like I'm an-other person to him, a stranger, not the wife who has stood by him for 15 years."

Jessica is the petite, attractive wife of a Vietnam combat vet named Ed. Jessica met Ed just before he was sent overseas. They fell in love al-most immediately and she has been his faithful partner ever since. For over two years now, Jessica has been attending a woman's group at a lo-cal Vet Center. All the women share Jessica's pain, fears, and profound loneliness. They are all wives of Vietnam vets.

Although still living with Ed, Jessica feels alone and abandoned. Her husband, it seems, is involved with another woman. The other wives have the same complaint: their husbands are involved with another woman, too—the same other woman.

Her name is Vietnam. She is ugly and battle-scarred, but her power is great. Somehow this other woman still controls the men who knew her.

Saigon fell years ago, but the Vietnam war still rages in the hearts and minds of many vets, robbing them of emotional closeness with the ones they love and preventing them from enjoying fulfilling lives. A significant number of Vietnam veterans suffer from Post-Traumatic Stress Disorder (PTSD), the current psychiatric label given to a malady more commonly known as "shell shock," "combat fatigue," or "war neurosis."

Remembering is worse than being there.[1]

I wish I didn't have PTSD, but I do. Even when I'm happy, I'm sad. 'Nam is like a permanent dent in my heart and mind. Tonight I was at a party with my wife. My favorite music was playing. I felt love for her and even for life itself. But this happiness only made me acutely aware of the pain of my past.

As we did a fast dance, I found myself stomping the ground angrily, muttering, "Damn you, bitch. Damn you, bitch. You caused my buddy's death." When I started flashing, I knew it was time to leave. But, damn, where do I go to get away from my own head?

I want to write, to heal myself, but depression has immobilized me. Can I even move this pen?

This morning I could barely get out of bed. Would I ever get up? Would I ever want to?

The world is cold and bleak. There's nothing to live for. I can't bear the deadness inside me anymore. All I feel is anger and pain about Vietnam. Yet I'm sick and tired of thinking about that place. Why can't I turn off the memories?

I saw a pregnant woman crossing the street yesterday proudly caressing her belly. I hated her for being happy and wanted to rip her belly open, like I saw in 'Nam. Thank God, I never did anything like that, but I came close.

I want to be normal, like everyone else, and enjoy the good things in life. I have a wonderful wife, who has stood by me though all my depressions and explosions (not to mention my 10 years of drinking) and a beautiful sixteen-year-old daughter, too. But am I happy? Hardly ever.

I'm constantly worried that my daughter is going to be raped or in a car accident. Whenever her school bus is late, even two minutes, I break out into cold sweats, hyperventilate, and want to call the rescue squad. I keep thinking that God is going to punish me soon for things I did in 'Nam, or for things I was tempted to do by taking away mv child.

I can't forget. I can't drive in the rain or go to barbecues either. Hot, wet weather and burning meat remind me of 'Nam. In my dreams, dismembered bodies and teeth without the gold fillings float in the air, I make love to ugly Oriental prostitutes and then the dead VC come back to life—angry at me.

I can't go home for Christmas, either. First there's my father, the World

War II hero who thinks we lost the war because guys like me drank and drugged too much. And then there's my cousin Ralph, Mr. Success. "You could have gone to Canada, but, no, you had to go prove something. So don't cry now."

His old lady wears furs. Mine stands on her feet all day for $6.54 an hour. My career was shot to hell by 'Nam, but I don't care. Deep down, I hate myself—hate myself, hate myself, hate myself—for what I became in 'Nam, for things that weren't even my fault.

—A Vietnam Combat Veteran

The Vietnam veteran with PTSD is a case of unwept tears, unsuffered suffering, a numb heart full of pain, subject to unwanted rage reactions which express not only a deep sense of betrayal and alienation, but a profound sense of grief, helplessness, self-pity, and self-hate as well.

One veteran describes his PTSD as an "inner agony that has no name, yet has many faces." Some vets run from their PTSD with drugs and alcohol. Others dry heave every morning, mistreat their wives and children, and have difficulty keeping jobs. Some try to escape by over-controlling their wives and children or by overcontrolling themselves with impossible "to do" lists and other forms of workaholism. Still other vets withdraw from society altogether and live as virtual hermits in secluded parts of the country.[2]

The official definition of PTSD, adopted by psychiatrists and psychologists, states that for a person to qualify as having the syndrome, he (or she) must:

1. Have had a history of trauma;

2. Find him- or herself reexperiencing the trauma in the form of such things as dreams, flashbacks, and intrusive memories, or acting or feeling as if the trauma was occurring in the present;

3. Experience a numbing of emotions and a reduced interest in others, which were not present prior to the trauma, as well as difficulties remembering the event and tendencies to avoid people, places, and activities which arouse memories of the trauma; and

4. Experience signs of physical arousal (not present prior to the trauma) as indicated by two (or more) of the following problems: difficulties going to sleep or staying asleep, irritability and rage reactions, problems with concentration, startle response, and hypervigilance (or overprotectiveness).[3]

Associated with PTSD, but not part of the official definition of PTSD, are survivor guilt, phobias associated with people and places linked with the trauma, depression, substance abuse, panic disorders, and a persistent feeling of being permanently damaged, scarred, inferior, or "doomed."

In life, we all face crises, large and small, ranging from the loss of a wallet to the death of a loved one. Yet these events, while stressful, cannot be considered traumas. Traumas severe enough to cause PTSD are of such magnitude, horror, or duration that they overwhelm one's emotional and physical coping mechanisms.

Basically, PTSD is a normal reaction to an abnormal or overwhelming amount of stress. Imagine being in a car accident 20 times a month for 12 months in a row. Imagine being raped twice a week for a solid year. How would you feel? Even if these terrible things were not happening to you directly, what if they were happening to persons all around you and you were powerless to stop it? What if you knew that at any moment, you might be the next victim?

That's what it was like in Vietnam, for all but a few. In a war where bar girls had hand grenades and even babies were booby trapped, almost anyone, man, woman, or child, could be a possible enemy. There were few, if any, "safe zones." Death was everywhere.

Although PTSD is called Post-Traumatic Stress Disorder, many veterans developed PTSD while still in Vietnam. They covered the symptoms with alcohol or drugs or suppressed them in other ways for a variety of reasons. Some feared being seen as weak or crazy. Some feared they would be punished for not being able to fight. Still others did not want to be taken from the field due to their symptoms and thereby leave their units. In essence, loyalty to their comrades enabled them to hide their symptoms sufficiently so that they could fight to the finish.

For others, PTSD symptoms emerged after the war. One reason for the delayed onset of PTSD in some veterans is that during the Vietnam war men were sent overseas for one year only. When they broke down or became dysfunctional during battle, they were not as readily removed from combat as during previous wars. They were usually treated for their symptoms, told to hang on just a little longer or until their DEROS (Date of Estimated Return from Overseas), and were "quickly reinstated in the unit."[4]

Not only war veterans can acquire PTSD. Anyone who has undergone a trauma outside the range of normal human stress can develop this disorder. The symptoms of PTSD have been noted in prisoners of war, survivors of the Nazi holocaust and the bombing of Hiroshima, as well as among severe burn and head injury patients. PTSD has also developed among victims of rape, incest, and other assaults; among survivors of natural catastrophes, such as earthquakes, fires, floods, hurricanes, and tornadoes; among refugees; and among survivors of technological disasters, severe burns, organized crime, and other forms of stranger crime.[5]

While PTSD is found among survivors of natural traumas or catastrophes, it is more prevalent, more long-term, and more intense among victims of manmade disasters. Dr. Judith Herman argues that the effects of short-term or one-time trauma differ significantly from those of repeated or prolonged trauma, such as combat, concentration camps, or years of family violence.[6] In her studies, she found that chronically traumatized people can evidence profound changes in identity and in their ability to relate to others. Some suffer nearly continuously. They have very few periods of emotional calm or physical comfort. Sleeping problems, startle response, "tension headaches, gastrointestinal disturbances, and abdominal, back or pelvic pain are extremely common." Also common are "tremors, choking sensations, or nausea."[7]

According to Sarah Haley, who has worked extensively with Vietnam vets, trauma consists of being made into an object.[8] Whether one is assaulted by a tornado, rapist, or Viet Cong, at the moment of attack one does not feel like a human being with the right to safety, happiness, and health. At that moment, one almost becomes a thing, a vulnerable object subject to the will of a power or force greater than one's self. When the assailant is a natural force, such as an earthquake, the catastrophe can somehow be explained away as an accident of fate. However, when the assailant is another person, the victim's trust in other human beings, and in society in general, can be severely shaken or shattered entirely.

PTSD symptoms are not signs of mental illness. The person who manifests PTSD symptoms is "responding to specific experiences" and "needs help in identifying and resolving the issues raised by these experiences."[9] Neither is PTSD a sign that an individual is psychologically "weak" or "disorganized," as shown by the fact that PTSD has been found to develop among a variety of survivors of natural catastrophes, many of whom had no previous significant psychological problems.[10]

Furthermore, PTSD can develop in persons who witness trauma on a daily basis or are subject to "persistent and unrelieved" stress as part of their job.[11] This statement holds true even for individuals who are carefully screened for mental health problems prior to admission to their field. For example, PTSD has been found among rescue workers, fire fighters, health care teams, and police officers.[12]

As human beings, we must all confront the fact of our mortality. We and our loved ones will die someday, no matter who we are or what we do. Usually this awareness comes to us and stays with us more powerfully in our middle or later years, when we see our parents and their friends dying, or when we ourselves acquire an illness. However, victims of catastrophes, individuals who work with life and death experiences on a daily basis, and combat soldiers confront the existential reality of death sooner than most. Like survivors of car accidents and assault, the Vietnam veteran touched his death in Vietnam. In addition, the seeming senselessness of the war compounded his or her reaction to the wounding and killing all around, resulting in a cynicism and sense of futility that, for some, can last for many years. [13]

In the face of trauma, such as combat, torture, or rape, a person usually shuts down emotionally. Feelings are not felt, but suppressed, so that the individual can survive the traumatic event. As a result of this suppression, however, a range of symptoms may develop. Among Vietnam veterans, the symptoms of PTSD include the following: depression, anger, sleep disturbances, anxiety, a tendency to react under stress with survival tactics, loss of interest in work or activities, suicidal feelings and thoughts, fantasies of retaliation, alienation, negative self-image, memory impairment, cynicism and distrust of government and authority figures, hypersensitivity to injustice, difficulty with authority figures, tendency to fits of rage, problems with intimate relations, emotional distance from others, survivor guilt, avoidance of activities that arouse memories of trauma in the war, fear of losing others, and self-deceiving and self-punishing patterns of behavior.[14]

PTSD, however, is more than a list of symptoms. The fundamental force underlying the symptoms of PTSD is the veteran's reexperiencing of the trauma followed by his attempts to bury memories of the trauma and the feelings associated with the trauma. He will repeat this sequence over and over. This cyclical recurrence is an essential characteristic of the syndrome.

As more than one Vietnam veteran's wife has observed, her husband suddenly withdraws soon after openly sharing with her. "I was so excited when Tom finally talked to me about Vietnam," Joan told the women's group. "All these years, he hasn't said a word about it. Finally, maybe, I thought we could be close. He even told me he had more to tell me. But ever since he opened up last week, he's shut down more than ever. He won't even tell me what he wants for dinner and hasn't let me touch him for over a week.

"What did I do wrong? I didn't know exactly what to say when he told me about some of his firefights. I'm no psychologist, but I was sympathetic. Maybe I wasn't sympathetic enough. Did I turn him off somehow?"

Joan did not do anything wrong. She didn't turn off Tom either. Tom turned himself off. Like many wives, Joan was shocked and dismayed at her husband's withdrawal and assumed that she was responsible. But her husband's withdrawal is not the result of her behavior—it is a predictable feature of the cyclical nature of PTSD.

Tom, like many vets with untreated PTSD, is in a state of emotional numbing. He has shoved many of his emotions, especially those surrounding Vietnam, out of his conscious awareness. But this does not mean that these feelings are not there, nor that they do not motivate him.

Feelings are real and powerful. Although we can't see or touch them, they can heavily influence our behavior, our mental outlook, and even our spiritual life. Like Tom, we can push our feelings down in an attempt to make them go away, pretend that they aren't there at all, or that they are relatively unimportant. But eventually the stifled emotions will surface and clamor for attention: "Here I am. Here I am. Deal with me. Deal with me."

In the case of the Vietnam veteran with PTSD, the emotions and associated memories emerge in conscious or unconscious awareness over and over again in a variety of forms, ranging from intrusive thoughts and images to dissociative states. This process is called "reexperiencing the trauma."

It is as if the veteran keeps playing a video movie with a sad ending over and over again, hoping that perhaps this time the ending will be a happy one. Of course, his wish does not come true. The veteran is so absorbed with the unresolved traumas of his past that he has less psychic energy and emotion to devote to his job, his friends and family, and most importantly, to himself, in the present.

"My husband can't be there for me when I'm sick," explained Joan. "He loves me and wants to give to me; he just doesn't have it to give. Because of his PTSD, his emotional resources are limited."

Because much of the PTSD-afflicted Vietnam veteran's psychic energy is bound up with his war experiences, when there is a family crisis, it is not unusual for the veteran to shut down emotionally. According to the Vet Center survey, about 40% of the time it is the Vietnam wife or other family member, not the veteran himself, who takes charge and handles most of the practical and emotional matters involved.

The vet may avoid the crisis because he fears it will aggravate his memories and bring upon him the hell of reexperiencing the trauma. Reexperiencing the trauma may occur in the form of: intrusive thoughts and images of the Vietnam experience; dreams, nightmares, or night terrors; and flashbacks, both conscious and unconscious, sometimes called dissociative states.

During dreams or nightmares, the veteran may shake, shout,

scream, and thrash about with considerable violence.[15] He may or may not remember the dream upon awakening. However, the feelings of terror and fear contained in the dream may persist for quite some time.

The insomnia which plagues some veterans can be seen as an attempt to avoid such dreams and nightmares. Some vets overindulge in alcohol or drugs before they sleep, in hopes that these substances will obliterate the dreams. Others can only sleep with a weapon nearby or under their pillows.

Nightmares about Vietnam may be replays of real war events, scenes of probable or much-feared war events, or dreams that symbolize the conflicts and terrors experienced during war. Regardless of which kind of nightmare is experienced, it can easily create an inordinately high level of anxiety for the veteran because he is forced to relive traumatic events. In addition, the intense anxiety and fear that nightmares may generate can have residual effects. They can spill over into the next day and make the veteran feel uneasy and disoriented. They can paralyze his decision-making and other abilities, as well as put a halt to his ability to enjoy whatever good his day may have to offer.

Veterans hate their nightmares because the nightmares intrude not only on their nights, but on their days as well. Since traumatic memories tend to be stored as visual images, traumatic dreams often contain vivid images which can flash through the veteran's mind frequently through the following day or days. It does not take a psychologist to understand how being beset by traumatic images during the day can impede the veteran's daytime coping abilities.

The veteran's daytime coping abilities—as well as those of his wife or partner—may also be impaired simply because the dreams interfere with much needed rest. Some families are awakened by the veteran's cries and screams. In other cases, men wake up their wives and children after nightmares, to make sure they are still alive, to ask them for reassurance, or for help in searching the home for Viet Cong. Another disturbing element about the nightmares is that they are unpredictable, making the veteran feel as if he is "out of control."[16]

The feeling of helplessness is found in most of these nightmares. For example, "being trapped in a foxhole with V.C. pulling at me and trying to drag me further down into the hole with them"; "V.C. sneaking up on me in my sleep and not being able to wake up in time"; "being wounded and put in a body bag and being carried to the cellar and I am screaming at people that I'm not dead, but they continue putting me there anyway"; "being chased by men with no faces through jungle and then I fall off a cliff"; "malfunctioning weapon"; and "four or five days per week I am being killed by a gun, knife, or an injection."[17]

For some veterans, the nightmares began during the war; for others, immediately afterwards. Veterans who have made progress in therapy often find that their nightmares become fewer and less intense. (This is not the case in the initial stages of therapy, however, which is characterized by a temporary increase in PTSD symptoms, including nightmares.) However, even veterans who have been engaged in healing programs for quite some time may have a resurgence of nightmares at midlife or when exposed to new traumas or stresses.

Ralph, for example, had struggled five years in group and individual therapy to cope with his recurring nightmares of the ghosts of dead Viet Cong trying to kill him. Finally, the dreams became less frequent and horrifying to him, until his mother developed cancer and Ralph watched her die. Then his nightmares returned in full force.

"Just going to the hospital and seeing my mother waste away brought back memories of the hospitals in Vietnam full of dying, crying people," Ralph states.

Veterans have also reported increases in nightmares and other PTSD symptoms in response to being in vehicular accidents, to being victimized by crime, or to seeing bodies of murder or accident victims, especially if the victims are young men. However, it is not necessary to have a dramatic or life-threatening incident occur for a nightmare or Vietnam memory to be aroused. Even mildly stressful events can precipitate a mental tour of duty back in Vietnam.

For example, when Larry's cat became ill with a mild case of respiratory infection, the veterinarian assured Larry that his cat would be well within days and showed Larry the x-rays and other medical tests to prove it.

Larry went to bed assured that his cat would be fine, but that night dreamt that his front lawn was covered with the disemboweled remains of dozens of cats and dogs. In the dream, a neighborhood child came to his door and told him that a man with a backpack had killed all the cats and dogs in the neighborhood, put them on his lawn, then shot himself. When, in the dream, Larry looked outside the window at his lawn, a dead man lay next to the dead animals. A police officer then came by and arrested Larry for killing both the animals and the man with the backpack.

In dream analysis, Larry related that once while in Vietnam his unit had killed many peasants in a village. He had refrained from killing people who he thought were civilians, but tried to pretend differently. Larry did not fool his commanding officer, however, who pulled Larry aside and ordered him to "kill anything that moved—man, woman, or child."

By that time, however, most of the peasants either were dead or had fled. The commanding officer then ordered Larry to kill some animals that were found in the village, disembowel them, and put their bodies next to the corpses of the villagers. Larry obeyed the order. But as he stacked the bodies of the dead animals onto those of the dead people, the commanding officer told him that if any questions were asked about who had killed civilians in this village, he would say that he, Larry, had killed not only civilians, but animals, and disemboweled them to boot.

In his dream about the dead animals, Larry recreated this traumatic war experience. The policeman can be seen as Larry's conscience, up-braiding him for killing the animals, and the man with the backpack, Larry himself, the soldier Larry of the past, that is. During the war, the soldier Larry carried a backpack and killed animals (and people). How-ever the current Larry is a parent, a pet lover, and a humane person. Al-though the current Larry still has rages, fundamentally he does not want to hurt or kill anyone.

In the dream, the soldier Larry is dead. A possible interpretation of this is that the dead man is a symbol for the death of the soldier Larry and/or the death of soldier values, such as enjoyment in killing. In re-ality, after the incident where Larry was forced to kill the animals, his respect for his commanding officer, for the military, and most impor-tantly, for himself died.

Also significant is that in the dream, the man with the backpack (the soldier Larry) kills the animals, then himself. This suicide in the dream could be seen as an act of self-punishment, guilt, or shame at having killed the animals. These were the same feelings Larry carried with him for years after Vietnam.

Next to dreams, the flashbacks of Vietnam veterans are perhaps the most publicized forms of reexperiencing the trauma. Basically, a flash-back is a sudden, vivid recollection of the traumatic event accompanied by strong emotion. The veteran does not black out or lose conscious-ness but he does, temporarily, leave the present and find himself back in Vietnam. He may see the scenes of Vietnam, smell the smells, and hear the sounds. He may or may not lose contact with present reality and he may or may not find himself acting as if he is back in Vietnam. During such flashbacks, he may easily confuse his wife and children for the enemy. Wives report that sometimes their husbands alter-nate between recognizing them as their wives and seeing them as Viet Cong.

Veterans may be reluctant to acknowledge that they are "flashing" for fear of sounding crazy. Yet their histories may reveal many instances of "coming to" with a memory of having once again been engaged in a war experience, such as going out on patrol or driving on a road in the jungle. "These episodes may last up to several hours and are not without risk. Serious injuries have occurred when veterans have prowled around backyards and alleys at night fully armed, reexperiencing a patrol in hostile territory."[18]

While a few dramatic cases involving flashbacks have been well publicized in the media, most Vietnam veterans who "flash" do so more quietly, in the privacy of their hearts and minds, without public commotion. While "extreme public episodes are rare," "flashing" is not.[19] Neither is "flashing" peculiar to Vietnam veterans. It has been observed in survivors of Nazi concentration camps,[20] in World War II aviation personnel,[21] and among survivors of long-term sexual or physical abuse.[22]

Flashing also tends to occur among persons who have had to endure situations where there was an "intense, chronic, or pervasive loss of security" and lack of safety.[23]

Flashbacks can be conscious or unconscious. In conscious flashbacks, the veteran experiences vivid images of war events and can later report what he has seen, even if he had temporary amnesia during or after the flashback.[24] During unconscious flashbacks, however, the veteran may find himself engaged in unusual behavior motivated by some memory of Vietnam, but he has no conscious awareness of any thoughts or emotions about Vietnam, either during the time of the flashback or later. Upon examining the episodes in therapy, however, usually the episode will reveal itself to be a "repetition of some event(s) in the war."[25]

To the wives and children of Vietnam veterans, flashbacks are always frightening. When their loved one falls to the ground or commands them to "walk the point" with him, they fear not only for their own safety, but for his. His moves are unpredictable. He could easily hurt himself in so many ways. How can they protect him? How can they protect themselves? How long will it take until he "comes back" this time? What if he never comes back or kills himself to end his anguish?

Women in group have been held hostage anywhere from two hours to two days by men who have refused to let them out of their homes, or certain rooms, for fear that they would be killed by Viet Cong. Sometimes the home, or portions of the home, are barricaded with wire or rope. Phones are ripped off the walls, doors are chained shut, and if the vet has weapons, knives, guns, and ammunition may be made ready for the first intruder.

In preparation, women keep extra supplies of groceries and medications on hand. If the flashback happens to occur while one of the children is out of the home, the woman must use utmost tenderness and cleverness to obtain her husband's permission to get the child or to allow a trusted friend to do so. If she must go herself, she worries about what will happen to her husband or other children while she is gone.

If she has other children, she may want to take them with her, but the vet might insist that the children stay with him "for protection." Or perhaps he may not believe that she will return. If he keeps the other children with him, then he knows she will come home again. Sometimes there are physical struggles over the children. Special problems arise when one of the children is ill and must be taken to a doctor while the husband is experiencing an episode.

Women in these situations usually show extraordinary coping abilities. Many have managed to keep their husbands sane and alive, even while severely physically ill themselves or while caring for infants. Most of the women report little fear for themselves. "Mike would never hurt me or the kids," says Debbie. "Even when he confuses me with the enemy, I can bring him out of it by caressing his face and telling him, 'It's me, Debbie, your wife. You're home. You're safe. You're not in Vietnam. It's me, Debbie, your wife, I love you.'"

Debbie, like the other wives, usually dares not call the police. The mere presence of a uniformed person might drive their husbands wild. Some husbands have threatened to kill any police that would come. If the veteran has had violent episodes since his return to the United States, the wife has to take such a threat seriously. The women are also afraid to call the neighbors for help, for fear they too will be harmed. In some cases, the women are ashamed to tell the neighbors or do not feel the neighbors would be sympathetic. Furthermore, if the neighbors were told, they might become alarmed and ostracize the veteran and his family.

For the most part, women go along with whatever their husbands ask of them, whether it be hiding under the bed to avoid enemy attack or building fires in the backyard. Children also become involved. While younger children might think it's great fun to tiptoe around the living room with Daddy at two in the morning with a flashlight, older children are saddened, concerned, angered, or confused by their father's behavior. Sometimes younger children imitate their fathers. They may hide under the bed whenever a helicopter flies by or refuse rice and other "gook food."

Older children may not imitate their father as readily, but they may not understand their father's problem either. They may be afraid to ask questions for fear of precipitating another flashback or family uproar. If the flashback has occurred in public, or in front of friends, the child might be embarrassed and ashamed of his or her father. If the flashbacks are numerous, the child may resent the interruptions. On a deeper level, however, the child feels helpless and at the same time takes on adult responsibilities. Many learn to assist their mother in "bringing Daddy home." They may wipe his brow and whisper words of love and reassurance just like Mommy. They may regularly help their mother remove objects from the room with which their father could hurt himself.

As Dr. Arthur Blank points out in *The Trauma of War: Stress and Recovery in Vietnam Veterans*, flashbacks have not received the scholarly attention of mental health professionals.[26] Sometimes mental health professionals have misdiagnosed flashback behavior as "uncontrollable rage reactions" and oriented therapy toward helping the veteran with his poor impulse control. Veterans with PTSD would be better served by an exploration of the history of their war experiences and the personal meaning of that history.[27]

Another form of reexperiencing the trauma, which may be related to unconscious flashbacks, consists of suddenly feeling certain painful or angry feelings which do not seem clearly related to any particular memory of Vietnam. For example, vets have reported rage reactions, panic attacks, or intense psychic pain without any conscious thought of the war.[28]

"I can understand when my husband sulks or explodes after hearing about some vet killing himself or about some buddy dying in a car accident. But many times he gets moody or angry for no reason at all," explained one wife. Yet what this wife, and her husband, may not fully appreciate is that often there is a reason for the emotional upset, even though that reason may not be obvious to either of them. The reason may lie in the intensity of the vet's repressed emotions about Vietnam. The feelings may emerge even when they are not triggered by any specific reminder of the war or any particular war memory.

Since reexperiencing the trauma can be so painful and possibly dangerous, the PTSD afflicted veteran may find himself retreating mentally, socially, and physically. For example, one vet stopped going to shopping malls after flashing and falling to the ground in the middle of a department store. As a result of his PTSD, the vet may also experience some memory loss or impairment or have trouble concentrating or remembering current information.

Wives report that their husbands forget not only therapy and doctor appointments, but also where they have put money or when to pick up children from the babysitters. Perhaps the husbands are lying, but their forgetfulness may be the combined result of drinking or alcohol addiction and unacknowledged and untreated PTSD. As Dr. Blank points out in *The Trauma of War*, such mental difficulties are clearly more than boredom, laziness, or lack of intellectual ability. They can represent a form of escape, a "distressful impairment of the capacity to appreciate" the experience at hand.[29]

In sum, vets with PTSD alternate between reexperiencing the trauma and avoiding reexperiencing the trauma. Sometimes "triggers" in the environment can set off a memory. For example, the sound of popping popcorn or helicopters, the sight of plastic trash bags (reminiscent of body bags), or the advent of hot, humid weather can put a veteran psychologically back to the original event. Sometimes he may react with the exaggerated startle response so characteristic of Vietnam veterans. An airplane passes by overhead and suddenly he is out of bed, reaching for a weapon, waiting to shoot the Viet Cong. The only people to shoot at, however, may be his own family.

Midlife brings additional triggers: the deaths of parents and other relatives and the premature death of Vietnam veteran friends due to combat-related physical and emotional problems. Also potentially traumatic for PTSD-afflicted veterans is the departure of children from the home, the decision of sons or daughters to join or not join the military, and any aggravation of war injuries or psychological stress due to the aging process or inadequate health care. Media coverage of armed conflict in the Persian Gulf, Somalia, Chechnya in the former Soviet Union; of the carnage in Bosnia and Rwanda; and of other subsequent wars are also powerful triggers.

For many Vietnam veterans the contrast between the warm reception and support given to the troops who served in the Persian Gulf and the way they were treated plummeted them back into feelings of betrayal and rage. Vietnam veterans had to fight for and wait for over a decade for the establishment of Outreach Centers and other services for combat stress. In contrast, such services were available to Persian Gulf veterans immediately upon discharge.

Vietnam veterans had to wait decades for the effects of Agent Orange to be recognized. In the meantime, an undetermined number of Vietnam veterans have suffered medical problems and even died from Agent Orange-related problems. In addition, an undetermined number of Vietnam veterans have refrained from having children due to fear that the children will be affected by the Agent Orange in their bodies. Still others blame themselves for any birth or other defects in their children, thinking that their exposure to Agent Orange caused the problem.

In contrast, the Persian Gulf Syndrome was acknowledged just a few years after the Persian Gulf war, not decades later. And as early as 1994, legislation was passed paving the way for financial compensation for those Persian Gulf veterans who suffer from joint pain, dizziness, memory problems, parasites, and several seemingly incurable medical problems. Meanwhile, some Vietnam veterans are still waiting for their Agent Orange claims to be reviewed and respected.

"Those guys deserve it," states a Vietnam combat veteran referring to the recognition and increased services offered to Persian Gulf veterans. "But we deserved it too. I only wish I had known about PTSD and gone for help right after Vietnam, instead of 20 years later. Twenty years of my life were wasted and I put my family—and me—through hell, when that didn't have to be."

Also associated with PTSD, but not essential to the diagnosis of the syndrome, is increased irritability, with little or no provocation, and impulsive behavior. In an attempt to escape their memories, some vets frequently change from one job to another or move from one part of the country to the next. These many moves are sometimes forms of running from the past or a desperate searching for a geographical cure for the hurting, confused self inside.

PTSD is, by definition, a delayed reaction to the war. Symptoms may emerge one, two, even 20 years later. Often stress in the present—economic difficulties, a death in the family, or the veteran's own midlife crisis—will bring out symptoms of PTSD which the veteran had previously been able to control. According to several Vet Center counselors, often it is a major loss in the family—the death of parent or child—that brings the veteran's PTSD to the surface and forces him to seek help.

Many women who have attended the Vet Center women's group report that their husbands were—or seemed—"normal" until the death of a sibling or parent. Tim, for example, had been working successfully as a dietician in a hospital for 10 years following Vietnam. His wife had noticed no signs of PTSD in him, except a tendency toward withdrawal, which she attributed to his family background. Also, he would sometimes drink too much. "But what man doesn't?" she reasoned.

However, last year, Tim had to deal with multiple stresses: the death of two nieces, a major car accident, and an overload at work. These combined pressures brought to the surface memories of Vietnam which he had previously suppressed. His drinking increased, as did his absences from home. While he was able to function at work, he found himself increasingly irritated with some of his patients, especially when they were rude to him. One day a patient was being particularly demanding and verbally abusive toward Tim. Unable to contain himself any longer, Tim threw the man out of the bed. What frightened Tim was not that he attacked this man, but that he wanted to kill him. Tim feels he would have killed the patient had nurses and the hospital police not stopped him. Fear of his own rage sent Tim to a local Vet Center for help.

The root of PTSD is a fear of loss—of personal annihilation, death, or dismemberment, or of losing others. Just as the concentration camp victims, rape victims, and prisoners of war are not insane for displaying the symptoms of PTSD, neither is the troubled Vietnam veteran.

War is seldom good for people. Even the ancient Greeks commented on the negative effects of war on man's psyche, as did Shakespeare and other writers. For decades, too, mental health professionals have noted the psychiatric effects of war and talked about "war neurosis."

Veterans of previous wars have suffered from PTSD even though their distress was not labeled as such. Among American troops, PTSD-like symptoms caused the evacuation of some 10% of enlisted men during World War I and, at various points, of many more during World War II. The psychiatric casualty rate was high during World War II despite elaborate psychological screening procedures which supposedly weeded out weak men prone to mental collapse. After World War II, however, military experts concluded that the trauma of war was often enough to impair even the "strongest" and "toughest" of men.[30]

World War I and World War II veterans who suffered from PTSD often kept their problems to themselves—or drowned them in alcohol. If it is not acceptable for a man to admit that he has inner turmoil today, it was even less so in the past. The fact that numerous World War II and Korean War veterans are still suffering from nightmares and other symptoms of PTSD has recently been brought to the attention of the U.S. Congress in an effort to open Outreach Centers to older veterans who have never received help for their PTSD.[31]

During World War I the psychological stress of war was first recognized by mental health professionals. During the "Great War," the "idea developed that the high air pressure of the exploding shells caused actual physiological damage," which, in turn, lead to numerous psychological symptoms that were later named "shell shock."[32] By the end of the war, the malady that seemed to afflict so many survivors was called "war neurosis."[33]

During the Korean War, the military, now aware of "war neurosis," provided immediate, on-site help to afflicted service men. Such assistance reduced the percentage of evacuations for psychiatric reasons from 23% during World War II to 6% during the Korean conflict.[34] During the Vietnam war, in an attempt to further reduce the psychiatric casualty rate, the one year tour of duty was adopted. The military reasoned that if men were subject to combat for only a year, they would be less susceptible to psychological breakdown.

The symptoms of PTSD in Vietnam veterans are almost identical to those suffered by World War II[35] and Korean war vets.[36] These symptoms have been found among Australian troops who served in Vietnam as well.[37] In fact, the psychiatric casualty rate among Australian Vietnam veterans is almost equivalent to that of American Vietnam veterans.[38] PTSD and PTSD-like symptoms were also found among hundreds of Israeli soldiers both during and after the Lebanon war, as well as among Persian Gulf veterans. Even the many welcome-home parades and medals given to Persian Gulf veterans did not dispel the development of combat stress among the troops. Some were traumatized by combat, yet others developed PTSD simply by witnessing friendly fire accidents or having to handle enemy corpses.

It cannot be overemphasized that having PTSD does not mean that the veteran is mentally ill any more than the earthquake victim is mentally ill for exhibiting stress reactions due to traumatic experiences.[39] Two recent studies found that while many vets evidenced stress reactions to the war, they were, nevertheless, psychologically healthy.[40] This phenomenon—the co-existence of stress reactions with healthy adjustment—has been found to be characteristic of survivors of other catastrophes as well.

"Most of the vets I know," writes David Harrington, a counselor of hundreds of Vietnam veterans and a Vietnam veteran himself, "are successful journalists, plumbers, lawyers, electricians, and, yes, advertising executives. They are bound together by one tie: Vietnam. Some suffer in a dignified silence. Others just can't do that."[41]

Summary

PTSD is a normal reaction to an abnormal amount of stress. The symptoms of PTSD include depression, emotional numbing, and avoidance of people, places, and things that remind the individual of the original traumatic event and can be suffered by anyone who has experienced an event or series of events which evoked feelings of terror and helplessness. The events must be threatening to one's life, or the lives of others, or of such magnitude of pain and horror that they would overwhelm almost anyone's natural coping mechanisms.

Women living with men who suffer from active cases of PTSD must cope not only with the normal stresses of marriage, but with the fact that their husbands suffer from emotional numbing as well as depression, low self-esteem, anger, survivor guilt, sleep disturbances, social withdrawal, and hypersensitivity to noise, rejection, and injustice. Some vets experience these symptoms regularly; others only during certain emotionally sensitive times such as the anniversary date of an important battle. "He loves me but he runs from that love all the time," says one wife.

As a result of all these stresses, the women are under constant pressure and may suffer from severe emotional strain. They may become depressed, isolated, anxious, and angry. As their emotional resources become depleted, they operate on "remote control," retreat from others and may become emotionally numb, just like their husbands.

♦ ♦ ♦

Questions And Information on PTSD

How Many Veterans Really Are Suffering with PTSD?

Of the approximately 3.5 million Americans who served in Vietnam, at least 58,000 died there. Approximately 300,000 more were wounded, 150,000 requiring hospitalization. Another 75,000 were severely disabled. Over 5,000 lost limbs, with over 1,000 sustaining multiple amputations.[42] Staggering numbers, but the number of Americans losing their emotional and mental health to PTSD may be even larger.

The 1988 National Vietnam Veteran Readjustment Survey, the largest study of Vietnam veterans and their families completed to date, found that approximately 15.2% of all male Vietnam theater veterans (or about 479,000 men) and about 8.5% of female theater veterans (or about 7,500 women) currently have PTSD. These statistics refer to theater veterans, or veterans who actually served in Vietnam proper, not to veterans who served during the Vietnam era, but did not actually go to Vietnam.[43]

Also excluded from these statistics are men and women who were in Cambodia, Laos, or elsewhere in Southeast Asia, but not in Vietnam proper. In some cases, these men were on missions so secret that it is difficult, if not impossible, to find documentation of their whereabouts and activities. The 15.2% figure also does not include the 11.1% of male theater veterans and 7.8% of female theater veterans who suffer from partial PTSD or sufficient PTSD symptoms to cause emotional pain, but insufficient enough to qualify as having the full-blown disorder. Including men and women who suffer from partial PTSD adds another 350,000 persons to the list. The study also found that about one-third of male theater veterans and one-fourth of females who served in country suffered from PTSD at some time in their life. While experts disagree on the true extent of PTSD, in agreement with the Vietnam Readjustment study, most put the figure at close to 1 million. Since PTSD is, by definition, a delayed response to the war, the number of vets eventually in need of psychiatric help may reach as many as 1.5 million or more.[44]

"With Vietnam (psychological casualties) are increasing without war activities . . . . We still haven't seen the peak," states Dr. Ben Jennings, clinical psychologist at the Tucson, Arizona VAMC PCT team.[45] In many cases PTSD or PTSD-like symptoms do not emerge until midlife or old age.

This phenomenon of PTSD symptoms emerging later in life has been found among veterans from previous wars. For example, a study of WW II POW's found that 22% had chronic PTSD, but 36% of these developed symptoms only after age 40. Of this 36%, about one-fourth had combat stress after the war, but managed to contain it—until midlife.

Consequently, Veteran's Medical Centers and Outreach Centers continue to see new clients, even though the war has been over for decades. How many more veterans will develop PTSD as they grow older is undetermined.[46]

In truth, we do not actually know how many Vietnam veterans suffer from PTSD. It was not until 1980 that PTSD was officially recognized as a "mental illness" by the American Psychiatric Association. Before that time, vets with PTSD were sometimes given psychiatric diagnoses that either excluded or minimized the role of the war on their psychological well-being.[47] As more and more mental health professionals become familiar with the nature of PTSD, they will be better able to detect and treat the syndrome in their patients.

The diagnosis of PTSD, however, can be a very challenging task, for PTSD can coexist with a host of other psychological problems— depressive disorders, alcoholism, anxiety disorders, paranoia, and even schizophrenia. The longer the veteran's combat trauma has gone unassisted, combined with stresses which the veteran has encountered since the war, the greater is the likelihood that he will develop additional disorders, especially clinical depression. In addition, some of the characteristics of PTSD are remarkably similar to those of other mental illnesses.[48]

On the other hand, a veteran can have PTSD and have few, if any, external symptoms of distress. It is perfectly possible for a vet to have PTSD and still function on the job and at home. In fact, one survey reports that about 80% of the Vietnam era vets have "adjusted well both during and following military service."[49] Notice, however that this 80% figure refers to Vietnam era vets (the 9 million who served in the U.S. military between 1964 and 1975), not to those 2.5 million who served specifically in Vietnam or to those who saw combat, the two groups which seem to be most affected by PTSD.

Another reason we do not know how many men suffer from PTSD is that some fail to seek help for fear of being labeled weak or unmanly. Some vets, especially those with relatives who supposedly made it through previous wars without any problems, feel it is shameful to seek counseling. Imbued with the masculine stereotype of the "real man" being one who is always strong and in control of his emotions, it is most difficult for some veterans to admit to themselves, much less to another human being, that they have any psychological problems.[50]

In addition, denial is a central feature of PTSD. Like alcoholism, drug addiction, and compulsive overeating, PTSD is a condition that tells its victims that they really don't have a problem. "That's what I told myself for years," explains one vet. "I thought if I ignored it, it would go away."

Some vets even pretend that the war "didn't really happen." This denial serves as a major defense against feeling the extremely uncomfortable feelings that often went along with the Vietnam experience—specifically, fear, guilt, grief, and rage, as well as moral confusion.

What Was So Special about the Vietnam War?

"What was so special about the Vietnam war?" I am often asked.

"All wars are hell. World War II and Korean war vets had a hard time too, but you don't see them running around, exaggerating their problems to get sympathy and benefits from the government. PTSD is a bunch of baloney," the reasoning continues.

"Whatever problems those guys have now, they had before the war. Besides, the war was fought by rejects. That's why we lost."

Wrong. The men sent to Vietnam constituted the best educated army America has ever fielded. "Seventy-nine percent of the men who served in Vietnam had a high school education or better when they entered military service. In comparison, only 63% of Korean War vets and only 45% of World War II vets had completed high school upon separation from the military."[51]

Another unique feature of the Vietnam war was that it was America's first "teenage" war. The average age of the American soldier in World War II was 26, but in Vietnam, it was 19. During late adolescence, the personality is not yet formed and the individual is more vulnerable to stress. According to many experts on PTSD, the age of the Vietnam veteran when he entered the service played a decisive role in the development of PTSD.[52] Dr. John Wilson explains: " . . . late adolescence (is) the time of life when people put their identities together, their occupation, their sex role, their commitments, the normal developmental process that leads to a human identity.

"So if you take a nineteen-year-old soldier and subject him to tremendous war stress for a year . . . you end up with people who in their own words say, 'I'm a different person,' 'I'm changed,' 'I don't fit in,' 'I'm twenty and feel like I came back fifty.' This diffusion of identity is a universal feeling among people suffering from PTSD."[53] Vietnam vets are sometimes called the "old young men" because they went to war at a significantly lower age than soldiers of previous wars, yet emerged "old men" with "aged hearts." [54]

For some of the teenage soldiers, it was not only their first exposure to death, but their first time away from home and their first time in another country. "I felt like I was back in the stone age," says one vet.

It is widely acknowledged, both by Vietnam veterans and the general public, that the combat performance of individual soldiers was not the sole or major factor accounting for the outcome of the war. Most combat vets strongly believe that we lost "because the nation's political leadership would not permit our troops to win a traditional military victory."[55] Even 75% of the general public "agrees that it was a failure of political will, not of arms," that was responsible for losing the war.[56]

Although the Vietnam war was not the first twentieth-century American war in which guerrilla tactics were used, it was the first in which guerrilla warfare predominated. And the guerilla warfare was particularly savage. The prevalence of specialized, well-hidden booby traps, often aimed directly at castration or dismemberment, is a major reason why permanently disabling wounds were sustained at a "far greater rate in Vietnam" than in previous wars.[57] "The percentage of Vietnam veterans who suffer from amputation or crippling wounds to the lower extremities is 300% higher than in World War II and 70% higher than in Korea. Multiple amputations occurred at the rate of 18.4% compared to 5.7% in World War II."[58]

In contrast to previous wars, during the Vietnam war the serviceman typically entered and exited alone. Each soldier had his own DEROS (Date of Expected Return from Overseas Service). Units were constantly in a state of flux, which "undermined unit integrity, cohesiveness, and emotional support." Furthermore, the "one year tour of duty led to the adoption of a 'survivor mentality' and a 'short timers' syndrome' which often undercut the soldier's capacity to make a full commitment to the war effort."[59]

What Effect Did the Atmosphere at Home Have on the Vietnam Vet?

In the fall of 1968, as I stopped at a traffic light on my walk to class across the campus at the University of Denver, a man stepped up to me and said, "Hi."

Without waiting for my reply to his greeting, he pointed to the hook sticking out of my left sleeve. "Get that in Vietnam?"
I said, "Yeah, up near Tam Ky in I Corps."
"Serves you right."
As the man walked away, I stood rooted, too confused with hurt, shame, and anger to react.
—A Vietnam Veteran[60]

It was not only the unique military and political features of the Vietnam war that contributed to the development of PTSD among its surviving warriors, but the disappointing homecoming. Instead of a hero's welcome, many vets describe being greeted with either apathy or hostility. For many, their "good warrior ethos" was destroyed not only by experiences overseas, but by the view of significant segments of the American public of the Vietnam veteran as a deranged, drug abusing "babykiller."

In previous wars, men may have felt guilt for killing, but their guilt was at least partially absolved because they were seen by friends, family, and society as "good warriors," that is, as heroes who killed as part of their duty. In general, the Vietnam veteran did not have the advantage of this societal absolution. Hence, Vietnam vets can be seen as suffering from two traumas, first the trauma of war and secondly, the trauma of an unwelcome homecoming.[61] As research has shown, vets with PTSD are characterized by a "negative perception of their family's helpfulness in their return home."[62] In many instances the veteran received indirect or direct messages that he should not talk about the war or his feelings about the war.[63] Such sharing would simply create too much anxiety and discomfort in the family members. One veteran told how he had to go hide in a closet to cry because his open expressions of grief were not tolerated by either his parents or his wife.

What Effect Does Combat Experience Have on PTSD?

While it is not necessary to have been in combat to have PTSD, study after study reveals that the greater the exposure to combat, the greater the severity of the PTSD. In addition, PTSD has been found to be prevalent among those who saw or participated in the abusive random violence that is part of any war.[64]

It is not clear whether there was more random violence in Vietnam than in previous wars. Some argue that Vietnam was not unique in its legacy of atrocities, only in the fact that the atrocities were more publicized than in previous wars. On the other hand, special factors did operate in Vietnam which, in some cases, induced extra killings.

In "Some Remarks on Slaughter," W. B. Gault, a psychiatrist who served in Vietnam, describes six psychological, social, and mechanical factors which contributed to the slaughter of defenseless Vietnamese civilians:

1. "The universality of the enemy"—the fact that the enemy was everywhere;

2. "The cartoonization and dehumanization of the enemy"—Asians were not perceived as human, but as strange childlike creatures—"dinks"—who did not value human life anyway;

3. "The dilution of responsibility"—the fact that entire squads simultaneously attacked villages or crowds;

4. "The pressure to act" to prove that one was masculine or to execute revenge;

5. "The natural dominance of the psychopath" in war situations; and

6. "The ready availability of firepower."[65]

Many combat veterans are well aware that they are not the first soldiers in history to be unnecessarily cruel. Most will say they would not have done some of the things they did in Vietnam had they not been under so much stress and seen atrocities committed on their friends by the Viet Cong. Nevertheless, some vets feel that they, in Vietnam, were more animalistic and brutal than previous warriors. The resulting sense of shame and self-hate can be intense.

In some cases, however, the vet may be experiencing this shame and self-hate on an unconscious level. He may not even be able to articulate any such feelings. If asked if he has a self-image problem, he may say "no." After all, shame, self-hate, and a negative self-image are not signs of masculinity. Yet, if the veteran is not able to acknowledge his shame or self-hate and deal with it in an open, constructive manner, he may act it out destructively. For example, he may project his own feelings onto his wife or children or some other family member. If, on some level, he sees himself as incompetent, evil, or bad, he may find himself criticizing his wife or children for what he sees as their misbehavior.

Vets who believe that manliness means exerting power and control over others may be especially prone to lashing out at their wives or children, mothers, or pets when they are feeling out of control of their own lives or out of control of their own emotions due to their PTSD.

"I am a murderer, I deserve to be punished," is implied in the veteran's low regard for himself.[66] Some vets may not wait for society or God to punish them. They punish themselves, with a relentless internal self-beating, often unconscious, often masked as boredom or depression. Or they abuse alcohol, food, or drugs; find themselves unwittingly making a series of mistakes on the job or at home; or find other ways of defeating themselves. Still others push away families and friends lest they inadvertently reveal their "secrets" to these significant others and thereby lose their love and respect.

The vet's basic fear is that if his wife or child knew the truth about him, they would reject him immediately. Perhaps he has heard stories about vets who shared war stories with their wives only to have the partner turn cold or begin divorce proceedings. However, if the vet retreats into his shell or verbally puts down his family, this can be a means of temporarily shoving them out of his life so that they will never guess that he has committed certain acts or experienced certain feelings which he has judged to be immoral or cowardly.

For example, some vets are tormented by the fact that, after a certain amount of exposure to combat, or despite their moral scruples against killing, at times they actually enjoyed the fight and got "high" on blood. Other vets are troubled by the fact that in certain instances they were cowardly and that their cowardice may have caused the death or injury of some of their friends. Back home reflecting on his past, the vet may ask himself, "Was that really me? If it was, then what kind of person am I? How can I face myself, much less others? Would my wife continue to stay with me and my children continue to respect me if they found out what happened in Vietnam?"

Of the approximately 2.6 million troops actually stationed in Vietnam, only about one-fifth served in the first echelon combat arms where the enemy was regularly pursued and engaged on the ground. However, given the guerilla nature of the war, actually 40% to 60% either fought in combat, provided close combat support or were at least fairly regularly exposed to enemy attacks.[67]

PTSD is not restricted to combat vets, but can be found among those who experienced near-death or life-threatening situations or who were surrounded by death. Medics, nurses, doctors, therapists, as well as transporters, body bag counters, embalmers, administrative officers, and numerous civilians who served in Vietnam have also developed PTSD.

Similarly, during World War II, war neurosis was found not only among combatants where the "threat of annihilation and destruction . . . was very real and imminent," but also among soldiers in graves registration units and in air corps emergency fire squad units.[68]

Like Vietnam veterans with PTSD, World War II veterans can have their PTSD reactivated by reminders of the war. For example, during the re-enactment of D-Day in 1994, World War II veterans living in nursing homes were found wandering the halls looking for their platoons or thinking the war was in progress. At first the nursing staff thought these men were demented. But later it became clear that they were suffering from PTSD reactions due to media presentations about D-Day.[69]

How Did the War Affect the Veteran Spiritually and Morally?

"Even the best of men couldn't begin to realize what the war did to human beings. How it made good men bent and worse men blind."
                                                    —An Army Medic in Vietnam[70]

PTSD is more than a psychological problem, it is also a spiritual and moral problem. War has always been a spiritual problem in that most religions teach "Thou shalt not kill." Yet, throughout history, governments, and even certain religious groups, have made exceptions to this general rule for purposes of defending the nation or the faith itself. For example, killing is prohibited in the Muslim faith, but a "Holy War" is permitted. Similarly, the Catholic Church sanctioned the Crusades.

Under such conditions, where the warrior kills for a purpose which he understands and in which he believes and where the killing is confined to a clearly defined enemy, a warrior can kill and still consider himself "good." In Vietnam, however, the enemy was not clearly defined; neither were the goals. Some who went to Vietnam believing in God came to question God's existence or God's benevolence. How could God allow this war to happen? Those who went to war unsure about their religious beliefs often emerged even less sure. For atheists, the war just confirmed the fact that there is no God.

When they returned home, they rejected religion and made it difficult for their wives to continue normal churchgoing activities. Some wives withdrew from their religious communities under these circumstances. Others increased their spiritual activities because they found them a tremendous source of energy and strength.

For some veterans, the war intensified their faith with profound religious experiences on the battlefield. There are reports of being protected by guardian angels, feeling close to God, even "seeing the Lord." Some men who had near-death experiences report spiritual awakenings of great beauty.[71] If their wives are atheists or agnostics, however, the vet's spirituality or religious fervor may create yet another marital barrier.

The majority of vets with PTSD, however, left Vietnam spiritually empty and in moral pain. Their participation in the war conflicted greatly with the spiritual or religious values they had once held.[72]

The veteran may have additional problems if he happened to serve in a unit that developed a hedonistic pseudocommunity. In this pseudocommunity it was "okay" to abuse alcohol and drugs and be sexually free, as it was to freely kill. Moral restrictions were ignored because the soldiers were far from home and because of the constant threat of death. Yet many young soldiers often had conscious or unconscious ambivalence about these experiences.[73]

The veteran's unresolved conflicts about his participation in some of these hedonistic activities may contribute to his withdrawal from his wife and family and from the faith he once held. He may feel he is too much of a "sinner" to go back to his synagogue or church or to participate fully in family activities surrounding religious holidays. Baptisms and bar mitzvahs may be especially painful since they illustrate the contrast between how he was when he went through those ceremonies himself and what he has experienced since.

As a result, religious holidays, like patriotic ones, can be very difficult times for the Vietnam family. Even if the vet forces himself to participate for the sake of the family, his wife and children know his heart isn't in it, which changes the entire tone and meaning of the event. Consequently, the religious event, which could have brought the family closer, ends up driving the family further apart and creating more pain.

What Is the "Predisposition" Theory?

In its crudest form the predisposition theory states that Vietnam veterans who are "cracked," that is, have PTSD, were "cracked" before they ever set foot in Vietnam. The predisposition theory does not deny that war is traumatic. But it attributes the veteran's resulting psychological problems primarily to his pretrauma personality characteristics (his defects, flaws, and weaknesses) rather than the war experience.

Obviously, PTSD is only complicated by any previous problems or traumas. It is only reasonable to expect that men who had social or psychological problems prior to their tour of duty in Vietnam would be more adversely affected by the war than their better adjusted fellow soldiers. However, under the circumstances in Vietnam, even well-adjusted, well-educated men cracked. In fact, given the circumstances of the Vietnam war, acquiring a combat-related disorder can be considered a more normal response than repressing the war experience or coping with it in other ways.[74]

Is PTSD the Only Reaction to Trauma?

PTSD is just one of several possible reactions to trauma. As Dr. Judith Herman points out in her book, *Trauma and Recovery: The Aftermath of Violence—From Domestic Abuse To Political Terror*, other common reactions include depression, somatization, and dissociation.[75]

Depression

What happens to a car that is driven cross-country 50 times without a tune-up, oil change, or tire rotation? What happens to a car that is well-maintained but is driven coast to coast 1,000 times?

Would some parts start to wear out? Might the car eventually cease to function altogether?

People aren't cars. However, what happens to a car due to overuse or inadequate care is similar to what happens to people when they undergo repeated traumas or prolonged severe stress and consequently don't have the time, money, or ability to take care of themselves. Under such conditions, their emotional and physical reserves become taxed to the point where they can easily develop a clinical depression.

In Vietnam, soldiers could not take adequate care of themselves on any level. Physically, they did not have proper food and rest and were subject to extreme temperatures. Emotionally, they had to repress their feelings or face ridicule, punishment, or temporary insanity. For some, there was social and sexual deprivation, and for all, deprivation of whatever family or community life they had known prior to the war.

Combat, combined with the struggles which often followed, stressed the bodies, minds, and emotions of many soldiers to the point where parts of their physical and emotional selves eventually "wore out." If, in addition, they abused alcohol or drugs, their physical health suffered even more. The cumulative effect of all these stressors easily set the stage for the development of a clinical depression.

The term *depression* as used here does not refer to the normal down periods experienced by almost everyone: that is, to temporary feelings of sadness, more commonly known as "the blues." Rather *depression* refers to biologically-based, clinical depression, which usually needs to be treated with psychiatric medication as well as psychotherapy.

Trauma can also trigger episodes of manic depressive illness, paranoia, panic attacks, and other disorders, especially if there is family history of such problems.* For example, David's grandmother and father suffered from clinical depression. Yet David showed no signs of depression until Vietnam. Despite David's family history of depression, however, his depression can still be considered war-related. If David had not seen combat, he might never have become depressed. And even without a family history of depression, David might have developed the problem, as have so many other combat veterans.

Trauma can also induce depression if the veteran suffers from major or long-term war injuries. Even people without a history of trauma are candidates for depression if they acquire a severe or chronic illness (e.g., cancer, heart disease, Parkinson's disease, or diabetes). The physical, emotional, interpersonal, and financial costs of such illnesses can easily deplete individuals to the point where they become clinically depressed.

Trauma and stress can also trigger medical problems, which in turn can induce clinical depression. Many illnesses are known to be stress-related, for example respiratory illnesses including asthma and bronchitis, certain allergies, anxiety-induced heart conditions, skin problems, and urinary or bladder infections. While it isn't clear that stress causes these problems, repeated trauma and unrelenting stress does break down the immune system, leaving the individual more vulnerable to illness. If the stress continues, the survivor will have difficulty finding the rest and peace of mind necessary for recovery.

It has been my informal observation that PTSD-afflicted Vietnam veterans and their families often become ill when subjected to additional emotional, financial, or other stressors. Formal research, such as that conducted by Dr. Bessel A. van der Kolk of Harvard University and others, has found a correlation between the development of physical illnesses and being subjected to repeated traumatic episodes.[76] In addition, almost any medical problem can be aggravated by psychological or economic stress.[77]

Latent psychological and/or physical problems may emerge not only during or after the traumatic events, but years later, often due to

* This reference to family history, however, is not intended to support the "predisposition theory" described in the previous section. The "predisposition theory" alleges that only those veterans who had problems before the war developed problems afterwards. This theory minimizes the effects of military experiences and has been used by some to deny veterans needed treatment and benefits.

I do not support the predisposition theory. However, it cannot be denied that a person's psychological, medical, social, and genetic history can play a role in how (not whether) he or she reacts to a traumatic event.

retraumatization or a midlife crisis. A veteran can be retraumatized if he becomes victimized by a vehicular accident, criminal assault, natural catastrophe, family violence, or multiple personal losses, or if one of his family members or close friends is traumatized.

Midlife can also retraumatize the veteran because events common to midlife can reactivate war issues. For example, if a parent or older relative dies, the veteran once again confronts one of the core issues of combat—that of one's own mortality and the loss of loved ones. Midlife events which have the potential to be retraumatizing include the illness and death of parents or other relatives; children leaving home for school, marriage, or careers; a diminishment of sexual interest and other kinds of energies; or the loss of youthful appearance and vigor.

John, for example, never suffered from asthma until he was 50 and his last child left home. At that time, John went into a state of psychological shock and mourning. Through his children, John had been able to feel young again. Even though John felt he buried his youth in Vietnam, he was able to capture moments of youth through his children. He delighted in their spontaneity, playfulness, and hope for the future, qualities he had lost but which he could vicariously enjoy by simply watching them.

When John's last child left home, John was devastated. Beyond the normal feelings of loss parents can have as their children leave the nest, John was losing more than his children; he was losing his connection to some of the feelings which gave life meaning.

That same year, John was given a new supervisor, one who acted very much like a commanding officer John had had in Vietnam. John had almost fragged this C.O. because of his cruelty and incompetence. The absence of his last child, combined with daily contact with what seemed to be a reincarnation of one of the most hated officers in John's unit, sent John back into the worst aspects of his Vietnam experience.

To make matters worse, the supervisor constantly berated John. Yet John felt he could not talk back, lest he lose his job. In Vietnam, John couldn't talk back either. If he had talked back then, he would have been punished severely. For example, he might have been beaten or sent on the most dangerous missions.

In Vietnam, John learned that his life depended on not talking. Now his economic well-being seemed to depend on the very same survival tactic: silence. Within months, John developed a severe case of asthma.

At work, John sometimes literally held his breath to refrain from expressing his rage. At times he felt like he was suffocating from lack of air. Emotionally, his pain and grief were suffocating him. In addition, he was trying to suffocate the anger which his new supervisor triggered in him. On a psychological level, John's medical problem was doing the grieving, raging, and talking he dared not do openly.

Somatization

David's asthma can be considered an example of yet another possible response to trauma: somatization. Somatization occurs when the body expresses the pain, anger, and other feelings associated with the trauma in the form of physical pain or impairment. As Dr. Judith Herman points out, somatization tends to occur more commonly in situations such as John's, where speaking up is dangerous and may be punished or cause for social ostracism or rejection.[78]

Somatization does not mean that the sufferer is mentally deficient or a manipulator who is trying to "pull a fast one." Somatization also does not mean that the pain isn't real or that it is "all in the head." The pain is true bodily pain. The illness is genuine. But the body is also expressing the feelings or memories that cannot be easily or sufficiently put into words because, if expressed, they will put the individual in jeopardy.

In combat veterans, somatization can take the form of physical pain or an increase in the pain of war injuries. On October 1, 1969, for example, Bill's arm was blown off. Around October 1 each year, Bill has phantom pains in his shoulder. "I don't like to complain about not having an arm, or about the fact that I still have to deal with infections, bleeding, and other problems because of that arm," says Bill. "But I guess the phantom pains do the complaining for me."

Dissociation

Have you ever been driving to a familiar place and missed the exit on the highway because your mind was somewhere else? Have you ever left your keys or wallet somewhere by accident because you were stressed out or "on overload"?

Such experiences of forgetting are common to everyone. They are minor forms of "dissociation," or a problem in memory where certain parts of reality are overlooked and other parts are focused on intently.

Without dissociation, we could not study for tests or even watch a movie because any concentrated activity requires paying attention to one part of reality and blocking out another. Many a Vietnam wife probably wishes she could "dissociate" from her family problems so she could simply enjoy a quiet walk or afternoon to herself. To truly dissociate, she would have to not only temporarily forget or dim some of her memories, but diminish, or almost obliterate, her feelings about those memories.

True dissociation can involve not only a blocking of information or memories, but a numbing of the emotions associated with that information or those memories. Hence a veteran may not recall a firefight or may be confused or vague about the specifics of the battle, but also report that he cannot remember his feelings at the time and that he has few feelings about the event today.

Like many symptoms, dissociation varies in severity and in the amount of havoc it can create in someone's life. Yet dissociation can also be a lifesaver. For example, the ability to dissociate helps abused children to do their homework and soldiers to bear the unbearable conditions. However, when dissociation is extreme, it can make keeping a job and maintaining good family communication almost impossible.

Veterans often described dissociation as "tuning out" or "numbing out." When a vet dissociates, his feelings become disconnected from his experience. He feels distant from what is going on about him, almost as if he is an observer rather than a participant in his own life. Amnesia about all or part of a specific traumatic event may also develop.

When the veteran dissociates in the present, he may truly forget all or part of the recent past or the present. His statement, "I don't know why. I just forgot," may be the truth.

If your husband dissociates, you may try to be understanding when he gets home hours late because he "tuned out" driving home and drove to another state. But you will also be worried and angry. You may resent his dissociative survival mechanism when he forgets to pay bills or pick up the children as planned.

In addition, at times you may be truly confused as to whether his not keeping his word at times is due to dissociation or whether tuning out is an excuse for being irresponsible. Since you may not be able to discern what dynamic is operating in your husband during a particular incident, you may want to consult with a trained professional, as well as with your husband.

Post-traumatic stress disorder depression somatization, and dissociation are not mutually exclusive. A veteran can suffer from all these reactions (e.g., he may have post-traumatic stress reactions with episodes of clinical depression or dissociation).

How Did the War Affect the Veteran Physically?

Paula took her two cats to the vet. The first cat became so agitated at being locked up in a cat box and transported to a strange place that she hissed at the veterinarian and scratched anyone who came close to her.

Even with the help of three trained assistants, the nine-pound cat's clawing and frantic movements could not be contained enough for the doctor to examine her.

In contrast, Paula's second cat went limp. From the moment she was placed in the cat box, she barely moved. She delighted the doctor because she was placid and easy to examine. But after her visit to the vet, the cat no longer delighted in life. She no longer purred when petted and was non-responsive to any signs of affection from Paula that day and for days afterwards.

The first cat's frantic fighting mode and the second cat's "shut down" mode seem to be extreme opposites of each other. Yet they are all part of the same phenomenon: the stimulation of the adrenal glands due to perceived or real threat or terror. The first cat's adrenals were stimulated to produce adrenaline, which put the cat in a "fight" mode. The second cat's adrenals pumped out noradrenaline, which put the cat in a "freeze" or "numbing" mode.[79]

These two cats, accustomed only to their owner's home, were temporarily traumatized: both the one who went wild and the one who went limp. For these cats, leaving the security of their safe place (home) and being put in unknown territory with strangers felt life-threatening and dangerous.

As the example of the cats illustrates, trauma can affect not only the emotions and the mind, but the physical self as well, specifically the central nervous system. When psychologist Abraham Kardiner studied the effects of war on veterans of World War I, he used the word "physioneurosis" to indicate that war had altered not only the thinking and feeling states of the warriors, but their physiology as well.[80]

Just as veterans sometimes continue "to live in the emotional environment of the traumatic event . . . the bodies of traumatized individuals continue to be on the alert for a return of the trauma and tend to react to even minor stresses with physiological emergency responses. . ."[81]

These emergency responses include the "three F's": fight, flight, freeze. Under conditions of danger, the adrenal glands release either adrenaline or noradrenaline. Adrenaline enables the warrior to move quickly and powerfully, whether to fight with renewed strength or to run (flight) with increased speed. In the example of the cats above, the first cat became so empowered with adrenaline it fought off three human beings, which is like one human being combating three elephants. In contrast, the second cat had a noradrenaline surge. Unlike adrenaline, noradrenaline leads to numbing responses. Hence some warriors freeze in battle and find themselves unable to move.

It is also possible for some veterans to be temporarily frozen (by noradrenaline), then empowered with adrenaline shortly thereafter or vice versa. Some veterans have been puzzled by the fact that one minute they could barely move, but the next minute, they found themselves fighting as if they were invincible. Upon reflection, they are angry at themselves for, on the one hand, being too "frozen" to kill and, on the other hand, so energetic they killed "too much" or took foolish risks with their lives. What they fail to realize is that their flight, fight, freeze responses were, to one degree or another, out of their control. Their bodies automatically went into fight, flight, freeze reactions as a means of self-preservation.

Under the influence of increased adrenaline flow, there can be increases in heart rate, blood sugar level, muscle tension, and perspiration; dilation of the pupils; and hyperventilation (rapid shallow breathing from the upper lung versus more normal, gentle breathing from the lower lung). Hyperventilation, in turn, can lead to irregular heart rate and dizziness, shortness of breath, choking sensations, lump in the throat, heartburn, chest pain, blurred vision, muscle pains or spasms, nausea, shaking, and numbness or tingling of mouth, hands, or feet. It can also generate mental confusion and difficulties with concentration.[82]

At first glance, an adrenaline surge may seem preferable to a noradrenaline response, especially in battle. However, adrenaline surges can be problematic because they cannot be turned off at will. Soldiers in battle whose adrenaline surges cause them to fight as powerfully as possible are easily tempted to discharge excess adrenaline through abusive violence, needless killings, or other acts of destruction. Or they may attempt to quiet the excess adrenaline by using alcohol or other drugs.

The adrenaline surge does not excuse excessive violence, but it plays an undeniable role in such incidents, not only in combat, but back home, when the veteran is triggered by an event that reminds him of war. When family members of veterans with PTSD "walk on eggs," it is because they do not want to trigger their veteran into a rage reaction over which he may not have control. The veteran himself, aware of his potential for violence and fearing the adrenaline surges and their powerful inducement to violence, may withdraw from family life, social events, and other aspects of communal living lest he be triggered into an uncontrollable fight mode.

Combat veterans know how powerful adrenaline surges can be. They also know how even the strongest man cannot often successfully fight his own biology. Consequently, some veterans may avoid people, places, and events which carry with them the possibility of igniting anger or memories of the war. On the surface, it may appear to family members, friends, and co-workers that the veteran is standoffish or a loner or severely disturbed, because he needs to retreat. Yet the veteran's retreat may be highly socially motivated: he simply does not want to hurt anyone. Some combat veterans have even left good jobs rather than take the chance of being triggered into a rage on the job which could lead to an uncontrollable adrenaline-induced violent reaction.

The subject of biological changes which occur when a person is exposed to repeated or prolonged trauma is complex, involving changes in the functioning of neurotransmitters and other biochemical changes. A more complete discussion of the physiology of PTSD is beyond the scope of this book, but can be found in the references cited in the Recommended Reading List located at the end of this book. Let it suffice here to state that veterans who suffer from some of these biochemical changes are vulnerable to clinical depression, mood swings, explosive outbursts, startle response, and overreacting to subsequent stress.

The Vietnam wife, no matter how much she loves her husband, may find it difficult to cope with these symptoms. Like her children, she may attribute the veteran's mood swings and rage reactions to her behavior. Yet one of the prime causes of these symptoms lies in the changes in the veteran's biochemistry due to overuse of his emergency biological system.

Often medication can help to repair the damage to the central nervous system caused by trauma. When medication succeeds in reducing the intensity of these symptoms, the veteran feels more in control of himself and consequently, may feel safer about interacting with his family and others. However, while medication can help control these symptoms, it cannot eliminate them entirely, unless, of course, the veteran becomes overmedicated and incapable of any kind of response, either negative or positive.

The biochemistry of PTSD is one of the new and promising areas of research in the field of traumatology.

2

Living with the Ice Man

He loves you, but he doesn't trust you and he wants to run away from you—that's the double message you get from someone with PTSD.

Looking back on the early years of my marriage, I don't know what was harder for me—Jim's anger or his depressions and his numbing. That numbing—it was, and is, one of the biggest problems we have. Sometimes I can't get through to him no matter what I do.

At first I tried to pierce his wall gently. No success. So then I tried rejection and anger. Maybe if I rebuffed and scorned him, he would come around. That worked—sometimes. But if his wall was really up, I could throw a first-class temper tantrum and he'd just shrug his shoulders and walk out the door.

I soon discovered that pressuring Jim for a response, whether I used loving tactics or not, was self-defeating. Either way, I'd usually drive him further away from me.

But he would always come back. He loves me. I know he loves me. And he's a good man, an honest man, who is only hurting himself. But in hurting himself, he hurts all of us—me and the kids.

"Why doesn't Daddy go with us to Aunt Vicky's or Grandma's or the

mall?" the kids used to ask. Now they don't ask anymore. They just accept Jim the way he is. I'd like to tell them that because of Vietnam their father just can't take crowds and loud, noisy places and parties, but I just don't know how.

I came to group complaining about Jim's numbing, not realizing that, over the years, I had become numb myself. Just like Jim, I am afraid of the feelings inside me—the years of pent-up anger and hurt and my sense of loss about what I thought my marriage would be and what my marriage really is.

Sometimes I stay away from group because I don't want to face my feelings. When I face the truth about my life, it hurts so bad I pray for the numbing to come back.

—Wife of a combat vet

Have you ever cut yourself and not felt the pain immediately? Have you ever been whiplashed in a car accident, but not felt the soreness or fatigue until several days later? The body often emits a natural anesthetic which permits us some time to take care of our wounds and to do whatever is necessary to protect ourselves from further injury. When the pain is overwhelming, we may even go into shock and lose consciousness entirely. Our bodies simply cannot tolerate the pain and nature, mercifully, spares us.

Just as, in self-protection, the body may temporarily anesthetize itself against physical pain, the psyche, in self-protection, can numb itself against onslaughts of unbearable emotional pain. During combat in Vietnam, the soldier had to turn off his emotions. Feelings had to be put aside because feeling them would have been not only personally confusing, but life-threatening. If the combat vet had connected with his grief during battle, he would have been less able to give and take directions or otherwise figure out what to do next in order to save himself and others.

This deadening, or shutting off, of emotions is called emotional or psychic numbing. It is a central feature of PTSD and has been found not only among combat vets, but also among survivors of other traumas— survivors of the Nazi holocaust and the bombing of Hiroshima; victims of earthquakes, floods, and fires; and victims of physical assaults such as rape, incest, child abuse, or muggings.

In the face of a traumatic event, emotional numbing is an entirely appropriate response, for it helps a person "to pass through a period of trauma or excessive stress" by dulling his or her "awareness of the death, the destruction, and the terror and the anguish about him [or her] and of his [or her] own helplessness in such a situation."[1]

Problems occur, however, when the individual remains in the state of numbing long after the original traumatic event. In these cases, the emotional numbing is carried over to other areas of life or to present day situations where there is no danger. Then it can severely "interfere with human living," especially with personal relationships.[2]

Vets with unresolved PTSD are often "stuck" at the numbing stage. Until recently, the Vietnam veteran was aided in the numbing of his wartime experience by two outside factors: military training which not only dehumanized the enemy, but which also "punished . . . [men] who experienced or expressed fear, sadness or grief or tenderness" by labeling them "faggot, sissy, or some other derogatory label";[3] and a society that for the most part did not want to hear about the veteran's wartime experiences.

Only in the past several years has our society begun to reflect on the Vietnam experience and appreciate its impact on the men who served. Before now, despite the well-publicized agony of the Vietnam war, much of the American public was in a state of "psychic numbing" about the war.

Some vets came home to supportive families and friends who were willing to listen and not judge. However, many found that their friends and family at home were not interested in their emotional experiences and traumas. The vet's soul-searching questions, if he dared to ask them, were even less welcome.

One wife explains: "An unprecedented media blitz had made us all aware of the political morass, the atrocities, the ambiguities. We knew the veterans were not heroes even before they did, but we were not sure just what they were. And so we told them simply to get on with their lives (and ours); to bury whatever it was they had seen and felt, to become 'normal' again. We refused to allow them to defuse. We didn't know how to hear men cry; we were unable to find out how they had changed.

"We weren't being cruel. We just wanted to love them as they had been and still were in our fantasies. We hoped that we could make them smile. But . . . we were the first to see that the problems would not disappear in some washday miracle, would not respond to our nurturing."[4]

In addition, unlike previous wars where soldiers shared war stories with surviving members of their units during the long journey home, the typical Vietnam veteran returned home alone, with no opportunity to "decompress" or share experiences and feelings with his comrades. For the Vietnam veteran, there was no gradual comedown or psychological debriefing. In contrast, some efforts were made to debrief veterans of the Persian Gulf and the results were positive. The Vietnam veteran, however, often was in the jungle one day and back home the next.[5]

One vet explains: "I got out of Vietnam on the sixth of June, got home the eighth. All of a sudden I found myself at one in the morning standing outside Oakland Air Force Base in my dress greens. I was out of the Army. I wish I would have had a barracks to go to or an EOD unit to settle down and relax and talk to people that could listen to me and understand—I wish it wouldn't have been so abrupt because it did fuck me up."[6]

Another vet killed a man an hour before he was put on a plane back home. Twenty-four hours later, in his mother's living room, he wanted to talk about it. "Oh forget it," his mother said. "Why do you want to upset everybody?"

Many vets complain that upon return home they were expected to recover from their war experiences quickly and to resume "life as usual" almost instantly. After Vietnam, however, life could no longer be "as usual" for them or for their families. In addition, feeling forced to pretend to be normal or untouched by their combat experience imposed yet another psychological strain on the already stressed veteran.

Psychic numbing exists in different degrees, in different ways, in different vets at different times. There is no set pattern. However, the result is the same: a distressing inability on the part of the PTSD afflicted veteran to form a meaningful, sustained emotional connection with another human being.

The Effect of Numbing on Relationships

The last time Lisa and Allen held hands was in 1973. Their last hug was 11 years ago. "And that's only because he forgot my birthday again and I reminded him," Lisa explains. "Allen was never that sentimental, but since 'Nam, he's done nothing about my birthdays or our anniversaries.

"If I didn't force Allen, he wouldn't show up at our son's soccer games, either. Last time I had to beg Allen to come. He came, all right, but he left after a half hour.

"Jeff wondered what happened to his Dad. I told him his Dad was sick. What else am I going to tell a teenager in his 'awkward years'— in front of his all-important friends—that his dad has PTSD and can't relate to people?"

After several years of having their anniversary passed by unnoticed, Lisa finally insisted that Allen take her out to dinner. Allen agreed, provided that the restaurant was not an Asian one. On the way to the restaurant, Allen kept reminding Lisa that birthdays, anniversaries, cards, and flowers no longer held any meaning for him. After the life and death situations he had encountered in Vietnam, most social formalities and "middle class sentimentalities" seemed trivial to him, if not outright silly.

Allen's low tolerance for formal dinners was born in Vietnam where, on several occasions, he had been given contradictory orders and found himself in situations which baffled all human reason. He had also suffered immensely from the heat and a variety of jungle rashes and had seen children starving to death. At one point he had been near starvation himself.

Lisa was not heartless. However, she was tired of hearing about the war. "While we were waiting for the waiter, all I heard about was how in 'Nam, combat vets never ate in fancy restaurants, about how the restaurants were booby trapped, about how lucky I was to be a woman, not a man, and to have escaped Vietnam—the whole bit. I wanted to leave right then and there, but then I figured it was probably better that he talk about the war than go into numbing.

"Besides, if I had suggested leaving, Allen would have either blown up at me, punched a hole in the table, or tuned out entirely. Sometimes I don't know what's easier to take: the numbing or the anger.

"So I sat there pretending, wondering how I was going to get through three hours of this, when we ended up leaving early anyway because the waiter was Oriental.

"We went home, Allen went out drinking, and I went to bed alone. This is the thanks I get for 15 years of being a loyal wife."

A majority of research studies support the existence of feelings of detachment and problematic interpersonal relationships among veterans with PTSD.[7] It must be remembered, however, that many of these studies are based primarily on veterans who seek help at Department of Veterans Affairs Medical Centers or at Vet Centers, not on the Vietnam veteran population as a whole or on Vietnam veterans who seek help with private mental health professionals. Therefore, the results of the studies cannot be generalized to the entire Vietnam veteran population. However, in the Vet Center study, over 95% of the Vet Center counselors polled observed that coping with the veteran's emotional numbing—his tendency to shut off emotionally and to be reluctant or unable to share on a deep emotional level—was a common problem for wives of PTSD afflicted veterans. In addition, almost 90% of those polled reported that vets with PTSD have greater difficulty disclosing themselves and expressing themselves with their wives or girlfriends than non-PTSD afflicted veterans. It may well be that it is primarily women whose husbands suffer from numbing who seek help.

In some cases, the numbing of emotions is so severe that the veteran is rendered almost totally incapable of relating to others, especially women, on more than a superficial level. Some of these more alienated veterans are literally homeless street people, who wander from one part of the country to the other, unable to commit themselves not only to a family, but also to an institution or organization.[8] Some of these men have had such devastating experiences in Vietnam that they have been unable to reintegrate into the mainstream of society, much less establish a relationship with a woman.

Other vets work two jobs or 10- to 14-hour days, filling their lives with work, not people. Such a heavy work involvement may be an economic necessity. However, the wives of such vets point out that even during nonwork hours, when the vet could be with the family, he chooses solitary pursuits or "blanks out" in front of the television. Sometimes he does not even watch television with the family, but has his own set in another room.

Other men deliberately choose to work evening shifts, rather than day hours. They prefer to work alone and in relative quiet. By working nights, not only do they have fewer co-workers to deal with on the job, but when they return home, they can sleep rather than deal with their wife and children. The night job also functions to prevent the veteran from attending numerous social and family affairs.

A few of the women who have attended the Vet Center woman's group have even had husbands who worked in other states, cities, or counties, but who, nevertheless, wanted to remain married—even to have children. Yet the veteran may visit his wife only 10 or 12 times a year, sometimes less often. Usually it is the veteran who decides on the visits. He appears on his wife's doorstep when he wants to see her, not when she wants to see him.

Sometimes the visits are announced, sometimes not. "I can't go anywhere because he expects me to be home waiting for him all the time," explains one wife. "But sometimes he doesn't show up when he says he's going to. Then I get depressed. But I'm afraid that if I complain, he won't come see me at all."

The wife who tolerates this degree of distance and instability may have been raised to expect very little from a man. Or perhaps she comes from a dysfunctional or abusive family of origin and is used to inconstant love and affection. Even though her Vietnam veteran may not be giving her the attention and support that is considered customary or ideal in a marriage or relationship, what she is receiving from him may be far more than what she received from her family of origin or a previous cruel husband. Sometimes a woman in this situation has few career ambitions, was given no job motivation other than financial survival, or was reared to be a traditionalist in desiring to center her life almost exclusively around a man.

Her dreams of love and marriage, however, are shattered by the reality of a husband who is more like a part-time lover. Even when she is with her husband, she is often disappointed. He may be affectionate, but more often he is cool and distant, even though he may have traveled many miles to see her. His coolness may have been born from the sorrows and betrayals he experienced in Vietnam or afterward. But the sources of his behavior, however legitimate, do not make his behavior any easier for his wife to tolerate.

"Sometimes I wonder why he comes to see me," one wife states. "He doesn't want to talk that much and when we're in bed, he's like an ice man. He says he doesn't care whether we have sex or not, doesn't care whether we stay married or not. If I start crying, he'll tell me he loves me, but he just can't help it, he doesn't care about anything."

The couple does not always engage in sex during these visits. But if they do, the woman often feels as if she has been with a stranger rather than with a husband. However, she usually hesitates to bring up her complaints for fear of further alienating an already alienated man.

For most of the Vet Center women, however, their partners' psychic numbing and emotional distancing is not so extreme. While some of the men are described by their wives as being almost chronically numb, other husbands are described as fluctuating between being emotionally present and "walling" out their families with what one woman aptly calls an "invisible sheet of ice." The vet may have periods where he is a family man, followed by periods where he is almost always absent from family functions. Or if present, he may be emotionally unresponsive and detached. Furthermore, he may suddenly freeze at a family function, stare into space, or leave abruptly, especially if Vietnam is mentioned or if there is some trigger from the war, such as a passing airplane or a sudden noise. He might also distance himself by starting an argument, which gives him an excuse to leave the room.

Some men freeze during intercourse as well, perhaps because of an intrusive memory or because the emotional and physical closeness is intolerable. As the vet retreats into his shell, the woman may be left frantic, wondering what to do next and questioning her sexual desirability.

"I can tell the minute he walks through the door whether or not his 'wall' is going to be up for the night," says Lisa. "If it is, there's no chance of sex or any kind of communication. Allen wants to be alone so much of the time, sometimes I wonder why he's married at all."

Typically, Allen wants two or three hours to himself after work before he can join the family. Sometimes his need for solitude conflicts with the children's schedules, so that he often misses spending time with them. When he is with his family, he seems uninterested or distant.

Lisa has read about PTSD and understands why Allen is silent and needs to absent himself. But on some level, she still wonders if there is something she does or says that causes Allen's coldness. The children, however, have little comprehension of their father's problem. Like their mother, they have come to accept their father's numbing as normal. A depressive blanket seems to cover the family and the major weight of the family's emotional life falls on Lisa.

"I don't even explain to the kids anymore why their father doesn't eat with us or isn't there to help them with their homework. If we plan to go on a picnic or game or even to my mother's for Christmas, and Allen, at the last minute, decides not to go, I've learned to go ahead without him.

"It's hard . . . but it's better than staying home with an angry vet or with someone so numb that sometimes he's like a statue."

When Lisa first sought help, almost all of her complaints about Allen's numbing had to do with the effects on their children, not herself. "I don't care about me, only the kids," she would repeat. Eventually, however, Lisa was able to experience her own deep sense of rejection and hurt at Allen's walling her out.

"It's painful to love a man who, although he might love you, is incapable of showing it. And it's not the big rejections—the major blowups, the horrible name calling, things like him not being there for Christmas—that do me under. It's the hundred little ways he ignores me every day. One hundred little rejections equal one big depression."

While the veteran in numbing may not intend to shut out his wife, she often experiences his numbness as a personal rejection. Even when she learns in group that her husband's iciness and need to be distant from her has more to do with his war experiences or his family background than her own physical, emotional, or sexual desirability as a woman, she may still feel rejected.

"Intellectually, I know it's the numbing, but emotionally, I need more from a marriage. Living with a Vietnam veteran is like being on a starvation diet," states one wife. Many wives complain of emotional neglect, or of not knowing whether they are "on" or "off."

The anxiety of not knowing whether she is going to be greeted with smiles, anger, or a blank look is especially prevalent among women who are adult children of alcoholics. For example, as a child, Lynn used to help calm her alcoholic father after his drinking binges and soothe her mother after her parents' frequent fights. Even before she reached puberty, both parents were turning to Lynn for "mothering" and comfort.

The little girl in Lynn had a legitimate right to want to be taken care of, rather than thrust in the role of caretaker. However, Lynn repressed her natural child desires and received much praise from her parents and other relatives for her abilities to keep the family together and make her parents and her sisters feel better.

Eventually she came to feel as if the continuation of the family depended on her. Whenever one of her parents was upset, she interpreted it as the result of something she had failed to do or had done wrong. She felt she needed to be perfect to keep the family from falling apart. As a child she had a persistent nightmare in which her home was blown up because she failed to please one or the other of her parents.

Today, however, as the wife of a combat vet who suffers from intermittent numbing, Lynn is experiencing the same emotional instability in her home as she did when she was a child. Once again, she feels responsible for the continuation of the family. During her frequent anxiety attacks about whether or not her husband will be pleased with her, she hyperventilates, perspires, and burns much of her emotional energy. She worries about how her husband's emotional state is going to affect her children. She is often running in two directions, trying to cheer up her husband and smooth things out for her children as well. When home life isn't happy she fails to see her husband's role in the situation, but focuses on her own inadequacies and minor imperfections.

Because her present home situation is similar to her childhood situation, Lynn's anxiety attacks tend to be intense and, at times, frighten her immensely. Her conclusion, that she is "neurotic," creates even more self-doubts and anxiety for her.

Wives can encounter additional problems with the veteran's numbing as their children grow older or if they marry the veteran at mid-life and bring to their marriage adolescent children from a former marriage. Teenage children may have heard about combat stress or the Vietnam conflict and seen movies or other media presentations on the subject. They can use the veteran's symptoms or knowledge of the war as a club against the veteran (or their mother) in their attempts to assert their independence and individuality from their parents or in the usual clashes with parents over dating, money, schoolwork, chores, and other teenage issues.

For example, a teenager might call her father or stepfather a "baby-killer" in retort for being disciplined or scolded. Or she may say, "You lost the war because you were too drunk to really fight. So don't tell me how to run my life." Or she may challenge her mother's directives by calling her mother stupid, as proven by the fact that her mother married a "crazy Vietnam vet."

Such statements can easily trigger the veteran's rage toward, or withdrawal from, that child, and perhaps from the family entirely. From the veteran's point of view, he has been "zapped" by friendly fire. Rather than retaliate, he may withdraw into an extreme state of numbing. Or he may retaliate, physically or verbally, then become numb later.

Whereas younger children might feel rejected by the veteran's numbing, older children may reject their father or stepfather because of his numbing or his unpredictable moods. They may arrange to see their friends outside the home or when their father is not around because they fear he may go into his "thousand mile stare," or begin to cry, sulk or yell and embarrass them in front of their friends.

In one instance, a daughter of a Vietnam veteran did not want her father to attend her engagement party. She knew her father hated crowds and formal affairs, such as she had planned. She had seen him go numb, or make a scene, at previous formal family functions. While she loved her father very much and was understanding of his PTSD, she just could not take a chance that he would ruin her special day. Even if he acted appropriately, she'd feel as if she had to watch him constantly to be certain he was not becoming overly anxious or depressed.

The veteran pretended to understand his daughter's position, but inside seethed with anger, shame, and hurt. He increasingly withdrew from the family and considered abandoning them and living in the streets. His wife tried to effect a compromise between her husband and her daughter, but both were rigidly entrenched in their positions. At one point, the veteran asked his wife to choose between him and their daughter, an impossible choice for this wife and mother. When she could not choose, the veteran threatened to commit suicide and left home. Outside intervention was necessary to help this troubled veteran family.

◆ ◆ ◆

Repressing Grief

Psychic numbing involves the repression of two powerful emotions: grief and anger. Grief repression has been cited many times as central to the vet's inability to emotionally connect with others.[9] The wall the vet builds around himself to keep others out is essentially a reflection of the wall he's built around his own heart to shield himself from his own pain and grief.

Some vets are afraid to grieve, for fear that once they start they might never stop. Having repressed their grief through numbing, they fear that once they begin to sorrow over one memory or incident, they will be flooded by other memories and drown in grief. So they fight their grief, trying to keep a tight lid on it, rather than experience the pain.

The depression which many vets experience is, in reality, repressed grief. It is often easier, or more comfortable, to be depressed than to actively hurt or suffer. Although depression is a way that grief can be expressed, it is not actually grieving. In order for healing to occur, the grief must be experienced in full, perhaps a little at a time and usually more than once, before the individual is able to let go of the loss and become more fully involved in the present.

Vets with PTSD often find themselves in the midst of deep depressions every year around the anniversary dates of the deaths of friends or certain other traumatic experiences. During such depressive episodes, the vet may continue to go to work. However, his working capacity is often impaired. At home his involvement with the family often comes to a standstill.

Typically, wives severely curtail their outside activities and don't come to group during these periods. Even though their husbands may not be talking to them, they feel that their husbands need them around. At such times, the husband may be unwilling, or, in the wife's view, unable, to watch the children while she is gone. The men may also be unwilling, or unable, to perform other household duties, leaving more work for the women. "How can I remind him to take out the trash when he's doing all he can to fight his depression and keep himself together enough to get to work the next day?" one wife asks.

While some of the wives are understanding, others wonder if their husband's psychic numbing is an excuse to escape responsibilities. Even some male counselors at veterans hospitals and centers, some of whom are Vietnam veterans themselves, recognize that some vets use PTSD symptoms as a way to get their wives to do more of the work, especially chores which they dislike or consider women's work.

In some cases, it is relatively easy to determine whether the veteran is using PTSD as an excuse or not. But in others, the situation is complex. For example, Mike refuses to drive his daughter to cheerleader practice or to her basketball games. This angers his wife, who works full-time and must add another trip onto the end of her already long workday. "Why can't he do it?" she shouts in a marriage counseling session. "After all, he only works 10 hours a week. I work 40. What is this? The middle ages when women did everything?"

But Mike insists that his sanity will snap if he sees one more basketball or pompom girl.

When Mike's daughter first became a cheerleader for her junior high school's basketball team, Mike did all the chauffeuring. Yet he did not approve of his daughter's participation. Even though he had been a basketball champ in high school, he now viewed basketball and all competitive sports as microcosms of the military system. Furthermore, he thought that cheerleading was a sexist institution. Nevertheless, he could not fight his daughter's desire to join the cheerleading squad nor his family's reaction to his objections.

It was not until the third or fourth basketball game, however, that Mike finally discovered yet a deeper source of his dislike of basketball. During this particular game, one of the players was knocked down. His knee cap was broken and his nose began to bleed profusely. As he was carried off the gym floor, he moaned loudly and left a trail of blood.

Mike's daughter began to weep, "Look at the blood! Look at the blood!"

As Mike looked, the heads of the basketball players seemed to pop off and, within seconds, their young bodies had become dismembered corpses strewn around the gym floor. Then, when his daughter leapt into the air yelling a cheer, Mike imagined her uniform full of blood stains and her legs bleeding with knife wounds. Howling in pain, she died in mid-air.

The sight of the blood and the young boy falling had brought to the surface a memory from Vietnam which Mike had almost totally repressed. It so happened that the number of combatants involved in this particular firefight, and their distribution and location on the battle ground, was remarkably similar to the number of boys involved in the basketball game, and their location on the gym floor. Furthermore, a member of Mike's basketball team, a friend whom Mike had encouraged to join the military, had died in that fight.

Mike had never dealt with his grief regarding that fight or his guilt regarding the death of his friend. Neither had he ever dealt with his horror at seeing the legs of a young Vietnamese girl hacked with knives. Soon afterward, he sought help at a local vet center.

One year later, however, he was not over Vietnam. His overworked wife, however, was waiting for the day when Mike would be able to relieve her of some of the chauffeuring. Furthermore, her son was going to join a little league next year. Then what "Vietnam problem" was going to prevent Mike from helping out with the driving? Would Mike at least allow his children to join a car pool? Up to this point, Mike did not trust his children with anyone but himself or his wife.

Mike's wife felt he was paranoid and impossible. Mike, on the other hand, felt he was only being cautious. "No one outside the family can be trusted," he insisted. Besides, if anything happened to one of the children, he would kill the offender, and then himself.

"It's not the work I mind," Mike's wife explained. "It's Mike's attitude. Our daughter knows he doesn't like her being a cheerleader and she feels bad about it. She feels guilty about going against her father. In fact, she was ready to quit the team after Mike broke down during that game. But I made her stick with it.

"She deserves to have a normal life; so does our son, even if our family isn't normal because of Vietnam.

"Our kids need outside activities more than most kids because our home life is so depressing. Mike's depressed. I'm depressed. We're struggling to keep our marriage together and make ends meet. I don't know how we're going to end up, but I do want these children to have some good memories of their childhood."

As a compromise, Mike agreed to assume additional household chores and not make derogatory comments about sports. In addition, he felt he could tolerate picking up his daughter one day a week, provided he could wait in the parking lot and not have to observe any games. Furthermore, his daughter had to change from her cheerleader uniform into regular clothes. He did not ever want to see that uniform again.

Peter's refusal to help his son move into a college dorm illustrates how combat stress can trigger repressed grief during normally problematic life transitions, making these normal life transitions exceptionally painful, if not retraumatizing, for the veteran, and a horrendous ordeal for the veteran's family. A child's leaving home for college, a military career, a job, or marriage can be difficult for many parents, even under the best of circumstances. There may be mixed feelings, for example. On the one hand, the child's departure is an emotional loss for the parents. On the other hand, there is cause for rejoicing in that parents can credit themselves for having succeeded in raising a child to the point of near maturity.

It is also a time of some fear. The child, now almost an adult, may fear facing the world without a protective parent nearby. The parents, on the other hand, may fear allowing their child to venture forth into a world of people, few of whom have the same attitude of parental love and protectiveness toward their child as they do.

As Douglas Scaturo and Peter Hayman write, "For the combat veteran who has frequently observed the loss of significant friendships often instantaneously, randomly, and brutally on the battlefield, the normative transitional events of family life may take on exaggerated emotional proportions by the standards of those who have never been traumatized."[10] Thus the event of children leaving home is experienced not only as a step toward the child's independence and maturation, but also as agony and betrayal. A child's leaving, however appropriate or innocent, brings to the surface the veteran's "feelings of total abandonment, isolation, and helplessness previously experienced during combat."[11]

The situation in Peter's and Nora's home illustrates the difficulties Vietnam families encounter when a child leaves home for college. Peter's son had won a basketball scholarship to a well-known college which was out of state. Peter himself had loved playing basketball as a youth, until a war injury prevented him from pursuing any sport whatsoever. He could barely walk, much less run. Unconsciously, perhaps, Peter's son excelled in basketball not only for himself, but for his father.

Peter was always so enthralled when his son excelled in another game. At the same time, his son rejoiced that he could bring some joy to his crippled, suffering father.

Peter had supported his son's applying for basketball scholarships at various out-of-state colleges. Consequently his son could not understand the intensity of his father's grief and anger when he announced he was going to accept a scholarship from a college 500 miles from home.

"How can you leave us?" Peter growled at his son.

"But Dad, you helped me apply for the scholarship yourself and you always wanted me to play basketball."

"Get lost, I never want to see you again. Maybe I'll kill myself."

Peter's son was angry, hurt, and confused. Peter's wife, Nora, was livid. She berated Peter for spoiling their son's victory in winning a major scholarship. Calling Peter selfish and inconsiderate, she ordered her husband to make amends to their son by personally helping him pack and move to the college.

Peter was in no mood for orders and called his wife selfish and inconsiderate for asking him to engage in physical activities, such as moving, which he could not perform well due to his war injuries. Peter stormed out of the home, furious, but also feeling guilty and ashamed.

He knew he had mistreated his son, yet he felt so cheated and betrayed by life that he couldn't help but become enraged at the thought of having to separate from someone so precious to him.

Memories of dead war buddies flashed through Peter's mind and he began to tremble thinking that his son might fall into harm without his protection. Suddenly his rage turned into tears. What if his son would die, away from home, like his buddies did.

"I'm overreacting. I'm overreacting," he told himself, but he still could not make himself feel differently. Inside he was shaking and bursting with emotions he could not name.

Nora requested an emergency meeting with Peter's counselor. Peter wept openly in front of his son about the pain of saying goodbye, not only to him, but to others who were now dead. For the first time, Peter's son understood that his father's reactions to him were not signs of disapproval and rejection of him as a son, but expressions of his father's profound love for him, his father's deep fears for his safety, and his father's war grief.

For Peter, the son's leaving home for college was a reliving of his war experience where he lost many friends. Although Peter currently had a few friends outside the family, his family was the center of emotional life. Now one of the major purposes of his life, his son, was walking out the door. No wonder he was shattered.

Nora, on the other hand, had also invested herself in the family. Like her husband, or any parent saying goodbye to a child leaving home, she was racked with feelings of pain and loss. But Nora had never threatened suicide because of her son, as had Peter. Nor had Nora ever gone through months and months of deep depression with the only joy in her life being her usefulness to her son. But Peter had clung to life many times only because he knew that his suicide would devastate his son.

"I remember once coming home after having a flashback while driving. It was of the Tet offensive where scores of guys died. I nearly died on the highway because I lost control of the car and nearly hit some people.

"Driving home, I decided I was a danger to society and should kill myself. But when I got home, my son, who was six at the time, was waiting outside for me. 'Daddy, Daddy, where have you been?' he asked. 'I've been waiting for you a long time. Hurry up, Daddy. I want to show you the "A" I got on my homework.'

"After that, I realized I couldn't kill myself. My son needed me."

Now that his son was leaving home, Peter would have to find new people to love and additional purposes for living. This would be hard for Peter since, like many veterans, he tended to isolate himself.

In a later counseling session, Nora suggested that Peter join some veterans organizations or make some other attempts to find new friends. Or he could become involved in some educational or social projects in which he could have direct contact with other children who needed attention. He could even start paying attention to her. She needed attention, as did their marriage.

Now that their son was gone, they would have more time for each other.

But Peter would not consider any of these ideas. This made Nora so furious she stood up in the middle of the counselor's office.

"See," she told the counselor. "He won't do a thing to help himself. All he does is moan and groan about the pain and make us all suffer, but when I give him a positive suggestion to make things better, he refuses to even try. All he wants to do is hide from life, all alone in his little room."

Nora then began to sob. "Peter's not the only one who is heartbroken that our son is going away. I'm going to miss our son too, even if I was never suicidal in my life. Now with our son gone, I'll need my husband even more. But he won't be there for me. Why? Because I'm not important. Why? Because I didn't fight in Vietnam.

"Peter, just because I'm not a Vietnam veteran doesn't mean I'm a nobody. My feelings matter too."

Peter remained unmoved.

"Your eyes are fixed on the floor and you have a sad look on your face. Are you feeling anything now?" the counselor asked Peter.

"I don't know. I just can't react. I want to respond to my wife, but I can't. I'm numb."

"What do you think of your wife's ideas?" asked the counselor.

"They're good logical ideas, but they are unacceptable to me."

"Why?"

"Because acting on them would insult my friends who died in Vietnam and my son, too. No other boy can replace him."

"Explain to me how making new friends is a betrayal of the men on the Wall. I really want to understand," said the counselor.

Peter could not explain, but deep in his heart he was certain that there was a strong connection. As Yael Danieli explains, for many trauma survivors, not only war veterans, but survivors of concentration camps, refugees, or other traumatic experiences, fully grieving and saying goodbye to the dead "perpetuates the hell" experienced by the survivors when they saw that the dead among them were not recognized or appreciated. Therefore, embracing the new, on a feeling level, can be experienced as abandoning the dead, which is tantamount to discounting and forgetting one's own memories of what was a permanently life changing experience.[12]

While society might want the Vietnam veteran to forget, or deny, his experiences, he cannot do so without annihilating a part of himself. Therefore Peter's decision not to expand his world after the departure of his son is a form of honoring the dead and, on some level, an act of self-preservation. Yet to his wife and others, the decision seems like a needless sacrifice that leaves not only Peter, but his wife, relatively isolated. Furthermore, the devastating impact of the son's departure on Peter left Peter with little to give his wife emotionally to help her with her sense of loss and adjustment needs.

At transition times, when couples need to turn to each other for support and comfort, Nora was left standing alone. Her husband's reasons for not being able to be there for her were legitimate and, to a large degree, out of his, or her, control. Yet that does not mitigate the fact that Nora was not receiving the tenderness, affection, and love she needed and expected from her husband at this time.

In such situations, there are no "good guys" or "bad guys," but rather two hurting people, who could provide each other with a considerable amount of comfort and support if they could only connect.

◆ ◆ ◆

Fear of Loss

Often vets with psychic numbing can function quite well at work, where emotional awareness and responsiveness are not required. However, at home, where emotional exchange is essential, the vets may fail miserably. Their wall may not always be up but, some wives sense, it is always there.

Being with relative strangers on the job is usually much easier for the PTSD-afflicted veteran than being close to those at home, where he might forsake his wartime vow "never to care about anyone."[13] "I swore I would never again let anyone matter to me, so I couldn't ever hurt that much again," states a veteran, remembering the combat death of his best friend.[14]

In the other cases, however, the vet does not react with withdrawal, but with a hyperstate where he cannot do enough. He may even become the rock on which the entire family leans. However, even when he is helpful and protective, unless he has been through PTSD therapy or otherwise learned to deal with loss, he will usually not be emotionally present. For example, while he can help make arrangements for a funeral, he may not be able to help others with their grieving, just as he himself may not be able to grieve at such times. At the same time, however, he may be wondering what is wrong with him that he does not feel sad or cry.

It is not clear why some vets respond to family crises by pitching in and helping and why others respond by disappearing, both emotionally and physically. According to the Vet Center counselors, the vet's response to loss may depend not only on his upbringing but on the way in which he saw, smelled, and felt death in Vietnam—in other words, the sheer amount of death and destruction he witnessed during his tour of duty. The way he reacted to loss in Vietnam can provide clues to his civilian response.

If, in Vietnam, he responded by going out and killing someone, he may have an angry outburst when there is a loss in his family. If he responded by numbing himself with alcohol, drugs, or emotional withdrawal, he may respond in the same way in the present. If he was in a unit that was mobile or under frequent fire, he may not have had the opportunity to mourn the death of his buddies and learned to numb himself emotionally.

Vets also respond differently to loss depending on whether or not they feel some sense of responsibility for the loss. If a vet's father dies of cancer, he may have no feeling of responsibility for his father's death.

If, however, his child dies of cancer, he may feel that the death is his fault since he was exposed to Agent Orange. Similarly, if his wife or child is injured in a car accident, he may know he was not to blame. If his child is molested by a babysitter, he may berate himself for not being more selective in his choice of a sitter.

Similarly, if his teenage son or daughter is murdered or harmed because of involvements in the drug trade or becomes involved in criminal activities, the vet may blame his perceived deficiencies as a parent for these events. His wife, parents, and others in the family may also blame him, which only increases his self-hate, shame, and guilt.

As more than one wife has affirmed, some vets stay emotionally distant from others because they are afraid that everything they touch will wither and die. On a subconscious level, the vet may blame himself for the family member's illness or injury, feeling that the "bad karma" or "death taint" which he acquired in Vietnam has followed him home. There may also be an element of guilt. Some vets feel that they are going to be punished for some of their thoughts and behaviors in Vietnam through the death or injury of one of their family members. Mike, for instance, was certain that God was going to punish him for not stopping the killing of an innocent child in Vietnam. Someday God would take away one of his own children.

Another example is Marie's husband, Dan. Shortly after Marie married Dan, her child by a former marriage contracted leukemia and died. From the time the child first became ill until she died some two years later, Dan refused to drive Marie to the hospital, talk to the doctors, or help in making any of the necessary decisions about the child's treatment.

When his stepdaughter would come home from the hospital for visits, either Dan would disappear or act as if she wasn't ill or in need of special attention. Sometimes Dan would even argue that the child's medications were not necessary because she was not really sick.

At night, when Marie reached out to Dan for comfort, he would either get angry with her or lie next to her like a mummy, looking at her as if she was crazy. "You're overreacting," would be his only comment.

As the child's health deteriorated, Dan became colder and colder, absenting himself from the home even more. Sometimes he would promise to visit the child in the hospital or come to a doctor's conference, but he would never appear. "I just can't stand hospitals," he would say.

Since Dan had been close to her daughter, Marie knew that Dan's iciness was due not to his insensitivity but to his inability to feel his grief. One night, when Marie and Dan were informed that there was no longer any hope for the child, Dan began to mutilate himself with a razor blade and angrily shouted that he would kill the doctor if the child died. He also felt he had contaminated the child.

After that evening, however, Dan showed no further emotion, not even at the funeral. Despite her understanding of PTSD, Marie was enraged. "He didn't help with any of the arrangements, hold my hand—nothing. I can forgive him his drinking, his other women—everything—but, at that moment, when I was burying my child and needing him the most, he wasn't there for me. I know my husband has PTSD, but this is carrying it too far!"

This same vet evidenced an almost identical reaction when his wife's grandmother died. Immediately after the phone call announcing the grandmother's death, the vet left the room. He ignored his wife all day, even though she was weeping. When dinner wasn't ready on time, he said, "Okay, I'll forgive you this time, but you should be over this thing by now."

Similarly, when a veteran's wife or partner becomes ill herself, the vet may be deeply concerned, but he may not show it. Often he may be reluctant to drive the woman to the hospital or the doctor's office and does not want to listen to her descriptions of her illness. He may even deny the existence of the illness to the extent that he blocks the woman's attempts for necessary medical treatment.

Some women have been forced to wait until their illnesses significantly progressed before they were allowed to seek medical attention. If they had sought a doctor without their husband's permission, their husbands would have been greatly offended. "He's so sensitive," the women often say. "If I go ahead and make a doctor's appointment without getting his okay, he'll interpret it as me being against him or not trusting his judgment. He's always putting me to the test, even when I'm sick."

In violent homes, the vet may even deny his wife the money necessary for medical care or punish her with a beating for seeking medical attention without his permission. Furthermore, as a form of economic battering, the vet may not give his partner the funds to visit a sick relative or to attend the funeral of a dead one. In such cases, his need to control the woman by economic means interacts with his wish to deny the existence of illness and death. It is highly probable that the vet suffers from personality problems in addition to his PTSD. In cases of extreme abuse, the vet's behavior more closely fits the patterns associated with abusive or character disordered personalities rather than the patterns associated with individuals who suffer primarily only from PTSD.

Another pattern that might develop is that when the wife becomes ill, the vet's symptoms increase. If the vet is emotionally or economically dependent on his partner, as she assumes a relatively helpless and dependent position, he may become frightened and regress emotionally. Hence, the wife must deal not only with her own medical problems, but with a husband who is becoming increasingly dysfunctional. He may become more helpless and dependent himself, or he may become more antagonistic to others in the home. He may increase his alcohol or drug intake, or even regress emotionally to the point of competing with any children for the wife's now limited attention.

He may even compete with his wife for attention. For example, if he is ill, he may feel that his illness is more severe than his wife's, even when this is not the case. His wife might have pneumonia but his cold is 10 times worse.

Wives often ask if such behavior is a formal part of PTSD. Theoretically, it is not. While emotional withdrawal is an expected part of the illness, if the vet regresses severely or acts in an extremely childlike manner when there is illness in the family, his behavior may be more related to some other psychological problem which coexists with his PTSD.

It must be emphasized that, according to the Vet Center Study, less than one-half of the vets with PTSD tend to respond inappropriately to family illness or loss. Some of the wives report that their husbands are extremely attentive when they, or one of their children, are ill or when there is a death in the family. In fact, extreme protectiveness, almost to the point of overprotectiveness, is also characteristic of some Vietnam veteran homes. While at times wives and children experience the vet's protectiveness as love and caring, at other times, they feel stifled and restricted by his constant concern about their health and safety.

For some veterans, the pattern of withdrawal from the family during injury, death, or another crisis is cyclical. "There are months, or years, where he's right there for me during times of trouble. But then are other months, or years, where I can't rely on him at all for help," explains one wife. Other veterans are described as trying to be helpful, but ultimately abandoning the scene of the crisis—the hospital, the funeral parlor, or wherever—because they could not tolerate the pain.

Furthermore, some of the very individuals described above demonstrated loving, caretaking behavior toward sick children and wives, after the wife, or a friend or counselor, pointed out to them what behavior was needed. In addition, it may well be that it is primarily women whose partners are unable, or unwilling, to be supportive during family crises who are seen at Vet Centers. Women whose husbands respond more appropriately may not need outside assistance.

Nevertheless, for the women who seek help at Vet Centers or Department of Veterans Affairs Medical Centers, it is not unusual for their vet husband to withdraw in times of family trouble, even in instances where his wife or child has been physically assaulted. At such times, one might think that a Vietnam vet, with his warrior background, might want to take justice into his own hands and wreak vengeance on the assailant.

In some instances, this is definitely the case. For example, some of the husbands have physically attacked drivers who crashed into their wives' vehicles. Yet, in other instances, vets have responded to their wife being in a car accident, raped, or mugged, or their children being beaten at school as if nothing had happened.

Alice, for example, was raped and mugged in her office building one evening after work. When she phoned her husband, he sounded extremely concerned and sympathetic and said he would come get her immediately. Three hours later, he had not arrived. Alice took a cab home.

When she walked in the door, her husband stared at her bloodied, torn clothing blankly. "Did you remember to bring home the milk?" he asked.

"I could have killed him, but I was too exhausted," states Alice. When she asked him why he had failed to pick her up, he stated that he "forgot." Then he went to bed in a room other than their bedroom.

To this day, he still claims that the rape never happened.

Similarly, when the family's dog died, Alice's husband seemed undisturbed. "It's just an animal," he muttered, even though the dog had been a family pet for 10 years. After this dog died, however, no other pets were allowed in the home and the family was not permitted to even mention the name of the dead dog. Alice recognized that her husband suffered from severe war trauma, but she could not tolerate his degree of numbing. After five years of marriage, she filed for divorce. After losing his wife, Alice's husband entered treatment and eventually realized that his PTSD had made him self-defeating in many areas of life. Part of his self-destructiveness ruined his relationship with Alice. Due to Vietnam, and before entering treatment, he had not been able to envision himself as a success in any dimension of life, especially in a relationship with a woman.

In a previous example, a Vietnam veteran named Peter reacted with grief and anger at his son's going away to college. However, in other cases, combat veterans have had no reactions to the departure of a child, or even the death of a child.

In contrast, the veteran's wife may be experiencing intense grief and pain at losing one of the major emotional investments of her life—her child. When she turns to her husband for support he may have assumed the "it don't mean nothing" position so often taken by soldiers in Vietnam toward the dead and dying around them.

"What are you crying for?" the veteran may tell his wife. "Our child isn't dead. And even if he were, it ain't nothing."

At this point, the Vietnam wife can easily feel abandoned, betrayed, and enraged—the same feelings her husband had on the battlefield when he saw young men die all around him and was told, or made to feel, that he should not, or could not, react.

If the veteran becomes retraumatized in a vehicular accident, criminal assault, or natural catastrophe; if a member of his family is traumatized; or if the veteran is in mid-life and is experiencing the changes and losses normal to midlife, his losses are multiplied. If his usual ways of coping with loss cease to be effective for him, he may, for the first time, seek psychological or spiritual help.

This discussion of inappropriate responses to loss is not intended to slur the character of Vietnam veterans as a group, a group which has already been slurred and misunderstood enough. Rather, the purpose of the discussion is to point out the possible effects of the grief repression and psychic numbing acquired in Vietnam on the veteran's ability to cope with losses in the present. In some cases, especially in cases involving physical abuse or severe verbal abuse, the vet's response to loss may also be rooted in problems other than PTSD, as well as in a strong belief in male prerogative of a man's "right" to be cruel to his wife.

♦ ♦ ♦

Social Isolation

"It doesn't take much to remind me of 'Nam," says Arnold, who has been in therapy for PTSD for over a year. "And when I remember, I don't feel like going out and pretending to be happy either. I used to pretend—to please my wife—but now I'm sick and tired of it."

His wife, Polly, however, is sick and tired of staying home. "We can't go to parties because Arnold can't stand small talk. We can't go to movies either, because sad ones make Arnold depressed. Comedies depress him too, because they remind him of his depression. Basically, Arnold isn't interested in people or fun anymore."

"I feel different from everyone else," Arnold explains. Arnold is also afraid of how he might react if someone mentions Vietnam, particularly if they make a derogatory comment about Vietnam veterans or a statement betraying gross ignorance about the war. Also, Arnold feels it is inconsiderate of him to impose his depression and cynicism on others. "Why should I ruin the party with my depression?" he asks. Like many depressed persons, he feels socially undesirable when he is "down" and only wants to be with others when he is "up," which, due to his mood swings, is often unpredictable.

Since Vietnam, Arnold has visited his father only twice. Arnold went to Vietnam very much a "hawk," preparing to make the military his life. He also wanted to make his father, a career officer, proud of him. Yet experiences in Vietnam made Arnold question certain procedures and personnel. Although Arnold still feels that the war was justified, he did not re-enlist and abandoned his plans for a career in the military.

He now distrusts most government institutions and prefers not to have any contact with "the establishment," whether it be the Department of Veterans Affairs, the Department of Labor, the IRS, or the local unemployment office. Despite his exceptionally high I.Q., Arnold has chosen to stack cans at a local grocery store rather than go on to college. He has also chosen to stack the cans at midnight, so as to keep his interactions with others to a minimum.

Arnold's father does not understand his son's survivor guilt and nightmares, nor his alienation from society. To him, Arnold is a disgrace to the family, not only because Arnold is not a better provider for his wife and son, but also because Arnold was not "tough enough" to endure the stresses of war.

Arnold's father lost a leg in World War II. While stationed in the Philippines, he saw "plenty of combat," as well as starving children shot to death for rummaging through garbage for food. "If I can get over that, why can't Arnold get over Vietnam?" he asks. "Besides, what's a mental problem compared to a wooden leg?"

As Arnold's case illustrates, social isolation and social alienation are frequent characteristics of the PTSD afflicted veteran. They not only reflect his depression, they perpetuate it. Deprived of human companionship, the vet can sink deeper and deeper into himself and into negative thinking. The vet's reduced interest and ability to relate to others, however, is not only detrimental to him, but to his wife and children.

In light of his experiences in Vietnam, social gatherings and other occasions often appear meaningless or superficial to him. He may, in some instances, belittle or trivialize his wife's desire to see friends or go out or he may request that she decline invitations and stay with him. In other cases, he urges her to go ahead without him. Yet often the woman stays home anyway, feeling morally obligated to be with her husband or protective of her children.

Almost universally, the women in group complain about their husband's isolative tendencies. But they also tend to accept his social isolation and their subsequent "hermitage" as a given. "Until he gets over his PTSD, I'm going to be a hermit too," states one wife.

Most of the women have given up trying to pressure their husbands into attending social functions or family gatherings. "It's too much pressure, not only on Arnold, but on me," says Polly. "If I insist that we go out with another couple or to my sister's, then I have to worry about whether or not Arnold's going to make a scene or feel so uncomfortable that he'll take it out on me later.

"Now I automatically say 'no' to every invitation. It got too embarrassing to be always cancelling out at the last minute and coming up with new excuses all the time.

"Even though Arnold has been in therapy for over a year, his emotions aren't stable yet. I never know what kind of mood he's going to be in before we go out. If something about Vietnam comes on the radio or one of his Vietnam buddies call, I can usually just forget our plans.

"Besides, we usually fight before we go out anyway. So now we don't make any plans. Nobody calls us anymore and we're stuck with each other."

Arnold has dropped most of his old friends from before the war, not an unusual pattern among vets with PTSD. While Polly has kept some of her friends, Arnold doesn't feel he has much in common with them and Polly usually sees them on her own, but she has limited time to do so. Most of Polly and Arnold's current friends are other Vietnam veterans.

"But they're mainly his friends, not mine," says Polly, "and when they talk about Vietnam, they expect me to leave the room. I guess they don't think a woman can take it.

"I used to leave meekly. But now I protest. After all, it's my living room they're sitting in—my food they're eating.

"After a while they forget I'm there and I fit right in. It's okay, I guess, but it would be nice to have conversations with people about something else besides Vietnam."

Despite Polly's wish for a broader scope of friends, she is grateful that Arnold at least socializes with other vets. Some vets do not even have this outlet. The husbands of many of the women who attend group are often virtual loners with few contacts outside their wives, and perhaps a few select friends.

Perhaps this is one reason these women attend Vet Center, VA, or other groups—to establish social connections.

Arnold socializes primarily with other veterans because he feels safe with them. They understand him and won't attack him psychologically. Communicating with similarly emotionally scarred vets is meaningful to Arnold, whereas light social banter and most forms of "chit-chat" are not.

After Arnold received his 100% service connected disability for PTSD, he was able to spend more time with his veteran friends and found himself spending time in homeless veteran and other veteran projects. These involvements gave meaning to his pain and enhanced his self-esteem. At the same time, his wife, Polly, felt Arnold should be spending time with their teenage children or helping her around the home.

"The children are leaving for college soon. Arnold may not want to spend time with them, but I do," says Polly. "If only Arnold would help out more at home, I could be more of a mother to the children before they leave the nest."

Polly also wanted more concrete assistance from Arnold because as she approached her late 40s, she found herself tiring more easily. "I'm not the superwoman I used to be," she comments. Due to the demands on her time at work and at home, Polly did not have time for social or recreational clubs or outings. The only group she was able to attend was her Vet Center woman's group and even that required a major effort on her part.

Special problems can arise when the woman has children from a former marriage. In some cases, vets have asked their wives to minimize their involvements with these children, and in a few isolated cases, have even requested that the woman send the children back to their natural father or, if the children are over eighteen, that the children must leave home. While no woman has yet given in to such requests, the resulting tensions, not only between the couple, but between the children and the veteran, are obvious, in some cases leading to teenage children leaving home voluntarily over the mother's protest. In other instances, Vietnam wives have had difficulty obtaining "permission" from their husbands to visit their children who are already living in another state with their natural father. In many of these cases, the veteran has been described as being extremely jealous of the wife's former spouse, more than of her children.

When the Vietnam vet wife first comes to group, her initial feeling is often that of relief. At last, she doesn't have to explain her situation in great defensive detail and can communicate almost instantly with the other women without lengthy introductions. She can also share her conflicting feelings about her husband's social isolation and the social isolation which his problems impose upon her.

On the one hand, she may feel that her first obligation is to her husband. She respects his PTSD and wants to be supportive. On the other hand, she is lonely, feels cut off from family and friends, but is weary of figuring out new and better ways of preventing clashes between her husband and others.

"I agree that both Arnold's father and my mother are narrowminded about the war," says Polly, "but I still think that our son should know his grandparents."

After a lot of arguing, Arnold agreed that Polly's mother could visit. "But the minute my Mom walks in the front door, Arnold's already out the back.

"At first I was humiliated at Arnold not being there when my Mom came to visit. Now I don't care, for me, but I don't want my son to grow up in a home where Grandmother and Daddy can't even sit down and have a cup of coffee together."

In marriage counseling, Polly requested that Arnold be at least willing to greet her relatives and visit with them for a half hour before he made his exit. Arnold agreed, provided he did not have to interact with the relatives during the rest of their stay and that Polly ask them to refrain from saying anything about the war.

Obviously, long family affairs, such as Thanksgiving dinners, are out for Arnold and Polly. They are also problematic for other women, many of whom purposely elect to spend holiday times with their children and husband, either without their relatives or with their families of origin yet without their husbands.

Summary

Psychic or emotional numbing is a natural and normal human response to being relatively helpless in a situation of great danger. In order to cope with the crisis, the individual tends to shut down emotionally and focus all his attention on surviving. Problems arise when the emotional numbing lasts beyond that needed for survival or is extended to situations which are not life-threatening.

Numbing almost always causes havoc and misunderstandings in marriage and other relationships requiring the expression of deep feelings. The veteran's difficulties in acknowledging his feelings, his fear of loss, and his fear of emotional pain often prevent him from establishing an emotionally close relationship with his wife. In some cases, the vet's numbing alternates with periods of emotional openness. In other cases, he may shun emotional relationships with women entirely or be able to relate to his wife on only a very limited basis.

The veteran's wife may interpret her husband's coldness as a personal rejection. As a result, she may build her own defenses against the veteran, have low self-esteem, and become numb to her own emotions, just like her husband. The vet's wall is a formidable barrier to marital communication, leaving the wife feeling shut out and alone.

3

PTSD and Sex

Come here, lie with me
And take away the pain
Then go away
I never want to see you again.
—Vietnam Veteran, August 1986

Bruce's body is covered with scars, but he is still a very sexy man. Even if he
wasn't a Vietnam vet and endowed with all the aura (and the muscles) of a
warrior, he would still be sexy to me. Quite frankly, one of the main reasons
I married Bruce was because I was so sexually attracted to him. Bruce is a ter-
rific lover, but when I get into bed with him, I get into bed with Vietnam too—
with the memories and the mood swings and with the times where it feels as
if Bruce is just using me to forget. Other times, because of his depression
caused by PTSD, he is almost totally uninterested in sex.

I can tell whenever Bruce doesn't want sex. Either he acts like I don't ex-
ist, or he starts a fight just to keep me away. I used to think there was some-
thing wrong with me because he didn't want me, until in couples therapy, he

explained that sometimes he just can't handle his PTSD and his job, much less the emotional and sexual demands of a relationship. At such times he wants—and needs—to be alone, free from other people, to "get himself together."

But on any given day, he can't predict how long a period of "cooling out" he may need. Sometimes all he needs is an hour or two. Sometimes the whole evening. Meanwhile I'm supposed to take care of the kids and everything else and then be ready for that magic moment when he decides he wants me. And when he wants me, he wants me right then. No matter how tired I am from a rough day at work or from being home with sick kids, when he's ready, I'm supposed to turn into a heated sex kitten.

Sometimes I give in to Bruce. Sometimes I don't. But if I give up other plans or push myself to have sex with him and then he all of a sudden stops right in the middle due to some Vietnam thing, I get mad. Maybe its selfish of me, but I'm tired of having to be understanding all the time.

After 10 years of marriage, I want something more out of sex than just sex. I want to feel cherished and loved, and emotionally close to my husband. For me, it's hard to keep up the passion when there's no communication.

But Bruce has periods when he can't communicate and if I insist on talking, he'll just withdraw even more. At such times, when he wants sex, I hate to turn him down, even if I'm angry with him, because his wanting sex is a sign that he's trying to get out of his depression and isolation. At least he's reaching for pleasure instead of pain. So I go to bed with him even when I don't feel like it, even when we haven't talked for days, or there's all this silent fighting going on. Sometimes I fake orgasm too, just to make him happy.

In this day of women's liberation, it's not easy to admit such things. It's even harder to admit that many times I go along with Bruce sexually because it's easier that way. Sex reduces his anger level and stops him from picking on me and the kids. Over the years, I've learned that if Bruce has his sex, for the next few days there's more peace at home for me and the kids.

—Bruce's wife, Laura

Sex is important, not only as a physical means of releasing tension, but as a means of communicating affection and love. Sex is also a means of reducing individual loneliness. Through physical merger with another person, human beings seek not only physical thrills and the pleasure of sensual excitement, but also validation and appreciation of themselves as unique individuals.[1]

"The way we express ourselves sexually—our most intimate way of relating to another person—reflects how we value ourselves, how we value the other person, how that person values us. It reflects all the things that mean warmth, love, affection and security to us—and which we therefore seek and cherish."[2] This is especially true for women raised before the so-called "sexual revolution." Most of them were taught to equate sex with love and with emotional, if not financial, security.[3] In contrast, some younger women, like many men, have been given cultural permission to enjoy their sexuality with a variety of partners. The majority of the Vietnam wives seen so far, however, hold relatively-conservative sexual values. Due to their upbringing or their religious convictions, they tend to feel that their sexual expression should be reserved only for men with whom they have a strong emotional commitment.

Typically, the Vietnam wife's sexual values were ingrained in her prior to the sexual revolution. Hence, almost all the Vietnam wives seen so far have held traditional values regarding sex and love. While some Vietnam veterans returned home to find their wives or girlfriends sleeping with other men, these are not the women who usually come to Vet Centers for help. Rather, the Vietnam wife who seeks help is almost always one who remained sexually and emotionally faithful to her husband during his tour of duty and who continues to remain true despite her husband's PTSD. Even if her husband has had prolonged periods of sexual apathy, has insisted on sex regardless of her feelings, or has had sexual flings or otherwise manifested some form of obsession with sex, she has remained faithful, never seriously considering the possibility of an affair with another man.

In fact, when approached by other men, most of the wives I have worked with felt guilt along with the exhilaration of being seen as sexually desirable by another man. A number of wives have even felt guilty about masturbating, even when self-gratification was made necessary by the veteran's physical absence from the home, his sexual lack of interest, or his disregard of his wife's sexual needs.

Dora, for example, jokes about sleeping with the handsome young teller at her bank who propositions her almost every time she makes a deposit. "If my husband stays out all night again, I'm going to meet that teller for drinks," she often says. Once she even made a date with the teller, but, as expected, quickly broke it. Not only did guilt overpower her, but she was just too angry at her husband to consider having a relationship—even a primarily sexual relationship—with another man. Besides, her major desire was for love, not sex.

Most of the wives say that they value the comfort of being held and the pleasures of talking intimately with their husband in bed more than any purely physical gratification. Yet, as a result of the women's movement, often the women do expect sexual pleasure, if not orgasm, as part of their "due" in marriage. However, the wives of some troubled vets have been disappointed to find that not only their dreams of emotional intimacy, but their hopes for sexual gratification, have been shattered by the "other woman"—Vietnam. Not only has this "other woman" disturbed the veteran's emotional peace, but she has intruded even on his sexuality, robbing both him and his wife of one of the most important sources of human physical and emotional gratification.

This chapter presents some of the ways in which PTSD has affected the sexuality of the afflicted Vietnam veteran and his wife. The ways in which PTSD affects the veteran's sexuality and his sexual relationships, however, have not been well-researched. To date, there have been only five studies of the effects of the Vietnam experience on the veteran's sexuality. In the first study, questions about sexual intimacy were mixed with questions about other forms of intimacy.[4] Therefore, no conclusions can be drawn specifically about the relationship of PTSD to male sexuality. In the next two studies, researchers found no evidence that combat was related to sexual problems.[5] In the fourth study, however, 90% of individuals with PTSD (including non-Vietnam veterans who suffered traumas) were reported as experiencing reduction of sexual capacity and interest. Extramarital affairs were also noted.[6]

Similarly, the Vet Center study I completed, as well as clinical experience with Vietnam wives and veterans, has found that many veterans had sexual concerns or were reported by their wives or their counselors to have sexual difficulties.[7] Over 86% of the Vet Center counselors polled report that vets with PTSD often experience periods of sexual dysfunction. Yet counselors caution that such sexual problems do not characterize every vet and are not necessarily symptoms of PTSD. Rather, these sexual difficulties reflect the depression and anxiety suffered by vets in the readjustment process. In addition, approximately 67% of the counselors found that vets with PTSD often desire sex on demand.

These results must be interpreted with caution. The sample of Vietnam families on which the results are based may be biased in that it consisted of individuals and couples in sufficient emotional distress that they sought help. Since this is not a random sample, these individuals cannot be considered representative of the entire Vietnam veteran family population.

In general, it is difficult to draw any firm conclusions even from formal research. Studies of prisoners of war from previous wars have found that the prison camp experience often results in long-term sexual uninterest, impotency, and other sexual dysfunctions, especially if severe malnutrition and physical abuse were involved.[8] However, some of the wives of Vietnam POWs who have attended group report a totally different picture—not only are their husbands sexually interested and almost always sexually potent, but they insist on sex on a daily basis.

Once again, I want to stress that there is no "typical" Vietnam veteran or Vietnam veteran wife. In sexual matters especially, there is wide variability. However, even in my limited sample, certain patterns emerged. In general, Vietnam wives report four areas of sexual concern related to their husbands' PTSD: his sexual uninterest or impotency; his insistence on sex on demand; his separation of affection and romance from sexual activity; and his extramarital affairs or other forms of obsession with sex.

These patterns are not necessarily constant over time for any given veteran. For example, some vets experience periods of sexual apathy or impotence when undergoing depressions due to PTSD. But when they find some relief from their PTSD, their sexual functioning returns to normal. Similarly, some vets desire great control over their marital sexual encounters. However, the wives of even the most controlling veterans describe their husbands as having periods when they can let go of directing every sexual move and "be normal." According to the wives, the husband's need to be watchful during sex or to reenact his role in combat in the bedroom seems to be related to some of the symptoms of PTSD, specifically increased withdrawal and irritability or nightmares. Given such fluctuations in the veteran's sexual behavior, the Vietnam wife is often confused about what to expect sexually from her husband. If she is not assertive about her sexual needs and seeks instead to please her husband, she may not know whether to put on her flannel nightgown or her sheer negligee.

♦ ♦ ♦

Sexual Impotence and Apathy

"Sex, what's that?" more than one wife has said, describing her husband's long-standing sexual apathy or sexual impotence.

Three of the possible major causes of impotence or lack of sexual interest or abilities in Vietnam veterans with PTSD are the depression and emotional numbing associated with PTSD and the potential negative impact of midlife losses. Depression and emotional numbing, especially when they involve anger turned inward or repressed grief, can lead to sexual uninterest, anorgasmia (lack of orgasm), or various other forms of sexual impotence even among persons who did not serve in Vietnam.[9] For example, Vietnam wives who say they are uninterested in sex often suffer from depression and emotional numbing as a result of having stifled their negative feelings toward their husbands, especially their anger at all the demands made upon them as a result of their husband's PTSD. Furthermore, they are often in a state of mourning about their own lives—about the years spent loving and caring for a man who does not, or cannot, return their love in kind. Under such emotional conditions, it is very hard for Vietnam wives to achieve high levels of sexual arousal on a consistent basis.

In the early years of her marriage when her husband sexually ignored her, Dora used to masturbate for relief. However, today she hardly ever does so. "I used to think I stopped because I was approaching 40, but that's supposed to be a woman's sexual peak. I guess it's my husband, not my age. Since I've numbed my anger at him, it's no wonder my sexual feelings have also gone dead. Funny, now that I think about it, the last time we had good sex was after a fight when we both told each other how much we hated each other. Maybe the sex was good because we finally let out our feelings."

As described in the previous chapter, psychic numbing occurs on three levels—the emotional, the mental, and the physical. Physically, the muscles constrict. According to Wilhelm Reich, in *The Function of the Orgasm: The Discovery of the Orgone*, this muscular constriction can result in genital disturbances.[10] Furthermore, "sexual energy can be bound by chronic muscle tensions."[11]

Some Vietnam wives experience little feeling, on either an emotional or sexual level, during sexual intercourse. True, they may have pleasurable sensations, even orgasm, but they are distressed to find that they experience their sexuality in a detached and distant manner. "It's like my body doesn't belong to me," explains one wife, whose statement reflects a severe degree of psychic numbing. Similarly her husband, like some of my other Vietnam veteran patients, while able to achieve erection and orgasm, describes his penis as "numb," and his orgasm as "dead." When physiological causes are ruled out, this muting of sexual feeling and pleasure can perhaps be related to the overall numbing of emotions in both the veteran and his wife.

Furthermore, sexual pleasure and potency can be inhibited, if not totally obliterated, in almost any man or woman, veteran or nonveteran, by the presence of anxious, painful, or other negative thoughts or memories.

Have you ever begun to worry about your bills or the health of one of your family members in the middle of making love? What was the effect on your sexual interest? If you were the victim of rape or some other form of sexual abuse, how easily could you blot out the memory of being violated? Wouldn't it take time to be able to respond sexually again, even with someone you loved and trusted?

If the Vietnam wife has had painful sexual experiences, memories of her past may intrude on her present sexual experiences with her husband. Similarly, veterans who witnessed or participated in sexual acts in which there was also pain or violence may recall these events when they begin to become sexually excited. On the simplest, most innocent level, perhaps gunfire went off while the veteran was making love. Or perhaps the veteran witnessed or participated in rape. Or perhaps he or one of his comrades was attacked or "set up" by a Vietnamese prostitute or girlfriend. Such memories, even if they are not in the veteran's conscious awareness at the time he is initiating sexual contact, may function to decrease his level of sexual involvement. They may even result in an inability to achieve and maintain an erection. Unless the wife is aware of the many possible causes of erectile failure in men, especially in men with PTSD, she may interpret her husband's impotence as a sign of her lack of sexual attractiveness. This is especially the case if one sexual failure precipitates the vet's almost total sexual withdrawal.

For example, if the veteran experiences a sexual "failure" due to certain memories, he may be reluctant to initiate sex or respond to his partner's sexual overtures in the future for fear of failing again. After repeated sexual "failures," he may withdraw from sexual activity altogether. Consequently, neither the vet nor his wife receives the emotional and sexual stimulation conducive to full sexual expression. Once this vicious cycle is established, the wife may also resign herself to a sexless marriage or feel like a sexual failure herself, just like her husband.

This has been the case with several vets I have counseled. Although they very much wanted to have sexual relations with women, they could not bear the embarrassment of repeated sexual failures. In general, their wives or girlfriends were described as being understanding and accepting of their impotence. Nevertheless, the men preferred to keep relationships at a nonsexual level.

Survivor guilt can also play a role in the veteran's sexual relations, with some vets reporting guilt feelings during the sex act. "Here I am, making love to my wife, when my buddy will never make love again. Just the thought of it kills my desire," explains one vet.

When the veteran is impotent or quickly loses his erection or interest in sex, his wife will usually have trouble reaching orgasm unless her husband uses manual or oral means of stimulation. Few of the wives, however, have proven assertive enough to ask their husbands to help them climax outside of intercourse.

When my husband can't make it, that means his PTSD is bothering him and I know better than to press him for anything, much less sex. He pretends he's sleeping, but I know he's awake, thinking. The depression, or anger, just oozes out of him.

If I ask him to touch me, I'm afraid he'll call me "selfish." Here he is suffering, and what am I thinking about? Myself. A few times I did ask him and he did what I wanted. But he did it mechanically, without love and no emotion whatsoever. It was no fun and made me feel like a whore.

So I don't ask anymore, I just accept sexual frustration as part of living with a Vietnam vet. If our sex gets interrupted because he gets into a mood, I just roll over and pretend that I'm asleep. He's left me hanging sexually so many times, I've learned not to get too turned on when we start. Slowly but surely, my interest and enthusiasm for sex has diminished.

Wives and girlfriends of veterans who were raped by American soldiers or by Vietnamese enemies during the war are particularly sensitive to the fact that their veteran's memories may be exceptionally intrusive and troublesome. What they may not know, however, is that their veteran may withdraw sexually because he is plagued by sadistic thoughts. These sadistic thoughts may arise, in part, from an urge to retaliate against his abusers. For example, Fred was sexually abused by Viet Cong guards during his six months as a POW After he was released, he sought to kill his abusers, but they could not be found. He still harbors considerable rage toward them, however, which mere vocal ventilation does not begin to relieve.

Rationally, he knows his girlfriend is not "the enemy" and does not want to hurt her. But emotionally, he still finds himself making her the scapegoat for his unresolved anger toward his abusers. Although he has never been aggressive with his girlfriend, he is troubled by sadistic thoughts toward her. For example, during intercourse with her, he noticed that as his sexual excitement increased and his urge to penetrate her increased, he wanted to "pierce" her and "rip her open."[12]

These thoughts troubled him greatly, so greatly that he now shuns sexual activity not only with her, but with other women, in order to avoid the pain and shame of having such sadistic thoughts and to avoid the risk that he might lose control and actually act on his sadistic impulses.

If a veteran actually witnessed any mutilation of female breasts or genitalia or any intercourse with dead women, his sadistic fantasies may be particularly vivid and problematic for him. He may be especially repelled by sex if he has found some satisfaction or pleasure in the sadistic thoughts or, if in Vietnam, he found some satisfaction or pleasure in observing or participating in sexually sadistic acts.

A vet need not have been exposed to sexual abuse during the war in order to suffer the intrusion of wartime memories in his sex life. Such memories can be evoked by the mere sight of a naked body or any scars resulting from the war. Hence wives, especially those wives who have invested considerable time and energy in maintaining trim figures or other forms of attractiveness, are often disappointed, and in some cases devastated, to find their men almost immune to their loveliness. They often fail to understand that every time the veteran takes his clothes off, or sees a woman disrobe, he may begin to—automatically and unwillingly—think of Vietnam. Jim explains: "Nudity was part of the death there. It was nothing to see naked bodies, wounded, dead, cut up or whatever." Before Vietnam, Jim had associated nudity primarily with pleasure. But now it is paired in his mind with pain and violence.

Jim was not wounded in Vietnam, but for those vets who were and who still bear physical scars, disrobing and exposing their scars to themselves and their partner may serve as yet another reminder of the war. If, in addition, the veteran was wounded in or near the genital area or in or near sexually sensitive areas, his injuries or the mere sight of his scars may contribute to his sexual difficulties.

While some vets are proud of their scars and consider them signs of manhood, for others the scars engender pain and anger. Many of the vets I have counseled brush off their scars or injuries as "nothing," ever mindful of the fact that they managed to survive, while others died, or that they could have been injured more severely, as were others. "Sure there's a hole in my leg, but at least I have one," says Ron. "Some guys lost both or everything."

Where psychic numbing exists, there may also be a denial about the pain of having been injured or disfigured. A vet with a wooden arm insisted that the loss of the arm "didn't bother him at all." In fact, he felt superior to vets who were "cry babies" about their physical and emotional problems resulting from the war. He had never grieved his loss and instead comforted himself with feeling like a true patriot for having sacrificed for his country. Quite possibly his sense of superiority over other vets who openly complain about their injuries may stem, in part, from his suppression of his own sense of loss. He claims to be sexually virile, but he has been unable to sustain either of his two marriages, either sexually or emotionally.

While some wives say that their husbands complain about their injuries almost constantly, other wives report that the "no talk" rule applies to war injuries as well.

Ron's body is covered with scars and punctured with gunshot wounds. Looking at his body objectively, it is ugly, horrible really. But I love him and don't mind caressing his ugly spots. I just close my eyes and kiss parts of him that would make most people shudder.

I only wish he had told me about his body before we had sex the first time. I was shocked. But since he didn't say anything, I didn't either. Besides, I knew he was testing me. He kept staring at me to see how I would react.

But his eyes had a faraway look, too, and I could tell he wasn't really thinking about me, but about Vietnam.

We've been together five years. Our sex life was great in the beginning, but now it's almost dead. We never talk about his scars, or Vietnam. After the first couple of months together, he couldn't get an erection. I told him I didn't mind, that I just wanted to hold and love him anyway. But he'd push me away and sometimes wouldn't come to bed at all.

I've caught him masturbating a few times, so I know he's not impotent. But he's definitely disinterested in me. I thought—hoped—his disinterest would be temporary, but now we're just like two friends living in the same house.

Ron feels that Vietnam ruined his sex life. Yet even veterans who are not physically scarred sometimes say that Vietnam ruined sex for them, like it ruined other aspects of their lives. Several studies have found that battlefield trauma is related to "diminished interest in previously enjoyed activities."[13]

Some vets with PTSD have so much emotional pain to deal with and so much disillusionment about their country, the military, and by extension life itself, that sex seems unimportant, if not meaningless.

For example, Harvey went to Vietnam an idealistic nineteen-year-old. His unit fried steaks and drank beer while watching whole villages and many Americans be blown to bits. Harvey became emotionally numb and his numbing was reinforced by his unit's jokes about the nearby slaughters.

Once Harvey and two friends were attacked by a group of Vietnamese women carrying razor blades. The women were aiming for a particular artery in the leg, which, if slashed, could make a person bleed to death. Rather than shoot the women, Harvey kicked them in the face, which made him wonder if he was a "good guy" or a "bad guy."

At the same time Harvey marveled at the women's motivation. Didn't these women in ragged pajamas know he could have blown them away in a minute? Why were they willing to risk their lives just to kill a handful of American servicemen?

Harvey began to question the U.S. involvement in Vietnam. "Am I on the wrong side?" he dared to wonder. However, such questions severely conflicted with his dedication to the military and the patriotic fervor which had sent him to Vietnam in the first place. Since the conflict couldn't be resolved, Harvey entered a state of mental numbing which only compounded his emotional numbing, rendering him sexually uninterested, even in Vietnam.

After returning to the United States, his sexual uninterest was aggravated by discovering that his wife had been unfaithful to him. He forgave her but she continued to betray him. After he divorced her, he had a short period of promiscuity followed by a long period of celibacy. Obviously Harvey's experience with the Vietnamese women, in addition to his experiences with his first wife, made him wary of being close to women.

In his present wife, Sue, Harvey feels he has finally found a loyal and loving partner. But Sue is allowed into Harvey's world and into his bed only a little at a time. Harvey wants Sue to want him sexually and to pursue him. Yet sometimes he feels threatened by the very sexual aggressiveness which he asks of her.

Sue is baffled. "Does he want me or not?" she wonders. She also wonders why she must pay the price for Harvey's past experiences with women. When Sue is physically ill or emotionally troubled, Harvey becomes highly anxious and then withdraws. At such times Sue wants moral support and physical affection, not a cold or empty bed.

There are many valid reasons for Harvey's behavior toward Sue, but Sue's emotional and sexual frustrations are equally real and painful. Already she is experiencing a lessening of sexual desire, as well as other signs of depression. Before she met Harvey, she liked to have sex almost every night. Now if they make love only once or twice a month, she says she "doesn't miss it." But in reality she does miss the soothing effects, not only of orgasm, but of the entire sexual embrace.

When either the vet or his wife is in denial about their pain, their psychic numbing may contribute to their sexual uninterest. But when either the vet, or his wife, is in therapy and their pain is beginning to surface, this can also result in a temporary uninterest in sex. When in pain, the vet may not want to be physically touched. In fact, his woman's touch utterly repels him. Some wives report that their husbands do not allow them to touch them for days.

When the Vietnam wife is in pain, she may feel like her husband, who is also uninterested in sex or in touching. However, she usually tries to explain to her veteran why she is not interested in physical intimacies. Sometimes she will even offer to be with him sexually despite her sexual uninterest. Yet, according to the wives, when the veteran is in a sexual "funk," rarely does he give his wife the courtesy of an explanation, unless, of course, the veteran has made so much progress in therapy that he is able to recognize and acknowledge his own emotional states. In addition, the wife's problem may be compounded by the fact that the veteran's sexual apathy toward her is often accompanied by an almost total emotional cutoff from her. Not only does he not make love to her, but he doesn't want to talk or communicate with her either.

Quite naturally, the wife who has not been informed about the nature and power of PTSD can easily interpret her husband's withdrawal as a personal rejection or as a certain sign that she is not physically or emotionally appealing. She may suffer a mini-depression as a result of her husband's coldness or she may match her husband's withdrawal by withdrawing also. Or, out of a desire to reconnect with the man she loves, she may make a sexual advance, only to be rejected and further plummeted into depression and self-doubt.

Jim's wife, for example, felt lonely without emotional and sexual contact with her husband. When after 10 days he had failed to even hug her, she woke Jim at 4 a.m. in hopes that he would make love to her. He was furious.

Damn her! That bitch! I told her not to wake me up in the middle of the night. She knows I have trouble sleeping. But a few weeks ago, it was I who woke her up at 4 a.m. and told her that was my best time for lovemaking. Maybe she thought she was doing what I wanted.

I don't know and I don't care. I never thought I'd get so calloused that I wouldn't care how my wife felt. But right now all her desires to love and kiss me are just a pain to me. Outright nuisances! I wish she'd just go away.

I've been thinking about 'Nam lately. The thoughts just interfere with everything. My depression takes over and I'm an utter flop in bed. My wife never minds when I can't perform. She always says she loves me just the way I am.

Yet I can't stand to even talk to her and I despise her for loving me, maybe because I despise myself somehow. I turn my back on her too, because I don't want her to see my face. I want to hide what's going on inside of me—the fear, the anger, the hate. I want her to go away, but I also need her. Without her I have nobody.

After she woke me up, I had nightmares. I tried to turn them off. I could actually feel myself trying to maneuver my eyelids so that the ugly drama would stop. But I couldn't stop the dream, the horror. At the end of the dream, I was so angry I wanted to kill somebody, something. The last thing on my mind was sex.

At the end of the dream, I was standing in the middle of a street, lost, confused, just like the first day I got back from 'Nam. I didn't know where anything was. Suddenly my wife appeared. She was there to help me, but I wanted her to go away because she couldn't possibly understand what I had been through.

In my mind, I began to tear her down, repeating to myself what was wrong with her. Yet I knew it was not her character defects that were making me mad.

I was mad because she was emotionally unscarred and I was mad that she, with all her love for me, couldn't take away the fear and anger in me, couldn't stop the panic.

I'm angry at her because she didn't have to go, because she didn't have to suffer, because her life has been so smooth in comparison. Sure, she's had her share of problems, but nothing like what I went through.

When I get like this, I feel crazy—here I am, pushing away one of the few people in the world who really cares about me.

Despite Jim's PTSD, he and his wife do have many tender moments. Nevertheless, too often in Jim's view, his Vietnam experience has impaired his ability to love. Furthermore, for him, as for other vets, Vietnam spelled the death of any belief in romantic love. Few of the vets I have seen still believe in romantic love and, among couples counseled, romanticism is almost nonexistent.

"Romantic love died in Vietnam, right next to my friends," explains Jim. "After you've seen enough death, injustice, and horror, you can't believe in love anymore, at least not the mushy kind of love that's in the media and songs.

"For me now, romantic love is a joke. How can I think now that getting lost in someone's embrace is going to take away my pain? When I hear love songs now, I get angry, then sad. I'm angry because I remember the times before 'Nam when I was young and innocent and half-believed those songs. But the stress over there and the stress back here since has rotted me out so much I'm no longer capable of feeling like that any more."

Another vet has similar feelings. "The most horrible feeling in the world to me is not pain or anger, but not being able to love, to be in bed with someone who I think is almost everything I ever wanted in a woman and still have no feelings. The sensuality of touching her, even my orgasm, is dulled by the lack of feeling in my heart."

For most of the wives too, romantic love is now an adolescent fantasy. The harsh realities of having to work full time, of a husband with unpredictable mood swings, and of the intrusion of the war upon their lives, has nearly eradicated their romantic dreams. In fact, some of the wives consider themselves veterans also.

For example, even though Jim's wife has never seen Vietnam, she feels she has served "combat duty" just by being a Vietnam wife. Like her husband, she has lost much of her romantic feeling about her marriage. "I wish I could feel romantic toward Jim—he deserves it. But there's just too many holes in the wall, too many bills to pay, and too many hurt feelings on my part. I still love Jim, but it's sad, sad, sad, not to be able to love him like I used to."

Some vets are in touch with their sadness about their impaired capacity to experience romantic love. Others vets, however, are not. As a result, they may abruptly leave parties or gatherings where there is romantic music because, as they tell their wives, they can't tolerate the superficiality or "phoniness" of the other people. But what they also can't tolerate is their own anger and pain or the feeling of being different from everybody else.

Their wives can feel different too. Jim's wife explains: "At parties, I watch Jim like a hawk. The minute I see him getting too hot—or too cold—I know it's time to make some excuse and get him home. My friends wonder why I can't relax and make small talk at parties. But how can I? I'm always afraid that someone will say the wrong thing about 'Nam and make Jim go off or turn into a zombie."

Some veterans accept diminished sexual interest and activity as part of their PTSD. But others have attempted to fight it, using a variety of means to sexually stimulate themselves. Some have found that they can achieve erection or orgasm through the use of marijuana, cocaine, or other drugs. Without the drugs, they are impotent. Others have used pornographic videos or other pornographic materials. Still others insist that their wives adopt exotic positions or don erotic outfits. In instances where the vet has been habitually physically abusive to his wife, sometimes erection could be achieved only after the woman was physically assaulted or sexually humiliated; for example, after she was called derogatory sexual names, after her sex organs were abused or ridiculed, or after the veteran exposed her breasts or genitalia in public. Sexual abuse of Vietnam wives, however, is probably best explained by the veteran's psychological problems other than PTSD.

In my experience, men who have had to resort to such means to achieve sexual potency often, on some level, feel ashamed or inadequate because they cannot achieve erection and orgasm "naturally" as they put it. While abuse of the woman is obviously morally unacceptable, it can be argued that there is nothing inherently wrong with using sex videos or other visual means of stimulation. Yet the very men who use such means often feel it is wrong due to moral considerations or their view that their sexuality should not be dependent on external props. When the external props no longer work, they may panic and seek professional help. Or they may decide to become celibate.

After experiencing several sexual failures with his wife, one vet began to frequent topless bars in hopes of being aroused. For a while, his efforts proved successful. After viewing women at the bars, and sometimes sleeping with them, he was able to have successful intercourse with his wife. Eventually, however, his go-go dancers failed him. No matter how young or voluptuous they were, he couldn't "get it up." His subsequent desperate search for younger and more attractive go-go girls also failed. It was at this point that he began to acknowledge his depression, not only about Vietnam, but about certain life situations prior to his tour of duty.

The Vietnam wife who must tolerate her veteran's drug or alcohol addiction, his pornographic interests, or his other means of achieving sexual arousal often feels insulted and humiliated. Is she not enough? Why does he have to look elsewhere for sexual stimulation? Furthermore, she feels reduced to the status of a sexual plaything. When her veteran makes love to her, she frequently feels that the lovemaking is more an expression of his intense need to prove his masculinity to himself, rather than an expression of love.

If the Vietnam wife must also contend with her husband's extramarital affairs, she feels slapped in the face. Yet even if other women are not involved, the Vietnam wife whose husband suffers from sexual problems often feels not only sexually disappointed, but more importantly, emotionally abandoned. She has experienced a major loss: the loss of her hope for a mutually loving marital relationship. In marriage, she had hoped for a man's tenderness, adoration, and protection. But instead she found Vietnam—flashbacks and nightmares, emotional walls and emotional pain, power trips and insecurities, or a raw male sex drive, devoid of the usual preliminaries or of any romantic gestures. If the woman, like her husband, is incapable of grieving, depression will set in. Rather than recognize her loss, she may develop her own symptoms or find means of avoiding her husband sexually.

She may simply be cold toward him, always be tired or busy, or start arguments with him. Or she may gain significant amounts of weight. While her weight gain may be seen as a way to "punish" her husband, in my view it is primarily a means of expressing her sexual and romantic frustrations and disappointments or a means of punishing herself. She may be punishing herself because she feels like a failure as a woman due to her husband's lack of emotional and sexual responsiveness toward her.

◆ ◆ ◆

Paranoia In The Bedroom

During the war, the veteran needed to be on constant alert. Combat readiness—if not overt paranoia—were qualities necessary for survival. Carol Vercozzi, in *The War That Refused To Die: Vietnam Again*, explains:

"If the message of the military was black-and-white, the soldier's world was a hundred shades of green. Everything he had learned about order and logic and reason, even the things he had been taught about the war . . . fell apart in Vietnam. Nothing was real . . . He stopped trying to apply reason, accepted that what you expected would not happen, that no one can be trusted, that everything outside yourself is subject to no rules you can ever uncover . . . Death was the new 'reality principle' and the paranoid combat-readiness state was the only hope of staying alive."[14]

In the bedroom, however, states of paranoid combat readiness are, to say the least, not conducive to satisfying sexual relations. Patterns vary from one couple to the next. Sometimes the vet's paranoia results in impotence: he becomes too frightened of the woman, or the sex act, to engage in sexual activity. In other instances, the vet's paranoia takes the form of not trusting that the woman really loves him. He may require that the woman "prove" her love by engaging in longer or more frequent sexual activity than she desires or by trying certain sexual positions or practices which he, not she, desires.

If she is not cooperative, she is accused of being "unloving," "ungiving," a "cold fish," or "frigid." Some women have been taunted with pickles, squashes, or cucumbers when they have not desired intercourse. Some wives feel they must go along with their veteran's sexual desires or risk becoming the "enemy" and consequently, the possible target of his anger or other form of retaliation.

The vet's paranoia in the bedroom may not be constant. Some husbands act paranoid some days but not others. Others undergo monthly or cyclical changes, alternating between periods of emotional stability and "normal" sexual relations and periods of severe mood swings and troubled sex.

The root of paranoia is fear, fear of being attacked or losing control. Certain aspects of the sexual relationship may serve to trigger such fears in the vet. Simply taking off his clothes or lying down may make him feel vulnerable and defenseless. He may also be threatened by shutting the bedroom door or by having the lights off. His wife, however, may want the bedroom door closed for privacy. Or she may want the lights dim or off for romantic or other reasons. Conflicts inevitably result.

More fundamentally, however, sex can be threatening to a vet, or to any man, because it requires "giving in" to a woman and surrendering to his sexual desire. While a man might very much desire sexual pleasure and release, he may fear the loss of control which such surrender implies. Or perhaps he views surrender as "feminine."[15] Similarly, women who have difficulty achieving orgasm have often been described as unable to "surrender" to their partner or to their own sexual impulses. Just as women sometimes have trouble "letting go" sexually for fear that their partners will hurt them, men can have the same fears.

◆ ◆ ◆

Staying In Control

"What if she bites me?" asks one vet, explaining his fears about oral sex. For him, letting go sexually is difficult because it increases not only his physical, but his emotional, vulnerability. For him, as for others, sex is the only time he feels emotionally close to his wife. Only during sex are his defenses down. While he describes the intimacy he experiences as sweet, he is also frightened by it. "I can't let her under my skin," he says, "so I limit the sex. I don't want to get hooked on anybody anymore. What if I lose her, like I lost others?"

For some vets, giving in to a woman's sexual requests, or even to their own desires for the woman, feels like "giving in to the enemy." Yet the "ability to surrender" is a "prerequisite . . . for orgasm."[16] In some bedrooms, the woman actually be comes the enemy. Perhaps she disappointed or "disobeyed" the veteran in some way, thereby crossing the line from friend to foe. The vet may view her as someone to be conquered. Yet the very process of sexual conquest requires that the veteran let down his defenses and surrender to her.

For a few of my patients, such surrender has been impossible. As a result, they experience various degrees of impotence. Or they arrange their sex lives so that they maintain almost total control over the sexual situation. For example, only the vet, not his wife or girlfriend, is allowed to initiate sex. Or he only will have intercourse facing the woman's back, never looking at her face.

Another way the vet can maintain control is to not permit the woman to stimulate him, orally or manually. He stimulates himself and uses the woman only for penetration. By stimulating himself, he not only protects himself from the possibility that the woman might hurt him, deliberately or by accident, but he can also monitor his own level of excitement and exert greater control over the timing and intensity of his orgasm.

If he does allow the woman to stimulate him, he may be very specific about how she is to do so. She may be allowed only to touch certain areas of his body or to exert only certain amounts of pressure at various places. In one instance, a woman was instructed to caress only one particular segment of the rim of her husband's penis and no other part of his body, with only one of her fingers, not her entire hand. When she failed to follow directions, she was accused of not loving her husband and of trying to hurt him. Sex would be discontinued.

In still other cases, sex is divorced from affection at the veteran's request. This can be a way for the veteran to control the degree of closeness between himself and his partner. "If we have sex, we can't cuddle and talk. It's just sex, nothing else. But when he wants to be close and have us just hold each other, then the rule is that we can't have intercourse," explains one wife. "I guess my husband can handle only one form of contact at a time."

When the veteran rushes sex, when he wants to strictly control every sexual move, or in other ways enters into a paranoid or aggressive state in the bedroom, the Vietnam wife usually experiences minimal emotional satisfaction and minimal sexual arousal. Her attention is diverted from sexual pleasure to self-protection. Instead of concentrating on what she needs from her husband sexually or how to best arouse him, she's wondering what he's going to do next. Will there be violence or verbal abuse? Will he flashback? Where are the children? Where are those weapons from Vietnam? Will he pull them out to empower himself sexually, to protect himself, or just to re-enact the past? If so, then what?

At the same time she is furiously processing the possibilities of what might happen and outlining what she may need to do to save herself, she is also trying to appease her husband sexually so as to minimize his agitation. Does he want her passionate? Does he want her quiet and receptive? Whatever he wants, she complies.

Under such conditions, sex becomes sexless, at least for the woman. Her sexual needs are often not considered, much less met. Insufficiently aroused and substantially diverted, both mentally and emotionally, from experiencing the sensuality of the moment, she may have difficulty enjoying sex as a sensual experience or achieving orgasm.

Yet, no woman thus far has seemed particularly concerned about not achieving orgasm. Those women who complain about the inadequacy of their sex lives do not complain about not having a climax, but about not feeling loved or cherished. In fact, wives tend to be more concerned about their husbands not achieving orgasm than about their own lack of sexual fulfillment.

In three cases, the vet refused to have orgasm with his wife. He would initiate sex, get himself excited, then withdraw just prior to his orgasm and hers. While the reasons for this self-denial are not clear, two factors seem to be involved: a desire to punish the woman and orgasm anxiety.

All three vets frankly stated that they stopped intercourse just prior to their climaxing in order to "get back at" their wives. "I don't want her to have the satisfaction of knowing that she can make me come—that she has that much power over me," one vet stated.

◆ ◆ ◆

Sex Now

While some wives complain of infrequent sex in their marriages, others moan that their husbands insist on sex a certain number of times a week or day. For these men, sex is sometimes an imperative. When refused by their wives, they feel desperately unloved. There is an urgent quality to their desire which cannot be attributed solely to their need for sexual gratification. In the view of some wives, their men are not just seeking sexual release in the sex act, but security, self-esteem, a sense of superiority, or "victory" as well.

The vet's intense need for sex may not be a daily occurrence. While some wives describe their husbands as always or almost always insisting on sex, others point out that their husbands seem to vacillate between being like "regular men," who are impatient, mildly aggressive, but also understanding, and being like "warriors" who demand gratification as their due—or else.

On one level, this intense need for sex can be related to the veteran's loneliness. Socially isolated people are often lonely. Although they may desire to be separate, their isolation often results in their becoming "stroke deprived," they do not receive the smiles, the hugs, the compliments, or any of the visual, verbal, or physical "strokes," large or small, which naturally come about with supportive others.

In this state of deprivation, the vet may turn to sex to meet his social and relationship needs. Sex becomes a substitute for in-depth emotional communication, or even for casual socialization. One vet called sex the "total stroke." For a long time, he believed that sex would satisfy all his hungers: his hunger for sex, as well as his hunger for human companionship and intimacy. Like many persons, he confused sex with love and with emotional closeness.

When sexual activity without communication left him unsatisfied, he increased his sexual activity. Even after more sex, however, he still felt restless and empty inside. Eventually he found that some communication with his sexual partner and more time spent socializing with others, not more sex, helped satisfy him.

On another level, the vet's need for sex can be intense because, biologically, sexuality is the "antithesis of anxiety."[17] As has been repeatedly proven in studies of both men and women, anxiety interferes with sexual performance, especially with orgasm.[18] Conversely, it is difficult if not impossible to be anxious while highly sexually aroused.

Hence, for some vets, sex is more than sex. It is a form of tranquilizer or sedative for their anxieties and other tensions. Not only does sex provide a sense of physical peace, but an emotional peace as well. "Sex takes away my anger," explains Tom. "After satisfying sex, for a few moments at least, all seems well, both within and without."

In this sense, sex can be used like a mood-altering drug. When the vet begins to feel pain, fear or confusion, he may feel overcome, not only by the specific emotions, but by the sheer fact of having such a powerful emotion. Not knowing what to do with his feelings, he may feel anxious and out of control. That his emotions are throwing him off base and won't go away on command also threaten his sense of masculinity.

He doesn't like the strength or power of his emotions. "Real men" are supposed to be in control of their emotions, not the other way around. It may be acceptable for women to let emotions dominate them, but former warriors cannot let emotion get the upper hand.

At this point, the vet needs a means of cooling his emotional waters, of feeling in control, of asserting his masculinity. Sex can obliterate, or at least temporarily mitigate, anxiety, emotional upset, and personal insecurities. Like alcohol and drugs, sex can be used as an escape, not only from emotional realities, but from other realities, such as children, bills, and other responsibilities.

In addition, sex helps affirm the vet's sense of manhood. Perhaps he feels emasculated in certain areas of his life, for example, on the job or because of a lack of a job. But when he is with a woman, he can, at last, "feel like a man." At least one person, his wife or girlfriend, is (literally) "under him."

Furthermore, for some vets, orgasm functions as a form of shock treatment for their depression. "If I don't have at least three orgasms a day, I get so blue I can't stand it. The minute I start feeling down, I reach for my wife. If she won't cooperate, I do something else," explains Peter, who also needs to exercise daily in order to combat his depression. When his wife refuses him sexually, it is not just sexual frustration which he suffers, but the full weight of some of his symptoms of PTSD.

The women, however, protest at being used as human tranquilizers. "I'm tired of being his pill!" is the cry of the wives, who become especially resentful when their husbands' approaches follow days of being ignored or being taken for granted.

"Peter and I don't have a relationship, we have a sexship," says Jo. "I'm supposed to be there for him sexually, ready to jump in bed, whenever he needs me, no matter what else is going on. I could be upset, the kids could be crying, my mother could be on the way over—it doesn't matter. He wants it when he wants it, just like a baby.

"If I don't go along, he says he'll go find someone else. Sometimes once a day isn't enough. He wants sex two or three times a day. I just can't do it, so he goes out on me."

When sex is sometimes used as a means of dealing with emotions or life situations, as in the case of Peter, the need for sex may become progressive and all absorbing. One woman is not enough, so two are needed. Eventually two women are not enough, so three are needed. Or a different type of woman is sought.

Some vets become obsessed with sex, hoping that by having more or different types of women, they will find peace within. Their spare time may be spent in sex stores and watching sex videos. Or sex can become a major preoccupation in other ways, perhaps by counting the number and measuring the duration of various sexual activities. Sexual flings are not uncommon. More than one wife has had to put up with her husband's affairs. "It's not that Peter and I don't have sex," says Jo, "but it's never enough for him. So he has all these floozies. I think he's trying to recapture his youth or something."

◆ ◆ ◆

Sex, Midlife, and Aging

As Vietnam veterans and their wives enter and pass through midlife into their senior years, their sexuality, like every other aspect of their lives, will be affected to one degree or another by the physical, social, and emotional changes associated with aging. As with any other couple, their state of emotional and physical health and their financial stability will play key roles in their interest in and ability to respond sexually to each other. Problems in any of these areas are likely to diminish the importance of sex in the relationship, as well as their actual sexual abilities.

Veterans with progressive illness, whether war-related or not, or whose war injuries become more painful or more severe due to subsequent injuries or medical problems, may be in so much physical distress that sexual interest is negatively affected. Or they may need to take medications that reduce the sex drive. Certain medications given to control diabetes, hypertension, rage, anxiety, depression, and insomnia are well-known for suppressing sexual responsiveness. For this reason, some veterans have refused to take these medications.

"I'd rather be a raving maniac or go into the black hole [of depression] than lose my sex drive," states one veteran. On the other hand, having rage, anxiety, depression and insomnia can also cause a loss of sex drive. When a veteran is more rested, less depressed, or less anxious as the result of properly administered medications, he may feel better and, consequently, feel more alive and interested in the sensual aspects of life. As the medication permits him to gain increased control over his symptoms, he may also feel more confident in interacting with others and hence may interact more frequently and more meaningfully with others, including his wife or girlfriend. On the other hand, sometimes even such improved functioning cannot overcome the dampening of the sex drive due to medication. Consequently, taking certain medications known to improve many areas of functioning, except for the sexual, can impose a double-bind on the veteran who values his sexuality and his sex life.

Sexual interest and abilities have also been found to wane among men in their 40s and 50s who have histories of prolonged alcohol or drug addiction. When these men were younger, their bodies may have been able to sustain the negative physical effects of substance abuse. But as these men age, the toll addiction has taken on their bodies can become increasingly evident. Along with any number of health problems due to substance abuse may come diminished sexual interest and ability.

It is not just that the alcohol or drugs in themselves have had detrimental effects on the veteran's health, but that the lifestyle associated with substance abuse is not known for improving one's health. Often poor nutrition, inadequate sleep, and poor self-care are associated with chronic substance abuse. Simply stopping the drinking or the drugging does not repair the physical damage wrought by years of self-neglect. In order to regain physical health and sexual stamina proper nutrition, rest, and attention to medical problems need to follow.

Yet for a veteran to restore himself to physical health, he first needs to feel he deserves to be well. Only then will he spend the time, money, and energy to take care of himself. Yet the PTSD-afflicted veteran is often suffering from intense survivor guilt, self-hate, and low-self esteem. Consequently he doesn't feel worthy of good self-care. If the veteran is, on some level, punishing himself for what he did or did not do during or after the war, he may not take advantage of available services and opportunities for medical or psychological help.

In other instances, the problem is not that the veteran doesn't allow himself to use available services to improve his health, and by extension his sexual self, but rather that the services do not exist, are of poor quality, or are beyond the financial range of the veteran.

In addition to physical problems, money worries can also render a veteran impotent. If the veteran's PTSD or poor physical health creates job, and hence financial, problems the veteran may find himself increasingly financially dependent on his wife. The psychological impact of this on men who were trained to see themselves as family breadwinners and protectors of women and children can increase their depressions.

Veterans who have had to depend on their wives as the stable source of income may find themselves increasingly uncomfortable with this arrangement as they see their wives grow older and become more easily tired from the strain of dual roles—one at home and one on the job.

In addition, as Vietnam wives grow older, they may develop depression or medical problems themselves, resulting in part from the limited time and money they have had to spend on their own self-care. Some wives in their 40s and 50s have developed cancer, heart problems, MS, or other medical problems which have impaired their ability to work with the vigor they had in their younger years.

A wife's cancer, heart condition, or fatigue level due to aging and stress can bring a couple closer together or drive them further apart. Global generalities cannot be made. However, in instances where the veteran truly loves his wife and is healed enough to be emotionally connected with her at times, his wife's impaired health may increase his sense of guilt over his unwanted but nevertheless real limitations in providing for his family.

For example, George worked part-time as a mechanic, but frequently changed jobs because he could not stand corrupt supervisors or unmotivated or poorly skilled co-workers. In Vietnam, corrupt leaders and poor mechanics had endangered his life, and the lives of others, many times. George took great pride in doing quality work. It was almost a matter of life and death for him, as it was in Vietnam.

George's wife, Sarah, worked as a teacher's aide. Because her husband changed jobs so frequently, he was not able to maintain any company-based life or health insurance for very long. Therefore Sarah felt compelled to keep her job for insurance purposes, even though, after their children were in high school, she wanted to go back to school and move ahead vocationally.

George wanted a lot of time to himself and Sarah felt frustrated in establishing emotional intimacy with him. Their sex life, however, was "fantastic." Even when George would isolate himself for days, Sarah wouldn't even think of divorcing him. "He's the best lover I ever had," Sarah explains. "Besides, all men are deficient one way or another."

When Sarah was 45, her mother became seriously ill and needed home care. Sarah wanted to leave her now much-loathed job, but could not because her family needed her health care coverage. By now, George and Sarah's children were teenagers and could make their own meals and do their own laundry. Therefore Sarah could go straight from work to her mother's home and help with her care. Sarah also spend most of the weekend at her mother's side.

Nevertheless, Sarah made a point of being in bed with George as much as possible. Since they usually made love around 11 p.m., by 11 p.m. Sarah was usually showered, perfumed, and ready.

But George wasn't ready at all. He felt so guilty that his wife couldn't quit her job at this time of family need because of his perceived inadequacies as a provider. He also felt guilty because he could see the fatigue on his wife's face. She was still pretty to him, but he knew that she looked older than her years because of decades of strain and he felt guilty about that.

He also felt guilty because he could not volunteer to help Sarah in taking care of her mother because he could not stand to be near sick or dying people. He had seen enough of death in Vietnam. The problem wasn't that he didn't like his mother-in-law, the problem was that he adored her.

She had been kind and nurturing to him, a far cry from his biological mother who was so involved with drinking during George's growing years that George had spent most of childhood "mothering" his mother and his brothers and sisters.

While George grew up parenting his siblings, he was never parented himself until he met Sarah and her family. Sarah was nurturing toward George, but her mother was even more nurturing.

Now George's mothering mother-in-law was thin, bald, and coughing up blood. George couldn't stand it. Between his guilt and his grief, George shut down, emotionally and sexually.

Sarah did not understand. She thought George no longer desired her physically because her face was falling and she no longer had the figure of her youth. When George refused her sexual overtures, Sarah wept uncontrollably. In her time of grief, she needed George's arms around her more than ever. The only way she knew to be held was in sex. She didn't know how to ask to be held just to be held.

She wept and wept not only because she felt sexually rejected, but because she was about to lose her mother. At the same time, she was grieving her own loss of youthful energy and appearance. She was also facing the reality of wishing that she would live forever, a wish many of us hold to dearly until the death of a loved one or a near-encounter with our own death forces us to face the reality of human mortality.

George had confronted the reality of human mortality in Vietnam, a hundred times or more. But Sarah's first meaningful encounter with death was her mother's illness. In sex, Sarah, like some veterans, was wanting not only sex and love, but comfort and affirmation of her existence.

Sarah's tears were a plea for George to hold and caress her. But the more she cried, the guiltier George felt. He knew Sarah needed him and now he felt inadequate not only as a provider, but as a lover. George did not know how to put his feelings into words and experienced his guilt and inadequacy internally. As the pressure mounted, George exploded—unfortunately, at Sarah.

"What's wrong with you? Your Mom is about to die and you want sex? What kind of woman are you anyway? And how come you are crying? Your mother's the one who is dying—not you," George said.

Sarah was now humiliated to the core and furious. Who was the one who spent hours caring for her mother during her free time while he, King George, sat home and watched T.V.? And who worked at a job she hated for the sake of the family while he, King George, switched jobs whenever he wasn't happy? Why, if she left a job every time she was unhappy, their family would be in the poorhouse.

As Sarah continued to lash out, George lashed back. Sarah retaliated, followed by another insult from George. And so the evening went until one of them left the bedroom and slept on the couch.

There is such needless pain and suffering in this story. The tragedy here is that Sarah and George could have given each other so much love and comfort, if only they knew how to speak their feelings to each other and ask each other for what they needed. Sarah, for example, could have asked to be held and George could have easily done so, whether or not he was capable of sexual intercourse. Even if Sarah had wanted sexual release, George could have assisted Sarah with that, provided she not require his having an erection.

As Vietnam veterans and their wives go through the various crises of midlife and aging, their sexual drive and abilities may be diverted and perhaps diminished by competing demands on their energies (e.g., medical problems in the family, the loss of a job, or just the physical changes inherent to aging). However, the couple does not need to be deprived of the much-needed pleasures of touching and caressing simply because one partner is (at least temporarily) impotent, frigid, or sexually uninterested.

Men in their 40s and 50s also need to realize that they are no longer 19 and may not have the "instant" erections of their youth. They may need additional sexual stimulation from their wives in order to achieve and sustain an erection. However, the veteran may be reluctant to accept his need for additional help from his wife and the wife, in turn, may be reluctant to provide it. She may have been raised to feel that stimulating a man as may be required is immoral or unfeminine, or she may feel ashamed to participate in certain kinds of sexual activities for other reasons. If she harbors resentments against her husband, they may be expressed by her not wishing to take an active role in sexually stimulating him.

Sex education of a new sort is needed for the couple in midlife, including an expanded definition of sexuality. Sexuality needs to be seen in its fullest form, including a full range of sexual and sensual touching, including massage, as well as intercourse and climax. The physical contact between husband and wife may change due to time, and stress, but it is important in midlife and old age because it is the one gift a couple can give themselves and each other.

As the Vietnam veteran and his wife say goodbye to their youth, they may need each other and their intimate moments even more than when they were more active. Fortunately there are many excellent books on the subject of sexuality for middle-aged and older persons. Even more fortunately, wrinkles and gray hairs do not kill the sex drive. It is my wish that couples reading this book not be deprived of what can be a source of tremendous satisfaction in their middle and later years— a mutually gratifying sexual and emotional intimacy with each other.

◆ ◆ ◆

Venereal Disease and PTSD

Venereal diseases (VD) are not symptoms of PTSD. Yet a number of wives have contracted herpes or one of the more traditionally sexually transmitted diseases (STD), such as syphilis or gonorrhea, from their husbands. In a few cases, wives mythologized the origin of the diseases so as to avoid the truth of their husband's infidelities. For example, one wife believed her husband when he told her that he caught herpes from the air in Vietnam. She was quickly brought to reality by her physician, at which point her denial turned into anger and tears.

After this wife's confession about herpes, other women shared that they too were infected, if not with herpes, with other sexually transmitted diseases. They were certain that they had contracted these diseases from their husbands, since they had been sexually faithful.

"I feel scared, scarred, and stuck. Now that I have herpes [or some other STD] no other man will want me," was the feeling of most of the STD suffers. They all resented their husbands, but after that seemed to divide into two groups. The first group was women who felt they "deserved" the herpes or other STD due to some moral or other failing on their part. This group sadly accepted having a STD as their "lot" in life. These women stayed with their husbands and if they did divorce, tended to do so for reasons other than being infected with a STD. The second group consisted of women who were so outraged at having been infected with a STD that they divorced their husbands precisely for that reason.

Infidelity is usually a cause of marital discord in any home; however, since herpes and other sexually transmitted diseases, especially the HIV virus, have become major health hazards in our society, infidelity has become more than an emotional insult. It has become a life-or-death issue. For example, early in her marriage to Tim, Mary Ellen tolerated his sexual flings. When the media began publicizing the existence of herpes and the HIV virus, however, Mary Ellen began to be concerned. Her husband discounted her fears and when she wanted to use a condom during their sexual relations, he refused. "I don't like them," he would say.

Mary Ellen was afraid she would catch something from her husband, but she did not insist on the condom. She was not being masochistic or suicidal. She was trying to keep her husband. Since she wanted her husband to forsake his other women, she tried to make their sex life as pleasurable for him as possible. If he didn't want to use a condom, she would not force the issue.

As she learned more about the HIV virus, however, and as she learned that her husband slept with women who prostituted themselves for drug money, Mary Ellen refused to sleep with her husband at all. "How do I know who he's been with?" Mary Ellen now says. "I can't die of AIDS just for his pleasure. I have children to live for, grandchildren too. I want my husband, but I'm not willing to die for him."

Even some wives who suspect infidelity are finding themselves increasingly reluctant to have sexual relations with their husbands. "It used to be my ego was hurt when I felt he was with someone else. But now my life is at stake. I'd rather go without sex than to an early grave," states one wife.

Most certainly, the existence of dangerous STD in our society make relationship issues, especially those of trust and fidelity, even more important to the Vietnam couple than ever before.

Wives' Responses

In general, women have trouble being intimate with a man who is unhappy or angry, who is emotionally distant, or who is verbally or physically abusive. Some women, however, especially physically abused wives, cling to sex as a major means of keeping their marriage alive. While it is impossible to make global generalities about the sexual response of Vietnam wives to husbands with PTSD-related sexual problems, several patterns do emerge.

*Denial of sexuality leading to sexual avoidance of
the veteran*

Some women respond to their husband's sexual dysfunctions, to his insistence on sex on demand, to his obsession with sex, or his sexual flings by turning off their sexuality. They may go to bed with him, but over the years they may lose touch with their own sexual rhythms and desires. They may even deny that they have any sexual drive or desires at all. When they do engage in sex, it is usually in response to their husband's need, not their own. In this, the Vietnam wife is not different from many other married women, who learn to adapt their sexuality to their partners' timing and tastes.

The Vietnam wife, however, is under special pressures. She knows her husband is troubled and if sex is paramount to him, she may go along with his sexual desires to help promote his mental health and keep the peace at home. When she is aggressive in bed, her aggression may not be a reflection of her own sex drive, but a response to her veteran's request, if not insistence, that she be more active sexually. Hence sex becomes more like work than play.

In recent years, with the onset of the sexual revolution, sex has become an achievement situation for women, as well as for men. It is no longer enough for a woman to lie in bed passively. Now she may feel pressured to "perform" by having an orgasm or at least displaying heated passion. In addition, a new phenomenon has emerged—women insisting on their "right" to sexual fulfillment and demanding that men bring them to orgasm.[19]

However, Vietnam wives who make such demands on their husbands are, in my experience, relatively few in number. In most cases, the woman allows her sexuality to be monitored by her husband's desires. If he wants her to be sexually aggressive, she will be so, even to the point of pretending more passion than she is actually feeling. In a few instances, women have forced themselves to be sexually aggressive to please their veteran, only to have him eventually become angry, accuse the woman of trying to emasculate him, and insist that she allow him to take control.

Given such a double message, even sexually alive women could throw up their hands. "It isn't fun if you're always being judged," explains one wife. "Or if the rules keep changing," adds another. As a result, the woman's sexual desires and most certainly her sexual spontaneity might become inhibited, leading eventually to the woman's avoidance of, if not outright hostility toward, marital sexual activity.

Decreased self-esteem

When the Vietnam wife experiences love during sex only on occasion, she begins to feel like a whore even though she is making love with her own husband. She feels debased because she feels she is being used as a sex machine. Yet she may engage in sex with her husband anyway, out of a sense of duty or because of her husband's insistence, or because he is, or seems, desperate. Or she may pity her husband. "Sex is the only time he feels alive. How can I deny him?" is a statement I have heard over and over. Or she may fear that her veteran will become enraged or that he will "go crazy." He might regress further and further into his PTSD if she does not comply. Yet she often feels like a robot. "I don't know why I do it with him. I don't get anything out of it sexually or emotionally. He hardly touches me. We don't talk. What's the point?" asks Jean.

Jean has been in group for over a year. She is long past the point of blaming the poverty of her sexual relationship with her husband entirely on herself. Today she clearly recognizes that her husband's PTSD and other psychological problems are contributing to the lack of love and good sex in their marriage. Yet even Jean, like most of the newcomers who come to group, on some level attributes her sexual and emotional difficulties primarily to herself, rather than to her husband's problems. "If only I was 'better,' then he would love me more," is Jean's underlying thought. More specifically, "If only I knew how to relate to him better," "If only I was prettier," or "If only my breasts were fuller, or my thighs slimmer, or whatever, then he would respond to me."

Despite her awareness of her husband's PTSD, Jean's self-esteem suffers because, as a woman, she has been socialized to look to male approval and male responses as a measure of her self-worth. Even the women with significant career achievements and successes and well-established identities outside their homes suffer from feelings of inferiority and inadequacy when their husbands avoid them sexually, or when their sex life seems to lack love and tenderness. They often find it hard to love themselves or to validate themselves as women when the man they love either ignores them, treats them like a sex object, or fails to give them the love and affection they desire.

While many of the wives might feel like failures as women on some level, they also realize that the lack of sexual gratification and emotional intimacy in their marriage is not all their fault. Most women are quick to point out that their husband's inability to be intimate and his fear of being close derive from several sources, including Vietnam. Despite their understanding of the sources of their husband's difficulties, most of the women nevertheless eventually voice resentments toward their husbands for failing to love them properly.

Anger, resentment, and feelings of betrayal usually exist in the women, right alongside their self-blame. Obviously, the woman's anger toward her husband, like her husband's anger toward her or toward his Vietnam experience, can dilute, if not totally obliterate, her sexual response.

In cases where the veteran is sometimes loving and attentive during sex, but other times not, the Vietnam wife becomes not only depressed but confused.

"Sex is great when Tyrone is his regular self. But when he's under pressure or something snaps him back into 'Nam, the regular Tyrone disappears and a warrior takes his place. He begins to heave and the blood in his veins visibly pulsates. Then I never know what to expect, in bed or anywhere else," says Beau.

Like other wives in group, Beau experiences many pleasurable times with her husband, who can be extremely tender and loving as well as self-centered and cold. His "PTSD moods," as she calls them, are unpredictable. At times they last for days, at times for months. In considering whether or not to stay married to Tyrone, she does not know on which Tyrone to base her decision—the regular Tyrone or the warrior one.

A few wives are so devastated by their husband's sexual rejection or iciness, they desperately pursue him sexually. If they can but engage him in sex, even purely carnal sex, then they feel loved and assured of their worth. So far, this pattern has evidenced itself only among some of the physically battered women who have attended group. As Lenore Walker, who has studied hundreds of battered women, points out, battered women typically use sex to create an illusion of love and as a means of establishing harmony in the home.[20] Yet the price they pay is loss of self-respect. Whenever a woman uses "sex in order to create love she may feel she is prostituting and degrading herself."[21]

♦ ♦ ♦

Sexuality and Role Overload

Sexuality is more than any specific sex act or variety of sex acts. It encompasses all of a person's feelings about his or her physical self, as well as his or her general attitude toward life. A highly sexual person is usually a vibrant self-actualized person whose enthusiasm for sex is mirrored in his or her enthusiasm for other activities.[22]

The sexual person enjoys and rejoices in his or her physical self, including but not limited to the aliveness that comes from sexual energy. Depressed persons are typically not sexual in this sense, even though they may reach for sex as a means of self-validation or become obsessed with sex as a means of avoiding other problems.

Fun sex, as opposed to "duty sex," requires an atmosphere of play and lightness, not the seriousness, strains, and sadness which often surround the Vietnam veteran with PTSD and his equally burdened wife. Sex is also robbed of its potential for maximum emotional and physical gratification when the couple is saddled with financial instability. The vet may be physically handicapped. Or his emotional problems resulting from the war or from job discrimination against vets may have reduced his career opportunities. There may be other headaches as well, such as conflicted relationships with the extended family, troubled children, and the normal emotional and physical fatigue of everyday life, all of which can lessen the quality and quantity of the couple's sex life.

In some couples, the sense of responsibility, as well as the actual responsibilities, are shared. Both the vet and his wife do about the same amount of work and worrying. In other cases, however, one of the couple assumes psychological responsibility for the family's burdens to a greater extent than the other and actually does more than half of the work. Typically, this is the individual who suffers not only from physical but also from mental fatigue. This partner's life becomes organized around work and other responsibilities, not pleasures or emotional needs.

Sometimes it is the veteran who assumes the role of the "responsible one." He is the one who says no when his wife calls him to bed or asks for a night out because he's finishing up some work or worrying about the broken water heater or the unpaid car repair bills. Or perhaps he feels his free time is better spent helping one of the children. In light of the family's many problems, his wife's request seems irrelevant, if not outright irresponsible or frivolous.

In my clinical experience, however, it is the Vietnam wife, rather than the veteran, who usually assumes the sense of responsibility for the family's emotional and financial well-being. Obviously there is a bias in this sample. Most likely it is primarily women who feel burdened by an enormous sense of responsibility for their families or who have relatively irresponsible partners who seek help.

As the family's official worrywart, sex and other forms of relaxation are not high on her list of priorities. When her husband wants to go to a movie or a mall, she wants to finish the ironing and other chores and go to bed early because the next day she's working overtime to help pay some bills.

As the following chapter on multiple roles will explain in greater detail, role overload is a given in the lives of many Vietnam wives. Saddled with multiple responsibilities both outside the home and in it, the Vietnam wife typically operates in her "responsible adult" mode, rather than in her "playful child" mode. It is as difficult for her, as for any other overcommitted person, male or female, to turn off the "responsible adult" mentality and become the "playful child" in bed, or elsewhere. Breaks or periods of relaxation or physical exercise are necessary in order to make the transition from responsible adult to playful child.

"Even when we're on vacation, there's no vacation from his PTSD," explains Jean, who feels her playful child died long ago. Her enthusiasm for sex, as well as for other forms of recreation, has also died a slow death in the traffic jams or got lost somewhere in the endless "to do" lists which accompany being a working wife and mother.

In addition, she has to work overtime in order to have the leave necessary to accompany her husband to his doctor's appointments. He refuses to go alone. Furthermore, Jean is afraid her husband will explode or even start fights if she is not along to smooth the path and calm him down should one of the medical staff be, or seem to be, insulting or incompetent.

"I've been on the go since 6 a.m. and what aggravates me more than anything is that after group I have to stop at the grocery store and pick up milk and cupcakes. The cupcakes are for my son's ball game tomorrow. The milk is for my other baby—my husband. He called me today in the middle of a staff meeting at work to remind me that we were out of milk.

"'Why can't you go get the milk?' I wanted to scream. But I know better than to yell at a combat vet. In his view, I'm the woman, so I'm responsible for the home, the groceries, the laundry, our son—the works. Sure, my vet helps, but only when he feels like it.

"I can handle doing all the work, but what I can't handle is having to turn into a sex kitten every night. I hate those women on TV who can work all day and purr all night. Some nights all I want to do is go to sleep. But all he wants to do is fool around. Sometimes he isn't even interested in sex, but he wants me to be there panting anyway. If I'm not in heat, he wonders if I have another man, or if I don't love him anymore, or if this group has turned me against him. I tell him repeatedly that I love him, that I enjoy sex with him, but sometimes I'm just too tired.

"Well, he just can't understand that, nor can he understand the enormous emotional burden I feel for our son. My husband is a very good father, except when he's into his PTSD. Then he gets depressed or into one of his moods or can be gone for hours, if not days, at a time. Even if he's around, he just sits and doesn't talk to us. I can't count on him to take Pete to his ball games or be involved in any of Pete's school activities. Since I work, I can't be there all the time either. But I make all the arrangements for my son to get to his events and I try to spend a lot of time with him on weekends.

"Of course all this arranging takes time and energy, which my husband thinks is done by a magic secretary. Then on weekends and my days off, he thinks that I should have hours and hours totally free to play around with him in bed. But, as a working woman, my days off are not days off. I have all these chores to do, as well as a need for time for myself. Instead, I feel pressured to turn into some kind of sex goddess, or at least be there sexually. Sometimes sex feels like another job to me, rather than a pleasure. I'm ashamed to admit that there are times when I'm in bed with my husband that I'm planning my grocery list or thinking of all the phone calls I have to make after I get up.

"Pretty sad, isn't it? I wish I could be more spontaneous and totally absorb myself in sex, like I used to, before our son was born and before PTSD came into the picture. Basically, I'm a very sexual woman and my husband is very good in bed—when he's not into his PTSD, that is. But I'm just too wound up from all I've done during the day and from realizing all that I have to do the next day to let myself go. I wish I could be more playful, but I'm not.

"It is frightening to realize how much a job, a home, a child, and a Vietnam veteran can take out of a woman, but reality is reality. We have to eat. He doesn't make enough. So I have to work, which means that not only my sexuality, but other things suffer."

While Jean resents her husband's expectation that she be sexual and alluring after a hard day's work, she also berates herself for not measuring up to his desires. Yet she, like so many other Vietnam wives, fails to realize that her veteran's ability to relax, play, and have the physical and psychic energy for sexual fun, is based on somebody else, specifically the wife, assuming the physical and emotional responsibility for much of the family's life. When the Vietnam wife takes care of most of the bills, the housework, the children's emotional and physical needs, she is essentially giving her husband the free time, and more importantly, the peace of mind, to pursue recreational activities and to achieve a mental and physical state which permits sexual desires to surface.

Jean's husband can go out twice a week with his friends and attend therapy a third night, knowing that Jean is cleaning the house and helping Johnny with his homework. Also, he can spend much of his weekend with friends or engaged in sports, because, once again, Jean is either managing the household or tending to Johnny. After having enjoyed himself with his friends or with his sports, he's ready to make love to Jean. But Jean's energies have been drained by having fulfilled many family responsibilities, as well as by the lack of free time in her life. While her husband has had the time to recharge his "pleasure batteries," she has not.

Not only does Jean's husband spend more time relaxing and playing than Jean, but he has a different mindset about life. Due to his PTSD and his sense of male prerogative, he is able to detach not only from his own problems, but from the problems of the family. For example, Jean reports that her husband forgets the nights he keeps her up for hours talking about Vietnam or having flashbacks. "The next night, he acts as if nothing happened," explains Jean. "He's ready to be Tarzan and I'm supposed to be Jane. But I'm still tired from the night before and still in a state of confusion and upset over his emotional condition.

"Because he feels fine at the moment, he forgets about all the times he's in a rage or in turmoil. But I can't forget. Nor can I pretend that everything's all right. He thinks everything is all right as long as we are making love. It's like he's never heard me say that no matter how good he is in bed, if he doesn't deal with his PTSD—really deal with it, not play at dealing with it—and change some of his attitudes about women, then I might leave him."

When Jean's husband gets depressed, he takes leave from work, goes camping or fishing, or travels to see his war buddies. When Jean gets depressed, she goes to work, fixes Johnny's meals, and does the dishes anyway. Happy or sad, sick or well, Jean is working almost all the time. Most likely if she was relieved of some of her physical and emotional responsibilities, her natural interest in sex, and other forms of fun, would come back.

Vietnam wives need not have jobs outside the home in order to suffer from mental and physical fatigue like Jean. The Vietnam wife who is home most of the day with small children may also find herself swamped with chores, as well as saddled with concern, if not agony, over her husband's mental health and the future of her marriage. In addition, she may suffer from the lack of stimulation, the loneliness, and the unfair lack of recognition and appreciation which often attend being a full-time homemaker in our society.

More than one full-time Vietnam wife and mother has sat in group weeping over the fact that her husband cannot comprehend how caring for a home and small children all day can be not only tiring, but frustrating, and certainly not conducive to being sexually alive at night. These wives feel they do not have the "excuse" of working outside the home in order to say no to sex or in order to explain their lack of sexual interest. Hence they sometimes feel under special pressure to be sexually enticing and available. Yet the very pressure from their husbands to be more sexual is a turnoff, and combined with the many strains of being a full-time homemaker and mother, such pressure from her husband can produce a highly anxious, and therefore sexually uninterested, woman.

Yet the Vietnam wife, despite her many emotional and physical responsibilities, is not inherently any less sexual than any other woman, as shown in the responses of Vietnam wives to a popular exercise used in group entitled "Your Free Self." After the Vietnam wife is thoroughly relaxed, she is asked to imagine her "free spirit"—what she would be like or what she would like to do if she were not feeling so responsible for her husband, the children, the laundry, the office, or if she were in a relatively problem-free marriage. To help her get in touch with her playful child, she is asked to remember any time in her past when she felt free of multiple demanding responsibilities. Under such circumstances, many Vietnam wives fantasize themselves as extremely creative and erotic.

♦ ♦ ♦

Sexual Deprivation And Depression:
A Vicious Cycle

While the Vietnam wife sometimes wishes she were more sexual in order to please her husband, she frequently forgets that often when she wants sex, her husband is simply not at home at night or is sexually uninterested or impotent due to depression or the prolonged effects of drug or alcohol abuse. She also forgets that if the two of them had greater communication and emotional intimacy, her sexual interest might soar. Yet the diminished frequency and quality of her sexual relationship with her husband only serves to widen the emotional distance between herself and her husband and to increase their communication problems.

In addition, the lack of sexual contact or meaningful sexual activity also perpetuates any existing depression in either the vet or his wife. While the vet and his wife may be depressed for different reasons, both suffer when their sexual relationship is suffering.

Since sexual activity and orgasm require energy, they are often seen as draining. However, suppressing sexuality and fighting the need for sexual release also require energy. While a person may feel depleted immediately after intercourse, ultimately the sexual release functions to create more energy and an elevation in mood. When the Vietnam wife states that she is too tired for sex, part of her fatigue may stem from the very lack of sexual touch and fulfillment itself.

Summary

Sexuality is an issue in many homes, but especially in the homes of PTSD-afflicted veterans. The veteran's sexual response may be diminished, or twisted, by the intrusion of wartime memories or survivor guilt into his intimate moments. Or the vet may fear the physical and emotional vulnerability inherent in disrobing and in the sexual act itself. If he is unable to maintain an erection, or otherwise enjoy his sexuality due to his PTSD, he may avoid sex altogether.

While some vets avoid sex, and some have periods of sexual uninterest, in some instances vets are interested in sex almost all the time. An intense need for, and preoccupation with, sex may reflect the vet's need to combat his depression and anxiety and to forget not only Vietnam but his problems in the present. Sex may make him feel good, if only briefly.

Meanwhile his wife may feel like a sex machine, a human tranquilizer, or a sexual reject. If her husband alternates his behavior, she may feel like all three. Whether the veteran avoids sex or is obsessed with it, the Vietnam wife's self-esteem suffers if her needs to be cherished and loved, to be listened to, and considered important by her husband are not met.

In homes where the Vietnam wife does the majority of the housework and child care, sheer fatigue may deplete her sexual energies, especially if she is simultaneously working outside the home. And underneath the fatigue, which is real, lies anger. Even if she can't admit it, her sexual rejection or lack of response often betrays her anger at him for failing her sexually or for sexually using her. Primarily, though, she is angry at her husband for failing to meet her needs for intimacy and emotional bonding.

Some wives resign themselves to sexually unfulfilling marriages. They tend to find comfort in their children and their work, not other men. Some wives admit their bitterness, others bury their bitterness with denial or excess food. In many instances, the sexual happiness of the Vietnam veteran and his wife can be viewed as yet another casualty of the Vietnam war.

4

The Reality of Multiple Roles

As the wife of a Vietnam combat vet with a flaming case of untreated PTSD, I have several full-time jobs. My full-time job at the office is just one of them. In fact, it is the easiest one of all.

First, and most important, I am a mother, and being the wife of a vet, this means that usually I function like a single parent. I don't know whether it's PTSD or male chauvinism or a combination of both, but the bottom line is that I am responsible for almost every detail of my children's lives. When they were young, I packed their lunches, went on their field trips, and ironed their clothes. When it was time for them to go to college, I did all the applications work, all the packing, and all the crying.

I am also responsible for most of the details of my husband's life—arranging his medical appointments, explaining and protecting him from his parents, my parents, the social workers, and the neighbors. I take care of all his paperwork too and since he's one of those vets who hates the IRS, I take care of all the family finances as well.

When my husband is in a good mood, he vacuums, does the dishes, and irons my blouses. But I never know how long his good moods are going to last and I can't count on anything getting done unless I do it myself. I hate to start a fight over something as trivial as an undone chore.

But all those undone chores pile up, and before I know it, I'm working all the time. Sometimes I get so tired I can't even fall asleep. But other times I purposely stay up until two or three in the morning just to have a little time to myself, and a little peace.

I wish I could socialize and do more for myself, but I don't have time. When the kids were still at home, I had to think twice before I left them alone with my husband. He wasn't abusive to them, but since he refused to get help, I had to be around him as much as possible in case he had a problem. If something had happened to him while I was gone, the kids could not have handled it without me. He wouldn't have been able to handle it either. Now the children are older, but I still don't feel comfortable leaving them alone with him. Seems like everybody is used to me being around most of the time to take care of everything.

I do everything for everybody else. I don't do anything for myself because that would be selfish. Yet when I do what everybody else expects me to do, no one ever says "thanks." Sometimes I feel so unappreciated that I want to run away from home.

—Melanie, mother of three and wife of a combat vet

Most of the Vietnam wives who have sought help work outside the home, some for personal fulfillment, but most out of economic necessity. Even in homes where the veteran receives a disability check for his PTSD or other war-related problems, it may be economically necessary for the wife to work to make ends meet, especially if the couple is supporting or assisting children or grandchildren or is paying off previous debts. In some cases the veteran is unemployed or only partially employed and receives no compensation from the government. In other cases, the husbands, while employed full time, have expressed considerable job dissatisfaction to their wives. In the remaining cases, the husbands have shown great pride and dedication to their vocations. However, among this group, in many instances the veteran's employment record has been marred by one or more outbursts of temper or physical attacks on an employee or supervisor. Both the veteran and his wife usually trace the outburst to the husband's PTSD.

Many vets lost career opportunities due to the reduced educational and job training benefits available to Vietnam vets as compared to World War II veterans. The Vietnam vet also returned home to an economy suffering from inflation and unemployment and to employers who were hostile or ambivalent toward him because of his veteran status. Today, the old stereotype of the Vietnam veteran as a crazy, angry baby-killer is slowly being replaced by the new stereotype of the Vietnam veteran as a "macho" or Rambo hero. However, even today, vets report that negative stereotypes about Vietnam veterans still exist. Furthermore, such negative stereotypes were certainly active years ago, when many vets were seeking employment. At that time, some vets purposely did not mention their Vietnam service in job interviews or, if asked, denied it.

The vet's real or perceived need to hide his identity as a Vietnam veteran may have contributed to his job dissatisfaction and other job problems. Furthermore, the tendency of some veterans with PTSD to have interpersonal difficulties on the job and to mistrust authority figures has left them jobless, job hunting, or going from one job to the next. Add to this any subtle discrimination against being middle aged or partially disabled and it becomes obvious why veterans often have difficulty attracting job offers.

The resulting instability deeply affects the wives who find themselves in financial limbo or in the process of constantly rearranging their work plans and schedules, the children's schedules, needed appointments, and any social plans to accommodate their husband's job changes, job hunting, or lack of employment. "I can't plan and there's no routine," states Dora. "If my husband gets a job, then maybe we can afford something we need or pay a certain bill. But I never know until the last minute. Then, once he gets a job, I never know how long he's going to keep it.

"Obviously we can't plan the chores—or even our own schedule. If my husband needs the car for a job interview, then our son can't get to his ball practice. No sense paying for the uniform if he isn't going to be able to participate.

"What we really need is a second car, but we can't afford one until George gets a job. But I'm not complaining.

"George's had six jobs since 'Nam, but some of his war buddies have had more than that. And at least my husband keeps trying to find work."

However, George is not motivated to work full time or to pursue an upwardly mobile career. Like some of his war buddies, he is turned off by middle-class values such as success and material gain. Problems arise, however, when the wife still desires a dream home with a two-car garage.

As wives approach midlife, they may have relinquished their dream of having a model home. "It simply isn't going to happen. I accepted that the same time I accepted turning 49," states Barbara. "But what I can't accept is having to work full time until I'm an old lady.

"It's one thing to be a superwoman when you are in your 20s and 30s, managing a home and career and always feeling like you are cheating one because of the other. But if I have to work until I'm 60 or 70 because of my husband's job problems, I'm going to be furious . . . and exhausted.

"I missed out on being with my children when they were little due to my husband and his PTSD. But now—today—I'm missing out on being a grandmother because of my job. My daughter just had a baby and it's killing me to be at work when I want to be with her."

Some wives are angry because they have had to remain in unrewarding jobs due to their husband's financial instability. In a parallel manner, some veterans have had difficulties accepting or keeping relatively menial or "unexciting" jobs because these jobs stand in such stark contrast to the positions of considerable authority or more adventuresome positions they held during their tours of duty in Vietnam. "Do you know what it is to have to work 9 to 5 in an office and take orders from someone you don't respect after having been in command of millions of dollars' worth of equipment in Vietnam?" asks a former officer. He resents having to write memos before he can do anything. In Vietnam, he had power of life and death over dozens of men and made his own decisions.

Regardless of the source of the veteran's employment difficulties, when he is unemployed or sporadically employed, his wife is not just a contributor to the family's income, but often the family's primary or sole source of funds. Hence all of the woman's issues and problems, whether with her veteran or within herself, exist in the context of a multiple-role lifestyle. The fact that she works both inside the home, as well as at an outside job, pervades every aspect of her life and emotional being. Yet it is a reality which she herself, as well as her partner, family, and friends (and many therapists) overlook.

The strains of having primary responsibilities both inside and outside the home are obvious. Yet they are often overlooked because of media images of the working wife or mother as one who glides from one role to the next without anxiety, conflict, or effort, with her makeup intact and her figure perpetually slim. In addition, there is the cultural expectation that a woman should be able to do it all, or at least most of it, without complaining. "I don't know why we think that we have to do it all, but we do," the women in group often say.

In the past, women were strangled by the notion that women who worked outside the home were neurotic, unfeminine, or otherwise "abnormal."[1] But today women are strangled by society's denigration of traditional feminine roles. For many women, it is no longer enough to be a wife, mother, or homemaker.[2] In addition, economic changes during the past two decades have necessitated that many women work outside the home for sheer survival of the family or to improve the family's standard of living.[3]

Handling a full- or part-time job in addition to home means increased demands on time and energy, which often result in overload and fatigue. With additional roles come additional commitments: more people to respond to, more appointments to keep, more deadlines to meet.[4] In addition, the Vietnam wife must come to understand and grapple with any office politics as well as her interpersonal dynamics at home.

Essentially the Vietnam wife working outside the home faces the exhaustion of having at least two full-time jobs, one at home and one at work. In addition, she often has a third job, that of arranging all her roles. Since the cultural expectation is often that the woman's outside job is peripheral to her essential home roles, it is usually the woman who makes the arrangements necessary to execute all the various roles—for example, the phone calls regarding child care and the transportation of children to and from school events. In most cases, the woman attempts to arrange that her working role does not interfere with her domestic role. However, the logistical difficulties involved, especially when children are young, can be enormous.

The Vietnam wife's burden is compounded by the fact that her sleep may be interrupted by her husband's nightmares or flashbacks, his anger or depression, or his unpredictable comings and goings. Or she may have to spend the night in the car or at a friend's because she fears his anger. Furthermore, due to tensions in the home, the Vietnam wife often goes to work not only without sufficient physical rest, but without mental peace.

Since her husband's emotional capacities are impaired due to PTSD, she is often the emotional center of the home. Both her husband and her children may look to her for nurturing, guidance, and strength. Furthermore, she often assumes an active role in her husband's recovery by encouraging him to seek help, arranging his therapy appointments or helping him to obtain his benefits. If he cannot tolerate bureaucracies or waiting, then it will be she, not he, who calls the doctors and the hospitals, contacts the veteran's benefits offices, waits in line at the pharmacy, and does whatever else is necessary. If he must appear himself, usually she feels she must go with him, to keep him calm should he feel he is being treated unfairly or should he notice any incompetence or insensitivity on the part of the clerks or the medical staff. If he is hospitalized, there are frequent visits and in some cases, participation in family therapy or conferences with doctors, all of which require time, energy, and effort.

Her children might also have special needs. They may need to attend therapy or Al-A-Teen meetings. Children from violent homes often have learning problems which require tutoring or extra parental assistance. In most cases, it is the mother, not the father, who helps her children with the homework. In addition, the Vietnam wife may be making special efforts to involve her children in outside recreational or social activities in order to offset the depressive mood in the home or compensate for their father's lack of involvement. In any of the above cases, the working woman's scheduling problems are even more complex.

At the same time, however, the Vietnam wife usually cannot afford the services that make being a working woman easier, like maid service, frequent restaurant dinners, or professional nursing or cleaning help for an elderly or infirm relative. If money is tight, she must also consider economic factors in executing her multiple roles. For example, she may need to shop at discount grocery and clothing stores, even though the stores are out of her way and the lines are long. She may also be unable to afford convenience foods, increasing her time in the kitchen.

Consequently, she feels pressured for time. Yet, she often feels she cannot complain about her time pressures to her partner because they seem trivial compared to his trials in Vietnam.

If I mention to George that I feel pressured, he just laughs at me and says, "You should have been in Vietnam. Then you would have seen real pressure. Why are you complaining about having to go to the grocery store again? At least you have one to go to, and a car to get there with. Why, when I was in the jungles . . . " and on and on.

All I know is that my life is not my own. During the weekdays, my job consumes me. Then at night, I do everything and spend all my time getting me, and everybody else, ready for the next day. My weekends and holidays are not my own either. I clean, cook, take the kids shopping.

Sure, I'm not surrounded by V.C., but my daily list of "things to do" would blow away the minds of most men. All they have is one job—I have at least six: cook, laundress, chauffeur, cleaner, shopper, banker, not to mention my full-time job and being a mother.

My husband laughs at my lists, but I couldn't survive without them. He doesn't understand that I'm working practically all the time. Neither do my kids.

I don't know if they learned it from TV or what, but they complain when I'm five or 10 minutes late to take them where they need to go, as if I'm late because I was taking a bubble bath or doing my nails.

No. I'm usually late because I'm finishing up chores they said they would do, but didn't do. Yet I hate to nag the kids because they've got enough on them with their Dad in and out of the hospital with his PTSD.

But I do blow up at them sometimes. Then I feel guilty because I really do want to be a patient mother and give them quality time. But how I can I be patient when I have so much to do?

♦ ♦ ♦

Sex Role Stereotyping

Sex role stereotypes die hard. Often the woman faces the dual problems of a partner who is unwilling or unprepared to share domestic tasks and her own difficulty in giving up doing the traditional homemaking tasks which once defined her value to her family.

Some of the women I have seen report that their husbands are excellent with the children, but not so excellent with domestic chores. The majority, however, report that while husbands help, they often feel and act martyred in doing so. Veterans who share domestic responsibilities often view themselves as helping or doing the woman a favor, rather than sharing responsibilities. In general, they do not receive reinforcement for their work at home from friends, family, or community, except perhaps for their involvement with their children.

If the vet has agreed to do something for the home or for the children, he may "forget" to keep his promise or decide to do it later. The woman then has the dilemma of choosing to press her husband to keep his commitment and risk being called a nag or a bitch, or to suppress her resentment and do the work herself.

The Vietnam wife has special difficulties in getting her husband to complete his responsibilities at home or to assume more of them. She is usually well-aware of her veteran's sensitivity to being "ordered around." On the other hand, she wants her vet to do much more. Yet she knows she might meet massive resistance if she makes her requests known. "He'll say he has too much pressure at work or from his PTSD to do anything more around the house," one wife reports. "He'll just get mad and walk out," says another. "If I push him too far, he might take it out on me and the kids later, or get into a funk and make me feel guilty," says yet another.

Often the woman is put in the impossible situation of having to choose between overextending herself or seeing one of her children's needs go unmet. For example, their child needs to be driven to music lessons or a sports event. The veteran has promised to take his child, but at the last minute, he says he cannot take the traffic.

He's had an exceptionally hard day. Somebody mentioned Vietnam and it set him back emotionally. It was enough for him to deal with his emotions and stay at work all day without him now having to go out again. He needs to be alone, to collect himself. What his wife is asking him to do seems minor compared to the pain, anger, or frustration he feels inside. Besides, taking kids places is "women's work."

The wife might have had a hard day too. She is exhausted, but she cannot disappoint her child. Also, she may feel for her husband, have empathy for his pain, and not want to add to his burden. In addition, she may know that if her husband is in such a negative mood, even if she insists that he keep his commitment, she will most likely not get what she wants. Furthermore, there will also probably be a scene between them, which will only upset her child and other family members.

In order to spare the child, her husband, and herself the stress of yet another marital conflict, the woman usually ends up doing the driving. Furthermore, the child expects the mother to do the driving. After all, isn't this what mothers do, take care of children? Never mind that the mother has worked all day. She is expected to be a source of boundless energy at night and compensate for the fact that she works all day by doing whatever she can for her children at night.

In addition, in some homes, one or more of the children is sensitive to the fact that their father has been "put down" as a Vietnam veteran or has problems due to the war. Hence they may greatly resent their mother "putting down" their father, even if the mother's complaint is legitimate. If their father has war injuries or is handicapped due to the war, the child's resentment at the mother for asking the father for more help may be even greater.

"When George and I fight, it's torture for our son. If he's supposed to go to a party, and George and I argue over who is going to take him, our fight ruins his fun. By the time we decide who's going to take him, he's decided not to go. He knows that his father has back problems from the war and doesn't like to drive. On the other hand, I work longer hours than my husband, so I feel he should help out more at home," says Janet.

"But it doesn't matter who's right or wrong. When George and I fight, our son gets hurt and doesn't want to go anywhere.

"Bad enough my husband is a recluse and is trying to turn me into one. But I don't want our son to be a hermit. So, I do all the driving."

In some Vietnam vet homes, there is a complete or almost complete role reversal. The vet is on permanent disability due to war injuries, unemployed, or only partially employed for other reasons. He becomes a househusband and the woman works full time. In some instances, the role reversal works smoothly. "It took a lot of training, but I finally got my husband to have dinner ready on time and to do the dishes afterward without me having to tell him 10 times," says one wife.

"At first he used to call me at work to ask me about every little thing. But after I told him that if he could handle the Viet Cong, he could certainly figure out the vacuum cleaner and the mop, his phone calls stopped."

But not all wives are this fortunate. Most find that their husbands do not househusband automatically; they need to be reminded to complete certain chores. Sometimes the woman tires of doing all this reminding and begins assuming some of the domestic chores herself. In some cases, one chore at a time, the woman eventually reassumes many of her previous domestic responsibilities.

Furthermore, when the househusband vet becomes depressed due to PTSD, he cannot be relied upon to keep his commitments. If there are no children in the home, the woman can let go of certain nonessential household chores until her husband regains his strength. But if there are children, much of the work cannot be left undone. The woman has no choice but to do it herself.

For example, Kate, who worked full time, and her husband, Ron, who worked 10 hours a week, established an elaborate division of labor chart. Ron's heart wasn't in it, yet he realized that the old days when men could read the newspaper while their wives cooked dinner and cleaned the house, were over. Kate, who managed an office by day, wanted to rest after work—"not too much, just a little bit." After hammering away at Ron for years about the unfairness of it all, Ron reluctantly agreed to carry his own weight and stop assuming that his wife was a superwoman who could do it all without any feeling of resentment.

The first week Ron attempted to do his chores. But he wasn't used to doing three things at once like his wife. Furthermore, when he got tired or bored, he wanted to quit, even if he hadn't completed everything on his list. After all, he reasoned, he had stressed himself enough in Vietnam. He was home now, not in the military. Breaks and slight infractions of the rules were permitted here. Beside, folding the laundry was really not a life-and-death issue compared to loading machine guns with ammunition.

For two consecutive days when Kate came home from work, she found half of Ron's chores undone. The first day she found Ron taking a nap. She was angry about the chores but she was also glad to see that Ron was able to get some rest. He suffered from insomnia and nightmares and Kate worried about him. The next day, however, the chores weren't done and Ron wasn't sleeping. He was out with his friends. Once again, Kate was resentful over the chores but a part of her was glad. In fact, she was delighted that her husband was finally socializing, rather than isolating himself, which had been his pattern. On the other hand, she was determined not to do his work for him.

The next day she picked the children's clothes for school out of the laundry but left her clothes, and left the filled dishwasher untouched.

That night she quietly confronted Ron and he promised to do better next time.

Two days later the laundry was still unfolded and the dishwasher was still full. At this point Kate was tempted to do Ron's chores for him. It seemed easier than nagging him or having him say that she was making "a big deal about nothing." In fact, Kate calculated that just in terms of time, it would probably take her longer to nag Ron into doing the work than to simply do it herself. But she left the chores undone, set the table with paper plates, and wore a dirty blouse to work.

She planned to confront her husband once more, but he was so angry that particular evening that she felt it best to drop the subject until a better time. A few days later she considered approaching him but he was so distant and depressed that she once again decided to wait. In the meantime she quietly unloaded the dishwasher and did Ron's laundry chores.

For the next few days, she waited for Ron to be in a good mood and for the right time to talk to him about the chores. The right time never came. Meanwhile, the household's needs continued and the children needed clean clothes. When Kate did speak with Ron he seemed so aggravated or distant that she quickly dropped the subject. Even though Kate was angry and resentful about the situation, within weeks she had reassumed responsibility not only for the laundry and the dishwasher, but for several of the other chores which had been Ron's tasks.

In many cases, it is not only her husband's resistance to helping with the domestic work which burdens the multiple-role Vietnam wife, but her own difficulties in giving up traditional homemaking activities. In assuming responsibilities outside the home, the woman experiences the loss of a clearly defined, socially approved feminine identity.[4] When she finds that she no longer has time to make cakes for the church bake sale or to be a room mother for her children's school, she may be criticized by others. If she tells her husband she cannot attend yet another Vietnam conference with him or take in a homeless vet, he may criticize her too. But more importantly, the woman may criticize herself and feel pain at not being able to be the type of mother, wife, or family member she could have been were she not employed outside the home.

"It hurt not to be there when my baby took his first step and to have to have a baby sitter tell me about it," explains one wife. This same wife feels deep guilt that she cannot do more for her invalid father. "I'd like to visit him more, prepare his favorite dishes, but I can't, because I work." She would also like to attend more Vietnam veteran parades and other such events with her husband, but she's simply too exhausted and overextended.

For the multiple-role woman, the security of the old home roles is gone. In the world of work, she must face new situations, take risks, and be evaluated on the basis of her skills, not her personality or her recipes. If she is in a low-paying or dead-end job, or if she is experiencing some form of sexism at work, she may begin to seriously question the "glamour" of being a working woman.

The woman's self-doubts about her working role are only increased when she encounters a loss of approval from others. While social mores have changed and working women and mothers are much more acceptable today than they were 10 or 20 years ago, it is not unusual for some of a woman's relatives to question the woman's departure from domesticity.[5] If the woman must work for economic reasons, she may be "excused." But to the extent to which she works for her own enhancement of skills, for stimulation, or for pleasure, she may be regarded suspiciously.

"After Dan got out of treatment for PTSD and was able to work again, my family expected me to quit my job," explains Marie. "When I tried to tell them that I'd go crazy home all day with four children, they told me they thought I was crazy. Didn't I have enough to deal with, what with Dan still quite not his old self and the problems with the children?

"If I told them that I liked to work, they wouldn't understand. For me, working, even if it's at a job I hate, is easier than being home all day, dealing with all the tensions and problems there. Actually, working is a vacation in comparison.

"My husband understands why I like to work, but my parents and in-laws have combined forces and convinced our kids that I should stay home and be 'more of a mother' to them. Now what do I do?"

The social system may not support the woman either.[6] Despite some improvements in recent years, the woman may still have difficulty finding adequate child care, part-time work, or flexible work schedules. In some instances the veteran proves to be a thoroughly reliable baby sitter. But when he is not available, due to his work schedule, or is untrustworthy, the woman may have "great practical, even sometimes insurmountable obstacles" in arranging her roles. At the same time, her colleagues and superiors may question her investment in her work, given that she is simultaneously committed to a family.[7]

Many Vietnam wives are already socially isolated because of the veteran's tendency to isolate himself or his jealousy of the woman's involvements with other persons. This pre-existing social isolation is compounded by the isolation which stems from the demands of working and the pressing needs of the family. Typically, the working Vietnam wife does not have time for recreation, social, religious, or community activities. At work she may not fit in with younger, single workers. In her neighborhood or in certain social groups, she does not fit in with full-time homemakers "whose interests, responsibilities and schedules are different from hers." [8]

Everyone, both men and women, has multiple roles. Men function as workers, fathers, sons, citizens, and in other capacities. Even traditional women have numerous roles such as sexual partner, companion, family social secretary, house manager, housekeeper, cook, laundress, interior decorator, caretaker of older relatives, and hostess.

Invariably, there are conflicts between the roles. Any person, male or female, who manages numerous responsibilities must often juggle competitive demands and, eventually, compromise. For the multiple-role Vietnam wife, as for all working women, conflicts between home roles and job or career goals are inevitable. Of particular importance, however, is how she reacts to these conflicts.

In the case of the stay-at-home woman, her various roles are not viewed as mutually exclusive. While the stay-at-home mother must often choose between taking care of her children and taking care of her home, all her roles are service- or family-oriented and therefore considered appropriate for women. In the case of the working wife or mother, however, career goals and job obligations are viewed as being competitive with, or noncomplimentary to, her home roles.[9]

In contrast, for a man to be simultaneously a father, husband, and worker is usually considered normal and appropriate. In reality, many men experience considerable conflict and difficulty in integrating their career and home lives. However, unlike the multiple-role woman, they do not also struggle with the societal attitude that their roles are mutually exclusive. Neither do men struggle with the peculiar tug-of-war between roles which working wives and mothers experience due to the low status ascribed to women's home roles.

In this day and age, very few women feel that they must strictly adhere to the traditionally feminine role which restricts her to home and family-oriented activities and which dictates that she be passive, dependent, and always emotional in relation to the world. Like their brothers, girls from middle-class homes are encouraged to achieve. At the same time, however, they are also instructed to be attractive, emotionally responsive, and appropriately feminine. Many girls are also told that any academic or professional successes they might have are secondary to finding a husband and having a family.

For many of the women who have attended group, it has been a monumental achievement to recognize that they have desires and ambitions outside of the family and to decide to take steps toward achieving those ambitions, even if those steps required that they be out of the home an extra evening or morning a week. Some of the women decided to take courses which would promote their careers. They had put off doing so until their husband recovered from PTSD or until such time as their course work would not inconvenience their families. However, after waiting several years and growing increasingly impatient, some of the women decided to go ahead and at least take one small step toward pursing their career objectives.

One wife explains: "My 'real job,' for which I'm not paid, is at home. But I am paid and receive more recognition and respect for my other 'real job' at the office. When I wanted to take a cooking course, nobody in the family objected. But when I wanted to learn computer programming to advance my career, you should have seen the fireworks.

"My mother-in-law refused to babysit for the kids, saying 'Isn't it enough you work all day? Now you have to go out at night, too? Who's going to mother those kids and take care of that husband of yours? Put your career off for later.' But when I took the cooking course, she thought it was great.

"I'm surprised that her guilt trip sank in, that it's still hard for me to do things for me, just for me. I was brought up to think I belonged to the family, but I thought I had outgrown that. I guess I haven't.

"But I'm going to go ahead and take the course anyway, guilt and all. If I have to go to school guilty, well, I'll just go there guilty, because if I put it off any longer, I might never get to it."

When the Veteran Is Physically Disabled or Becomes Medically Ill

When the veteran is physically disabled or becomes ill, the Vietnam wife may find herself in the role of nurse or medical case manager, in addition to her other roles. Albert, for example, had five physicians, each for a different medical problem. He never went anywhere without a small bag full of his medications. But the list inside this bag, specifying which medications had to be taken when and under what conditions (e.g., with or without food or water), was written and continually revised by his faithful wife, Penelope.

The frustrations involved in calling five doctors every time there was a medical change or problem was too much for Albert. If he was put on hold for more than a few minutes by the doctor's office, he would either hang up or curse the receptionist. Penelope decided it was easier for her to make all the calls herself than deal with an angry husband, or an equally angry doctor's staff. Yet calling all these doctors and trying to coordinate their efforts on her husband's behalf often added several hours of work to her week.

Even more taxing for Penelope were the times when Albert needed surgery or hospitalization. Albert's PTSD symptoms always increased at these times because Albert associated hospitals with war. Hospitalization also forced Albert to confront the issue of trusting authority figures. In Vietnam, Albert had had several negative experiences with military authority figures. He had trusted them with his life, only to witness them making foolish mistakes which nearly killed him.

Now Albert was trusting his life to medical authorities. What if they made mistakes or let him down as had other authority figures in Vietnam?

To the extent that an operation or a major medical procedure replicates the Vietnam experience for the veteran, the normal stresses of intensive medical care or hospitalization are heightened. At such times, the veteran may make even more demands on his wife for loving attention and selfless care. At the same time the wife is asked to give more to her husband, she is not receiving whatever help he was giving her or the family. While she may very much want to give to the man she loves, it is unrealistic to say that there are no costs involved to her and the family when the veteran becomes ill.

The Vietnam wife may function as a physical nurse, as well as a psychological one, when her husband is ill or disabled. She may also find herself in the role of "psychological nurse" (and the term is not used in a derogatory manner) to her husband as he sees fellow veterans die premature deaths or suffer from increased PTSD symptoms or other psychological disorders due to subsequent life stresses.

Albert, for example, fought during the Tet Offensive. After many years of counseling, he achieved a workable peace with his past. In fact, he was so grateful for his newfound life that he wanted to share it with other veterans by giving them hospitality and emotional support.

His wife, Penelope, was not quite prepared for her role as hostess and informal counselor to Albert's friends. A part of her resented that she had to share her husband with other veterans. Yet she knew that her husband's mental peace depended on his reaching out to other veterans who hurt. So she voiced no objection when Albert allowed fellow veterans to stay with them if they were suicidal or having severe anniversary reactions.

Penelope not only cooked for these men, but listened to them. She also helped her husband bear his grief as he began to lose his friends to premature heart attacks and suicides, as well as mental illnesses other than PTSD.

Albert could cope with veterans with newly-realized PTSD, or those veterans who after many years of denying or discounting their war experiences finally acknowledged their pain. But when veterans who had made substantial progress in dealing with their war stress subsequently relapsed or developed new mental problems, Albert felt not only grieved but also defeated, the same emotions that shrouded his Vietnam experience.

Albert and Robert, for example, met in alcohol rehab and became good friends. They identified with each other as combat veterans and supported each other in the struggle to stay sober. After several years of sobriety, however, Robert's father was murdered by a street thug. This loss sent Robert into a drinking relapse, which resulted in his wife seeking a divorce. After his wife left, Robert sunk into a catatonic depression.

With medical help, Robert eventually emerged from his nearly vegetative state, but he was not the same Robert who had joked and gone fishing with Albert in the past. The loss of his father and wife had broken Robert's spirit. He was staying alive for the sake of his mother and his children, but he had little hope for any joy for himself. Everything he did now reflected his loss of the life spirit. His speech was slurred and he was not able to leave home for long periods of time without having panic attacks. Fishing trips with Robert ended, as did their long phone conversations in the middle of the night. Both had meant so much to Albert.

To help ease Albert's loneliness, Penelope tried to force herself to go on fishing trips with him. But her efforts proved disastrous. Penelope didn't like fishing and, as hard as she tried to hide that fact, it showed. She also felt she did not have the time to be her husband's fishing buddy, as well as his wife and medical case manager.

The next "casualty" in Albert's life was Floyd. Floyd was Albert's best buddy. Floyd and Albert had met in a PTSD inpatient unit and had stayed in close touch for many years. At one point, Floyd was facing severe financial troubles. But the economic stress did not result in increased PTSD symptoms or in depressions, disorders which Albert knew much about. Instead Floyd began showing signs of schizophrenia, an illness which was totally unfamiliar to Albert.

As Albert watched Floyd increasingly withdraw from the real world into an imaginary world of his own, Albert became horrified, and grieved. "I've lost him. I've lost him," Albert moaned inside. Albert also felt angry and sad, abandoned and helpless. Not only was he losing one of his few good friends, but he was unable to help his friend.

While Albert grieved, Penelope kept the home running and provided her husband with extra emotional support. Yet there was no one to give her additional doses of love or attention or to help her when she needed an extra hand. Once again, she was giving more emotionally than she was receiving. She felt tired and resentful, but didn't think she had the right to voice her feelings because her husband was disabled and so distraught. She feared that he might become depressed, and possibly suicidal, and did not want to burden him with her difficulties. In her view, he had enough of his own.

Penelope found solace in her music and her faith. She was encouraged to stay in touch with her own family of origin, which luckily was very supportive of her and to try to make as much time as possible for those activities which strengthened her emotionally or spiritually.

Responses to the Multiple Role Dilemma

One common response to the problem of competing demands is the attempt to be "superwoman." Because the new values for women have not eliminated the old values, but have been merely superimposed upon them, many women expect themselves to fulfill traditional roles while working outside the home to the same extent as if they did not have job responsibilities.

Another not uncommon response to the multiple-role dilemma is overeating. According to the Vet Center survey, approximately 20% of the wives seen were not just chubby or slightly overweight, but obese. Although definitions of obesity vary, in general obesity is defined as excess weight which is life-threatening. If a woman is more than 40% over her ideal weight, she is considered severely overweight or obese.

In some instances the Vietnam wife's extra pounds have already created health problems for her. But even if the woman's health is not yet impaired, psychologically the excess pounds usually decrease her self-esteem and her sense of control over her life.

For almost all the obese Vietnam wives seen so far, overeating has been a coping mechanism, not only since their marriages but since early childhood or adolescence. They turned to food for comfort or as a means of alleviating stress. Now married to Vietnam veterans who usually have not completed the healing process, they are beset not only with the stresses of the multiple-role dilemma, but also with the stresses of problem-filled marriages. They turn to food once more.

Hardworking Vietnam wives who have little time or energy for pleasurable activities and those whose sex lives may be either sporadic or unfulfilling may be easily tempted to turn to food for gratification. However, this does not mean that the veteran is responsible for his wife's difficulty with food.

Just as the alcoholic or drug-addicted veteran is responsible for what he does to his body, so is the wife responsible for what she puts in her mouth. Food is a fast fix; it is also an easy fix. Since women tend to do the shopping, cooking, and feeding of the family, food is readily available. Furthermore, unlike drugs or alcohol, food is legal, but it can serve the same purpose.

Food can sedate the emotions and anesthetize the woman to pain, anger, and hurt. Food can also be used to quell inner turmoil or as a way of dealing with—or not dealing with—relationship difficulties and external stress. The physical act of eating is not only pleasurable, but tension-reducing.

Dora, for example, is overwhelmed with demands, both inside and outside her home. Her sex life with her husband is troubled, as is her entire marriage. In the midst of feeling overwhelmed by responsibilities and wondering what the outcome of her marriage will be, she turns to food to give her a lift, to make her feel better, and to give her the energy she needs to execute her multiple roles.

But she doesn't really need the calories to complete her work. Furthermore, any good feelings she might get from the satisfaction of having eaten something delicious are temporary when her scale, her clothes, and her husband remind her that she is fat.

Yet Dora can't stop eating. For her food is a way out. Like many Vietnam wives, Dora feels that her whole life is being "gobbled up" by the needs of her PTSD-afflicted husband, her children, and her full-time job. In response, she gobbles up whatever she can find.

When she gets home from work, she simultaneously juggles making dinner, helping her son with his homework, and worrying about her husband. What psychological state will he be in when he gets home? Will he get home at all tonight? She has situations at work that she needs to figure out. She is also exhausted. But she can't just finish the dinner dishes and go to bed. She has to pay the bills her husband "forgot" about and do the laundry he promised to do.

Dora is tired of worrying about her husband, of constantly placating him, of doing his work for him, and tired of all the fighting. When her son asks her to take him to the crafts store to buy clay for a school project, she wants to scream. Instead she gulps down the leftovers from his lunch box and finishes off the ice cream. Then she has to go to the grocery store to buy more ice cream so her husband doesn't find out that she binged and yell at her again.

Under the intense pressure of so many obligations and feeling unsupported by her husband, Dora often gives up. "I might as well eat, what else is there for me?" she sometimes asks, not realizing that what she really needs is more rest, more love, and more time for herself. Like many Vietnam wives, Dora wants desperately to exert more control over her life but doesn't know how to do so. Feeling powerless, she turns to bingeing, but that only makes her feel less in control and gives her less, not more, physical and emotional energy with which to cope with her multiple roles.

Helping the Multiple-Role Woman

In group, when women discuss their multiple roles, the purpose of the group discussion is not to help the women become more efficient in doing it all. Rather, group discussion is focused on how the multiple-role woman can learn to appreciate herself more for what she does do. She is also encouraged to examine how she might structure her life so that all her various roles are expressions of her individuality rather than her conformity to some sex-role stereotype of the ideal woman. Specifically, Vietnam wives who work outside the home usually need help in:

1. Understanding that family problems are due not to personal inadequacy but to characteristics inherent in her multiple-role situation.
2. Accepting conflict as inevitable.
3. Making choices and reconsidering assumptions about the female sex role.
4. Acknowledging personal strengths and assets.
5. Acknowledging legitimate dependency needs and feelings of helplessness.
6. Learning to ask for help.
7. Learning self-nurturing.
8. Exploring alternative ways of fulfilling roles.
9. Expanding career horizons.
10. Expanding social and other personal growth horizons.

Most of the Vietnam wives I have counseled have high expectations of themselves. They want to be thorough and excellent workers, as well as loyal, sensitive, giving wives and mothers. When problems arise, the Vietnam wife tends to define the problem as her inability to manage or cope. Given a lifestyle that includes the schedules and tasks involved with work, school, child rearing, marriage, and homemaking, as well as the intense emotional needs and unpredictable behavior of a veteran who is suffering from a stress disorder, occasional interruptions in the routine and unfulfilled expectations are inevitable. The woman needs to be reminded that these occurrences are natural, not signs of her personal failure.

In fact, the woman may need to be continually reminded that conflict is inevitable and that conflict or other problems in the family are not the result of her personal inadequacies. She also usually needs help to appreciate the complexity of her lifestyle and the weight of the multiple burdens she is carrying. Part of her burden stems from the traditional assumption that it is the responsibility of the woman to take care of everyone's needs. Not only does the woman tend to believe this, but her husband, children, parents, and other relatives do also. Therefore, it is often difficult for the woman to ask her husband, her children, or other relatives for help.

At the same time, the woman may fear success in her career. Often she anticipates that her achievement will threaten her husband, who is perhaps struggling emotionally and financially, or that she will be ostracized as a "women's libber" by him, his family, or even her own friends and relatives.[10]

Summary

All working women who are also wives or mothers struggle with the burden and the conflicts inherent in having two major commitments— one to their families and another to their jobs. In our society, women of all ages, especially middle-aged women, may also find themselves caring for older relatives or for grandchildren. If so, they have even more major strains on their emotional and physical resources. In addition, women usually are also assigned the job of arranging all their roles so that they do not conflict with one another and so that they can meet the needs of the entire family.

Unfortunately, in many families when the woman assumed a working role outside the home, there were few subtractions made from her home roles. This is especially the case in Vietnam homes where the veteran holds traditional values about the woman's role and is reluctant to participate in child care and housework. Consequently, even the most hardworking and efficient Vietnam wife will inevitably have times when she is overwhelmed by the demands on her time and energy. Beneath the surface, she will also be angry and resentful of all that is expected of her in her multiple roles.

The Vietnam wife's multiple-role dilemmas are similar to those experienced by other working women. However, the Vietnam wife's burden is increased significantly by her husband's PTSD and any resulting employment or emotional dysfunctions. Often the Vietnam wife carries with her to work the mental agony of worrying about her husband's psychological condition and possible self-destructive behavior. At the same time she must be careful to be productive at work and in no way endanger her job since her income may be essential for the family's survival.

In addition, because of her husband's PTSD, she often assumes major multiple caretaking functions with respect to her vet. She may arrange his appointments and serve as a buffer between him and the world. If he is unable or unwilling to perform as a parent then she also shoulders the massive responsibilities of being both mother and father to their children. She also has the responsibility for explaining their father's actions to the children, as well as coping with the children's reactions to their father and her husband's reactions both to their children and their reactions to him.

Self-care, fun, and pleasurable activities fall by the wayside as the Vietnam wife goes endlessly from one chore to the next, from one crisis to the next. When she becomes tired and depressed, she wonders what's wrong with her. Like many multiple-role women, the Vietnam wife tends to interpret the conflicts and stresses in her life as reflecting some personal deficiency on her part. In truth, however, many of her problems are inherent to the multiple-role lifestyle, not the result of some personality problem on her part.

5

Alcohol and Drug Addiction

I feel very confused. I'm just beginning to understand PTSD and why my husband acts like he does. To see a good person run himself and me into the ground is heartbreaking.

I don't understand the drinking, how can anybody drink so much? I don't understand the lying, can't he ever tell the truth?

Even though he's the man, I'm in charge of all the money and bills. He's an alcoholic and a drug addict and he cajoles and threatens me—does anything he can to get money out of me, whether the bills are paid or not. When I won't give in, I'm accused of not caring about him. Then Vietnam is thrown in my face, as if that excuses all behavior.

Alcohol and drugs have caused him to steal my checks, forge my name, and pawn my possessions, never telling me, letting me be sued and put in financial binds. He's supposed to pick the girls up from school, but I can never count on him. Many times he's left them there because he was off on some drug deal or he passed out at a bar. Also, because of his PTSD, his mind strays a lot.

I don't know what the kids think about all this. Maybe they're too young to understand. But already they sense that I'm nervous a lot and they seem to resent my preoccupation with their father. "I wish you wouldn't be so busy worrying about Dad and spend more time with me," my youngest told me yesterday.

I've tried to talk to my husband, but have had no success.

If I try to discuss my feelings or respond with something he doesn't want to hear, then I am hit to make me shut up. I worry about my daughters— because they see and hear all this. I'm scared for myself too, afraid that he'll pull me down with him.

—Terrie

Living with PTSD while juggling multiple roles is stressful enough, but when the Vietnam wife must also contend with her husband's alcohol or drug addiction, her daily life stresses are multiplied in manifold ways. Financially, emotionally, socially, and sexually her life becomes more complex and more unrewarding. Depending on the degree of her husband's addiction, she must assume a great degree of responsibility for her family's finances and the welfare of their children. When, and if, her husband begins to use essential family funds to write false checks or to sell family belongings in order to support his addiction, the woman may have to take drastic measures in order to assure the survival of the family.

Women become enraged when they find their credit cards abused by their husbands or when they find their grandmother's T.V. set at the local pawnshop. But they become especially enraged when their husbands embarrass or neglect the children due to alcoholism or drug abuse or when they drink or engage in drug transactions in front of them. Some Vietnam wives assume the role of protecting the children from finding out about their father's addiction or otherwise protecting the veteran's image as the good father or war hero. Or, if the women are honest about the veteran's problem, they must deal with their children's denial, hostility, grief, or other reaction to this information.

If children are not carefully educated about alcoholism or drug addiction, they may be angry at their mothers for implying that their father is a "wino," "drunk," "pothead," or "junkie." The children's self-esteem will suffer as they begin to perceive their family as being "different" because of both PTSD and the addiction. If the children go into denial, they may feel the alcoholism or drug addiction is a figment of their mother's imagination or they may blame her for it. For example, the mother may explain that father is not present because he is out drinking, only to have one of her children insist that father is not drinking but working overtime. Another child might mutter angrily, "If you'd be nicer to Daddy, he'd be home now."

In situations where the Vietnam wife denigrates her husband for his addiction, the children may resent her for talking against their father. Even if they agree with her about the inappropriateness of the father's behavior, they may have mixed loyalties and not like hearing negative facts about their father. Like most children, they might prefer to idealize their father and see him as good and strong or as a war hero. In addition, they may blame their mother for not being able to stop their father's drinking.

As children become adolescents and young adults, new patterns can emerge. For example, some teenagers know more about their father's addictive habits than their mothers. This may occur because the fathers confide in their children or simply because adolescent children are home with their unemployed or semi-employed fathers while their mothers are at work.

Some teenagers have tried to protect their mothers from knowledge of the full extent of their father's addiction by lying to their mothers. Such protective lying especially occurs when fathers have become involved in extramarital sexual relationships or in criminal activities as the result of their addictive habit. In some instances children have given their earnings to their fathers to support the father's substance abuse in hope that the father will not take money from their mother or the family funds.

In some homes, one or more of the children may become substance abusers themselves. Adolescent children of addicted veterans can develop addictions themselves for any number of reasons—because of the example set by their fathers, because of the emotional and social problems they develop resulting from the stresses their families are experiencing, or because of peer and other cultural pressures which have led countless adolescents to drug or alcohol abuse (regardless of their family dynamics). Yet, even when a crack-smoking 16-year-old tells his mother, "But you don't get mad when dad does it. If it's okay for him, it's okay for me," this does not mean that the father's crack habit is the sole or major cause of the son's behavior. Although having an addicted parent provides a role model of substance abuse for children, those children may have become substance abusers even if their fathers were clean and sober and even if their fathers did not suffer from PTSD.

Trying to determine the source of her child's substance abuse habit may plague the Vietnam wife. At the same time, she may also be plagued by panic, grief, rage, and feelings of helplessness and remorse. The women I have seen are furious with their husbands for modeling addiction and also at themselves for marrying or staying with a man who abuses drugs or alcohol. Some women have stated that had they realized that their children might become addicts as the result of their marriage, they might have separated or taken other action before this deadly problem began in one of their children. On the other hand, they wonder if they had indeed separated from the veteran, if the stress of a separation or divorce might not have led the children to drugs or alcohol.

On a deeper level, these mothers have expressed anger at whatever they perceive to be the cause of their husband's addiction—the war itself, the military, the lack of societal acceptance of the veteran after the war, or specific individuals or institutions which they feel hurt their husbands or failed to provide adequate or expected help at crucial times.

On yet another level, some of these sad Vietnam wives are also angry at their teen or young adult who is abusing drugs or alcohol. Some feel as if that child abandoned and betrayed them. Instead of being a source of support and satisfaction in life, this child has now become yet another source of anxiety, fear, and emotional pain, if not also a financial liability.

If there is a serious substance abuse problem in the family, the Vietnam wife may fear that the family will dissolve emotionally or go bankrupt. The Vietnam wife may fear not only for her safety, but for the safety of all family members.

For example, when Janice first came for help, she was concerned about her husband's use of crack, but only mildly so. Basically she felt that because her vet was intelligent and kind-hearted, he would overcome his deadly habit and she would be spared any abuse. Even when told by an expert that crack addiction was a progressive illness and potentially life-threatening, Janice needed to believe that "everything would be all right."

She proudly pointed to the fact that her husband respected her wish that he not use crack at home in front of their children. Yet one night her husband came home with some of his drug friends. They were all high. Janice protested, but her husband pointed out that since he and his friends had not taken the drugs in the home, technically he had not broken the rule about not using drugs at home.

"At least he's home, where I can watch him," Janice thought and said no more.

When one of her husband's friends began to make sexual comments about Janice's teenage daughters and tried to fondle her, Janice asked her husband to have his friends leave. But because her husband was high on crack, he could not respond to his wife's plea for help.

Janice then ran for help to her 16-year-old son. But he was in his bedroom using drugs "just like dad."

At her next therapy session, Janice stated that she realized she was in a situation that demanded action. Yet she was not ready to make any major life changes. Also, she was so afraid she had become numb and therefore immobilized. Maybe if she waited, the problems would go away.

But the problems only became worse. Janice's teenage son dropped out of high school and spent his days high or drunk. There were frequent phone calls from strange women demanding money from her husband. When one of these women threatened to hurt her husband or kidnap her daughters if the money was not forthcoming, Janice took her daughters and fled to a friend's home. Although she still did not want to divorce her husband, she would no longer live with him until he gave up drugs and could provide a safe living environment.

Her husband refused drug treatment and her son refused to come live with her. Eventually her husband disappeared and her son landed in jail.

Janice was heartbroken, as both a wife and a mother. In her view, the Vietnam war had robbed her not only of her husband, but also of her son. She grieved the death of her dream of a happy, loving family life. Furthermore, at age 51, after having spent 25 years living with PTSD, she felt "too used up" and "too burnt out" to begin again with a new man.

"What did I do to deserve this?" she wondered. "Is something wrong with me that all this happened?"

There is nothing wrong with Janice or her son or husband. They were all victims of a vicious cycle of untreated PTSD, leading to drug addiction, which, when left to follow its natural progressive course, can only lead to insanity or death. At least Janice was able to save herself and her daughters. Her son can also be saved, if he receives help.

"My husband may be somewhere in the United States, or in South America, or who knows where. Or he may be dead by now, killed by drug dealers or some thugs. In the world's eyes, he's nothing but a broken-down drug addict and a crazy Vietnam veteran. To me, he's an MIA—a Vietnam vet who is Missing in Action."

Approximately half of the women who have attended the Vet Center women's group have had alcoholic or drug-addicted husbands. However, this figure of 50% cannot be considered at all representative of the Vietnam veteran population as a whole. In fact, considerable controversy exists regarding whether or not Vietnam veterans have higher rates of alcohol and drug addiction than other veterans or than their nonveteran peers. Some researchers contend that Vietnam veterans, especially combat vets or vets with PTSD, have higher rates of addiction than other groups. Other researchers, however, emphatically state that drug addiction and alcohol abuse among Vietnam veterans is part of a worldwide problem of substance abuse and that service in Vietnam has not been established as a predictor of any form of substance abuse. In addition, there are no studies of addiction among children of Vietnam veterans. In many ways, their substance abuse can be viewed as part of a nationwide problem of youth turning to alcohol and drugs.

A search of the existing studies on alcohol and drug abuse among Vietnam veterans revealed an important distinction between alcohol and drug abuse. While it was found that drugs were widely used in Vietnam, it was not found that this drug use persisted upon return to the U.S.[1] In general, research has shown that "Vietnam veterans dependent on narcotics generally had high rates of recovery soon after returning to the U.S."[2] For example, the peak use of heroin occurred in Vietnam in the early 1970s when a high-quality, relatively inexpensive form of heroin became readily available. During these years, there was also an international epidemic of heroin use and great concern that the Vietnam veterans would bring their heroin and other form of drug abuse back home with them.[3]

This fear, however, did not materialize. One researcher found that less than 10% of Vietnam veterans who used narcotics in Vietnam were using narcotics one year after discharge.[4] Some studies have found that the rate of recovery from drug abuse among Vietnam veterans is substantially higher than the rate of recovery among other addicted groups.[5]

Much of the confusion in these and other studies of drug abuse among Vietnam veterans stems from the fact that some studies are based on Vietnam era vets—all vets who served during the years of the war whether or not they actually served in Vietnam—whereas others are based only on veterans who served in Vietnam itself. Also, definitions of drug abuse vary from one study to the next.

This confusion spills over into the research on alcoholism among Vietnam veterans, with researchers varying not only in their definition of Vietnam veteran but in their definition of alcohol addiction or alcohol problems and in the types of statistical methods used. Not everybody who drinks is, or becomes, an alcoholic. Similarly, not everybody who uses drugs is, or becomes, physically addicted to them. Yet such distinctions are not made in some studies or are made differently from one study to the next.

Some researchers insist that there are no significant differences in alcohol abuse between Vietnam veterans and other groups. More frequently, however, researchers have found that war veterans, especially those who saw heavy combat, have a higher level of alcohol consumption, binge drinking, and alcohol-related problems than comparable groups of other veterans and nonveterans.[6]

Regardless of what research studies show about the rate of alcohol and drug addiction among Vietnam veterans, it is the experience of many therapists who work with Vietnam veterans that PTSD and alcohol or drug addiction frequently go hand in hand. Some vets turn to alcohol or drugs in order to numb their emotions.[7] "He can't sleep, so he drinks or smokes a joint," more than one wife has stated. In a few isolated instances, husbands were not addicted prior to Vietnam nor during their Vietnam tour of duty. Upon return to the U.S., however, they turned to alcohol or drugs as an attempt to medicate themselves and suppress the symptoms of PTSD. More often, however, the use of drugs and alcohol was either learned, or reinforced, in Vietnam where both alcohol and drugs were readily available.[8]

By now, it is well known that alcohol, marijuana, opiates, and other drugs were widely used in Vietnam for entertainment, anxiety relief, or as a means of coping with the boredom, or the terror.[9] What is less known, however, is that Vietnam is the first war in which tranquilizing drugs and the phenothiazines were dispensed on the combat front.[10] One vet claims that it was his commanding officer who introduced him to, and forced him to take, certain drugs. "The sarge pulled me in his office my first week there and said that if I didn't take these drugs, he'd blow my brains out. I had never taken any drugs and didn't plan to—ever—even though almost everyone around me seemed high. 'Look,' the sarge said, 'Do as I say.'

"He waited there until I had swallowed the pills. At first I thought he was picking on me because I was a country boy from Boise, Idaho, but now I see that he was trying to save my life. If the others had found out I wasn't on drugs, they might have thought I was a spy. I might have gotten fragged or something.

"Turns out, I needed those little pills to do what I had to do and stay sane. After a while, those little pills made even the blood seem pretty."

Perhaps this was an isolated instance. Perhaps not. Such instances are not frequently reported in the available literature. In most cases American servicemen obtained drugs from the Vietnamese, not their commanding officers.[11] The military did, however, dispense certain mood and consciousness altering drugs to help control some of the medical symptoms which interfered with combat performance. For example, "antinauseants and potent antipsychotic agents like procholoperazine (Compazine R) and chlorpromazine (Thorazine R)" were "commonly used for symptom control in combat troops with diarrhea and nausea."[12] These drugs did have a psychological effect—mainly that of impairing the veteran's "capacity to integrate emotional experiences" regarding the war.[13]

Another factor contributing to the use of drugs or alcohol during the war was that the option of obtaining a psychiatric discharge was not as available to soldiers in Vietnam as to those in previous wars. The thrust of military psychiatry and psychology during the Vietnam war was to encourage soldiers to "hang on" until their one year DEROS.[14] Hence, for the soldier experiencing psychological difficulties during the war, yet obstructed from obtaining a psychiatric discharge, drugs and alcohol might have been a means of escape or coping.

Servicemen on drugs or alcohol who were disruptive were often given administrative discharges with the diagnosis of "character disordered personality," rather than PTSD.[15] The authorities often failed to distinguish true character disordered individuals from those who were using drugs and alcohol as a means of coping with acute combat reaction. Hence many men were not only not treated for their PTSD, but were also saddled with a diagnosis of character disordered personality, a diagnosis with an extremely negative connotation. It is the view of many clinicians (myself included) that combat is not a prerequisite for PTSD. For example, American civilians who worked in Vietnam developed PTSD. Furthermore, while substance abuse may have many origins in a particular individual, one of the functions of substance abuse for some vets is self-medication for the symptoms of PTSD.[16] Some of my patients used alcohol and drugs prior to Vietnam, but increased their usage overseas. Upon return to the United States, their alcohol or drug usage diminished but remained at a somewhat higher level than prior to the war. While alcohol or drugs were a part of their lifestyle prior to the war for various reasons, now another reason was added to the list—suppression of wartime memories and some of the symptoms of PTSD.

Alcohol helps the veteran to sleep, reduces his anxiety levels, and helps "ease muscle tensions and sometimes depression, irritability, and agitation." If the vet or his wife feel that using drugs or alcohol is "legitimate" because these substances help lessen the nightmares, the insomnia, or other symptoms of PTSD, then their denial of the dangerous effects of the veteran's addiction, on everybody, may be reinforced. The vet will have yet another justification for abusing himself and his wife; yet another excuse for accepting unacceptable behavior.

"I never know what I'm dealing with," states Rhoda, wife of an alcoholic veteran, "Don, his PTSD, or his booze." Rhoda has educated herself about alcoholism, knows that it is a disease and that she is supposed to distinguish the disease from the person. "But when Don is drinking, he becomes the disease and it's very hard to deal with."

As the wife of an alcoholic Vietnam veteran, Rhoda must contend not only with her husband's flashbacks, extreme irritability, and hatred of rice and anything Asian, but with his weekend drinking binges and his unavailability as a companion and lover to her and as a father to their children. "Don loves his kids," Rhoda is always quick to say. "But he has no idea what they're thinking about, or what they're doing in school. He's never abused any of us, ever, but he's usually off to himself or out drinking."

Rhoda is lucky. Her husband is only in the early stages of the disease of alcoholism. He is still able to function on the job and does not suffer from memory lapses or blackouts or any of the diseases which attend the later stages of alcoholism.

Although Don and Rhoda's sexual relationship is sporadic and their emotional communication is limited, Rhoda can still count on Don to go to work and not drink in front of the children. But that's all.

She pays all the bills, assumes almost total responsibility for the children, and never knows when, and if, her husband will be joining her for dinner, for the children's school play, or for their anniversary. So far, she hasn't found any bottles hidden throughout the house. "But it's coming," she predicts.

She knows the disease of alcoholism well. Her father was an alcoholic, as was her grandfather, and she saw them both progress through the various stages of alcoholism to early deaths. Rhoda is well aware of the latest view that alcoholism is primarily a physical disease, rather than a psychological one, but this understanding does not ease her loneliness or her fears about the future.

Rhoda first began to suspect that Don was an alcoholic when he would go shopping and forget to buy the food, but always bring home the liquor. Furthermore, when he would come home from work, he would head straight for the liquor cabinet. He didn't always take a drink at that time, but he needed to be sure that the liquor cabinet was full. Whenever it wasn't, he would become extremely anxious and even get up in the middle of the night to go search for an all-night liquor store. "He wouldn't always drink what he would buy," explains Rhoda, "But if the liquor wasn't there, he'd be a nervous wreck."

Rhoda also observed that liquor was always first on his shopping list and that he spent a lot of time in liquor stores just cruising down the aisles examining the various bottles. At this point Rhoda's husband was still in the first stages of alcoholism. If she had not had such a discerning eye, his drinking patterns may not have appeared different from the drinking patterns of others. During this first stage, the alcoholic is able to consume increasing amounts of alcohol without any significant impairment to his abilities. In fact, during the first stage, his functioning may even be improved by drinking.

During the middle stage, the alcoholic begins to experience some of the effects of the physical damage caused to his body by his drinking. He also begins to experience a loss of control over his drinking, an intense craving for alcohol, as well as important personality and emotional changes—nightmares, depression, insomnia, sweating, memory impairment, and tension. When Rhoda's husband reached this stage, she observed major mood swings in her husband and found that his sexual performance suffered, or became dependent on having consumed a certain amount of alcohol. During this second stage of alcoholism, alcohol, the poison, now becomes the medicine as the alcoholic comes to need more and more alcohol to counteract symptoms of withdrawal.

The third stage of alcoholism is characterized by extreme physical and mental deterioration and the need to drink almost constantly to combat withdrawal symptoms, which by now have progressed to include paranoia, convulsions, hallucinations, shaking, delirium, mental confusion, an inability to walk, and poor motor coordination.[17]

Like alcoholism, drug addiction is also progressive. Although the particular symptoms and stages of drug addiction are specific to each drug, as with alcoholism, drug addiction often involves physical problems. In addition, there are numerous interpersonal problems caused by excess moodiness, jealousy, irritability, suspiciousness and fearfulness which sometimes borders on paranoia, and in some cases, violence.

The symptoms of drug abuse and drug withdrawal are many and vary from one drug to the next. Some of the common withdrawal symptoms include panic, confusion, irritability and restlessness, dilated pupils, nausea and vomiting, abdominal cramps and diarrhea.[18]

The symptoms of drug abuse and withdrawal depend not only on the drug used, but on the amount and quality of the drug and its reaction with the individual's unique body chemistry, his environment, and any other drugs or alcohol he has taken. Often a wife can detect that her husband is on drugs if he becomes unable to keep appointments or other commitments or if he leaves his job for unexplained absences (especially on Mondays, Fridays, or the day after payday) or short bursts of energy followed by extremely low periods of productivity.

A wife can also suspect drug addiction if her husband spends an unusual amount of time in the bathroom or in other locked rooms, gives up old friends to take up with other drug-addicted persons, or becomes unable to keep a job or stay in school. Furthermore, she should not be surprised if her personal belongings are taken from her and sold or if her accounts and other assets are depleted by her husband's increasing need to support his addiction.[19]

Betty's husband used to squander her salary on drugs until she deposited her check in an account with just her name on it. Even then, he would present himself at the bank as Betty's husband and try to make withdrawals. Unsuspecting tellers complied with his wishes until Betty strictly instructed them not to allow him to make any withdrawals or to cash any of her checks, since at times he would forge her name on them. Afterward, her husband started taking her credit cards, charging items, then returning them to pay for drugs. Eventually Betty had to cancel her credit cards. Other wives have had to keep their credit cards, their bank books, and other financial papers and assets under lock and key for protection against desperate husbands.

It is not unusual for a woman, even for a woman who is relatively well informed about alcohol or drug addiction, to initially be in a state of denial about her husband's illness. It is only human to want to avoid painful realities and observing a loved one suffer from a life-threatening, financially and emotionally disruptive problem hurts. True, the woman may be angry at her husband for being an alcoholic or a drug addict, but beyond her anger is her pain.

Even if she does not assume a shred of responsibility for her husband's alcohol or drug addiction, if she loves or cares for him, just seeing him suffer causes her to suffer also. Even if she no longer loves him, but instead feels a loyalty to him as the father of her children or as the man to whom she has given many years of her life, she will also feel pain at observing him progressively deteriorate. Later on, her pain may well be mixed with anger, disgust, or even hatred toward her husband for the ways in which his illness has destroyed part of her life and the negative impact of his illness on the mental, and sometimes physical, health of her children. The older the Vietnam wife is, the more years she has invested in the veteran and the harder it may be for her to face such painful truths.

While a part of the woman's initial denial may stem from her reluctance to feel pain, part of her denial may also be rooted in shame and guilt at being married to an alcoholic or a drug addict. She may not want to acknowledge her fears about the possible disastrous consequences of her husband's addiction, not only to him, but to herself and their children as well. Rather than face reality, she pretends she didn't find the needles in the bathroom or the half empty liquor bottles in the hall closet. She may pretend to her husband that she doesn't know. More importantly, however, she pretends to herself, to spare herself the anguish of having to face the responsibility and difficulty of making certain changes in her life or decisions about the family's future due to her husband's illness.

If she is the adult child of an alcoholic, she may be reluctant to face the nightmare once more. Wilma, for example, hoped that if she pretended her husband didn't have a drinking problem, it would just go away. Similarly, as a child she wished that her father were not a "drunk" and believed that if only she wished hard enough her father would be "normal" like the fathers of her friends.

Wilma had spent much of her childhood and adolescence crushed between two warring parents, an angry, discontented alcoholic father and an equally angry, discontented mother. When her father would come home drunk at 3 a.m., demanding a meal he would never eat, Wilma's mother at first would comply. But eventually she would tell her husband to cook his own damn dinner and berate him for ruining the family with his drunkenness. At this point, Wilma would be awakened by the shouting matches, then asked to cook for her father, or to sweep up the broken glass from the liquor bottles which her mother had furiously smashed in protest to the father's drinking.

Even though Wilma sympathized with her mother's plight, Wilma also loved her father and resented her mother for nagging him and not supporting him. To Wilma, her father was her hero, in spite of his disease. When her father, a prominent physician, abandoned the family when Wilma was 13, Wilma blamed her mother, but she also blamed herself. If only she were a better or more lovable daughter, her father would have never left home.

After Wilma's father left, her mother went to work full time during the day and collapsed into depression during the evenings, leaving Wilma to mother the two younger children. But Wilma had always mothered her sisters, for as her father's alcoholism had progressed, her mother had become increasing preoccupied with him and his drinking (as well as her own distress) and left much of the housework and child care up to Wilma.

Now Wilma was finding herself mothering her husband. Women who are adult children of alcoholics or who are married to physically handicapped veterans or to veterans with severe bodily injuries are especially prone to assume a maternal or caretaker role toward their husbands, especially if the vet feels he has not been adequately compensated by the government. Wilma met Todd when he first returned from Vietnam. Laden with medals, handsome and smart, Todd seemed like a hero to her. Her teenage years had been so unhappy and lonely that when Todd proposed to her, she said "yes" almost without thinking. By marrying Todd she hoped to get away from her depressed mother and end her unconscious search for her missing father. Like many returning vets, Todd initially idealized his wife and for a brief while, Wilma and Todd had an idyllic relationship.

When Wilma married Todd, he was only in the first stages of alcoholism and his illness was not apparent. She first began to suspect that Todd was alcoholic when he would come home late because he had stopped off at a local bar or when he seemed to prefer to go drinking with his war buddies rather than stay home with her. But she so desperately wanted her present life to be better than her past life that she could not believe her new hero was an alcoholic, too. When her husband reached the middle stage of alcoholism and the signs of his illness became unmistakable, Wilma could no longer deny reality. Todd was drinking at five in the morning and there were cash register receipts for large amounts of liquor in the trash, as well as evidence of affairs with other women.

Wilma began to make excuses for Todd: he drank because his compensation check was late, because a war buddy had threatened suicide, or because someone had taken him to see a movie like *The Deer Hunter*, *Platoon*, or *The Hanoi Hilton*. Furthermore, Wilma began to berate herself. She felt Todd's drinking was her fault, just as a child she had felt responsible for her father's drinking. Although the women in the Vet Center group challenged her on this, Wilma's sense of inferiority and responsibility persisted.

After Wilma shed her denial, her next posture toward her husband was that of "enabler." Not realizing that her husband had a problem which she could not "fix," she attempted to try to "help" him by hiding liquor, by being as pleasant and loving as possible, and by protecting him from all reminders of his war experiences and the consequences of his drinking. For example, she made excuses for him to his relatives, his employer, and even to their own children. When he would become intoxicated and unable to drive, she would pick him up from any place in the city, any time of the day or night. When he blamed her for his drinking, she didn't talk back. Instead she hid anger and hurt and became more determined to "help" him.

Wilma did not want to be a "nag" like her mother and lose her husband the way she lost her father. As the adult child of an alcoholic, Wilma had a well-developed tolerance for alcoholic behavior and family chaos. But when her husband impulsively gave away a huge sum of money to some less fortunate Vietnam veterans at a drinking party, leaving no money for the family's bills, Wilma felt she had to confront her husband about his alcoholism, and she did so, many times. But she would quickly back off when he'd flare up at her. Even though he had never physically hurt her, she knew he had smuggled an M-16 home with him from Vietnam. While she feared the weapon, what she feared most was being abandoned. As an adult child of an alcoholic, her abandonment fear was profound.

Like many of the wives of alcoholic or drug addicted veterans, who do not value their own happiness, fulfillment, and peace of mind as much as they do that of their husbands and children, Wilma was shaken out of the stages of denial and enabling into the stage of active coping not so much by her own suffering, but by that of her husband and children. When her husband, under the influence, fell down some steps and nearly cracked his skull and when, on several occasions, he failed to feed the baby her dinner or strap her seat belt in the car properly, Wilma knew she could no longer be passive or limit her action to words.

In other cases, women have been forced to confront their husband's alcoholism (and their own enabling) due to his car accidents, job losses, or his arrest on drug charges. Or their children began to evidence unmistakable signs of low self-esteem and self-blame or to be ashamed to bring friends home for fear Daddy will be drinking, drunk, or high.

Unpaid bills, emptied wallets, and missing nest eggs also jar the woman out of her wishful thinking that the problem will magically disappear. More than one woman has walked into the Vet Center group shocked at the latest debt her husband's addiction has incurred for her, debts ranging up to $96,000. While financial hardships tend to be greater for the wives of drug addicted veterans than for the wives of alcoholic veterans, both groups of women suffer not only from the high costs of liquor and especially drugs, but from the spending sprees and poor financial judgment and planning that often characterize the addictive personality. In some cases, women have had to shoulder the expenses of their husband's gifts to mistresses.

Such circumstances have forced women with little previous experience or training in financial matters to become virtual financial experts and to take complete control of the family's assets. The veteran, however, often will protest this affront to his masculinity. But faced with her children's deprivation, the wife has often had no choice but to "be hard." She puts her husband on a strict budget, puts as many of the family's assets as possible in her name only, and makes almost all major financial decisions on her own. When she is impeded in taking financial control of the household by her husband's threats of violence, she may have to resort to stealing from her husband in order to meet household bills and pay for food.

Cleo, a Vietnam wife jailed for theft, tells how her circumstances led her from an unhappy home to an unhappy marriage and ultimately to prison.

My father abandoned our family when I was five years old. My mom had to work two jobs to keep bread on the table. She was grouchy and angry when she came home from work and didn't have much time for any of us. I can understand now why she was so irritable, but I didn't understand it then.

I had a lot of anger in me, but I was never an aggressive kid in school. In fact, I did pretty well considering that my older sister usually forgot to fix me breakfast. I was shy and never part of the gang. My shrink says that by the time I was in the fifth grade, I had an inferiority complex and that's why, in my teen years, I was easy prey to manipulative men.

Most of my boyfriends and my first husband used me. I think Johnny was the first man who really loved me. He bought me gifts and understood what I had gone through in life because he had been through a lot in 'Nam too. The only problem was that Johnny had gotten hooked on drugs over there. But at least he wasn't violent, like the other drug addicts I knew. Also, he had a good job, even though he was getting high a lot.

When I met Johnny, I had two children by my former husband. He had deserted me just like my father had left my mother. I found myself in my mother's position, working all the time and hating it. At times I would get so tired of carting the kids from one babysitter's to the next that I could scream. I was also tired of the loneliness and the constant worry about trying to pay my bills.

So when Johnny proposed, promising that he would help support me and the kids so I would only have to work a part-time job, I said "Yes" immediately. At last I would have some time to be home with my children, like a "regular" mommy.

The first few months everything was fine, except that Johnny kept quitting one job after another. He always found a new one, but he would never stay long enough to establish health benefits. Because I had quit my full-time job, we didn't have my health insurance either, which meant we had to pay our doctor bills out of our pockets.

Our finances were manageable, even with Johnny's drug bills, until my son developed a serious medical problem that ate up most of our savings. At the same time, Johnny seemed to be spending more and more time and money on drugs. I resented it, but whenever I'd mention the cost of his drug habit, he'd remind me about my son's doctor bills. He also threatened to leave me if I couldn't accept him the way he was. After all, he had accepted me the way I was, with all my hang-ups and problems.

Johnny was the only person I had in the world. Also, I couldn't afford to leave him. My children and I needed his income, even if he did squander too much on drugs. As he needed more and more drugs, our money got lower and lower and he started stealing. Then he asked me to steal too.

I had a government job then. The first time Johnny mentioned that I should help myself to the money lying around the office, I was shocked. But he assured me that the government had plenty of money and that as a lower-income private citizen, the government was always ripping me off anyway. Furthermore, the government had certainly cheated him, as a Vietnam veteran, out of his well-deserved benefits. Stealing from the government, he argued, was an act of justice.

I knew these were rationalizations, but I went along anyway. I was afraid of losing Johnny if I didn't help him get his fix. The first time I stole, I burned with shame. But afterward, it became easier and easier, almost a game, until the day I got caught and landed in jail. The worst part is that now my kids have a convict for a mother.

Like Cleo, some of the incarcerated wives and girlfriends of Vietnam veterans (seen at a local correctional facility, not at the Vet Center) were imprisoned for shoplifting or other forms of stealing in order to support not their drug habit, but their husband's. They often came from economically and emotionally deprived backgrounds. At least one-fourth of these women had been physically or sexually abused as children. They often stated that they "stole for love." Usually their husbands were drug addicted prior to Vietnam, but increased their drug usage during and after the war. While the imprisoned women often stated that they stole in order to keep their men "happy" and attached to them, some stole to protect themselves from physical assault. Drugs, they claimed, helped sedate their husbands' tempers and reduced the number of nightmares and flashbacks, resulting in fewer instances of wife beating.

Cleo's husband was not violent, but Viola's husband was. He terrorized both her and the neighborhood. She was glad to steal to buy drugs that would cool his heat and purchase her safety. While Viola was serving time for shoplifting, her husband was shot to death by another drug addict.

The Vietnam wife with an alcoholic or drug addicted husband needs first to educate herself about alcoholism or drug addiction. Suggested books are included in the Reading List. In addition, attendance at Al-Anon (for wives of alcoholics), at ACOA (Adult Children of Alcoholics) or at Nar Anon (for family members of drug addicts) could also help.

Secondly, she needs to emotionally detach from her husband's addiction as much as possible. Whether it takes one Al-Anon or Nar Anon meeting or a hundred, the woman needs to realize that she is powerless over her husband's illness. Confronting him, placating him, covering up for him, verbally attacking, or otherwise punishing him will not work. Just as she needs to let go of a sense of responsibility for her husband's addiction, she also needs to stop trying to "fix" her husband. The only way she can truly help him is to encourage him to seek treatment.

If he will not listen to her, she may consider approaching him through a planned intervention with others. The Johnson Institute in Minneapolis has trained counselors to assist family members and friends in approaching an addict in a united, firm, but caring manner.[20] The general plan is for family members, friends, and others to approach the addict and confront him or her in a non-blaming manner with their observations of his or her behavior and offer guidance and support in obtaining treatment.

Sortie, a counselor at this Institute, explains that intervention usually consists of three phases. "In the first, participants speak from the heart, saying, in effect, 'I care about you and I'm not going to lose you.' . . . [In] the second phase, if the patient is just not getting it and is minimizing the problem, participants offer specific instances during which the addict's behavior was out of control . . . In the final phase, participants present consequences if the addict does not enter treatment."[21]

Usually the third stage is never reached, because most addicts agree to seek help. A Vietnam wife can consider using this sort of intervention to help persuade her husband to seek rehabilitation for his drug or alcohol habit. However, it is suggested that her efforts be made with the assistance of a trained mental health professional.

In addition to the above two measures, the third step a Vietnam wife needs to take is to examine her role as an enabler of her husband's addiction. Without blaming herself for her husband's habit, or even for inadvertently supporting it by trying to be a "good wife" or family peacemaker, she needs to become aware of all the specific ways, both large and small, in which she protects her husband from the consequences of his behavior.

Next, she needs to assure her physical safety and that of her children, as well as the financial survival of the family. While she cannot control her husband's spending or other alcoholic or drug-influenced behavior, she can take charge of as many assets as possible, realistically assess her financial situation, and make a budget.

Some women hesitate to take such actions because they were raised to believe that finances are the man's responsibility and that they are not competent at making financial decisions. Even if a woman is unfamiliar with money matters, however, she can seek information and advice. Furthermore, if she is not a substance abuser and she has her family's best interest in mind, she is more likely to make sound economic choices than her husband who has not only PTSD, but an addictive illness as well. While the wife may fear taking the risks inherent in making financial decisions for the family, she needs to consider the fact that if she abdicates control of the family's finances to a man whose thinking abilities are impaired and whose objective judgment is clouded by substance abuse, she is allowing her entire family to sink into a form of economic suicide. Some women do not feel it is feminine to take economic control over the family. But poverty and economic hardship are not feminine either.

Finally, the woman needs to examine her personal life and decide what behavior she will accept from her husband and what behavior she will not. She can make such decisions without necessarily divorcing or formally separating from her husband. One wife had put off going to college until her husband recovered from a leg injury received during the war. Although he was left crippled, he was able to continue to drive his cab. She had thought his drinking would stop once his leg operations were completed, but she was mistaken. While she did not like his drinking, she decided to remain married to him. However, she would not remain in the house with him when he was intoxicated and potentially violent. Without criticizing him for drinking, she would simply go stay with friends. She always had a suitcase packed and extra money saved for gas or for a hotel should friends not be available.

At one point, however, her husband invited two of his homeless war buddies to come stay with them. One alcoholic was bad enough, but three, she just couldn't handle. They expected her to cook and clean for them and verbally abused and roughhoused her when she refused to do so. After five years in Al-Anon, she understood that their rude, aggressive behavior was a function of their alcoholism, but she also understood that she could not change them.

In group, she overcame her feelings of selfishness and guilt and decided that in order to assure her safety and to give herself the peace of mind and quiet necessary to finish her college degree, she would not leave her husband permanently. However, until such time as the war buddies moved out or became sober and her husband sought help, she would live with a friend. After two years, her husband tired of his war buddies and joined A.A. The couple is now reunited, but the veteran understands that the minute he resumes drinking his wife will move out. Furthermore, while she is willing to compromise and negotiate with him, she will no longer let his illness arrest her own emotional and professional development.

Not only does the Vietnam wife need to examine her own personal life carefully to see how her husband's drinking has affected her life goals, she also needs to take a close look at how her husband's alcoholism may be affecting her children. In most cases she will need to confront the painful reality that her husband's alcoholism has affected or will affect her children. Even children as young as one or two have been found to respond negatively to an alcoholic father. If the vet has forgotten to feed the child or otherwise mishandled it due to his drinking, the child may cry upon seeing its father.

Alcoholism is aptly called a family disease because the drinking affects everyone, not just the problem drinker. Over time, the whole family becomes isolated, not only from the community at large, but also from relatives, neighbors, and friends who must not know about the father's drinking or his PTSD. Children may even be asked not to invite friends home. Or, when a child becomes older, he or she may hesitate to have friends over lest the father be drinking. If the father also suffers from a severe and untreated case of PTSD, the child may also fear finding his or her father in the midst of a flashback or in some manner acting as if he were in Vietnam. Since both alcohol and PTSD can cause emotional regressions and flashbacks, when the two are combined, some vets exhibit very unusual behavior. A child may fear finding his or her father both drinking and crawling around the house as if he were in the jungle.

The children may feel responsible for their father's drinking. Young children may feel the father is drinking because they made too much noise or misbehaved. Older children blame their marks in school or their undone chores. As the Vet Center and other studies have shown, some PTSD-afflicted veterans are intolerant of children's noises and games and tend to be critical of their children when the children do not obey the rules of the house.[22] In some cases, the vet has imposed a military-like regime upon the household and severely scolds the children when they fail to "measure up" or "obey orders." If the father is drinking at the time of the scolding, or afterward, the children can easily conclude that his drinking is the result of their failure to obey his instructions.

While children from PTSD-afflicted alcoholic homes tend to blame themselves for their father's drinking and other signs of distress, they may also learn to hide their feelings and their needs. Because their father is so preoccupied with his drinking and his PTSD, and because their mother is so preoccupied with their father, the children are often left to take care of themselves.

Not only is mother often too busy, but often she is angry, crying, anxious, or withdrawn as well. Children can be as concerned, and as angry, at their nonalcoholic mother as at their alcoholic father. In light of her emotional expressiveness and fatigue, they may become frightened and insecure. If mother "falls apart" like father, who will take care of them?

Children of alcoholics are often characterized as having a profound fear of abandonment. They are afraid that if they do not help mother, or father, there will be no one left to provide for them. As a result, even at a young age, many of these children learn to hide their needs and to help take care of one or both of their parents instead.

All children do not react in the same way. However, almost all children in alcohol and PTSD-afflicted homes are exposed to inconsistencies and many family crises as well as to a considerable amount of anger and bitterness on the part of both parents. Not uncommonly, one or more of the children may adopt almost a parental role and try to help either the father or the mother. Since the mother is often trying to be nurse, doctor, and counselor to her husband as well as mother, homemaker, and wage earner, there are many times she simply cannot meet all the responsibilities thrust upon her. In such cases, it is not unusual for a child even as young as eight or nine to assume major household responsibilities—cooking, cleaning, babysitting, or even balancing the checkbook.

For example, Judy, who is a senior in high school, is the eldest of three children. She doesn't play sports after school. She doesn't hang out with her girlfriends. She doesn't participate in any extracurricular activities. She comes straight home to help her mother. She looks for her father's hidden bottles, helps prepare dinner, keeps track of the household expenses, does the cleaning, and spends the weekends taking care of her younger brother and sister. When asked to go to slumber parties or other social events, she usually refuses so that she can stay home with her mother. What if her father stays out all night and leaves her mother alone? Acutely aware of her mother's loneliness, Judy tries to be her mother's friend as well as her helper.

Judy also declines invitations because she feels she cannot count on her parents to drive her. There is only one car and if her father is drunk and needs to be picked up, her mother may not be available for transportation. Once Judy was left stranded at a party because her father was in a car accident. Another time, Judy's father just forgot. Yet another time, it was Judy's mother who, in her role overload, forgot.

Judy has suppressed her anger and is a "model child." Her brother, on the other hand, displays some of his aggressive feelings. When playing with other children, he needs to be right and to win or else he stomps off making threats. Since he idealizes his father, whenever he hears his mother talking about his father's PTSD or alcoholism, he overturns trash cans or tears up some of his sister's papers. He also suffers from insomnia and will watch hour after hour of war videos in order to get to sleep. His favorite videos are those with ample amounts of blood and slaughter.

This child's preoccupation with power and violence is, in part, natural for his age and for our culture. However his interest in death and killing also stems from knowledge of his father's war experiences. In this, he is like a minority of children of Vietnam veterans found in the Vet Center study who display an inordinate interest in power and death. In addition, his persistent need to watch such videos serves a psychological need related to his living in an alcoholic and PTSD-afflicted home. Specifically, the aggression and violence acted out in these videos can be seen as giving vicarious expression to the hostility and confusion which the child harbors within.

Summary

Alcohol and drugs became a way of life in Vietnam, as many servicemen used these substances in order to cope with the horrors and absurdities of war. After returning to the United States, some servicemen quit their alcohol/drug use but others had become physically addicted and continued to abuse these substances. Still others continued to, or began to, use alcohol/drugs in order to suppress their emerging symptoms of PTSD.

When the Vietnam wife confronts her husband's alcohol or drug habit, she often does not know if she is dealing with a true alcoholic or drug addict or with an individual who is self-medicating for his PTSD. In some cases, this self-medication evolves into an addiction, or at least into a life fraught with emotional and financial insecurity.

When there is heavy drug/alcohol usage in the home, the Vietnam wife can expect even less emotional and financial support from her husband than if he suffered only from PTSD. Furthermore, her husband's addiction, in combination with his PTSD, will detract from his ability to parent his children and can create an even wider range of emotional problems for the children with which she will have to cope, if not now, in the future.

While not all children react in the same way, feelings of shame, guilt, and low self-esteem are prevalent in the homes blighted by addiction and PTSD. In addition, the children sometimes have ambivalent feelings toward both parents. The Vietnam wife may find her children blaming her not only for the father's war-related problems, but for his alcohol or drug problems as well. Or she may find herself trying desperately to create some semblance of a normal home life.

Furthermore, as her husband's drinking/drug addiction progresses, she may find herself and her children increasingly alienated from family members and friends, from the community, and even from their own emotions. One or more of her children may become addicted, run away from home or marry early as a means of escape. Her children may blame her for staying with the veteran and subjecting herself and them to financial and emotional insecurity, if not emotional and perhaps physical abuse. On the other hand, if she leaves the veteran, the children may blame her for abandoning their father when he needed her the most.

6

Anger

In the early days, before Joel started PTSD therapy, there was a lot of verbal abuse. But by and large, Joel's anger at the time was not really focused on me. Although rationally I recognized that he was a loose cannonball ready to be fired, emotionally I pretty much blocked out the reality of his anger. That's not a healthy way to deal with things, but most likely he and I would not be together if I hadn't.

Nowadays, it's the eggshells under the feet, constant tension, a constant testing of the atmosphere to decipher Joel's mood, whether it be angry or depressed, that keeps the whole family wound up most of the time. Also, Joel is starting to blame me for more and more of his dissatisfactions. If a line is too long or one of the kids cries too loud, that's my fault. If his mother forgets to call or calls too much, that's my fault too.

Now that Joel is aware of his PTSD, he wants to run away even more. But he has no place to go, and that's my fault, too.

At my very first counseling session, the therapist suggested that I was a very angry woman. The idea was totally unacceptable to me. To me, anger was ugly and to be an angry woman, well, that was almost the same as be-

*ing a "bad" one. "Good" women, I had been taught, forgave quickly and did
not harbor resentments. They were also experts at turning lemons into lemon-
ade and at keeping their mouths shut when their husbands were upset.*

*Because my husband had seen so much death in Vietnam and was still
pulling shrapnel out of his skin, I didn't feel entitled to be angry. My problems
seemed petty compared to his. I was also afraid that if I aired my grievances with
him, his entire storehouse of anger from Vietnam would land on me or the children. Many times it has been in my best interest and in the best interests of my
children to follow my grandmother's advice and keep my mouth shut.*

—Andrea

Many of the women in group readily cry and easily admit to feeling
helpless and depressed, but rarely express any anger. Anger is a major
problem for them, as it is for their partners. Despite popular psychology
books which often suggest "let your anger out," old religious and societal sanctions against expressing anger still exist, especially for women.

Perhaps today's young women are being taught differently, but
most of the women who have attended group were raised to believe that
anger is not feminine. Rebecca, for example, was taught that anger was
a sin and that God would strike her dead if she ever sassed her parents
or expressed anger toward them or any other authority figure.

While Rebecca now laughs at this old-fashioned thinking, emotionally she is still bound by it. So are many of the other women. They
fear that if they express their anger, especially toward their partners,
they will be struck dead by a thunderbolt. In most cases, the thunderbolt the women fear the most is not a physical attack, but an emotional
one. As with many women of their generation, their self-esteem is
closely intertwined with their partner's view of them. Even women in
their 40s, 50s, and 60s, who have outgrown much of their dependency
on the opinions of others, may still be affected by their husbands' eval-
uations of them.

In addition, many of the women were raised to assume the traditionally female role of family peacemaker. They fear that expressing
anger will cost them what they have been taught to value most: family
peace and harmony. Some Vietnam wives also teach their children,
"Don't get angry in front of Daddy and upset him." Such a message either perpetuates the denial of the powerful emotion of anger from one
generation to the next or else forces the child or adolescent to find another outlet for his or her anger.

Under ideal circumstances children are taught by parents or caretakers to express their feelings in words and encouraged to speak those
feelings, even the angry ones. However, in the Vietnam veteran family,

if either the mother or the father knows only how to stifle anger or let it explode indiscriminately, the child or adolescent has no role model in the home for other ways of expressing anger. He or she will not know how to express anger in an open, direct manner or identify the frustrated need or disappointment which gave rise to the anger. Even if someone in the family has the ability to help a child express emotions, the families may be under so much economic or psychological stress that neither parent may have the time or energy to help a child learn how to identify emotions, how to express them accurately, or how to find constructive ways of coping with them.

When anger cannot be freely or safely expressed at home, some children act out their frustrations in school. Counselors who have worked with children of Vietnam veterans with PTSD report that school is the arena where children are most likely to vent the anger they cannot reveal at home. When children are young, their anger is usually expressed in terms of minor acts of disobedience toward the teachers or minor infractions of school rules.

As children grow older their behavior becomes more rebellious and, in some cases, more dangerous to others or themselves. Teenage girls and boys who become promiscuous, adolescents who engage in petty crime or abuse alcohol or drugs, and older children who run away from home may be acting out their anger, as well as other feelings toward their families.

Most of the women are angry. Some are in touch with their anger, others are not. Most have ambivalent feelings about their anger. On the one hand, they feel their anger is a legitimate response to being mistreated, unloved, and overburdened; on the other hand, since their partners suffered various hardships in Vietnam, they should be more understanding and patient.

However, this pattern may change when a woman reaches midlife. Upon the reflection characteristic of this time of life, a woman may begin to both appreciate and resent what she has sacrificed for the sake of others or for the sake of her value system. Like her husband, she may feel cheated and betrayed. Her husband may feel he gave his all in the name of patriotism, only to be unappreciated by his nation and deprived of social status and inner peace. Similarly, his wife may feel she gave her all for the sake of family values, only to be unappreciated by her family and devalued by others for being so "old-fashioned" or for not having achieved material success. In addition, as the Vietnam wife ages in this society, she, like any other mature woman, is deemed increasingly physically undesirable and expendable, as if she were a wounded soldier unfit for battle.

Regardless of their age, however, many women try to hide the full extent of their anger from their husbands. Some fear being hit. Others do not want to in any way interfere with their partner's therapy and recovery from PTSD. Still others keep quiet because their partners have talked about suicide, a real possibility for some Vietnam veterans. Although the Department of Veterans Affairs calls it a "trash statistic," research completed in California alleges that as many vets (some 58,000) have died by their own hand as were killed in Vietnam.[1] Equally distressing is the high number of deaths and injuries due to single car collisions and other "accidents" among Vietnam veterans, which could have been suicidal in nature.

Most of the women would readily describe their partners as angry. Some even call their men "human volcanos," ready to erupt at any moment. Indeed, the Vietnam veteran with unresolved or untreated PTSD is often a very angry man.[2]

In Vietnam, when friends were killed or atrocities witnessed, there was no time for the normal grieving process. Grief, like many other emotions, was suppressed. Both during the war and afterward, drugs or alcohol often were used as a way to avoid feeling grief, fear, homesickness, and many other feelings which the war created.

Anger, however, was one of the few emotions the soldier felt free to express in Vietnam and it was often the expression for a wide range of feelings. He could easily deal with anger or any other emotion by going "off" in the next firefight or engaging in some form of brutality, often without any official reprimand. "Kill or be killed" was the rule of the day. To assure survival, usually there was no time for moral considerations, or even much thought. "If it moved, we shot it," explains one vet.

Given the guerrilla nature of the war, responding with violence became almost automatic. Some vets describe being shocked at how easy and "pleasant" it became to kill. "There was a terrific release, a power rush," explains one veteran. "For a while, I thought I became addicted to killing."

The vet who described himself as "addicted" to killing was ahead of his time in coining the term "addiction" as applied to battle. Recently mental health professionals who have worked with veterans have used this term to describe the excitement, "rush," or "high" which some veterans experienced in combat and which some still experience when remembering combat or when engaged in potentially dangerous activities. According to some researchers, there are biological changes which occur in men when their lives are on the line. These changes minimize the warrior's awareness of danger and of physical and psychological pain and discomfort and help him to move rapidly and powerfully. The resulting state of excitement can be overpowering and extremely pleasant.[3]

Combat addiction has also been called "berserking." Dr. Jonathan Shay, a psychiatrist who has worked for years with combat veterans, writes of the love-hate relationship some veterans have toward the violence they were asked to perform. He calls the state of unrestrained violence or "going berserk," which war ignites, a state of "flaming ice."[4]

"No one has ever drawn a syringe of blood or cerebrospinal fluid from a berserk warrior nor mapped the electrical activities of his nervous system. No one knows how much of the large literature on the physiology of extreme stress can be applied to berserking, on which there is no established physiological literature. It is plain that the berserker's brain and body function are as distant from everyday function as his mental state is from everyday thought and feeling . . .

"Veterans are well aware of the sensations that accompany the berserk state . . . The heart pounds, the muscles tense, the senses are on extreme alert. This is widely known as the 'fight or flight' reaction . . . There may be a 'burning in the gut' or a feeling 'like electricity coming out of me.' Adrenal hormones reduce sensibility to pain and fatigue and sharpen the senses. Bodily strength at such times seems superhuman . . .

"Prolonged combat also brings bodily changes that deaden pain, hunger, and desire, resulting in an emotional coldness and indifference. The neurochemical basis of this change may be the release of opiate-like substances by the brain itself in response to terror and pain . . .

"The true physiological relationship between the burning rage of the berserker and his icy deadness remains uncharted territory. We see the paradox that the same human being may burn with fury while cold as ice, incapable of hunger, pleasure, or even pain from his wounds."[5]

The berserk state is an extreme form of the loss of restraint of aggression.. Not all who fought in Vietnam went berserk. However, most learned how to react quickly and violently to any danger, real or perceived. This quick action response, however, while appropriate to the combat situation in Vietnam, was no longer useful (or condoned) upon return to the United States. Vets had to quickly unlearn the violent tendencies that had been expected of them and served them so well during the war.

Yet, after the glow of coming home alive had passed, many veterans found themselves angrier than ever. First, at having been asked to fight in an unofficial war where political considerations often undercut military objectives and second, at the U.S. public in general and at those in their immediate families who they felt failed to acknowledge, much less appreciate, their sacrifices in Vietnam.

Some vets also brought home with them unresolved anger toward certain individuals in the war whose ignorance, avarice, or selfish career interests caused the possibly preventable deaths or injuries of buddies and others. Some of this anger was acted out during the war, with its well-known incidents of "fraggings" (or killing) of officers.

On a deeper level, some vets came home angry at themselves for surviving when others didn't, for acts of cowardice as well as any senseless killings or even for killing in the line of duty. "In my nightmares I see a VC I killed. As he dies, his face turns into my face. Now I realize that whenever I killed, I killed a part of myself," says one vet. Not uncommonly, vets in therapy report that while they may have felt little remorse about killing while in Vietnam, they now feel as if they lost "parts of their soul."

Nancy's husband, Bob, for example, was ordered to send three men into a dangerous area. He suspected this would result in their deaths, but he had to obey orders. In another instance, Bob was asked to repair some machinery under heavy enemy fire. His attempts to work efficiently were impeded by the moans of the wounded and the increasing numbers of dead around him. Furthermore, the tools he was given for the repair work were not appropriate for the task. Many died as a result of what Bob calls his "incompetence."

Upon return to the states, Bob never discussed these or any other incidents. Instead, he drank to drown his anger at himself, at the officer who had ordered him to send three men on a suicide mission, and at the person responsible for giving him the wrong tools. He quit jobs because he could not tolerate "stupid" orders and wanted to attack superiors who pointed out any of his mistakes. Bob also tended to suffer from rage reactions whenever he had to repair something in his home.

"After 'Nam, Bob could barely deal with his own feelings, much less mine," says Nancy. "So I learned to be quiet.

"If Bob was mad about anything, from the long line at the supermarket to something his mother said, he'd blame me for it. Even if I was trying to help him, he'd jump all over me. I've found that if something isn't my fault, I just leave the situation alone.

"Like last night, he was trying to fix our refrigerator. I could have done a better job of it, but didn't dare say so. Even when he started cussing and asking me for help, I stayed away. I knew if I went over there, even just to help, I'd end up getting yelled at or hit.

"The last time he fixed the refrigerator, he threw the tools all around, smashed some plates, and put a hole in the wall. Now there's another hole right next to it.

"At least I wasn't in the kitchen when it happened. Last time he said that it was my fault he put a hole in the wall.

"I don't care what women's liberation says. I'm staying quiet."

Nancy had suffered five years of intermittent physical abuse before she threatened to leave Bob. But the mental abuse was much worse. Bob has stopped the physical abuse, but Nancy, like many of the women, still "walks on eggs."

"It helps when I don't call him names back or make nasty remarks about Vietnam veterans," Nancy admits. "Therapy helps too. At least now he sometimes warns me, 'Get out of the way, Nancy, I'm having a PTSD attack.'

"Or sometimes he'll chew me out and apologize later, saying he was really mad about something about Vietnam, not about me. He's never had this awareness before. Before, anytime he had a feeling, any kind of feeling about anything, it would come out as anger—toward me, the T.V., the cat, anything, but usually me.

"Now that I understand PTSD I don't take Bob's explosions so personally anymore. But still, it isn't easy, and I'm still wondering when he's going to fix that hole in the wall."

While the Vietnam veterans with PTSD are subject to angry outbursts, the major problem presented by vets seeking help is more often the fear of becoming violent, rather than actually being violent. Sarah Haley, who has worked with many dozens of Vietnam veterans, describes the veteran as caught in the grip of a "paralyzing passivity" born of fear of losing control and hurting others.[6] Having learned what he could do in terms of killing and maiming others in Vietnam, the veteran often strives to suppress his anger for fear of hurting family members.

This "impacted anger," however, is a powder keg, which, on occasion, is ignited and can explode. Unfortunately, sometimes the targets for the anger are the very persons the veteran loves most—his wife and children. Sometimes the anger emerges dramatically. Stereos are smashed, pets are hurt, and women are slammed against walls or hurled through glass doors. But more often the anger emerges less violently, in the form of small cutting remarks or verbal outbursts over relatively trivial matters. These minor outbursts, however, can do as much to erode a relationship as a major physical assault.

For example, normally Rebecca's husband does not pick on her for not keeping accurate financial records, for not having been a virgin when they married, or for yelling at the children. However, if he is angry about some other matter, especially a matter having to do with Vietnam, he will freely vent such complaints. Intuitively sensing that her husband's anger runs deeper than the issues he is talking about, Rebecca does not fight back. What she would like to say, but doesn't is: "After all the women you had in Vietnam, you're complaining about me not being a virgin at the altar? And how dare you criticize my housekeeping and my child care, when you do precious little of either? If you'd help me a little, I wouldn't be making so many mistakes with the checkbook or need to yell at the kids so much."

Rebecca's husband also tends to criticize their children for not doing better at school. Yet he fails to reinforce his children for the efforts they do make, just as he often fails to acknowledge all that Rebecca does on behalf of the family. When children receive primarily negative reinforcement and very little positive reinforcement from a parent, their motivation to please that parent tends to decrease, not increase. This may only intensify the parent's criticism and establishes a cycle of mutual anger and hurt.

The child feels that if the father really loved him, he wouldn't be so judgmental. On the other hand, the father may feel that if the child really loved him, he or she would try harder at school. Without the feeling that his father believes in his child, that child may lose confidence in him- or herself or lose the motivation to self-discipline in order to achieve in school. As the child's grades worsen, the father's critical remarks increase, until either a confrontation or a stalemate occurs.

Stalemates often occur in Vietnam homes where the vet is overly critical because, over time, both the Vietnam wife and her children learn to "tune out" the vet. If the Vietnam wife or her children sense that they are being used as scapegoats, they will then have a good reason to ignore the vet or discount his comments. In addition, they will also be doubly angry—from the specific critical remarks and the second anger from being used as an inappropriate target for the vet's anger about his own issues.

Upon first coming to a Vet Center for help, however, many wives and children suffer from low self-esteem and guilt because they have taken their vet's destructive comments or actions to heart. They have yet to realize that often they are not the fundamental cause of his angry comments or behavior. As the result of counseling, some wives learn to tell if their husband is truly angry at them or if he is merely venting his fury about some other issue and using his wife as a whipping girl.

Often, however, the situation is mixed. The vet is aggravated about something his wife did, but the intensity of his anger is related to an unresolved Vietnam or pre-Vietnam issue, not to his wife's action. Similarly, as the result of therapy, sometimes children as young as 12 or 13 have been able to discern whether their fathers are really angry at them or whether they are really mad about something else, like Vietnam, or a flat tire, or a demanding boss. They may also come to recognize when their mother is scapegoating them too—when she is truly angry with them, or is, in reality, angry at their father, but merely taking it out on them because they are smaller and safer targets.

Once a Vietnam wife or child comes to realize that she is being used as a scapegoat, she may not only become relatively immune to the veteran's comments, but may lose some respect for the vet and disregard his wishes or directives. Even if the wife or child fails to recognize when the vet's anger does not belong to her, but believes instead that she deserves the vet's anger, she may also block out his rage or treat him like a crazy man. She may need to ignore the vet or set up some other protective barrier between herself and the vet if his angry or critical remarks are too painful or overpowering to be absorbed on a frequent basis.

However, if the vet's family denigrates him, either verbally or inside their own minds, and communicates this disrespect or disregard to the veteran, he may become furious. Even if the wife and child are not outwardly disrespectful, but merely, in self-protection or as a form of retaliation, ignore him, he may also become furious. At this point, he may either withdraw, or he may escalate his verbal criticisms in order to obtain his wife's or child's attention and regain a sense of power and control. In some cases, he may even feel he needs to resort to violence in order to be heard or command respect. After each explosion, the veteran typically redoubles his efforts to suppress his anger, which in turn leads to a further build-up of impacted anger. Unless the real cause of the anger is dealt with directly, the possibility of another explosion in the future is imminent.

Like the men, the women have their war stories too. Their chief complaint is that their husbands often use them as scapegoats for the problems having to do with Vietnam or with life in general.

"I don't know why the traffic jams are all my fault, too," says Rebecca. "But if we get stuck in one, Eric starts yelling at me and I get scared. Last time he put a hole in the windshield. Another time he nearly pulled out the steering wheel."

To avoid such angry outbursts, the vet might withdraw. As explained in the introductory section on PTSD, certain events or conditions, like national holidays, humid weather, barbecues, or Asian restaurants, may bring forth conscious or unconscious flashbacks to Vietnam experiences. During these times especially, but also at other times, the veteran, fearing loss of control, medicates himself with drugs or alcohol, sinks into a deep depression, or leaves home.

Time after time, women have reported that suddenly their men leave the room, go hide in the basement, or walk out of the house. Sometimes they are gone for many hours, if not days or weeks. Some men visit other Vietnam veterans, often traveling to other cities to do so, or go to the Vietnam Veterans' Memorial in Washington, D.C. Others simply go out to drink or to find drugs.

"Is this a marriage?" asks Rebecca. "When Eric goes off with his war friends, what am I supposed to do? And what am I supposed to tell our son? A lie—that Daddy's working overtime—or the truth—that Daddy's down at the Vietnam Memorial smoking pot?"

Left alone, the women feel unloved and abandoned. They also resent having to shoulder all the responsibilities for the household, as well as for any children. Not only must they answer their children's questions and help them with their emotional reactions to their father's absence, but they must also explain to relatives and friends why they are alone and why they do not know where their husband is or when he will return. In those instances where a woman's parents, relatives, or associates look down on her for having married a "crazy" Vietnam veteran, the woman's embarrassment, confusion, and anger toward her partner is doubled.

In one case, a husband left for four months; in another, nine months. The wives report that afterward their husbands came home "as if nothing had happened," offering no explanation about where they had been. So far, three women have been abandoned entirely. In two instances, the men clearly stated that they were leaving because they were afraid of hurting their wives. These men were not habitual wife abusers. They had lost control on only one or two occasions, but they did not want to lose control again. According to the wives, these men, now in other cities, work long hours, have practically no friends, and do not socialize with other women.

Most of the women entered their marriage or relationship with the expectation that they would be taken care of by their partner to some degree, both financially and emotionally. Some had never envisioned themselves as having to work outside the home, much less as having to be the "strong one." Yet, most of the women who have attended group are not only the emotional, but the financial, mainstays of the family, holding down at least two jobs—one at home, one at work.

Anita holds down two jobs while also caring for two school-age children. Her husband, Paul, has been unemployed ever since Vietnam and has been in and out of treatment for his PTSD for several years. Sometimes he is so depressed he can do little around the house. His major contribution to the family has been his disability check, which depresses him further.

In deference to Paul's ego, Anita keeps her complaints to herself and shares them only with the group. Like the majority of the women in the group, Anita feels deep loyalty to her husband and is very sensitive to the fact that he endured a great deal in Vietnam.

"Paul lost his hearing in one ear and has permanent back injuries. Half his unit was wiped out too. After all he went through, maybe I have no right to moan. But it's been 13 years of me being supermom. I'm worn out and I keep wondering, when is he going to get over this thing?

"I try to be patient, but when I come home and the dishes aren't even done, I blow up. Then he says I'm aggravating his PTSD."

Most of the men are described as being willing to help with only a minimal amount of household work or child care and some leave all the chores to their wives. In general, the men seem somewhat more interested in child care than in housekeeping activities.

Perhaps the women would be less resentful if their contributions to the family were acknowledged and appreciated. But most of the women report working long hours with minimal reinforcement or positive regard from their spouse or lover. "I know it's the numbing that makes him unable to show affection and I know that he's too depressed himself to even ask me 'how was your day?' when I walk in the door. But it still hurts," says Anita.

While most of the women are angry, they fail to acknowledge their anger because, on some level, they blame themselves for their partner's distress. According to the Vet Center survey, approximately 84% of Vet Center counselors polled indicated that the Vietnam wives they have seen suffer from self-blame for the veteran's depressions, his rage reactions, or his wide fluctuations in mood. Often Vietnam wives have mistakenly interpreted their veteran's emotional or sexual withdrawals as signs of some inadequacies in themselves as women. When their veteran doesn't talk, they wonder what they did to "turn him off"; when he explodes, what they might have done to "set him off."

In group, the women learn about Vietnam and PTSD. It comes as a surprise and a relief for them to hear that they are not responsible for the symptoms of their partner's stress disorder. The Al-Anon slogan, "C-C-C"—You didn't Cause it, you can't Control it, you can't Cure it—is emphasized.

Yet it takes months for the majority of the women to absorb this message. Most of the women, now in their early or late 40s, entered marriage with a 1950s mentality, believing that if only they were giving enough, then their husbands would be happy and all would be well. Many have tried to be the "perfect" wife and have expended a great deal of psychological energy trying to make their husbands feel better. Some have even become frantic in their attempts to "fix" their partner.

Yet they learned that their love was not enough. While they were wanted, they were also not wanted; while they were needed, sometimes desperately so, they were also functionally useless in the face of symptoms of PTSD. Yet if they expressed their feelings, especially anger, only more anger or rejection was sent their way.

Their men, struggling with PTSD, simply could not tolerate the emotional overload. Women who complained were frequently called "selfish" or "ungiving" or reminded that they could not possibly understand the horrors and deprivations endured in Vietnam. In some cases, the woman received the same guilt-evoking message from the veteran's family and friends: she should put her own feelings and needs aside until the veteran "got himself together." She should especially keep her anger to herself, since the veteran was already upset enough.

Some relatives and friends even overlooked the physical battering of the wife. Pat, for example, was physically abused throughout her seven-year marriage to Joe. She also supported him financially and was his only friend. She came to group severely depressed because the last beating had resulted in a miscarriage. She was also in danger of losing her job because of missing so many days from work due to her injuries.

With the group's support, Pat rallied the courage to ask Joe to stop the abuse. When Joe refused, Pat moved out, making her return conditional on his seeking help. Joe promptly moved in with his mother, who immediately called Pat and begged her to return to Joe, who was "falling apart" because he missed her so. The mother added that if only Pat were a "better wife" (and lost 20 pounds, too) Joe would be able to get over Vietnam and not be abusive.

It must be emphasized that the abusive men referred to above were not in treatment for their PTSD and had refused all help, not only for PTSD, but for their alcohol and drug addictions as well. It is highly probably that these particular combat vets were suffering from other difficulties in addition to PTSD.

One of my major therapeutic goals has been to help the women get in touch with their anger and learn how to deal with it in a constructive, rather than destructive, manner. While it has never been my intention to encourage women to blast their partners with anger or produce further alienation in sometimes already very alienated couples, mental health requires that women recognize, and take control of, the powerful energy contained in their anger. In some cases, the woman's marriage has been saved as a result of having her acknowledge her resentments and share them with her partner. Otherwise, she might have simply left.

Many of the women suffer from impacted anger just as do their partners. If a woman has repressed her anger over time regarding a series of incidents, then each new conflict with her partner brings to the surface not only the anger appropriate to that particular incident, but all the built-up angers from the past. Like her veteran, the woman becomes afraid of erupting and tries to keep her anger to herself. She may hesitate to speak up even about minor incidents, for fear of "thunderbolting" her husband with all her past angers or with threats of leaving. Rather than risk his retaliation or her shame at such an unfeminine display, many of the women have done their best to hold in their anger.

Whereas the veteran may turn to alcohol or drugs to sedate his feelings, his partner may use a more socially accepted drug—food. As stated previously, approximately 20% of women seen at the Vet Centers polled were significantly overweight. Some were even double their ideal weight. It is possible that these women literally swallowed their anger as well as other feelings. For example, when Sybil overeats, she is literally stuffing down her anger with food. On her way home from work, she often stops to buy one of her favorite binge foods. "It's the only way I can cope with walking through the door and having him ignore me or blow up at me," she explains. When her husband ridicules her body, Sybil usually vows to go on a diet. But the minute her husband walks out the door, she's in front of the refrigerator stuffing down her hurt and her rage with food.

In fact, whenever her husband denigrates her about anything, Sybil ends up eating, if not immediately after the incident, then a few days later. Sybil is one of those Vietnam wives who learned to be quiet. In addition, her self-esteem is so low that she doesn't feel entitled to be angry. "Fat slobs like me don't have rights," she once said. "I should be grateful he's still married to me." Whenever her husband disappoints her or cheats on her, she has difficulty expressing her anger toward him directly. Instead, she eats. "Each of his blondes has cost me 30 pounds," she sighs.

Sybil dares not admit it to herself (much less to her husband), but she harbors tremendous rage toward him. For example, Sybil claims to have forgiven her husband for his extramarital affairs. But her forgiveness, although sincere, is superficial, for she has never experienced the full depth of her fury.

"I've forgiven him," she tells the group, candy bar in hand. "After all, boys will be boys and this boy had to make up for the time he lost in Vietnam."

"Would you be saying that if you were thin?" asks a group member.

Sybil throws the candy bar across the room. "Hell, no! If I were thin, I'd kill him."

Like Sybil, other Vietnam wives have engaged in "revenge eating" in response to their husbands' extramarital affairs. On the surface it may appear that the woman is trying to punish her husband for his infidelity by gaining weight. Yet on a deeper level, the eating is a form of self-abuse. Upon introspection, many of the women blame themselves, not their husbands, for the affair. They think that if only they were sexier, more loving, more intelligent, more *something*, the affair would not have occurred in the first place. By overeating, the women are consciously or unconsciously punishing themselves for their perceived inadequacies as women by destroying not only their bodies, but their self-respect and self-esteem.

Summary

Coping with the veteran's verbal abuse and his outbursts of anger is a major problem for the wives and girlfriends of PTSD-afflicted veterans. The Vietnam wife often fails to understand that her husband's verbal tirades and his angry outbursts may reflect his unresolved angers regarding his Vietnam experience, rather than the appropriateness or inappropriateness of some action or inaction on her part. Similarly, children who are unnecessarily criticized by their father often cannot discern that the intensity and frequency of their father's stinging remarks stem primarily from his own problems, not their failings as children.

While the Vietnam vet is often portrayed as a violent individual, this image is false. In reality, the vet who suffers primarily from PTSD more accurately suffers from impacted, or suppressed anger, and consequently, from depression, which is often anger turned inward. When the vet is no longer able to keep a lid on his anger, however, rage reactions do occur. Yet, unless the veteran suffers from problems in addition to his PTSD, his rage reactions may be intermittent and followed by remorse and even greater efforts to suppress his anger.

Whether the vet is overly critical, explodes, or withdraws, his wife and children are often angered by his behavior. However, they often do not feel free to express their anger at the vet directly because they fear that the storehouse of anger he harbors inside may be unleashed upon them. Anger is also prohibited for Vietnam wives and children because of sanctions against women expressing anger toward men and against children expressing anger toward their parents. In addition, neither the wife or child may know to express anger constructively.

Nevertheless, the wives and children may be angry. Yet their anger toward the vet, like the vet's anger toward certain aspects of his Vietnam experience, goes underground, where it only tends to grow, rather than disappear. Like their husbands, some Vietnam wives harbor years of resentment and, because they have no outlet for their anger, suffer from problems such as depression, medical problems, and, in some cases, obesity. Some children also have been treated for depression, stemming at least in part from having internalized their anger toward their father, their mother, and the entire family situation. Depressed children may also be angry at themselves for not being able to rectify matters at home or not being able to alleviate their father's or their mother's emotional pain, anxieties, and other problems.

7

Battered Wives

I met Bill right after the war. He seemed kind and compassionate and was extremely charming. My parents and friends, however, protested my seeing him. They felt he had a "dark side." But I thought they were just prejudiced against Vietnam veterans.

Not until six months after the wedding did I find out they were right. Bill really did have a dark side. The abuse began slowly and insidiously. I didn't count his slapping me and sitting on top of me as abuse. Even when he threw things at me or locked me up in rooms, I didn't consider myself battered.

Me, an educated woman with a master's degree, battered? My shrink had to be out of her mind. When she first used the word battered, I was not even fully aware of what she was talking about. Sure, Bill and I had our difficulties. But didn't every married couple? He wasn't that bad, was he? If Bill was angry, it was my fault, or Vietnam's fault, I supposed. All I had to do to make things better was to keep improving myself and help Bill readjust to civilian life.

I first realized I was an abused woman last Veterans Day, when Bill pushed me out of the car into the rain. It was midnight and he had taken my house keys, my credit cards, and my paycheck. At that moment, I realized that

I spent my entire life avoiding his anger and arranging people, places, and things so as not to "set him off."

I had lost my identity in constantly placating him and I was sacrificing the emotional and physical health of my children just for the sake of a wedding ring. I couldn't even make a doctor's appointment for the children without obtaining his "permission" first, even though I earned most of the money in the family.

Up until this point, I had lived in denial, just like he did. Together we minimized my physical injuries and my mental sufferings and blamed everything on Vietnam. I firmly believe that Vietnam did play a role. Bill was a trained killer who had somehow not gotten the fight out of him. The military had flown him straight from the jungle back to his home town, with no time to unwind. He had also been asked to kill innocent civilians. Having learned violence as a problem-solving technique in Vietnam, he felt free to use it in our marriage. His war experience had also taught him that it was okay to push around women.

I left Bill several times, but he would always hunt me down. Once he kidnapped me and the kids from a friend's home. After the jungle of Vietnam, breaking into my friend's house was peanuts to him. He was skilled at scaling walls and other such tactics.

After each episode of violence, however, he was the most loving and wonderful husband and father imaginable. The children would scold me for having wanted to leave him. Since Daddy was being so "nice" now, they felt I should forgive him as I did them whenever they misbehaved.

My children were still in grade school then. They knew nothing about what went on behind closed doors or about all the sacrifices I had made to keep the peace at home.

When they became teenagers, they realized what was going on and urged me to leave him. When my son turned 14, he ran away from home and stayed with a friend. When my daughter turned 16, she threatened to do the same. I realized that although I was trying to save the family by staying with Bill, all I was doing was ruining it. I realized I had already lost my marriage in the sense of there being something beautiful between me and Bill. And if I didn't leave him, I'd have nothing left—no children, no home, no self-respect.

I finally moved out. But while I was married and trying to tell people about my marriage, they usually turned around and told me I was as 'sick' as Bill was. Even my therapist thought I was crazy. Very few people, it seems, understand the powerful forces that keep a woman trapped in an abusive situation. They also fail to understand how the Vietnam war could ruin a man. Sure, Bill had problems before the war, but I am certain that my life with Bill would have been altogether different if he had never gone to Vietnam and did not have PTSD. There was a lot of good in Bill, despite his abusiveness.

—Tessa, wife of a Special Services officer

All Vietnam veterans are not wife abusers. Yet domestic violence is a problem in some Vietnam veteran homes, as it is in society at large. While definitions vary, most researchers agree that a battered woman is one who has received at least two or three deliberate and severe physical assaults. The physical abuse can include a wide variety of bodily assaults: slapping, hitting, punching with fists, attacks with broken glass or weapons, burning, biting, pushing, slamming against walls, and shoving down steps.[1]

Battering is not inherent to PTSD. It is not a symptom of the disorder. Yet some vets do batter and, for some, the battering is PTSD-related.

If the vet adheres to the traditional male sex role stereotype, which dictates that "real men" should appear unemotional, always strong, and never confused, he might panic when his feelings about Vietnam rise to the surface. Feeling out of control and emasculated (by his own emotions, which, except for his anger, he may view as "feminine"), he may attempt to regain a sense of control and affirm his manhood by battering. Battering also helps release the mounting adrenaline caused by his pent-up emotions and inner turmoil.

The vet may also try to feel strong and "manly" by attempting to control his wife or girlfriend by other means, such as by making excessive demands on her, by restricting her financially, or by isolating her from others. However, if she resists his attempts to control her, or otherwise frustrates him, he may resort to violence in order to assume a position of dominance.

Vietnam veterans who batter are similar to other wife abusers in that they may batter out of a need to control and feel masculine and because they have few other means of expressing their needs and frustrations. However, physically abusive Vietnam veterans differ from other batterers in that their military training and experience not only gave them permission, but, in some cases, greatly encouraged them to give in to, rather than to restrain, their violent impulses. In addition, most vets received intensive training in a variety of fighting techniques. In some cases, wife abuse is the direct result of the vet's confusing his wife with the Viet Cong in the midst of a flashback or seeing her as "the enemy" in the midst of a paranoid state. However, more usually it is the vet's economic or emotional dependency on his wife or his need for her to provide him with physical or psychological comfort that precipitates battering in the home.

In my experience, violence in the home seems to erupt when the wife does not meet the veteran's expectation that she can make life smooth for him, when he feels threatened by her need for intimacy, or when he somehow feels emasculated by her strengths. While these dynamics also exist in nonveteran homes, in my experience they are especially prevalent in homes where the vet is still struggling with untreated PTSD, suffers from extreme emotional numbing and feelings of powerlessness, and, in addition, has not yet adjusted to recent changes in the woman's role.

While the vet was fighting in the jungles, the women's liberation movement was beginning to make concrete progress in emancipating women from their traditional roles. Upon returning from Vietnam, the veteran may have understandably focused on his own readjustment success rather than on social changes. To the extent that PTSD hinders personality development and keeps the veteran focused on Vietnam, rather than present realities, the veteran may still be holding on to what are now severely challenged, if not totally outmoded, notions of the woman's role. When his wife's behavior or attitude contradicts his beliefs about how a woman should be or act, he may batter in an attempt to reinstate the traditional sex roles with which he is more comfortable and which assign him a position of dominance.

PTSD-related wife abuse, as opposed to other forms of wife abuse, is usually sporadic and lessens when the vet learns to identify and express his leftover anger and grief from Vietnam constructively and when he learns to root his sense of mastery, competence, and achievement in developing his skills and talents rather than in dominating a woman. He also must learn to accept his own emotions and see them as part of the human condition, rather than as signs of "feminine weakness."

Renewed pride in himself, as a Vietnam vet and as a competent person, usually reduces his need to batter in order to feel powerful, important, or masculine. Stopping battering, however, is usually more difficult for the veteran from a violent home—one who saw his mother being beaten and who, perhaps, was beaten also. Socialized to see violence as normal, it may be harder for him to unlearn violence as a coping mechanism, especially if he still harbors unresolved painful and angry feelings regarding the abuse he saw or endured as a child.

Furthermore, if his mother spent most of her time avoiding beatings, or recovering from them, the vet may have suffered from inadequate physical and emotional nurturing as a child. In his wife, he may hope to find the mother he never had. When his wife fails to meet his needs, he may quickly become furious.

In my experience, the most severe and long-term cases of wife abuse exist in homes where the vet came from a violent family. Wife abuse is also especially prevalent in homes where the veteran is alcohol or drug addicted, where he suffers from a neurological disorder, or where he is character disordered or overtly paranoid. In all these instances, where PTSD interacts with another condition, it is difficult to determine which is primary—the PTSD or the other condition. However, the result is the same—a physically abused and emotionally scarred Vietnam wife.

While psychological humiliation and degradation almost always accompany the physical abuse, the threat of violence must exist in a relationship if it is to be considered a battering one. The woman must know that her partner is capable of directing blows at her and perhaps, ultimately, of killing her.[2]

Yet it is not necessary for a woman to be continually beaten in order to feel terrorized or humiliated into a submissive posture. One or two beatings or threats of violence, accompanied by infrequent inflicting of physical pain or actual torture, are sufficient to establish a pattern of male domination by force.[3] One wife, for example, twice was beaten soon after her husband's return from Vietnam. For 15 years since, she has kept quiet, hiding her innermost needs and feelings from her husband for fear of being hit. A few months ago, she summoned the courage to assert herself and ask some questions about a touchy issue. As expected, she was assaulted and now lives in fear. These infrequent assaults are enough to "keep her in her place."

Current estimates are that anywhere from one-tenth to one-third of all married couples engage in spousal assault.[4] However, many researchers, as well as official military and other government documents, note that wife abuse, like child abuse, tends to be underreported.[5]

More than one million abused women seek medical attention for injuries caused by battering each year.[6] Some studies show that at least 20% of the visits to emergency rooms by women are the result of wife abuse.[7] Four women a day in this country die as the result of domestic violence. In fact, wife abuse causes more injury to women than auto accidents, rapes, or muggings.[8]

Men from all social groups batter—rich men, poor men, white men, African-American men, professors, and even clergymen. To date, we do not know whether Vietnam veterans batter their wives more or less than any other group of men. Available figures indicate that anywhere from one-third to one-half of help-seeking Vietnam veterans admitted to striking their partners.[9] According to the counselors polled in the Vet Center study, approximately one-fourth of wives seen at their Vet Centers report not just mental, but physical, abuse.[10]

These data are somewhat dated, in that they were gathered in the late 1970s and 1980s, yet they are the only data available. Most likely, as veterans age, the severity and rate of wife abuse diminish. I base this statement on the general tendency for rates of wife abuse to be highest among couples in their 20s and 30s and to decline as the couples enter their 40s and 50s.[11] The rates may also be lower because of increased publicity given to the problems of wife abuse in recent years.

Among the women I worked with, however, many were hit at least once. However, only about one-fourth fit into the battered woman category where the husband exercises a financial and emotional, as well as physical, stranglehold over the woman. In these cases, women are not just hit on occasion, but thrown down stairs, slammed against (and through) walls, cut with knives, and locked in rooms without food or heat for hours. Some wives have been seriously sexually abused by their husbands, forced into obscene situations, or punched in the stomach, even when pregnant, causing some miscarriages.

I have also treated Vietnam veterans' wives and girlfriends who are incarcerated at a local correctional facility for a variety of crimes ranging from theft and drug dealing to attempted murder and murder. One of the women, Peggy, is serving time for killing her veteran husband, a man who, during his numerous flashbacks, would brutally assault her and their seven-year-old son.

"He thought we were V.C.," she explained. This man never sought help. Years after the war, he would simulate Vietnam by building fires in their backyard and sleeping outside. Whenever airplanes flew overhead in hot and humid weather, Peggy would anticipate a beating. In self-protection, she would hide at the homes of relatives and friends. But her husband would seek her out, drag her home, barricade her inside, and terrorize her, sometimes for days on end.

Peggy was afraid to call the police. Her husband had threatened to kill any police who came and then kill her. She had good reason to believe him, for he had souvenir guns from Vietnam and had been in a Special Forces Division where he had killed many persons. Furthermore, he had often stated that even if the police shot him dead or imprisoned him, he would not care. Life was meaningless to him.

Peggy felt trapped. The only way she saw out of her marriage was murder. "But I'm still not free of him," she would often say. "In my dreams, I see him running around in our backyard, acting like he was in the jungles, then coming at me. If I didn't kill him, he would have probably killed himself someday."

Another imprisoned wife, whose husband also failed to recognize his PTSD, reported that her husband beat her during nightmares about Vietnam and, on one occasion, tried to cut her ear off with a lid from an opened can of baby formula.

"I'm not a Viet Cong! I'm not a Viet Cong!" she screamed and hit him on the head with a broomstick until he "came back to the U.S.A."

While these examples may seem extreme, they are real, and while the figure of one-fourth may seem high, actually, it is not strikingly different from the figure given for the rate of wife abuse in our society as a whole—a figure that ranges from 10% to 50%, according to the studies previously cited.

It cannot be overemphasized that the one-fourth percentage is based on estimates obtained several years ago from only half of the existing Vet Centers, as well as on an extremely limited sample—help-seeking veterans, not on the Vietnam population as a whole. The percentages from these highly specialized samples cannot be generalized.

In addition, there is evidence that the increased public recognition given to Vietnam veterans in recent years has helped decrease the incidence of domestic violence. "In the last few years, there has been a reduction in the external causes of anger by the dedication of The Wall, by the willingness of television to discuss Vietnam, by therapy and rap groups conducted by Vet Centers, and by society's more accepting attitude toward Vietnam veterans," explains Mark Kaufki, Vet Center Team Leader, Wilmington, Delaware.[12]

"The Wall is a real focus for grieving," he continues. "It's as if society says it is okay to grieve. Veterans can do that now. Grieving can dissipate a lot of internal pressure," pressure that perhaps was relieved in the past through woman battering.[13] For example, a combat vet named Demo explains how The Wall helped him resolve some of his war grief, and rage.

By mid-1965, I had been in the 'Nam about 10 months. My first tour as a crew chief in a rescue chopper, I had helped load, carry, and care for men with every type of wound that can be received in combat. If we weren't being fired on, I always helped the corpsman when he was swamped.

When the firefights cooled out in our zone, we went back in for our dead. Charlie's sniper knew we didn't leave our dead behind, so they were usually waiting for us. After the dead were "tagged and bagged," we made a final run for body parts, arms, legs, and an occasional head, etc.; in case someone had taken a direct bomb hit, they could be confirmed dead rather than MIA. I was sure I had seen all the horrors of war and could handle it.

By my second tour (I just didn't fit in "the world" anymore), I had been retrained as a co-pilot. Although things had heated up, I was up front, in the clean part of the bird, and with all there is to stay airborne, it was easy to keep the death and dying out of my mind.

We were about 12 clicks southeast of Dung Ha on the way to an evac call, when the bird next to us took a direct rocket hit.

I'm sure the crew of four, two of which were my friends, felt no pain. Pieces of their rotor blades flew through our canopy and we almost lost control. A piece hit the engine and we were blowing smoke like crazy.

We found the flares, dropped down at the far end of the clearing. In case we couldn't get airborne again, another bird could get in.

When I looked in the cabin, my heart pounded. Shrapnel not only hit our canopy, but blew clean through our bird. On its way, it took off the left hand of our crew chief, a sergeant, and cut the new medic assigned to us in half.

I had just spoken to "Doc" a few minutes before. I applied a new tourniquet to the sergeant's stump; the one he put on himself was leaking like hell. I popped a vial of morphine, then tagged both halves of Doc.

As we inspected our bird for damage, the grunts brought the wounded Marine we had come to evacuate to the clearing.

I already hated him. Because of him, five men were dead, one was crippled for life, and there was a good chance we would never get back to a safe zone.

When I looked at the wounded Marine, I almost vomited all over him. He was burned so badly I could barely recognize him as a human being. His ears were gone, his eye sockets were burned out holes. All that was left of his nose was a small charred bone.

His lips were burned off and his teeth were hanging out through his cheeks and chin.

I grabbed at his dog tags to get his blood type and had to pull hard because the chain was burned into his neck and the tags burned into his chest.

I read them and total horror overwhelmed me. It was Nick, from a small town north of mine.

He and I had been altar boys together and on the church basketball teams together. We had seen each other at countless church dances, too.

I pumped three vials of morphine into Nick, but he was still trying to scream. He couldn't, though, because his tongue was burnt off.

I knew his brain was cooked because I could see his skull on his left side, but I gave him plasma, cleared his lungs, and held him till we got to an aid station.

The nightmares about Nick started when I was still in the 'Nam, not about his injuries, but whether or not I should have helped him die.

I kept seeing a shadowy figure in a housedress crying while leaning over Nick, still burned hideously with all kinds of tubes going in and out of him from head to toe.

After a few months and a few crashes later, my luck ran out. I woke up in a hospital in Japan, in a body cast from my chin to my ankles.

Being an only child, my parents flew to Japan to see me as soon as they got the news. Although she tried to hide it, I'll never forget the look on my mother's face when she saw me. My father, who left Greece when he was 13, brought six brothers to America, started his own business, and was stronger and worked harder than anyone I have ever met, before or since, couldn't stop crying.

It took quite a long time and a lot of surgery, but both legs work again. My back is tolerable and my right arm is 90%.

The dream changed while I was recuperating. Nick was still there, but instead of the shadowy figure, my mother had taken her place and that look showed through every time.

Every time I would have that dream, the next day it took all my will power not to lash out at someone, or something. I stayed away from women because I was afraid that if I got involved and had that nightmare, the poor woman might end up hurt. I'd wake up from that dream . . . shaking . . . and mad.

While working in Washington, D.C., my best friend asked me several times to go to The Wall. Each time I made an excuse. Finally, he talked me into it.

The closer we got to The Wall, the more afraid I became. Suddenly I was face to face with one of my biggest fears. In order not to have to look at the names on The Wall, I concentrated on the faces of the people walking in the opposite direction.

It was awful and wonderful at the same time, for on the faces of the people were all the emotions I was feeling.

For the first time I felt I wasn't alone in my confusion, my anger, my grief. I saw vets like myself, who looked relieved that they had made it and guilty they hadn't done more. I saw old people crying for their children and for their own loss and loneliness as well. Saddest of all, I saw young people trying to understand why so many had to die, so violently, and so far away.

I saw The Wall, finally. I don't mean I looked at it. I mean I saw what it was. It is a monument to those men and women who gave their lives for our country.

A few days later I went back. I couldn't help it. I searched until I found Nick's name on the wall. I waited my turn and with trembling hands I looked in the directory and found he died the day we brought him out.

I knew then that he had a closed casket funeral. His mother, father, and family never knew the horror I had seen. They could remember him the way he was, young and full of life. From that moment on, so could I.

From that moment on, the nightmare ceased and I didn't feel like beating up on people any more.

—Demo, Vietnam Veteran

The Wall helped dissipate the grief which could have led to destructive behavior for Demo, and for an undetermined number of other veterans. On the other hand, abused women and battering couples are less likely than others to seek help and, despite recent public awareness, may not report the abuse. Therefore, the true extent of wife abuse among Vietnam veterans is undetermined.

While wife abuse is not limited to any particular population of men, it has been found to be more prevalent among families experiencing financial pressures, frequent moves, and isolation from peer groups and family support systems—characteristics of some Vietnam veteran families.[14] A related problem is that in some homes, the vet is economically or emotionally dependent on his wife. He may sense his dependency and resent it. It insults his masculinity and sense of control. As a result, he may batter to maintain superiority.

Veterans, like other men, grew up in a society where the marriage license was sometimes perceived as a "hitting license." Furthermore, some veterans had extensive military training and wartime experiences which emphasized the value of power and violence and quick action responses.[15] As one veteran stated, "I was just a mealymouthed clerk until the military turned me into a trained killer. Is it any wonder I beat my wife?"

"The military portion of our society, which is a microcosm of the larger society, contributes to the learning of violence and specifically to the battering of women and children," explains Rick Ritter, a former Vietnam veteran who now specializes in helping vets who batter.[16]

"Basic training encourages woman hating, as does the whole military experience," Ritter continues. "Each man strives to outdo the next . . . to top him. Inevitably, someone has to be on the bottom. Somebody has to be the scapegoat, the enemy (when all else fails women are always available for that role in the mind of the military)."[17]

"Most men in basic training are teenagers—the time when their concept of womanhood is crystallized," writes Shepard Bliss in *The Military, Masculinity and the Men's Movement*. "Many men have their first experiences with sexual intercourse while in the military, not the best context for what can be such a loving act, but can also become an instrument of control, power and domination.

"Speaking about Vietnam, a soldier explains . . . 'You either had to be satisfied with masturbation or find someone to rape.'"[18]

According to Lydia Savina, who writes extensively on battered women, "During the Vietnam war, as in all wars, women were raped, mutilated, and tortured. Rape was often a method of interrogation, even though it was less than 10% effective. Assault on Vietnamese women was also sometimes a way for American soldiers to vent their frustrations regarding the war or to retaliate against the Vietnamese for the deaths of buddies or military defeats."[19] "After a hard day at the battle it was okay to go into town and brutalize a woman. If (we) had already won the land then it was okay to defile the defeated foe's woman as a conqueror," writes one veteran.[20]

"Certainly not all Vietnam veterans raped or otherwise victimized women. But some did, and those who did not actually participate in such crimes witnessed them or at least heard about them. Undoubtedly such experiences serve to lower inhibitions against expressing violence against one's wife or girlfriend in the U.S."[21]

One psychological factor leading to wife abuse among Vietnam veterans can be the unresolved grief and rage which underlie the symptoms of PTSD.[22] For some men, it is easier to lash out at a wife or girlfriend than to deal with the seemingly insurmountable amounts of pain and anger within. Some of their pain and anger may be leftover from Vietnam, but some of it stems from their frustration and disappointment with the present, as in the case of David.

"Why do I hit her when she's all I got?" asked David.

"Why do you think?" I asked.

"Because she's there, the safest available target."

"Who do you really want to hit?"

"The V.C., my C.O., my boss, myself."

David entered therapy in an extreme state of psychic numbing. As his emotions began to surface, he began to panic. The feelings seemed to overwhelm him at times. He felt out of control, almost powerless, over his inner life.

Most people do not like to feel powerless over anything. For men, especially, it isn't "masculine." They may batter as a defense against such feelings.

David, for example, frequently felt powerless in Vietnam. Once he was ordered to shoot into a deserted hut. David objected, but his C.O. insisted. As it turned out, inside the hut were two abandoned toddlers.

"I swear, I didn't know there were two kids in there, I swear," David bawled in one session. "And I could have killed my C.O." But David didn't kill his C.O. He didn't even say anything to the C.O. about the killing. Soon afterward, however, as a means of atonement, David began to visit a nearby village and brought small presents for the children. Five weeks later, the V.C. blew up the village. All the children were killed. "After that, I gave up," says David. "I didn't care about nothin' except getting home alive."

Upon his return to the United States, however, David's wife did not want to hear about Vietnam. He could not find a job he liked. He felt cheated by the government over his benefits. Once again, he felt powerless. Once again, he decided "not to care."

He claims to have put Vietnam out of his mind until 10 years later, when his wife, at 39, unexpectedly became pregnant. He was also in the midst of a midlife crisis. Only then did he begin to attack his wife immediately after she came home from work, threatening to throw her down the stairs or puncture her ovaries if she ever became pregnant again. Or, fearing his anger, he'd withdraw from her altogether and spend his nights in a park or go to the mountains for days. If she would not consent to an abortion, he planned to leave her. On the other hand, he felt that abortion was a form of murder. Seeing no solution to the problem, he became angrier and angrier at his wife, who he felt had tricked him into impregnating her. His wife, however, claims that the pregnancy was a total surprise.

As David's case illustrates, unresolved PTSD can play a key role in wife abuse, with a greater frequency and severity of wife beating occurring among couples where the veteran has yet to deal with his grief and rage. A significant event can sometimes precipitate an episode of wife abuse.

For example, incidents seem to occur when there is a death in the family or when one of the children is seriously injured. The veteran, in a state of psychic numbing, may show no apparent emotion about the event. However, when the wife begins to grieve or openly react, the veteran may batter her as an attempt to cope with the pain which her emotional response brings to his awareness.

In one instance, a vet's sister-in-law died in childbirth. The veteran showed no emotion until his wife picked up the phone to make plane reservations to attend the funeral. Screaming that there was no need for airline reservations because her sister wasn't really dead, the vet pulled the phone out of the wall and punched his wife in the stomach and face.

In another instance, a child received second-degree oil burns in a kitchen accident. The vet refused to accompany his wife to the hospital. In his view, the child was not injured. Even when the child returned home in bandages, the vet was emotionless and said nothing. The next day the wife began to cry as she changed the dressings on the child's wounds. The vet accused her of overreacting and choked the cat. When the wife intervened, the vet choked her.

Beatings also may occur on patriotic holidays or when a veteran encounters frustrations with bureaucracies—like delays in obtaining benefits and waiting in long lines—even though the wife may be the veteran's right-hand partner in the process of obtaining his rights. Mary Elizabeth, for example, was constantly contacting veterans benefits offices for her husband, Walter, who became irrational or depressed when he had to deal with government officials. Since Vietnam, Walter had been unable to work and she also was the sole support of the family. Yet Walter abused her, especially on patriotic holidays.

One holiday she phoned in the middle of the night. Walter had tied her to the bedpost for two days. He had not only assaulted her, but also used one of his knives from Vietnam to scrape designs on her stomach. When he left to buy some beer, he came back with a dozen live crabs also. He put Mary Elizabeth in the bathtub with the crabs and tried to recreate water tortures he had seen overseas. When a neighbor unexpectedly came to the door, Mary Elizabeth somehow managed to slip away and lock herself in her bedroom. She now wanted to kill herself.

My suggestion that her desire to commit suicide might reflect her suppressed anger toward Walter was not well received. Mary Elizabeth insisted that she understood why Walter was violent and listed all the traumas he had experienced in Vietnam which, in her mind, excused his behavior.

Similarly, Amy, who arrived at her first group meeting with a black eye and two missing teeth, felt that the military was responsible for her husband's outbursts. He had been wounded in Vietnam and did not receive proper medical care. Whenever he was in pain, he would prevent her from leaving the home and sometimes batter her.

While not all wives are so "understanding," many blame anything but their husbands for his behavior. Such thinking, however, is a form of denial which only serves to help the woman "forgive" and resigns her to a life of violence.

Other wives report that husbands hit them and then ask for forgiveness because, after all, it was just their PTSD acting up. There is, however, no excuse for a beating, not even PTSD.

Summary

While some vets recoil from all forms of violence after their firsthand experiences with blood and death in Vietnam, others find themselves "on guard" and "ready to attack" even at home. According to the Vet Center study, some 25% of Vietnam wives complain of physical abuse. This rate, however, is based on a limited sample studied many years ago and is not significantly different from rates of wife abuse found among other groups in our society.

In homes of Vietnam veterans, wife abuse tends to occur during certain flashbacks to Vietnam, in times of family loss or injury, or when the vet is feeling powerless over some aspect of his life, for example, his financial or employment situation, his personal relationships, or even his own emotions. Through battering he hopes to recapture a sense of control and to affirm his strength and masculinity. If the vet became anesthetized to violence in Vietnam, he may trivialize his wife's injuries, and thereby support her denial that she isn't hurt "that bad."

Battered Vietnam wives, like their husbands, sometimes blame Vietnam for the violence at home, not realizing that such violence cannot be entirely attributed to the veteran's PTSD. In fact, in cases of extreme or persistent wife abuse, usually the veteran suffers from problems in addition to PTSD.

Like other abused women, battered Vietnam wives often fail to realize the extent to which they are being abused until they are severely injured, or until one of their children develops a problem. Even if children do not become directly involved in the violence, they will suffer psychological damage from living in a home where they see their mother being abused. Since domestic violence tends to escalate over time, eventually the children will discover the parental "secret" and imitate the parental patterns of victim or aggressor. Like children from alcoholic homes, children from violent homes tend to feel responsible for the family turbulence and, in some cases, suffer from long-term guilt complexes over what they did or didn't do to cause the assaults or to prevent them from occurring.

When they become adolescents, they may act out the violence they have seen at home by being violent themselves. They may run away from home or stay absent from the home for long periods of time or they may develop addictions or other psychological problems as a result of having witnessed their father abuse their mother. Just as their mothers can develop PTSD from living in a state of constant danger, children who grow up witnessing violence can also develop PTSD symptoms of varying degrees of severity. As a result, they can suffer from memory and concentration problems which impair them at school or work and in their familiar and non-familiar relationships. They are at especially high risk for developing clinical depression, as are their mothers.

8

"But Military Wives Never"

I was born in a military family and, as a child, was proud of it. I thought it made me special. When my father served in World War II, my mother received a tremendous amount of support from the other military wives and members of the military community. I didn't like the frequent moves, but the warm reception we received at each new base almost made up for the home and friends we had left behind.

I was proud to be a military wife too, until my husband came back from Vietnam and both he and I were shunned, not cheered like my parents had been. In many ways, large and small, I found myself hiding the fact of my husband's tour of duty from the others on the base. Although Alex had served honorably, he was seen as being part of the war which had brought disgrace to the military and which had made the military a four-letter word to some people.

Popular military women's magazines and other military wife publications wanted no stories about Vietnam wives and there were no special clubs where we who had sent our men to the jungles could share our struggles and concerns. If we had trouble coping, well, that was our fault. After all, as military wives, we were supposed to be strong, keep a stiff upper lip, and stand by our man 100%, no matter how he might be destroying our peace of mind, as well as his own.

Given this atmosphere, I found dozens of clever ways of disguising the fact that my husband had served in 'Nam and invented yet another ingenious list of excuses for not attending certain military functions. Of course, nonattendance at social and other functions was a definite "no-no" for a military wife, but there were times I was needed at home. If my husband was severely depressed or being self-destructive, I had to be there to help keep him, and our children, together.

At the time I had nowhere to turn. Ten or 15 years ago, understanding of PTSD was just developing in our society. In the military particularly, PTSD was largely unheard of, or seen as an excuse for cowardice or as some kind of moral or masculine failure. Even today, among certain groups, the active duty Vietnam vet afflicted with PTSD is looked down on.

I left my husband three years ago, divorcing not only him but the entire military, the only life I had ever known. Of course I was accused—by his parents and mine—not only of breaking up the family, but of ruining my husband's military career and my children's financial security. I was also disgracing his particular unit, which boasted few divorces. Yet I could no longer live a lie.

My military benefits are gone and I live close to poverty with several children to support. The most painful part of the divorce, however, was giving up access to my husband, surrendering my desire to save Alex from his depression, drinking, and his bouts of combat memories. And he was getting worse. My most vivid memory of him is seeing him lying on the couch, disheveled and bloated from beer, bags under his eyes from the nightmares, saying he didn't have a problem. The only problem was me. If I would only leave him, he would be fine.

I pleaded with him to get help, threatening to divorce him if he didn't. But he simply couldn't share his psychological problems with anyone in the military. It would have felt like a complete emasculation to him, a total antithesis of the 'macho' hero he was expected to be. Furthermore, since there is little confidentiality of records in the military, he feared that his attempts to seek help would have become a matter of record and possibly held against him for the rest of his military career.

I often wonder how Alex is today. Rumor has it that he is deteriorating rapidly. But because he is a lifer and holds a high position, special exceptions are being made for him. He is also the object of much sympathy because he was "deserted" by his "irresponsible" wife. My years of loyal wifely service and personal martyrdom for the sake of the family count for nothing.

—The ex-wife of a high-ranking officer

Military wives have often been strangled by what the "good military wife" should do. For example, when Evelyn, a formerly battered military wife, sought help from her husband's commanding officer and the army chaplain, she was advised to stop wallowing in self-pity, "toughen up," and support her fighting man. Soon he would be going to Vietnam. She might lose him. No sense filing charges or making a fuss now. Besides, if she exposed her husband's wife (and child) abuse, it would hurt his career. What if he was demoted from officer to grunt status and had to fight in the front lines? If he died in 'Nam, it would be all her fault.

Brought up in a military home, Evelyn was indoctrinated into the "shoulds" of being a good military wife at a relatively young age. She was also brought up in a religious household, which emphasized the virtues of female submission, self-sacrifice, and the sanctity of the family. These "shoulds" were reinforced by her military neighbors and those in her husband's chain of command. As a result, she found it impossible to leave her husband until several years after his return from Vietnam, when his physical abuse endangered the life of their youngest son.

Like Evelyn, the military wife is under a special set of pressures related to the military community. The demands that community makes on her are numerous and difficult to follow even without a husband suffering from PTSD. If the husband is afflicted with PTSD, her life becomes almost unmanageable.

Military wives have listed the following demands as those most difficult for them to accept when trying to cope with PTSD as well:

• Always put her husband's career above her personal needs and the needs of the family;

• Be willing to tolerate frequent moves and separations from her husband without undue complaint;

• Be prepared to bear and raise their children alone;

• Assume complete responsibility for the children, the home, the car, and finances during her husband's absences, but then allow him to feel he is the head of the household when he returns;

• Be willing to give up anniversaries and birthdays and accept that the military comes first and the family second;

• Attend all parties and mixers and always act in a way that promotes her husband's career;

• Conform to group expectations and especially any expectations or orders from the "higher-ups";

• Always be compassionate, understanding, and obedient, and plan special homecomings for her husband;

• Keep her home spotless even if she works full time and doesn't have help;

• At all times, keep up the pretense of having a home life;

• Never, ever, under any circumstances, expose her husband's weaknesses or defects of character;

• In general, be willing to accept a subordinate wife role because not to do so would endanger her husband's status and potential for promotion.

One wife wrote, "I'm a perfect military wife. I've already moved 35 times in my life and taken full responsibility for all the moves and the children. I accept not being allowed to pursue my own career and accept the yo-yo of dependence and independence (being super-strong while my husband's away and acting helpless when he's back). But I cannot accept alcohol coming first, the Marines second, and me last. What should I do?"

This wife, like other military wives, was particularly bitter about the excessive use of alcohol which she felt was encouraged by the military. "The military made an alcoholic out of my husband," she says. She was also bitter about having to downplay her husband's involvement in Vietnam. Yet she, like others, felt there were many positive aspects to being a military wife, specifically, the feeling of belonging and security. "It was fun, like being in a big family. Even in the best of families there were secrets. Mine just happened to be that my husband was a Vietnam vet. Sure, I couldn't talk about Vietnam the way I wanted, and sure, there were cliques but I felt like part of the group. Money was tight too, but we knew the military would meet most of our basic needs."

Since the early 1990s, the career security thought to be almost automatic in the military has been threatened by cutbacks in military spending and other economic changes. Yet when these women first married, such disruptions were not foreseen. The women enjoyed the sense of security, the travel, the semi-mandatory socializing, and did not mind being constantly uprooted. But they also spoke of loneliness and the loss of their personal identity. "It's hard to make friends, because you and everyone else are always moving," explains Evelyn. "Plus, when your husband is gone and you have to handle everything, you get too busy to socialize, even though there's a lot of pressure on you to do so.

"But the hardest part is not being treated like an individual. You are not yourself, but someone's wife. Your husband's rank determines your life. It's like you don't exist." Evelyn found that almost everything she did, from cashing checks to buying cleanser at the commissary, was dependent on her husband's status.

Even military wives who are wage-earning members of the military in their own right are often rendered economically dependent on their husbands by the structure of the military. In addition, military values usually place the husband's career ahead of the wife's.

Evelyn's face is lined. Although only 49, she looks much older. Before Vietnam, her career officer husband physically abused her only on Saturday nights. In fact, during the early years of their marriage, there was no abuse. But soon after their first child was born, the beatings began. Evelyn has openly shared her story in the group several times. Like the traumatized vet with PTSD, she keeps telling and retelling the sad story of her own Vietnam, hoping that perhaps if she tells it often enough, the pain will go away. Yet, like a good military wife, she has never cried.

"I didn't know what to do when Hank started crunching my skull and punching my stomach with his fists," she explains. "I'm not a fighter and I was raised in a family where there were certain things you just didn't talk about. I didn't know you could talk to people about family problems."

The walls of their apartment on base were paper thin. Certainly the neighbors heard the beatings, but everyone, Evelyn included, joined in the conspiracy of silence that shrouded wife abuse until public exposure of the problem in recent years.

All four of Evelyn's children were born while Hank was away at training or overseas. She managed everything during his absences, but had to do a complete turnabout when he returned home. She didn't like having to do whatever he wanted, but she felt she had no choice. Her husband was aggressive and possessive and always picking fights. He was six foot six inches tall; she, five foot two. He weighed 270 pounds; she, 104. And he was a trained killer.

At times Evelyn had fleeting thoughts of leaving him. "But I had four kids and no place to go. As a military dependent, I would have been destitute without him."

Once she sought help from a military counselor, who, she claims, "sloughed over" her problem, did not believe her, and advised her to stay married. "If it's that bad now, how can it get worse?" he pointed out.

But it did get worse. After Vietnam, her husband insisted that she have another child and name it after one of his dead war buddies. When Evelyn wanted to go to college instead, her husband held a knife to her throat and raped her repeatedly until she conceived. "Nobody had ever heard of marital rape then," Evelyn remembers. "Besides, he said that since I was his wife he had a right to rape me."

When she miscarried, Hank punished her by cutting her 30 times on the face, neck, and arms with a broken bottle. Evelyn told the military hospital personnel that she had fallen through the glass shower door. They acted as if they believed her, even though on that particular base all shower doors were plastic, not glass.

After Vietnam, her husband was tortured by nightmares and self-hate and abused not only Evelyn, but mutilated himself as well. "In 'Nam they put a rifle in his hands and told him to 'go to it.' He killed—tortured—innocent men, women, and children or maimed them for life. The minute he walked off the plane from 'Nam, I knew he had changed, that he had all that on his conscience. I begged him to go see a psychiatrist or a priest, but he wouldn't hear of it.

"After 'Nam he started going into the bathroom and trying to scald himself or drown himself in the tub. I'd stop him. Other times he'd cut his arms and legs with razor blades, not enough to kill himself, but enough to get blood everywhere. He also plucked out most of his eyelashes, threw knives at pictures of himself, and went around saying he should be tortured to death.

"Once he gave me a gun and begged me to kill him. I didn't pull the trigger, of course, but he held my hand so tight I was afraid the gun would go off anyway.

"I felt so sorry for him then. I knew the way he was wasn't all his fault. After 'Nam, he'd isolate for days too, drinking and holding me hostage. Because he was an officer, when he'd call in sick, they believed him. They didn't know he was sitting on me in the living room for hours and not letting me go to the bathroom or take care of the kids.

"My three older children knew to go to a neighbor's house whenever he was into one of his moods. But my three-year-old was still around, in his room playing mostly. But every now and then he would come out and ask what we were doing on the floor. 'Daddy and Mommy are arm wrestling,' I'd say.

"There were other bizarre things too, like his insisting we make love with the lights on and the doors open, even when the kids were around, or opening the windows when it was below zero and making me freeze with him—or else."

Evelyn tried to talk to Hank's parents, but they were military and didn't want to face the fact that their son had PTSD and an alcohol problem. Evelyn approached her husband's commanding officer, asking him to urge her husband to seek help. But the commanding officer said that since her husband was an officer, he could not become involved and that if Evelyn continued to expose her husband's many problems, she would severely damage his military career.

For two years after her husband returned from Vietnam, Evelyn describes him as "unbalanced." There were two sides to her husband, the bad and the good. He could be so very loving and kind to her and the children, but then, turn around and choke her, or their youngest son, for wetting the bed, or any other reason that came up. This child also had a learning disability which the father could not tolerate or accept. When the child abuse became severe and Hank continued to refuse help, Evelyn finally packed her bags and left.

Evelyn was already separated from her husband upon coming to group. She came to group seeking greater understanding of PTSD and hoping to find ways of helping her husband, even though she was planning to divorce him. She was also seeking help for herself as she was coming out of her own numbing.

The extent of wife abuse in the military is unknown. Certain factors, common in the military, however, seem to affect the frequency and severity of abuse. Sociologist Murray Strauss found wife abuse to be more prevalent among families with two to five children and among families experiencing financial stress, frequent moves or separations, and isolation from peer and family support systems.[1]

According to a 1984 Army Family Advocacy Progress report, the majority of both military battered wives (some 65%) and military who batter (some 70%) are between 21 and 30 years old.[2] Furthermore, high school graduates are more likely to be spouse abusers than men with either more or less education.[3] With over half of all servicemen having a high school education and military training emphasizing the use of violence, the military wife is at a high risk for battering.

Yet official military statistics indicate a very low rate of spouse abuse and do not differentiate between families of Vietnam veterans and other military families. The rate is higher for overseas families (5%), probably due to the stresses associated with overseas postings.[4] Most experts, however, both within and outside the military, feel that these statistics grossly underestimate the extent of the problem.[5]

The same is true regarding civilian populations: most experts concur that the actual incidence of wife abuse is greater than the reported incidence, despite recent improvements and increased willingness to report spousal abuse. Similarly, in both civilian and military populations, the exact relationship between documented wife abuse and actual incidence of abuse is unknown.[6]

One of the major problems in estimating the extent of family violence in the military is the fact that although each branch of the military and the Department of Defense have a reporting system, the systems are inconsistent. Furthermore, "families, service providers and military personnel may be reluctant to identify or report domestic violence."[7]

If the civilian wife is reluctant to report abuse, due to shame, guilt, or fear of retaliation, how much more so the military battered wife? So often she desperately fears that reporting the abuse will jeopardize not only her husband's career, but her own financial security as a military dependent as well.

To avoid such consequences, many battered military wives do not seek help or turn to civilian resources instead. These civilian service centers, however, are under no obligation to report to the military and rarely do so.[8]

In perhaps the most exhaustive study of wife abuse in the Armed Forces completed to date, researchers L. West, William Turner, and E. Dunwoody of the Center for Women's Policy Studies in Washington, D.C., found that many cases of abuse go unreported because emergency room staff typically do not ask women if their injuries are the result of abuse.[9] (Although this report was completed in 1981, it is the only such report available as of the writing of this book.)

At the command level, there may be deliberate underreporting due to the stigma associated with abuse. According to Dr. Beryce MacLennan, "Chiefs of staff may not wish to give the impression that service life brutalizes individuals or places great stress on families or that their service has more violence than another."[10]

Like their civilian sisters, many military wives do not report abuse, because, on some level, they feel they "deserved it" or because they are not even aware that they are being abused. Unless the abuse is frequent and severe, they feel it doesn't "count." Yet under the UCMJ (Uniform Code of Military Justice), as under most state laws, it is a crime not only to abuse one's wife, but to threaten to do so. Although UCMJ does not consider spousal rape or indecent assault with the intent to rape punishable offenses, charges for forcible sodomy can be brought against abusive husbands under military law.[11]

Since 1990, domestic violence programs for abused military wives have grown. The problem today is not so much that services do not exist, but that military wives are still reluctant to report abuse or do not know where to start in seeking assistance. In addition, many wives still mistakenly believe that the violence will cease on its own, without outside intervention.

The days when military men could get by with almost murdering their wives are gone. While abusers are not always apprehended, anti-battering laws are on the books and in many cases are enforced, especially when the battering involves child abuse or child sexual assault.[12] Commanders can be charged for failing to conduct an inquiry into a battered military wife's complaint. In the West study, numerous military officers at a variety of bases voiced considerable concern about the detrimental effect of domestic violence on the serviceman's efficiency and on "morale and military readiness" in general.[13]

Usually military wives, like Evelyn, have appeared less disconcerted and disappointed by their husbands' numbing and other symptoms of PTSD than nonmilitary wives because, as military wives, they had learned to expect less from marriage than other women. Furthermore, during years of adapting to their husbands' many absences and the family's frequent relocations, many of the military wives had learned to become relatively emotionally self-sufficient. Often the military wife's strengths and self-reliance make her more tolerant of emotional distance and lack of communication within her marriage, more accepting of her husband's alcohol or drug addiction or his sexual flings, as well as of his PTSD.

Kitty, for example, was born in a small town in Kentucky. Her high school sweetheart, William, decided to join the military rather than fight a futile battle against the poverty of Appalachia. When he found out that he was going to be sent to Vietnam, he and Kitty married immediately as part of the glamour of a soldier going off to war.

William never talked about his Vietnam experiences, but going overseas was a culture shock for him. He had never been outside Kentucky and was naive in many ways. Although his Vietnam experience eroded many of his illusions about patriotism and becoming John Wayne, he decided to make the military his life. His only other option, he felt, was to join the unemployment lines in his hometown or settle for a low-paying, dead-end job like his father had.

As they traveled from base to base, Kitty was not only William's emotional support system, but his only tie to his past. There were only a few signs of PTSD until, some 10 years after the war, William decided to quit the Army. He was fed up with taking orders and had developed an intense hatred for one of his commanding officers. However, when William left the military, he began to experience some of the symptoms of PTSD more frequently, especially the nightmares. Since the military provides a supportive structure for military values, often men who served in Vietnam do not experience PTSD symptoms until they leave the military.

All along Kitty had not expected much emotionally from William. When she became a military wife, her rural tradition of female self-reliance and passivity matched perfectly with the military's expectations for wives. When William became depressed or abusive, Kitty did not go into shock. Growing up in an economically depressed area, she was used to unhappy, frustrated men, some of whom felt free to lash out at their wives. In her hometown, for example, wife beating was almost accepted and, as in many rural areas, there were few resources for abused women.

"You just don't talk about it" was the rule and that same rule applied in the military. Consequently, when William sometimes hit her, Kitty thought that hitting was a normal part of marriage which she was powerless, or had no right, to stop.

Another taboo subject was mental illness or emotional trouble. These were not talked about in Kitty's hometown or on base. Even while William was in the military and not at the height of his PTSD suffering, Kitty had noticed a few signs of emotional problems. Yet neither she nor William dared to break the taboo and seek help. Whenever she brought the subject up, William would go to bed or for a long walk.

Today William is back home in Kentucky—alone. Kitty is in college in a nearby state, pursuing a career of her choice, a career which she had postponed many times due to the military and her husband's problems. She now suffers from the fatigue, loneliness, and other hardships common to struggling single mothers. Yet she is certain that she did not want to resign herself to the limitations of her small town in Kentucky, nor to the limitations of a marriage with a husband whose long periods of emotional numbing were peppered with angry outbursts.

Even though Kitty is now divorced, she comes to group to better understand, and accept, what happened to her high school sweetheart. She also wants to better understand, and accept, herself—all of herself, even her fears and insecurities. While some women have difficulty accepting their strengths, Kitty has the opposite problem, accepting her feelings of helplessness and powerlessness. Since she was taught—by both her upbringing and the military—to keep such feelings to herself, it has been difficult for her to accept that at times she feels vulnerable or overloaded. She is afraid of being thought weak.

"I'm supposed to be strong all the time," she says. "In my hometown, women were supposed to take anything—the cold, the heat, the poverty, and even abuse—without complaining. I found the same expectations in the military. I had to 'hang tough' no matter what and accept whatever my husband was, or did. Now I feel I don't have to accept everything that comes my way, especially any threats or physical abuse."

Like Kitty, all but one of the military wives who have attended group report physical abuse as part of their marriages. In most instances the abuse was intermittent and confined to a few, significant episodes. In a few cases, when the wife was in the military herself, she physically fought back.

Helen exemplifies the contradiction of a military wife who is a high-ranking officer in her own right, but who at home is still "the wife." Yet Helen's submissive behavior at home, in contrast to her assertive behavior at work, is not truly a contradiction. As Del Martin explains in *Battered Women: Issues of Public Policy*, most women are "socialized to believe that their greatest achievement in life is marriage and motherhood and that failure of the marriage is the wife's personal failure."[14] A woman can easily hold a position of power and authority at work, but at home quickly resume the subordinate role for which she has been socialized from a young age.

Helen is now head nurse of a cancer ward. After Vietnam, her husband collapsed into an infantile, dependent role. He gladly did the dishes while she went to work. Every now and then he would attempt to work, but the stress from the job, combined with his PTSD, was too much for him.

At home, Helen's husband is restless. He expects her to be there for him when he wants her, leaving her little time for herself. Yet he is rarely concerned with her needs, or so it seems to Helen, except for those rare, but treasured moments, when it is obvious that he needs and cherishes her above all other human beings.

Helen resents her husband expecting her to be superwoman—to be able to handle the job, the home, the children, and him with no breaks and no complaints. But she also holds these expectations for herself and admits to being her own worst critic.

When Helen first came to group, she tried to help everyone else. She had done much reading on PTSD and spoke a strong feminist line. She was quick to tell other women not to "put up with it," and to put themselves, not their husbands and children, first for a change. She was also able to deeply feel the other women's anger and pain, but rarely acknowledged her own.

Helen had been a military wife before she decided to join the military herself. While her husband was in Vietnam (he served for two tours), she was busy advancing in rank. After Vietnam, her husband left the military, but he did not object to Helen continuing her military career. As both a military wife and a woman in a largely male-dominated group, she was trained and expected to be strong and independent, to hide her needs from others, especially her needs to be taken care of, to be protected, and to feel loved.

In her mind, as in the mind of many in the military, such needs were signs of weakness and cause for shame. Furthermore, as a child, she had been punished for showing her feelings and dependency needs. In her heart of hearts, however, even though she was almost 50 and considered herself liberated, she did want to lean on someone, "just a little bit." While she was extremely helpful and encouraging to the other women in group, taking their phone calls in the middle of the night, for example, Helen rarely called on the other women for support.

"If you can handle everything yourself, why do you come to group?" a group member once asked her.

Helen grudgingly admitted that she too needed help, and that having to be strong all the time had made her bitter and hard. Yet she saw no alternative to being an "iron woman." The standards which she felt imposed on her by the military were now a part of herself. She was jealous of the women in group who could cry, feel sorry for themselves, and express fears of "going crazy" or "falling apart."

"I want to be a basket case too, but I can't allow myself any of that," she explained. "I rigidly put my nose to the grindstone, day after day. There's no softness in me, no vulnerability. I don't like what I've become, but it isn't all my fault. Circumstances, like being a military wife, a wife of a Vietnam combat vet, and a military officer, have forced me to be like this.

"If I act any differently, femininely I call it, I'll be mocked at work. Also, it puts too much pressure on my husband if I show him I have needs. He can't take it when I have needs. He's the only one allowed to have needs. Yet I know that inside me there's a little girl aching to be held, aching to play. But I can't let her out. She has a lot of tears too, but she's not allowed to cry."

For the most part Helen continued to be as unselfish in group as she was in her personal life, rarely taking any group time to discuss her concerns. Once, however, the group encouraged her to take some of her own advice—focus on herself and plan some ways of nurturing herself which were not dependent on her husband. The most she could come up with were to insist on not being woken up in the middle of the night to hear war stories about Vietnam and on going to the grocery store only once a week, not whenever her husband or teenagers needed something. In fact, one of her teens could drive himself to the store and take over the shopping chore himself. Helen also decided to take some vacations by herself and to reconnect with relatives and old friends. After over a year in group, Helen also made some progress in accepting her dependency needs and feelings of helplessness as inevitable aspects of being human, rather than signs of personal failure.

Helen decided to confront her husband about two instances of physical abuse from the past. While her husband was not generally abusive, nor did she particularly anticipate any more beatings, she made it clear that she had changed from the time he first assaulted her. Then she had accepted the abuse without comment, not even going to the hospital when she needed to because he felt it would have endangered his military career. But now he had to listen: should he ever lay a hand on her again, if he did not seek help immediately and stay in therapy until he learned to control his aggressiveness, she would be gone, taking her children and her paycheck with her. In fact, their oldest son had threatened to run away from home if he had to witness another episode of domestic violence.

Summary

Military Vietnam wives are often strangled by the expectation that they be silent heroines and unacknowledged pillars of strength. They also tend to suffer from isolation when they encounter disparagement of Vietnam veterans or a lack of understanding of PTSD within the military. If their husbands are alcoholic or abusive, their isolation may be extreme. Since drinking tends to be accepted in the military, the military wife must often bear the brunt of her husband's alcoholic behavior alone. Similarly, if she is being abused, she may feel she must endure this to protect her husband's image. In recent years, however, there has been an increase in services available to the abused military wife.

The military wife is used to managing the household, rearing the children, and coping with all the daily crises of living. Since these responsibilities are a part of her role as a military wife, when and if her husband does not take part in these tasks as a result of his PTSD, she may accept that as natural.

She may be accustomed to a marriage where her emotional needs are not always met. The frequent travel and other separations that are part of military life have often forced the military wife to meet her emotional needs by herself or to deny them altogether. This geographic instability also hinders her from establishing friendships and other roots and increases her dependence on her husband at the same time it prevents her husband from being physically present, much less emotionally available.

When this isolation is compounded by the emotional numbing that is part of PTSD, the military Vietnam wife may feel, and actually be, emotionally alone. If she has internalized the "strong woman" norms demanded of military wives, she may be reluctant to admit to her loneliness or to any of her other emotional distress. All wives of men with PTSD have a stressful existence. Military wives, however, bear an especially difficult burden.

9

Wives of African-American, Native American, and Hispanic Vietnam Veterans

Coping with PTSD is like coping with racism. You need a lot of faith and a lot of hope because it's a constant uphill battle. As the wife of an African-American combat veteran, I know my husband is blighted with two ills—PTSD and an intense rage at the racism in our society—the racism which burned African-American homes while he was burning Vietnamese ones fighting for America and the racism that kept him from getting a job when he got back to America.

When Graham got off the plane after serving two tours of duty in Vietnam and went out to celebrate with his buddies, he was refused service at the restaurant. The manager even gave him the finger. Graham's white buddies were ready to pounce on the manager but Graham wouldn't let them. At the next restaurant they went to, Graham was served dirty water in a greasy glass and a beer with spit in it.

I found out about these incidents years later. Like so many Vietnam veterans, my husband never talked about his experiences. I only heard about them when his nightmares got out of control and he had to seek help. I don't know why he didn't tell me sooner. Maybe he thought we had enough problems or maybe he was trying to protect me.

I, like many African-American Vietnam wives, am also a child of the

1950s. The fifties, for the most part, were better times economically for African-Americans. Many men were able to work two jobs. They were paid less than a white with one job, but with their wives' income, many African-American families, like mine, lived comfortably, by pre-integration standards, that is.

Today, I expect and want financial and emotional security, just like a white woman. But PTSD has damaged my husband's ability to feel, and racism has destroyed his peace of mind. Unfortunately, when he's angry, his enemy no longer has a face or name. Since I'm the only one around, sometimes he blames me for the "system" or for what somebody in the war did or didn't do. I can tell when he's angry because he totally shuts down and withdraws from me.

Like last week. Someone walked into my husband's office and asked to speak to the manager. When my husband said that he was the manager, the person said, "No, I want to talk to the real manager."

I asked my husband if he was upset by this incident. "No, no, it's okay," he said. But I know he's upset and hurt and doesn't know what or who to blame—the system or himself.

When the white women in group talk about their husbands, I understand because I feel that way too. In a lot of ways, our marriage problems are the same. Yet I'm different. As an African-American woman, I have borne the brunt of both racism and sexism. My husband is different too. He had a double dose of rejection; first by the whites and second by the African-Americans who thought he was a traitor for fighting the Vietnamese when he should have stayed home and fought for civil rights.

I'm also different in that I never expected a life of luxury. I expected to work both before and after marriage and childbirth. Having to work was a given, not a blessing, not a tragedy, just a given. For example, in college I was one of only eight African-Americans on campus. I wanted to go to college to get a decent job. My friends—the white ones—had no intention of working after marriage. The only one who was serious about education as a means to a job was one girl whose widowed mother had had to work to support the family.

My conflict today is not accepting that I have to work, but harmonizing my independence and self-reliance with my marriage. It was my family tradition and my church that instilled in me the ability and the willingness to work to improve my situation.

So here I am, trying to be a so-called "modern" African-American woman with all these trends and at the same time struggling with Graham's PTSD. I know what my goal is. I want more sharing, financially, emotionally, and sexually in my marriage.

—Wife of an African-American combat vet

Bessie Taylor had three sons: Ross, Mitchell, and Sam. Although she worked long hours for not much over the minimum wage, she considered herself fortunate. For her, changing sheets and sweeping floors at a class B hotel in East St. Louis, Missouri was one step above tilling her sharecropper parents' fields just outside Birmingham, Alabama.

Her husband, Gus, was a janitor. But Bessie knew Gus was more than a janitor. During World War II, Gus, like many African-Americans had served valiantly (although in a segregated unit). Gus had wanted to make the military his life, but after he saw white soldiers being given preferential medical treatment on the battlefield and experienced color prejudice in other ways, he decided to quit the military as soon as the war was over. Furthermore, during his military career, he was accused of not being a "real American" because he was African-American and had slightly Asian features. Gus was the frequent butt of racial jokes. In addition, he had never received his well-deserved, often promised, promotion.[1]

However, Gus hid his bitterness and neither he nor Bessie was anti-American at all. In fact, they were very patriotic. While they didn't like racism, they accepted it as inevitable and raised their three sons to be God-fearing loyal citizens.

In 1959, when their oldest son, Ross, decided to pursue a career in the military, neither parent objected. The position of African-Americans in the military had improved since World War II. Although racism was far from dead, in general the military was now more integrated than ever before. African-Americans were even being allowed into the Marine Corps.[2]

After the bombing of North Vietnam in 1965, Ross was sent to Vietnam. Every night Bessie Taylor prayed on her knees that her son would return alive. The entire congregation of her church prayed with her, for they all knew that at that time 25% of the American death toll in Vietnam was African-American.[3] In contrast, young African-Americans constituted only 11% of the American population.

Some claimed that this disproportionately high African-American death rate was the result of African-American soldiers, like Ross, who heroically volunteered for combat duty. Others, however, attributed this death toll to racism.[4] Both radical and not so radical African-American groups claimed that African-Americans "were being drafted for genocidal purposes. Just to get rid of . . . " the African-American male.[5] This message was echoed by Hanoi Hannah, a North Vietnamese broadcaster who appealed to African-American soldiers to go home because, in her view, the American involvement in Vietnam was a racist, capitalist plot to eliminate African-Americans.[6]

In 1965, the African-American death rate was so high that the Pentagon deliberately reduced the number of African-American soldiers on the front line.[7] But this did not quell the Taylors' fear for Ross. When Mitchell wanted to follow in his brother's footsteps and enlist, the Taylors said "No!"

At that time, as part of the war on poverty, the military was actively encouraging African-Americans to join. In fact, during the mid-1960s, African-Americans were being "massively recruited." For many young African-American men, the military offered relatively fewer obstacles to economic and social advancement than other careers and occupations. Great numbers of African-American youth "responded to the call." [8]

Despite his parents' objections, Mitchell desperately wanted to join the military, not only for economic reasons, but for patriotic ones. Even though African-Americans had been mistreated in America, Mitchell loved America and believed in the cause of freedom and democracy. His parents agreed with him philosophically, but they still begged him not to join, especially since Ross had signed up for a second year in Vietnam.

Mitchell obeyed their wishes, made plans to marry, and began working in a print shop.

One month before the assassination of the Rev. Dr. Martin Luther King, Jr., Ross Taylor was shot to death, not by the Viet Cong, but by "friendly fire." The Taylors were not given this information, however. Instead they received a letter announcing their son's death as a hero. Gus Taylor pulled his hair, cursed God, and burned the letter, along with his Bible and all his souvenirs from World War II. Bessie Taylor also pulled her hair, but she would not curse God. Instead she prayed to understand the reason for her son's death, which only further enraged her husband.

Meanwhile, Mitchell rushed down to the Marine recruiting office and signed up for combat duty in Vietnam. There was no stopping him now. Even if his parents continued to oppose him, he would go to Vietnam and kill as many "gooks" as he could find to avenge his brother's death. Also, being one of the first African-American Marines seemed far more glamorous to Mitchell than pushing cartons in a print shop where he was often called "boy."

Mitchell quickly married his fiance, Sandra, and shortly thereafter, with his mother's Bible in his pocket, landed in Vietnam, unconsciously hoping to find his brother there, or at least, to discover more about how he had been killed. But the Vietnam which Mitchell encountered in late 1968 and early 1969 was not the same Vietnam as his brother had seen in 1965. Although the African-American death toll was now reduced, it was still disproportionately high. As Wallace Terry, author of *Bloods*, points out, by 1969 career African-American soldiers were being replaced by African-American draftees, many of whom were unwilling to adopt "Uncle Tom" roles. Due to the civil rights movement at home, especially after the assassination of Dr. Martin Luther King, Jr., African-American soldiers were more openly disgruntled about racism in the military than ever before. When they observed discrimination in positioning, medals, decorations, and promotions, many spoke out.[9]

As a result, they were often given "bad paper," that is, less than honorable discharges. In fact, African-Americans "received a grossly disproportionate number of dishonorable or 'bad paper' discharges," which negatively affected their veteran's benefits and career opportunities upon return home.[10]

Furthermore, there were numerous racial incidents, not so much on the front lines, but in the rear.[11] As Dr. Irving Allen, an African-American psychiatrist explains, "Conflict was expressed through graffiti, segregation, fraggings, and fights. For many men it was as if there two wars—one against the enemy and the other against other Americans."[12]

Some racial incidents occurred during basic training when African-American soldiers heard the Vietnamese people being ridiculed, belittled, and dehumanized as "gooks" who only deserved to be killed.[13] Some of the racial epithets and slurs used against the Vietnamese were strikingly familiar to those used against African-Americans. The slogan, "The only good gook is a dead one," was all too similar to "The only good nigger is a dead one."

But Mitchell closed his ears to the voices of African-American militancy. His goal was to avenge his brother's death. He jumped into combat with a ferocity that earned him much respect. In the jungles of Vietnam, Mitchell became close with many of his comrades, regardless of their race. He even became friends with a card-carrying member of the Ku Klux Klan, who changed his view of African-Americans after seeing Mitchell risk his life to save a white comrade.

When Mitchell's unit encountered mutilated American bodies (both African-American and white), they sometimes retaliated with the indiscriminate killing of civilians and livestock, other pointless destruction, the raping of Vietnamese women, and other violent acts. Although this violated Mitchell's religious upbringing, by now he was so psychically numb that he ignored the Bible in his pocket. He joined in the violence without thought—until he and his unit reached a village where some of the peasants had fuller features and darker skin than other Vietnamese groups.

As Mitchell's buddies forced a peasant to unearth his hidden rice and other food supplies, Mitchell remembered how in Alabama the KKK had forced his grandmother to dig up some of her hidden produce and belongings. And when Mitchell's buddies began to rape the peasant's curly-haired, full-lipped daughter (who reminded Mitchell of his wife) and forced the weeping peasant to watch, Mitchell remembered that his grandparents were poor peasants too. Furthermore, he had heard stories of how African-American men had had to endure the torture of watching their sisters, mothers, and wives be assaulted by marauding whites. "What if that was my mother or my Sandra?" he thought.

"Come on, Mitchell. Join in. What's wrong with you? Are you a faggot?" his friends called.

Despite his new awareness, Mitchell did not have the strength to resist the group. But when the peasants were about to be shot, Mitchell urged his friends to go shoot some water buffalo instead.

Full of self-hate, Mitchell threw his mother's Bible down the village well, which had just been poisoned by the American troops. Shaking with anxiety, he wanted to scoop up some of the poisoned water and drink it. But in her last letter, Sandra had informed him that he was now the father of twin boys. Mitchell decided to live, not for himself, nor for Sandra, whom he doubted he could ever love again, but for his two boys, one of whom was named after his dead brother, Ross.

Sandra's letter had also stated that his brother, Sam, had recently been arrested for simply driving through an all-white neighborhood in suburban St. Louis, probably due to his participation in a civil rights rally. Furthermore, the home of one of Sandra's relatives had just been bombed.

Sitting at the well, frozen with pain, Mitchell began to ask himself the same questions many African-American soldiers asked themselves: "What am I doing here? Why am I killing and hurting people who look more like me than the people who are hurting my relatives and friends back home?"[14]

As numerous studies have shown, compared to white Vietnam veterans, African-American Vietnam veterans suffer not only from higher rates of PTSD, but tend to have endured postwar stress symptoms for longer periods of time since the war.[15] The significantly greater readjustment problems of African-American Vietnam veterans can be attributed to the fact that they have had to deal with two stressors: first, the war, and second, racism, both in the military and back home. In addition, they have had to deal with the guilt and conflict inherent in the "gook identification" syndrome.[16]

According to psychologist Parson, the "gook identification" syndrome is the "conscious and unconscious emotional identification by African-American soldiers with the devalued, maligned, abused and helpless aspects of the Vietnamese people."[17] Even if the African-American veteran did not participate in any combat or abusive violence against the Vietnamese, he often experienced a sense of shame and considerable confusion about the purpose and morality of the project he was involved with.

In general African-Americans were less able to dehumanize the enemy than whites because the Vietnamese, like the African-Americans, were not white, were poor, and were struggling for their independence. African-American soldiers could also identify with the "tribulations, misery, and general suffering of the Vietnamese at the hands of a super power."[18] Research has found that African-American soldiers were more likely to express positive or neutral feelings toward the Vietnamese than white soldiers, were more likely to oppose the war, and were more emotionally disturbed by abusive violence and atrocities committed against the Vietnamese than were whites.[19]

For example, during his tour of duty, Mitchell encountered barracks decorated with the Confederate flag and GIs from other units who called him "boy" or "nigger." He was tempted to fight these other soldiers, but, remembering his goals, held back. After returning to the United States, he also encountered the Confederate flag, this time behind the desk of the first employer from whom he sought work.

"I had been promised the job over the phone, but the minute the manager saw my face, he decided he didn't really need any more help right then," Mitchell explains.

As Mitchell went from one job interview to the next, encountering one subtle form of racism after another, he remembered some little boys he had seen in Vietnam. They would run from one GI to the next, trying to sell their mothers or their sisters. Oh, how he used to laugh at them. "Animals, yellow animals," he secretly thought.

But now on the streets himself, almost begging for work, Mitchell felt that he was in the same position as those beggar boys. Mitchell's guilt about having hurt Vietnamese people was only compounded when an African-American employer refused to hire him because he had gone off to Vietnam and "killed his own kind." At times Mitchell felt that admitting that he was a Vietnam vet was like building the very gallows on which he could be hung.

Nevertheless, according to General Westmoreland and Wallace Terry, the service of African-American troops in Vietnam was superior.[20] However, African-American troops, like white troops, seldom received a hero's welcome and, like their white counterparts, they often returned home to families that did not want to hear about the war. In addition, some African-American Vietnam veterans had to deal with the taunts and rejection of those African-Americans who believed that African-

Americans who fought in Vietnam had betrayed their race by participating in a "white man's war," a war that was not only immoral, but illegal.

At the same time, employers were sometimes reluctant to hire the African-American Vietnam veteran, not only for racial reasons, but because he had served in Vietnam and was therefore potentially dangerous. To compound the problem, unemployment was higher in most areas than when the vet had left for Vietnam, especially if he had come from an economically deprived neighborhood. Studies completed in 1969 and 1970 showed that African-American Vietnam vets had double the unemployment rate of white Vietnam veterans or earned substantially less.[21]

Terry concludes, ". . . What can be said about the dysfunction of Vietnam veterans in general can be doubled in its impact upon most African-Americans: they hoped to come home to more than they had before; they came back to less. . . . The doors to the Great Society had been shut."[22]

Even before Mitchell returned from Vietnam and began to scream from nightmares, turning to alcohol in order to sleep, Sandra knew there was no such thing as a "handsome African-American knight" who would whisk her away from the realities of life into a land of bliss. Although she was pumped with the same romantic mythology as the white women in the group—that the right man would fill her life with excitement and meet all of her needs—Sandra was also raised in a tradition where most of the women worked and often functioned as the major, if not the sole, provider of the family, both emotionally and financially.

Throughout American history, for a variety of reasons, African-Americans often found it difficult, if not impossible, to find meaningful or productive work. Many could not find any work at all. The African-American woman, however, could almost always find work in white people's houses or in other low-paying, dead-end jobs.

African-American women, however, suffered from a double jeopardy. They were both African-American and female.[23] Like many women, they were often paid less than men for the same work or relegated to jobs without any possibility of advancement. As of December 1993, the Women's Bureau of the U.S. Department of Labor notes an earnings gap between men and women. ". . . No matter how we measure them, women's earnings are below those received by men . . . In 1992, for those receiving hourly rates, women's median hourly earnings were 79.4 percent of men's." The same discrepancies occur when considering weekly and annual earnings. The "earnings gap for hourly wages was 20.6 percent; for weekly earnings, 24.6 percent; and for annual earnings 29.4 percent." In general, African-American women earned less than white men, white women, or African-American men.[24]

Table 1.   1991 Median Earnings—Year-Round Full-Time Workers[25]

All women	$20,553
White women	$20,794
African-American women	$18,720
Hispanic women	$16,244
All men	$29,421
White men	$30,266
African-American men	$22,075
Hispanic men	$19,771

In sum, "despite their increasing educational attainment and their strong continued labor force experience, African-American women are still more likely than white women to be unemployed, to be in low paying jobs, and to account for a larger proportion of the poor."[26]

Sandra's mother, for example, supported a husband and four children on the salary of a laundress. Although Sandra's father sought work, East St. Louis was an economically depressed area and he could only find work sporadically. Like many of her neighbors, Sandra's mother accepted her role as the primary, and sometimes sole, support of the family and as emotional caretaker of the family. As research has shown, historically African-American women have held jobs outside the home while simultaneously seeking to fulfill domestic roles.[27]

Sandra's mother maintained her courage and strength through her faith and involvement in the church, where she was somebody important, director of the choir, not just a maid. She was not anti-male, but she taught all her daughters not to put their faith in men, but in themselves and in a spiritual being. She also warned her daughters never to give up all their money to a man, but keep some of their earnings for themselves.

Sandra was brought up in the church and she believed deeply. But she did not want to live her mother's life, struggling for every nickel and dime. In Mitchell she saw an ambition and determination that matched her own. When he asked her to marry him, she immediately agreed, even though she was only 19 and had hopes of going to college. She never dreamt Mitchell would lose his ambition, as well as his faith, in Vietnam.

The arrival of twin sons destroyed her plans for schooling, but not her dream of social and economic advancement. While Mitchell was in Vietnam, she worked as a salesgirl, never expecting not to work just because she had babies. In group, Sandra, like the other African-American women, never expressed the deep guilt which some of the white women have felt about leaving their children to work outside the home. While the African-American women regarded their maternal role as primary and had some home-career conflicts, they were of a different order of magnitude than the conflicts of the white women. Somehow, the African-American women, probably due to their historical role as workers, experienced their work role as less abnormal or deviant.

Sandra worked hard, caught on quickly, and, as a result of the increased opportunities made available to minorities in the early 1970s, slowly advanced to a supervisory position. When the department store went so far as to open up their managerial training to African-Americans, Sandra was the first to enroll and quickly rose to the position of manager of several departments.

But Sandra did not mention her vocational achievements to Mitchell. Nor did she tell him when she began to make more money than he. She kept part of her earnings in a secret account. She did not feel she was being deceptive; she simply did not want to insult Mitchell's masculinity.

During the civil rights movement, Sandra had been exposed to African-American liberation ideology and other ideologies which analyzed how the African-American man had been crippled, if not "castrated," by society.[28] Sometimes it was forgotten that the African-American woman had also been persecuted and "castrated," yet she also was viewed as the "matriarch" who was a "castrator of Black men."[29] Sandra did not want to fall into that category, especially since her husband had once implied that she was able to maintain her job only because she was "high yellow" and because she was willing to act subservient to whites.

True, Sandra did overlook some of the racial slurs that came her way. But she did so not out of meekness, but out of self-interest. Her goal was economic advancement and security. She wanted to move her family out of their roach-infested apartment in East St. Louis to something better. In Sandra's view, there was nothing to be gained by "acting touchy" and fighting a losing battle against the system.

Furthermore, in her case, the system had not treated her as harshly as it had her husband. She had been able to take advantage of some of the doors opened to African-Americans in the 1970s. In contrast, her husband, embittered by Vietnam, angrily refused to use his veteran's educational and medical benefits.

During the war, Mitchell was run over by an army jeep whose driver, high on drugs, had lost control of his vehicle. Mitchell's skull was fractured. He lay in a coma for several weeks. Upon reviving, he had lost much of his memory. Three years and seven operations later, Mitchell's memory and other mental abilities were restored. There was no evidence of the accident save for slight nervous tremors.

When he applied for compensation, the doctors were divided. Half attributed the tremors to his military experience, half to his drinking. In addition, Mitchell's military records were burned in a St. Louis fire. After these experiences, Mitchell vowed never again to ask the government for help.

When Sandra wanted to leave the slums of East St. Louis, Mitchell objected. How could they afford a home across the river? Sandra lied. She told Mitchell that her mother had given her the down payment for the home. Mitchell knew it was a lie, but he did not contradict Sandra. He argued that, as man of the house, he didn't want any handouts from her family, just like he didn't want any handouts from the government. But Sandra felt they had to move for the sake of the children and Mitchell relented.

After recovering from his last operation, Mitchell worked full time but his career advancement was hampered by his depression. Even though he had a high I.Q., he could not think beyond showing up at work on time, doing what he had to do, then going home to drink and forget it all. Basically, Mitchell hated his job. He was acutely aware of every form of racial discrimination, both subtle or overt. In Sandra's view, he sometimes imagined discriminatory incidents or remarks and made mountains out of molehills. In Mitchell's view, Sandra was naive.

Furthermore, Mitchell could not identify with those African-Americans in his office whom he felt fit the stereotype of the African-American male as "shiftless and lazy." He especially could not tolerate African-Americans who had not been politicized through some major experience with discrimination and who saw him as too serious, as "thinking too much," or as "living in the past." In addition, Mitchell felt avoided by both African-Americans and whites. Mitchell felt that they were all afraid of him because they knew he was a combat vet.

A major issue in Sandra and Mitchell's marriage was money. Even though Mitchell's drinking was not yet interfering with his work performance, alcohol was becoming an increasingly large item on the family's budget. Mitchell drank alone, but he also drank at a local bar, where he liked to treat others, especially other Vietnam veterans. He also liked to send extravagant gifts to his parents and his brother Ross's widow.

Sandra smoldered at the bills, but said nothing. She knew that when he treated his war buddies or sent gifts to relatives, he felt powerful, like a "real man." "I can't take that away from him," she'd say in group, until the day she discovered that there wasn't enough money for the basic bills.

At this point, Sandra felt she had to take action, but she could not confront her husband. Although she obviously "wore the pants" in the family, and Mitchell would do whatever she wanted, she did not want to "castrate" him or "emasculate" him by restricting the amount of money he could spend on liquor or on gifts to his relatives.

As usual, whenever she felt stuck between her role as family caretaker and her role as submissive wife, she decided to pray about what to do. Sandra prayed about almost everything, especially Mitchell's healing. She was certain that if only she prayed hard enough, Mitchell would eventually seek treatment for his alcoholism and his PTSD. Meanwhile, she was doubling up on her church activities, not only for purposes of spiritual growth, but because the church helped fill many of her other needs. Although she rarely admitted it, Sandra was lonely. Mitchell left her alone much of the time and church helped fill her emotional and social needs, as well as her spiritual ones.

While some African-American veterans emerged from their Vietnam experience with a renewed and deepened faith in God or a Higher Power, others, like Mitchell, became cynical and suffered from a deep spiritual despair.[30] Mitchell refused to attend church with Sandra or with his mother. He never participated in grace at family mealtime, nor would he tuck the children in bed because prayers were said, which greatly angered Sandra.

Eventually Mitchell stopped eating with the family and Sandra moved out of the bedroom. His screaming and sobbing during nightmares kept her up at night. Also, she did not like to be with him while he was drinking. While she rarely refused him sex, she did not want to put herself in a position where sex would be automatic.

Sandra took her sons to church often, for religious purposes, but because also she felt that her sons would be exposed to many strong African-American men there, men with a positive outlook on life. Mitchell objected. He did not want his sons to be "brainwashed." But this argument, like most others between Sandra and Mitchell, ended in a stalemate.

Sandra and Mitchell rarely talked. While Sandra was able to express her feelings, Mitchell could not relate to her on an emotional level. He could share with his mother, however, and with some of his female cousins. Sandra resented that he would not be open to her and that she knew very little about her husband's Vietnam experience. But she felt it would not be productive to press Mitchell or insist that he talk to her.

Although Sandra and Mitchell had little emotional communication, they did have frequent verbal conflicts over money and sex, with Mitchell wanting more sex and no limitations on his spending. But these conflicts masked the more complex psychological problems and power struggles between them.

Mitchell wanted to assert himself as head of the household. However, after seeing how women were treated in Vietnam, he did not want to bully his wife. Furthermore, he had utmost respect for Sandra. She had been faithful to him during his absence, had nursed him through his years of surgery, and had been a good wife and mother as well as an excellent provider.

Sandra also represented to him the spirituality which he had lost. Although Mitchell had given up on God, the second before he was hit by the jeep in Vietnam, he had prayed for help. Sandra told her church friends that it was a miracle that Mitchell had not been killed. But Mitchell reminded her that he had prayed for his brother Ross and Ross died anyway. So had many others died despite the prayers of their relatives. Actually, Mitchell didn't know what to believe about God. Yet a small part of him wished to regain his former faith. Hence he clung to Sandra and did not want to oppose her.

Sandra, on the other hand, was hesitant to leave Mitchell because she knew that African-American women outnumbered African-American men to such an extent that if she left Mitchell, she might never remarry or find another man. Yet, painful as it would be, she knew she could make it on her own, without one. Besides, Mitchell was but a shadow in her life anyway. In addition, she had tasted the power of self-determination. She was not only a successful mother, but a successful career woman. Her major problem was that while she was clearly in charge at home, she felt she had to act dependent and submissive for the sake of her husband's ego and her sons' developing masculine egos. If she "castrated" her husband, she would also be "castrating" her sons. Also, she did not want to see her husband go down the tubes.

On the other hand, she felt morally responsible to protect her sons from their father's cynicism and negativity and the family's budget from the potentially ruinous effects of alcoholism.

Like many of the military wives who have attended group, Sandra did not have, or did not admit to having, high or romantic expectations of marriage. She would often say that if only Mitchell gave up drinking, was willing to join in at least one family activity a week, and would talk to her, even about minor matters, she would be content. Deep emotional intimacy she could not imagine, much less hope for. Turning to Mitchell for emotional support also seemed like an impossibility.

While it is difficult to make generalizations about such a diverse and socially mobile group as African-American women, one consistent impression of the African-American women who have sought help is their high level of functioning and capacity for work. Yet, in meeting Sandra and other extremely functional, well-balanced African-Americans, the psychological costs for all the coping they have been expected to do and have done are not readily apparent. Sandra, for example, came to group extremely skeptical. She didn't believe much in psychotherapy. Furthermore, she certainly didn't believe it was she that needed help, only Mitchell.

Much like her mother and Mitchell's mother, Sandra grew up submerging her own needs. Whenever feelings of helplessness or personal insecurity would arise within her, she would reject them. Such feelings were not acceptable and they would certainly not help her in her struggle for survival.

Like many of the African-American women who have attended group, Sandra had great difficulty sharing her fears and stating her personal needs for attention, comfort, and support. She has never cried in group nor lost control of herself at home. While some of the white women openly weep in group and admit to having "hysterical fits" where they would destroy their husbands' belongings, smash plates, or run around saying they are going to run away from home, so far no African-American woman has behaved or reported behaving in such a manner.

Part of the African-American woman's reluctance to share may be cultural. As psychologist Erwin Randolph Parson explains, African-Americans in therapy may show less emotion than whites because, during the centuries of slavery, as well as afterward, they learned to wear a mask.[31] This mask served an important purpose for it hid "from the white man the extent and intensity of their (the African American's) feelings of frustration and the anger that went along with this."[32] In addition, in the days of slavery, the only possessions slave owners could not take from African-Americans were their "inner feelings, thoughts, and beliefs." Therefore, "for many African-Americans sharing too much too soon with a therapist is not only culturally impossible but is an indication of a failure of family tradition, as well as a sign of mental disease."[33] For the African-American Vietnam veteran, sharing is often complicated by the "additional mental burden of shame at having killed third world brothers and sisters in the war."[34] For his wife, sharing personal problems in a predominantly white group run by a white therapist may also be extremely difficult. The African-American woman may fear that she will be adversely judged by the others, including other

African-American women, or she may feel disloyal to her husband if she shares her marital problems with whites.

For example, approximately one-fourth of the African-American wives seen were in battering or prebattering relationships. But they took longer to share their situation with the group than white women in similar binds, because, as they stated, they did not want to perpetuate the stereotype of the African-American man as a violence-prone individual. In addition, some were more reluctant to call the police than white women. While battered women frequently are reluctant to call the police, some African-American women voiced an additional concern. They were hesitant to turn their husbands in to the authorities because they did not trust what would happen to a African-American man in the hands of the police. Involving the police was, for some of the women, not only a violation of their loyalty toward their husbands, but toward their race.[35] In addition, some women felt the police would fail to protect them because of their color.

Some of the African-American abused women, however, would head straight for the phone the minute their husbands would raise their fists. A number have been extremely assertive in obtaining protection orders and other legal help. However, more than the white women, African-American women tended to fear entanglements with bureaucracies and authorities. When some of them left their husbands, they did so quietly, without involving attorneys, police, or mental health professionals.

In general, the African-American women I have seen appear less conflicted about combining motherhood with work roles. They have tended to express less anxiety and guilt about pursuing careers or working outside the home. In addition, they seem to suffer less from fear of success than white women, who are often afraid of losing their femininity if they successfully compete in previously predominantly male arenas. However some women, like Sandra, have difficulty in that they want to maintain their self-reliance and independence, while at the same time maintaining relationships with their husbands.

Although all the women who attend group need help in differentiating which of their problems are due to internal conflicts, which are due to their husbands' PTSD, and which are due to external realities, the African-American woman can also examine the role of racism or racial conflicts in her life, and in the life of her husband. While not all of the woman's problems can be attributed to racial factors, some are. She may need to acknowledge how her life has been affected by social forces outside of herself.

While the African-American woman should feel free to discuss racial concerns, it cannot be assumed that all her concerns are racial. If she does not want to discuss any racial conflicts, she should not be pressured to do so. Perhaps she does not need, or want, help in this area. Furthermore, she may be uncomfortable discussing racial problems or differences if the group is predominantly non-African-American.

She may also be hesitant to discuss racial matters, because at times she may be confused about the role of racism in her life, as well as in the life of her husband. "I don't want to be paranoid," said Doris, "but when my supervisor reprimands me, I'm never sure if his complaints are legitimate or if he's picking on me because I'm African-American." Doris readily admits that sometimes she fails to complete all that is technically required of her. "But the books are never thrown at the whites or the Orientals in the office—only the African-Americans."

In therapy, Doris has had the courage to take a good hard look at her behavior and identify the ways, both large and small, in which she may be contributing to tensions between her supervisor and herself. At the same time, however, she has finally mustered the courage to stand up to, rather than accept, certain racist and sexist practices and attitudes at the office.

Her husband, Fred, however, either forgets that many problems have racial, rather than personal, origins and drowns in self-blame, or he tends to blame almost all his problems on racism and forgets to look at himself. Either way, he is left feeling hopeless and powerless.

Doris' fiance died in Vietnam. She was still wearing black when she met Fred, soon after he returned from Vietnam. During their many years of marriage, Doris spent countless hours trying to talk Fred out of his paralyzing fear that "the system was out to get him." While Doris does not deny the existence of racism, she feels that Fred has lost many job opportunities simply because his attitude communicates a considerable amount of underlying anger as well as a sense of defeatism. Doris does not accompany Fred on his interviews. However, she can tell that he is alienating prospective employers simply by the way he speaks and carries himself while talking on the phone with them.

Whenever she feels he might be receptive to her advice, she gently suggests that he might be setting himself up for failure by anticipating discrimination or other forms of rejection and tries to encourage him to think about what he might be doing to hurt his chances for success. She also tries to pass on some interview tips.

Sometimes Fred listens. Other times his smoldering anger at the racism he has encountered, both in the military and afterward, shifts onto Doris. He has never hit her, but he has verbally mocked her and accused her of "selling out."

"You have the wrong enemy!" she'll shout back, but Fred still resents that while he was in the rice paddies, Doris and other African-American women were going to school or moving ahead in good-paying jobs. In contrast, he feels that Vietnam has delayed his career development, not one year, but 10.

Upon his return from Vietnam, Fred tried to use his benefits to go to college. But the anti-veteran attitude of many college students drove him from school and into the police department. There he worked hard as a front line cop only to be repeatedly turned down for promotion. In his particular precinct, only Irish Catholics received promotion.

Fred quit in disgust and was unemployed for several years. As he struggled with depression and with doors closed to him because of his race and his status as a veteran, he tried to get compensation for a lower back problem he felt was war related. The government, however, was not in agreement and there were numerous phone calls and letters about his claim. Every time a letter arrived, Fred was certain the person writing was spying on him or out to get him.

"It's only a form letter from someone behind a desk," Doris would point out. "Don't take everything so personally. Whoever wrote this letter doesn't even know you're African-American."

But it was difficult for Fred not to personalize form letters or any other kind of interaction with a bureaucracy. The only persons he trusted were his mother and Doris.

Doris understood Fred's dependence on her but it exhausted her. She became weary of having to constantly reassure Fred that he was safe, but she never complained. She knew that Fred had had a particularly rough time in Vietnam, not only because he had served on the front lines, but because at one point he had been called upon to help quell rioting African-American troops.

"I don't think he'll ever get over having to hurt some of the brothers. He was on both sides, but on no side, and both sides made threats on his life. Fred's greatest fear is that someday he'll accidentally run into someone from that part of his past."

When Doris first came to group, she was sad, not angry. Whenever Fred encountered yet another frustration or failure, she would wrap the black kerchief from her fiance's funeral around her hair and grieve. Fred, on the other hand, had difficulty feeling raw grief. At times it seemed as if Doris was doing his grieving for him. Every time, she would pull Fred through his disappointment. Then, when he was back on his feet, she would collapse into a short-term depression that caused her to miss a few days of work. She also developed insomnia, was easily startled, and began worrying that she too had PTSD.

At first Doris felt her only hope was to convince Fred to return to school. His GI benefits had expired, but she had been setting aside money and acquired a minority loan for him. With Doris's support and the help of several Vet Center counselors, Fred was able to complete some legal training. He is currently working for a firm which helps disadvantaged groups. He is productive and effective on the job and grateful to have found a constructive outlet for his anger and his pain.

Wives of Hispanic Veterans

Like African-American Vietnam veterans, Hispanic Vietnam veterans constitute a minority within a minority in the U.S. Also like the African-American Vietnam veteran, the Hispanic Vietnam veteran often suffered from economic and educational disadvantages prior to the war, from the "gook identification syndrome" and various forms of discrimination during the war, and from economic and vocational distress following the war.[36] In Vietnam, writes Harrington in the National Hispanic PTSD Conference, "Hispanic veterans . . . suffered the highest ratio of casualties of any community in the nation. Hispanics were 7% of all troops and 20% of all killed. One of two Hispanics who went to Vietnam served in a combat unit. One out of every five Hispanics who went to Vietnam was KIA (Killed In Action). One of three was WIA (Wounded in Action). Discrimination against Hispanics began right with the recruitment process. For example, in New Mexico in 1970 Mexicans were 27% of the population, 69% of all draftees and 44% of all combat deaths."[37]

In addition, the Hispanic Vietnam veteran had to and may still currently be dealing with the stresses of the acculturation process.[38] Meanwhile his wife, sister, and mother were earning and are still earning even less than African-American women.[39]

According to Lillian Baragas, who works with Hispanic Vietnam wives, Hispanic wives seeking help are often very depressed and have low self-esteem. "They believe their veteran's behavior is caused by something they're not doing and their roles as wives and partners are not being fulfilled."[40] Given the strong family and church orientation of Hispanic culture, women are often encouraged to be supportive of the veteran and strongly discouraged from seeking separation or divorce. At the same time, however, Baragas says, "Friends who don't understand PTSD are going to tell her she's crazy for staying with the veteran."[41]

Often Hispanic Vietnam wives, like their husbands, do not seek the help of mental health professionals or Vet Centers, seeking help first from their family and church. "Counseling carries negative connotations in Hispanic society," Baragas explains.[42] She has found that Hispanic women find it "difficult to self disclose in group settings."[43] However, relatively structured educational programs on PTSD have helped Hispanic Vietnam wives understand that they are not the cause of their husband's distress.

Wives of Native American Veterans

In recent years there has been considerable interest displayed in the purification healing rituals of Native Americans and their helpfulness in assisting veterans with post-war adjustment. However, to date, there have been no studies completed on the wives of Native American veterans and their unique concerns.

Summary

Like their husbands, African-American and Hispanic Vietnam wives suffer from a double jeopardy. Whereas their husbands labored, and in many instances continue to labor, under the burden of discrimination because they are nonwhite as well as Vietnam veterans, the wives are subject to the dual oppression of sexism and racism.

National statistics show that on the average, African-American and Hispanic women earn less than white women. In addition, African-American and Hispanic Vietnam wives are living with men whose PTSD tends to be more severe and of longer duration than that of white veterans. For many African-American and Hispanic vets, PTSD is intensified by the "gook identification syndrome." Their PTSD is exacerbated by multiple experiences with racial or ethnic discrimination both before, and after, the war. In general these veterans have greater difficulty finding jobs than their white counterparts. Furthermore, a number of African-American veterans suffered from rejection not only from the white community, but from those members of the African-American community that saw them as "traitors" for fighting a white man's war.

In contrast, Vietnam veterans of Native American Indian origin sometimes came from tribes that were able to separate the war from the warrior. Such vets were given honor and homage upon their return. Their re-entry into society was facilitated by tribal re-entry ceremonies. Yet even those Native American Indian vets who were greeted and treated like honorable heroes by their tribes were not oblivious to the fact that in society at large, they were scorned and not respected.

While there is little information available about Indian Vietnam wives, clinical experience and the Vet Center study reveal that African-American and Hispanic wives suffer from the same depression, isolation, and frustrations as white Vietnam wives. Yet African-American wives appear less conflicted about their role as a major source of emotional and economic support for their families. They do, however, feel that they want and deserve the same economic security and emotional and sexual fulfillment in their marriages as their white sisters.

10

PTSD and Children

When Dad left [for Vietnam] I was not told too much why he had to leave and what he was going to be doing . . . I cried terribly when he left, and emptiness and fear flooded my body and mind.

My father came home with a hearing impairment . . . His resentment today toward his deafness is still eating him up inside, because it has gradually gotten worse over the years.

He had changed a great deal when he got home. His nightmares and diving in the bushes from his fear from the war were a few things I heard and saw. His drinking got a lot worse, and so did his anger. Violence entered our house for the first time roughly a year later from his return from 'Nam. He physically abused me and the rest of the family. Verbal abuse almost all the time. I never, never knew what to expect . . . Him being so unpredictable aroused a tremendous amount of paranoia in my daily living.

It seemed like he had his own war he was fighting inside himself, and with the effect of alcohol he couldn't control his unbelievable rage that would explode in front of anybody.

My resentment toward my mother grew also. I felt she didn't care for us kids or else she would protect us from this insane man. It was terrible, horrid fear in her eyes and face when Dad would lash out and attack us as if we were the enemy.

A lot of bitterness, hatred, anger, resentment, and absolutely no pity for him was all I felt for quite a few years. I felt I was trapped in a vicious circle of fear with no way out and no one around to understand me and talk with. I became an extremist for destruction and hate and blame toward myself. I held myself responsible for my father's behavior, because I felt I was unacceptable and hated in his eyes.

For over 10 years it never dawned on me my father's behavior might be caused by what he went through in Vietnam.

I was ashamed of myself and felt extremely guilty for all the years of condemning my father to hell when he was already in a living hell of guilt, remorse, and hatred toward himself.

I can assure you I have been deeply affected directly from the war in Vietnam. I couldn't be excused from it because it came home with Dad and lived in our house for a good portion of my life.

Today, though, I am trying to learn and understand the destruction the war placed on our combat vets and Vietnam era vets. It tears me up inside to see their unmistakable misery within. I have seen it with my own eyes with my Dad.

I will never forget the craziness and insane behavior from both myself and my father in the past. But my awareness and acceptance is the biggest asset I have today. I am working on all those feelings I have suppressed for several years and to me, this is the best thing I can do for myself. To keep trying and keep loving him for who he is and where he's been, and to understand it was not me who should be responsible any longer for his behavior.

—Kid of a vet[1]

Not much research has been completed on the children of PTSD-afflicted Vietnam veterans. Clinical reports are also scarce. Therefore, this chapter does not necessarily apply to all Vietnam veteran families seeking help and certainly not to all children of those many Vietnam veterans who do not suffer from severe cases of PTSD or who are somehow able to contain their PTSD in such a manner so as not to affect their families.

This chapter is based on the reports of mothers who have attended the Vet Center group, collaborative work with child psychologists and other counselors who have worked with the children directly, the results of a national survey of Vet Center counselors regarding the effects of PTSD on children, and existing articles and other publications on children of Vietnam veterans with PTSD, adult children of World War

II veterans with PTSD, children of Holocaust victims, adult children of alcoholics, and children of incest survivors.

"Birth reminds me of death," writes Harry, a brain surgeon who served in Vietnam. "When I first saw the shriveled mass that was my newborn daughter, I felt pangs, thinking about how all the guys that died in Vietnam were once little babies like that. Some of them died like that—as shriveled masses.

"As much as I hate to admit it, right there, in the delivery room, I decided not to love my daughter. What if she would get sick and die on me, or betray me in some other way, I simply could not handle it.

"It makes me wonder what it's all about, why we struggle so hard in this life, only to die in the end. Sometimes I wonder why I bother to live at all."

As Harry's last statement reveals, he is severely depressed and at times suicidal. More than once he has had to ask his wife, Nelda, to lock up the firearms he brought home from Vietnam in a safety vault and hide the key from him. Even though Harry never shot anyone nor was shot at, he, like many medical professionals who served during the war, suffers from many of the classic symptoms of PTSD, especially survivor guilt.[2]

Yet Harry finds it difficult to admit that he suffered any psychological effects from the war. During his medical training, he was taught to "develop a high degree of clinical detachment."[3] Such emotional detachment, he learned, was absolutely necessary in order to make the "right medical decisions," but it also served to harden him to his own emotional reactions to the war. In addition, Harry is reluctant to admit to having emotional problems because he is afraid of losing his colleagues' "respect; or worse (his) job or practice."[4]

If it weren't for Nelda's insistence, Harry would not have had the courage to seek help. Although therapy was helping him with his depression, Nelda did not see much improvement in Harry's attitude toward their three children.

While the literature suggests that many Vietnam veterans are extremely capable and involved fathers, the overwhelming majority of wives seen at the Vet Center describe their husbands as emotionally withdrawn from the children and assuming little, if any, responsibility for the children's physical care or emotional development.[5] In addition, some wives complain that their husbands are excessively demanding, critical, or controlling of the children, treating the children as if they were privates in barracks.[6] In one home, for example, children were required to salute the father. In the Vet Center study, some 73% of Vet

Center counselors polled report that vets with PTSD tend to withdraw from their children and some 80% report that vets with PTSD tend to be overcritical of their children.

Perhaps it is primarily women whose husbands are not actively involved with their children who seek help. Nelda's complaint, "I'm a married single parent," has been echoed by almost every mother who has attended group. This does not mean that their husbands do not love their children, but rather that their PTSD interferes with their desire to be good fathers.

In the 1970s and 1980s, during the era of changing sex roles, many men sought to become more involved with their children. Many mothers, even stay at home mothers, expected their husbands to spend quality time with the children, as well as to assume more of the physical child care duties. But this change in attitude toward traditional sex roles does not seem evident among veteran families with young children seen thus far. Almost always the majority of child care of preadolescent children seemed relegated solely to the mother.

Candice Williams, who has worked with hundreds of Vietnam veterans and conducted women's support groups, explains, "In Vietnam veteran families, there is often overattachment to culturally stereotyped roles," despite the "tremendous role changes [that] have occurred in the family during the past decade."[7]

The exceptions to this statement are Vietnam veterans who have assumed major caretaking responsibilities toward their grandchildren. Some children of Vietnam veterans cannot take care of their own children because they need to work or finish school or because they are incarcerated or away from home for other reasons. Under such circumstances, they might leave their children with "grandma and grandpa."

When grandma (the Vietnam wife) works full time, grandpa (the Vietnam veteran), who is home on disability or because he cannot work, may become the primary caretaker of his son's or daughter's infant, toddler, or preschool child. Hence some Vietnam veterans who never changed a diaper for their own children are now not only changing diapers, but mixing formulas and going to parent-teacher meetings for their grandchildren.

Some of these veteran grandfathers have found immense purpose and joy in caring for their grandchildren. These infants, preschoolers, and grade school children are too young to be aware that their grandfathers were socially stigmatized and called "babykillers." They look up to their grandfathers and love them with a pure kind of love that only very young children have to offer. The innocence of these young children and their absolute trust and dependency on their grandfather has, in some cases, melted the veteran's "wall" more effectively and more lovingly than years of psychotherapy.

"I will get paranoid at times," relates Andrew, who served three tours in Vietnam. "But no matter how paranoid I get, there's one person I know isn't out to get me—my grandson.

"When he puts his hand in mine and asks me to help him do something, I feel like a million dollars. He looks up to me and loves me the way no one in my family, or anyone in the world for that matter, ever has or ever will."

Andrew wishes he had had the same tender feelings toward his own children when they were young as he has toward his grandchildren. So do his wife and grown children, who can't help but wonder what their lives would have been like if Andrew had shared his "good self" with them as he does with the grandson.

"I was too confused after Vietnam to be any kind of father or husband. Vietnam was too fresh in my mind," Andrew explains. "With age, I've mellowed out some. Therapy has helped too. So now maybe I can enjoy my grandchildren the way I should have enjoyed my own children."

For Andrew, as for other vets, caring for grandchildren was perceived as a second chance to be a good parent and find fulfillment in the parent role. It can also be a form of restitution for children lost in Vietnam. Andrew lost a baby son in Vietnam. Andrew had repressed all memories of losing his Vietnamese child and girlfriend until he joined a therapy group and began having nightmares of his girlfriend's village going up in smoke. While in Vietnam, he blamed himself for not having provided for the safety of his girlfriend and their child, even though he had no way of knowing that his girlfriend's village was targeted for destruction.

Ironically, the very love Andrew had for his Vietnamese family contributed to his need to distance himself from his American family. In order to protect himself against the grief involved in possibly losing his American family someday, Andrew walled himself off emotionally.

His self-protective position, however, evolved unconsciously, not consciously. Andrew, like other vets who find it difficult to love fully, did not will or command himself to build a wall around his heart. He did not consciously decide, "I am going to limit the love I have for my wife and children so I won't hurt so much if I lose them the way I lost the woman and child I loved in Vietnam." Rather, his psyche automatically, as a form of self-preservation, erected the wall so that it would not be devastated by yet another unbearable loss.

While Andrew's wife is pleased that he is capable of loving their grandchild, she can't forget how disappointed she was that Andrew was not involved in raising their children. "Grandchildren have brought out the best in Andrew. But our children, it seems, brought out the worst," she comments.

Here Andrew's wife is speaking from the pain and disappointment she felt as a young bride who bore children to the man she loved. She thought Andrew would be thrilled with the healthy babies she brought into the world. Instead Andrew embraced them half-heartedly, out of duty, not love. At the same time, Andrew began to withdraw from her emotionally, as a direct result of her having the children. Given this situation, Andrew's wife's bitterness is quite understandable.

For Andrew's wife, as for Nelda and many of the younger mothers who have sought help, the image of the "liberated couple" where husband and wife happily and equally share the housework and the child care is an impossible dream. Nelda would be grateful if Harry would just show the children some fatherly love and stop criticizing them just for being children—for making noises, not being on time, acting contrary at meals, balking while dressing, or whatever. Although Nelda works outside the home and could certainly use Harry's help with some of the routine household and child care chores, her heart's desire is not to have Harry change diapers or fix lunches. Rather, she prays for the day when Harry will stop destroying the children's self-esteem with his critical comments and unrealistic expectations.

"I could see the scars on the children even when they were young. Even when our daughter was two, she understood Harry's critical remarks. Harry didn't think a two-year-old could understand when he was making fun of her, but she did. And he thought his children didn't miss him, but they did—and still do. Even though he hurts their feelings by not showing up at their games and school events, they love him anyway.

"He's their father and they need him. They need strokes from Dad, as well as from Mom."

There is nothing closer to most women's hearts than their children. Among almost all of the wives and girlfriends of Vietnam veterans I have counseled, their children are their prime concern, in most cases overriding their worry for their husbands or for themselves. When a child is hurting, that child's pain usually becomes the mother's major focus of attention and the dominant topic of group discussion or individual therapy.

Even the incarcerated Vietnam wives I have worked with, women convicted of crimes, such as murder, attempted murder, or theft, women who are street smart and heavily invested in presenting a tough image to the world, would almost always break down, or at least ask for help, when talking about their children.

Like many other Vietnam wives seen at the Vet Center, Nelda feels her children's pain. She even feels it when they aren't feeling it, but denying it instead. In an attempt to help her children, Nelda tries to compensate for her husband's absences and other deficiencies as a parent by giving her children extra attention and love. But she is tired of being her children's emotional band-aid and furthermore, she fears, and realistically so, that all her love and extra efforts cannot undo Harry's emotional damage to the children. "Do you know how I feel when I see my son giving up on a project because his father has called him 'dumb' or 'lazy'?" No matter how hard she tries to convince Harry Jr. that he can succeed at a certain project, he has internalized his father's low image of him to such an alarming extent that he gives up almost immediately.

While Nelda is enraged at the destruction of her son's self-esteem, she is also sick and tired of being accused of being a "bad mother."

"Here's me, doing everything, and here's my husband, the critic. Why am I to blame every time the children misbehave or have a problem at school?" Nelda often asks with disgust. Even though she knows her husband's accusations are not true, she, like her son, has adopted her husband's low image of her. On some level, she sees herself as an inadequate mother, even though every piece of objective evidence points otherwise.

As Harry and Nelda's story illustrates, the major problems experienced by children in homes afflicted with PTSD are emotional. If the veteran's PTSD expresses itself in irritability, outbursts of temper, frequent flashbacks, or erratic behavior, the children are often frightened and anxious, not knowing what to expect next. "I've got to be home all the time to keep the children from falling apart in case he (the veteran) falls apart," explains Beth, mother of three. "Only when he goes on camping trips do the kids and I get a break."

While younger children learn to go to their rooms when Daddy goes "off," older children may leave for the evening. Or they may stay home and try to help their father. "Even if I leave home for the weekend, I take my father with me in my mind," explains Beth's oldest son, Tom, age 14, who is more troubled by his father's crying spells and negative attitude toward life than by his father's anger.

In Tom's home, as in other homes, the veteran's dramatic emotions and mood swings, or his severe depression, usually determine the emotional climate of the home. Aware of their father's volatility and emotional sensitivities, Tom and his sisters have learned, like their mother, to "walk on eggshells." As frequently occurs in Vietnam homes, the children are not told why their father is so troubled, or so distant. As a result they often blame themselves for their father's unhappiness or his withdrawal from them.

A Vet Center counselor who has worked with children explains: "In the majority of these troubled families, the children have been given little explanation for their father's difficulties and the stresses of family life. Inevitably they attribute much of the blame and responsibility to themselves, just as do the children of divorcing, alcoholic, and otherwise troubled parents. The patterns of communication among family members are often very sparse so that there is little opportunity to acquire a more accurate or different explanation. Indeed, the child's sense of responsibility may be heightened by the frequent exhortations of 'Be quiet. Be good. Don't upset your father.' Thus, these children may grow up feeling alienated from their fathers, responsible for the difficulties in the family, and isolated from community supports."[8]

In Tom's home, however, the father has recounted his traumatic experiences in Vietnam so frequently that, by now, Tom is bored with his father's war stories. "I can't stand hearing about it anymore!" Tom sometimes shouts. "Forget the past, Dad! Live in the present!"

But Tom's father can't forget the past and such outbursts on Tom's part engender unresolvable father-son disputes, which leave the veteran father feeling misunderstood and unloved by his own family and Tom feeling guilty for further upsetting his father and for not having suffered as much as his father did. Although Tom wants to help his father, he feels helpless to do so. Yet Tom often willingly restricts his activities in order to be with his father. At the same time, he resents the burden his father's emotional pain and problems have imposed on his life.

While Tom has never been rejected by his peers or neighbors, in some communities children have been ostracized for having a Vietnam veteran father, especially if their father has committed an antisocial act in the community, has emotionally regressed, or had flashbacks in public. In other cases, children may be seen as different because their father has adopted an unusual or nonconforming lifestyle or form of dress. In families where there are frequent moves, the child's educational progress and friendships may be disrupted.[9]

If the veteran is prone to rage reactions, the children may fear inviting their friends home lest their friends witness the father's anger. The Vietnam wife herself, while greatly desiring that her children have a normal childhood, may discourage her children from having guests for the very same reason. She may also be aware that the noise, play, and activities of children, especially if they are young, may trigger her husband and increase his anxiety level.

If the children are adolescents and enjoy listening to loud music with their friends or staying up late with them, the veteran may react negatively to the presence of his teenager's friends. The noise level may make him irritable and he may experience the presence of guests in his home late in the night as a form of invasion of his personal space.

The psychological problems experienced by children of Vietnam veterans as a direct result of the veteran's PTSD generally occur in one of seven different family settings:

• Families such as Harry and Nelda's, in which the mother functions as a virtual single parent due to the veteran's emotional conflicts or withdrawal;

• Families in which the mother is so chronically stressed or depressed that she turns to one of the children excessively for emotional support;

• Families in which there is "secondary traumatization"—where one or more of the children overidentifies with the veteran, exhibits some of the father's symptoms (or other symptoms), or attempts to "rescue" the veteran;[10]

• Families in which there is an overprotectiveness of and overvaluation of the children by the veteran;

• Families in which there is physical, as well as emotional, abuse of the mother or the children;

• Families in which there is alcohol or drug abuse as well as PTSD;

• Families in which the woman has children from a former marriage.

These categories of families are not mutually exclusive, as will be shown by using some of the same families to illustrate different family problems. Furthermore, the children, like their mothers, tend to suffer from self-blame, low self-esteem, difficulty expressing anger and aggression, and conflicts in establishing themselves as unique individuals apart from the family system. According to the Vet Center study, some 82% of the counselors polled indicated low self-esteem to be a problem in children of Vietnam veterans suffering from PTSD. Approximately 56% of the counselors polled noted that children tend to feel responsible for the veteran's emotional well being.

While some homes are characterized by close attachments among family members, in other homes there is considerable emotional distance and anger. The children may respond to their parents' anger with anger of their own, or with various forms of emotional distancing. They may turn up the stereo when Dad or Mom begins to yell. Or perhaps they simply plug themselves into the T.V. set using headphones. According to Ellen Salom, who conducted groups for children at a Vet Center in Philadelphia, when children are asked to draw pictures of their homes, they sometimes depict homes where each family member is in a separate room.[11] Such pictures suggest a high degree of emotional alienation and lack of communication in the family. On the other hand, in other families there is solid bonding, although usually it is the mother and children who form a tight subunit in the family which excludes the veteran.

Many of the psychological patterns found among children of traumatized Vietnam veterans are similar to those found among children of World War II veterans with PTSD and among children of the survivors of the Nazi concentration camps.[12] In his study of World War II veterans with PTSD, for example, Robert Rosenheck found veterans reluctant to discuss their war experiences with their children. "This reluctance," writes Rosenheck, "derived from embarrassment and guilt about acts of brutality they had committed as well as from the fear that they would become upset while discussing specific incidents. They were also afraid that unpleasant details would frighten and alienate their children.'"[13]

The Effects of Distancing on Children

While veterans complain about not feeling emotionally closer to their children, their children often exhibit various symptoms in response to their father's lack of emotional involvement with them. (The observations made in this section could also apply to grandchildren in those situations where the grandfather is the prime caretaker or otherwise exerts a great deal of influence over the child unmitigated by other adults or caretakers.) True, the father's intention in distancing himself from his child may not be a rejection of the child. Yet children tend to view their father's alienation as rejection. If, in addition, there is name calling or other forms of emotional abuse, the child may become convinced that he or she is not loved or accepted by their father. In some cases, when a veteran calls his child lazy or some other negative label, he may think he is teaching the child the right values, like the value of work. However, children usually experience such name calling as humiliating. It makes them feel that they are not good enough for their father.

The child's reactions to the father's emotional distancing appear to be age-related. Among pre-schoolers, there may be increased separation anxiety, evidenced by increased clinging to the mother, increased fearfulness, and even increased aggressive behavior. "Whenever Harry walks into the room, Donna starts screaming," explains Nelda. "She won't let him feed her either." Then Nelda is blamed for not teaching the children to love their father. Mothers of slightly older preschool children have reported increased temper tantrums following their father's absences from the home, as well as decreased interest in playing with other children.

Between the ages of four and seven, children's understanding of the world is egocentric.[14] In their view, the world revolves about their needs and they believe that their thoughts and wishes can actually cause external events. Hence they easily blame themselves for their father's alienation, anger, or depression. Even if the child were to be given some education about Vietnam, the child would have difficulty digesting and comprehending such information. At this age, children still tend to believe that they are the major cause of all the activity around them. Furthermore, "In times of stress," notes Melanie Suhr, "even adolescent or older children can revert to (such) egocentric modes of thinking . . ."[15]

By the time children have reached the ages of seven or eight, their capacity for concrete reasoning has increased.[16] Now they are able to see cause and effect more clearly. Yet, since they are usually not told about the impact of Vietnam on their father, they may still personalize the father's alienation. In some cases, they feel great sadness and actively grieve for him. Nelda's middle child, Joleen, age 8, actually pined when her father failed to keep his promise to watch a certain T.V. show with her. Other mothers have noted depression in their children, a lack of interest in social activities, and much keeping to themselves in their rooms. "Daddy doesn't play with me because he doesn't like me," some children have frankly said with tears in their eyes.

At the age of seven or eight, children may also become involved in loyalty conflicts between the parents. A child may side with the mother or with the veteran. It is not uncommon for children who side with the veteran to also join with him in any denial of his PTSD, alcoholism, or other problems. Since some children tend to idealize their parents, they may find it hard to admit that one of their parents has a serious problem. In several cases, the Vietnam wife's attempts to encourage her husband to seek professional help have met with resistance not only from the veteran, but from his "ally," one of the children.

"Why are you trying to send my Daddy away to a hospital? He's not sick," children have told their mothers. Some have even threatened to run away from home if the mother carries out her plans. Children who ally with the veteran often blame their mother for their father's PTSD symptoms and other unhappiness. Or they may think she is trying to take the father away from them by pushing him to seek inpatient treatment. They may also fear that once father leaves, he may never return.

Or that someday their mother may send them away, as she did their father. These fears can usually be alleviated by careful explanations of what treatment involves and if possible visiting the treatment facility with the children.

According to the Vet Center study, some 42% of counselors polled found that children have ambivalent feelings toward the mother. "They're downright negative," writes one counselor. Another, however, notes that some children cling to the mother. In his study of World War II veterans with PTSD, Rosenheck found similar patterns. Some children sided with their mother and admired her efforts to help the father. Other children were highly critical of the mother for not being supportive enough of the veteran.[17]

Trauma specialists are now realizing that for some children separation from a parent may be traumatic in itself, in that the child is dependent upon parents for survival. Consequently, if a child was born prior to the father's going to Vietnam, his very departure in itself could have traumatized the child. The child, however, may blame his or her mother for the father's absence since she is the only one in his environment on whom the child can displace his or her anger at the father's departure.

If, later on, the father is hospitalized, the child's traumatic reaction to the father's original departure for Vietnam may be activated. Once again, mother may be the target for the child's anger at losing the father, even if the separation is temporary. Once again, mother is there and father is not. Also, mother is "safe." In general, the child knows that mother will not reject or abandon him or her even if he or she expresses anger toward her. In this sense, the child's expression of anger at the mother can be seen, in some situations, as indicative of the child's trust in her love.

At the age of seven or eight, children may not only begin to take sides, but, if there is much quarreling in the home, like children of divorcing parents, they may come to "distrust parents who are modeling painful, vicious behaviors."[18] Unable to trust either parent, the child feels insecure and may evidence not only depression, but rebellion at both parents' commands.

At the same time, like his mother, the child may have learned to be quiet. Among children of Nazi holocaust survivors, the same inhibition of angry feelings has been found.[19] These children have often kept their angry feelings to themselves because they did not want to cause additional suffering to their obviously already suffering parents. In a parallel manner, some children from Vietnam homes do not want to upset their obviously already upset father or their overburdened mother. In addition, the child may have been severely punished for aggressive or defiant behavior by the father. Given military training and background, some vets equate anger with disrespect and tolerate little disobedience from their children.

When Children Repress Anger

Young children, even adolescents, may stifle their anger because of their natural dependency on their parents. Generally, it is difficult for most persons to be angry at those on whom they are emotionally or financially dependent, for if the anger is expressed, there is a high risk of alienating the person whose love and attention or support is so desperately needed.

Children's repressed anger can eventually emerge in the form of self-mutilation, suicidal thoughts, and sudden outbursts of aggression. According to the Vet Center study, aggressive behavior on the part of children is far more common than self-mutilation. Some 76% of the counselors polled indicated that they had observed aggressiveness to be a problem among children of Vietnam veterans suffering from PTSD whereas only 10% found evidence of self-mutilation. Among the children whose mothers have attended group, self-mutilation, suicidal thoughts, and angry displays of temper have occurred primarily among sons, rather than daughters. In one case, a 10-year-old son habitually scraped his legs with razor blades, not enough to injure himself, but enough to leave noticeable marks. In another instance, a child scratched his head to such an extent that he became partially bald. Other examples of self-mutilation include head banging, self-burning, skin pinching, hair pulling, and extreme fingernail biting.

In most cases, such self-mutilation is a way of coping with emotional pain, rather than a way to control the parents through guilt or active attempts at suicide.[20] Generally the children are ashamed of their actions and commit them in private. Typically self-mutilation represents repressed anger or a form of grieving or pining for the father.

Suicidal depressions are another result of repressed anger, with several children contemplating suicide as a means of making their father "sorry" for not loving them or for not doing things with them or as a means of escaping the arguing and other forms of unhappiness at home.

In contrast to children who internalize their anger in the form of self-mutilation, depression, or suicidal thoughts are those who externalize their anger by fighting relentlessly with their siblings or peers at school or who destroy property at home. In some cases, the child blames the mother for his or her aggression. "You made my Dad sick!" or "Why can't you make Dad better?" tormented sons have cried out as they smash tables, walls, or stereo sets. In other instances, otherwise "perfect" daughters have been found tearing drapes off windows or smashing windows, saying "I hate you! I hate you, Mom," blaming the mother for all of the family's problems.

Another distressing development for the Vietnam wife is when her children learn to use emotional withdrawal as a means of punishing her or manipulating her into giving in to their desires. One wife, the mother of a teenager, feels that her son has learned to wall her out whenever he is displeased with her rules. "My son was not a problem when he was young, but now whenever things don't go his way, or he doesn't like the family rules, he threatens to abandon me or totally tunes me out. I couldn't understand where this behavior came from, since it wasn't evident in his younger years, until it suddenly dawned on me that he's treating me exactly the way his father treats me."

In other instances, anger stemming from the family situation is displaced onto Asians, specifically Vietnamese refugees. According to the Vet Center study, however, only 13% of the counselors polled found hatred of Asians, specifically Vietnamese, to be a problem among children. While the child may have learned from the father to hate Asians, they provide a relatively safe target for the hostility which the child feels toward his father or mother, but does not feel safe to express. While no violence against Asians has been reported, several children have verbally harassed Vietnamese refugees and relish telling anti-Vietnamese or "gook" jokes.

For example, Brian, age 11, was referred for psychological testing because his academic problems seemed to reflect an emotional problem rather than a lack of ability. His grades began to decline after the second grade and he became more hostile and aggressive with his classmates. He refused to sit near Asian children, and got into fights with children when he felt they were wrong. Right and wrong were big issues in his family since his father, a former combat vet, had become very sensitive to issues of justice and fairness as the result of his Vietnam experience.

Brian would also pull pranks and then lie about his behavior. When Brian's father returned from Vietnam, he was easily startled by sudden noises and often felt anxious around strangers. In a parallel manner, Brian became frightened by the ringing of the school bell and suspicious of strangers, even the psychological examiner sent by the school.

Despite his anxiety about strangers, Brian worked well with the examiner. He worked hard on the intellectual puzzles the examiner gave him until he was asked to put together puzzles of humans and animals. The cut up pieces reminded him of the gore in his father's war stories and he was unable to concentrate on this part of the testing. He also showed signs of anxiety when asked to define words like *knife* or to deal with words and concepts having to do with aggression. Whenever questions or pictures about vehicles came up, Brian exhibited an extreme fear that the vehicles would be blown up or crash, as his father had described occurring in Vietnam when vehicles were booby trapped or set with explosives.

When Brian had trouble with a test, he expressed fear that the examiner would yell at him, as apparently his parents did when he brought home poor marks. Even when he was assured he would have a second chance at certain items, he did not appear to believe the examiner and would give up.

As a result of the testing, it was recommended that Brian receive special educational services, as well as individual and family therapy. He was placed in a special classroom environment where he received more individualized attention. There was less expected of him there than in a regular classroom and he consequently experienced many more academic successes than in his regular classroom. Over time he became more self-confident and was less aggressive toward other students.

Counseling with a child psychologist also helped Brian separate his father's war realities from the reality of his own everyday life. Although Brian had trouble opening up to the therapist, eventually he revealed that much of his mental life was spent fantasizing about his father's experiences in Vietnam. Often his conceptions of what his father had experienced were severe distortions of what his father had shared with him. Some of Brian's ideas had become confused with movies and television programs about war.

In family therapy sessions with his father, Brian got a clearer picture of his father's war experiences, which enabled him to focus more on reality. Brian also needed many assurances that his father was no longer in danger, as he had been in Vietnam, and that the dangers his father had gone through did not exist in their particular neighborhood. The therapist and Brian's mother had reassured him many times but once his father said the same things, those reassurances became more effective.

The family therapy sessions also revealed that, in part, Brian was doing poorly in school in order to get his father's attention. Even being yelled at was better than being ignored. When it became clear to Brian that his father was willing to give him attention in other ways, Brian's school performance and emotional state improved.

The most significant breakthrough in family therapy occurred when Brian was finally able to articulate his anger at his father. Ever since he was a small child, Brian had been unable to show anger toward his father because he didn't want to aggravate and upset him, and because he feared his father's physical strength.

Even though Brian's father had never hit either Brian or Brian's mother, he had destroyed property. Once when he was angry at his wife, he smashed the glass door at the entrance to their apartment building.

"Don't you know we might get evicted for that?" Brian's mother shouted.

"Don't you raise your voice at me, woman. I'm the man in the house," Brian's father shouted back.

"But the property manager is going to make trouble for us."

"I can handle that puny runt. Remember, I've stood up to armed men."

"But what if a child had been standing near you and had gotten hurt by the flying glass?"

"Then it would have been the kid's fault for being there, not mine."

Brian's father's last words were probably said in anger. Most likely he had forgotten he ever said them. But Brian did not forget—not the words, and not the smashed door. He was afraid that if he made one wrong move at home, he would become the object of his father's powerful fist. Consequently, he acted out his aggressive feelings at school. Even the teachers and the principal seemed safer than his father. At home he was afraid to stand up for himself, even when he felt his father was being unjust.

For example, Brian's father suffered frequent fears about his family's safety. Whenever a family member went out, they were required to call home upon arrival at their destination. Sometimes after getting to a friend's house, Brian would quickly call home. "Hi, Dad. I'm okay, Dad. Bye, Dad."

Sometimes his father interpreted his brevity as a sign of disrespect. Other times he felt his son was hanging up on him. In therapy, he was able to tell of an incident in Vietnam when a command control operator had muttered some information to him quickly, almost inaudibly, then hung up on him. This left him with incomplete information and as a result he was not able to save some wounded Americans from the Viet Cong. As a result, he was intolerant of mistakes in his family as well as himself and hyper whenever somebody spoke to him on the phone quickly or inaudibly.

As a result of that session, Brian learned how to talk to his father when he was in a hurry. "Don't get hyper, Dad, but I'm talking fast because I don't have much time to play with my friends unless I get started right now. If there's something really important you want to talk about, I'll stay on the line. But if you just want to talk about the usual stuff, I'd rather wait until later."

In the presence of a third party—the therapist—Brian was able to speak directly to his father about things that were bothering him. The more he was able to do that, the less need he had to act out his anger in school.

This presentation of the various reactions children have to their father's PTSD and the descriptions of other troubled children to follow in this chapter are not intended to present a picture of all children of Vietnam veterans with PTSD as suffering from severe or irrevocable psychological damage. Simply put, some children can cope better than others.

While some children are severely emotionally hurt by the situations in their homes, other children display great strength and develop an advanced degree of emotional maturity and objectivity as a result of the stress. Furthermore, even those children who have been emotionally hurt by PTSD and related problems can, with proper intervention, be helped considerably.

"A child does not have to become ill to have been affected by parental trauma, and even negative effects have different impacts, extents, and durations," writes Joseph Albeck, an expert in the area of the intergenerational effects of trauma. "Furthermore, not all effects of parental trauma are necessarily deleterious. The possibilities for growth as a result of trauma in both generations, in addition to any injuries sustained, must not be overlooked."[21]

Albeck further states, and rightly so, that it is both impossible and arrogant for any mental health professional to make gross generalizations about the effects of parental trauma on children since so little research has been completed in this area. Therefore, the children of traumatized parents should not automatically be "pathologized" or seen as psychologically damaged.[22]

Why the Veteran Distances from His Children

In Harry's case, as in the case of other Vietnam veterans with PTSD, the roots of his emotional withdrawal and ambivalent feelings toward his children are usually much deeper and more complex than simple male chauvinism, sheer insensitivity, or outright cruelty. In fact, philosophically, some vets truly believe in women's liberation and men's liberation and very much want to be active, emotionally responsive fathers. Yet on a day-to-day basis, they find themselves extremely annoyed and impatient with their children.

According to the Vet Center study, approximately 85% of the counselors polled indicated that vets with PTSD have a low tolerance for children's noise and games. Some 51% indicated that vets with PTSD have special difficulty tolerating the "terrible twos" and some 79% have trouble with adolescent or preadolescent rebellion against parental authority. Of course, even non-PTSD afflicted parents may have problems with these stages of childhood development. However, in the case of the Vietnam vet, authority issues developed as a result of his Vietnam involvement may exacerbate his own unresolved issues and make rearing his own children an especially stressful experience.

"In all honesty, I'd rather be alone," confesses Harry, who also feels very guilty about his limited ability to tolerate his children. Similarly, a veteran treated by Sarah Haley (who has worked with many Vietnam veterans) feels guilty for snapping at his wife and children "for every little thing."[23] In fact, this veteran considered himself "'. . . a poor excuse for a father' when his three-year-old asked why he looked so sad and yelled all the time."[24]

Parenting requires an enormous amount of energy, which some PTSD-afflicted veterans lack due to depression or preoccupation with their war experiences. In this, they are like some of the survivors of the Nazi concentration camps, who, due to their focus on their traumatic experiences in the camps and their subsequent demoralization, have been found to lack the energy to parent.[25]

Vets with severe cases of PTSD or who are in inpatient treatment programs often feel they cannot handle the stresses of child-rearing while simultaneously trying to recover from PTSD. According to Haley, who has seen this in her work with veterans, "Fatherhood may overtax the veteran's ability to resolve a trauma. Any point during the child's development can impinge upon the veteran's depression, withdrawal or conflicts." [26] As a result, the vet may allocate the job of parenting to his wife, not realizing that his very physical or emotional absence from the home is the source of many of his wife's difficulties with their children.

In some cases, the trauma of combat or specific injuries have caused irrevocable physiological damage to the veteran's nervous system.[27] Even without physiological damage, however, PTSD-afflicted veterans often evidence the startle response to sudden noises and movements. Children may be strictly warned by their mothers not to surprise their father by jumping on him or in any manner approaching him from behind. The edginess some vets feel around others, especially children, can be seen as an exaggerated startle response.[28]

Combat memories also play a role in the veteran's ambivalent feelings toward his children.[29] As a result of combat experiences, some PTSD-afflicted veterans respond negatively to their children's aggressive play or to their children when they approach the ages of children they killed or saw killed in Vietnam.[30] One vet's PTSD lay dormant until his son became nine, the exact age of a young boy he inadvertently killed during the war.

This type of reaction is not atypical, even among noncombat veterans. Harry, like other medical personnel, often treated Vietnamese children. When his daughter turned two, he had to flee from her birthday party, remembering a two-year-old Vietnamese girl whose life he had failed to save. Some vets may not even want to have children as a result of their war experiences. For example, D. Harrington and Jeffrey Jay, therapists who conduct groups for Vietnam veterans, cite the case of Tony, "who had seen a friend knifed in front of his eyes. The friend, a corpsman, was treating a Vietnamese family of mother, father, grandmother, and infant that had been detained for questioning. When the corpsman turned from the father, the mother grabbed the corpsman's knife and stuck it through his back. In the instant it took the woman to stab the corpsman, Tony shot the entire family with automatic fire, including the infant. Ten years later, in group therapy, Tony, whose wife thought his bitterness and displays of indifference were reflections of her inadequacies, admitted that he would not have children because of his belief that a man who could react so quickly and so violently was not fit to become a father."[31]

Sometimes the veteran's memories, not just of children killed in Vietnam, but of any kind of person killed in Vietnam, are activated by simply watching children play. Haley cites an example of a veteran who had "never thought of the Viet Cong as people, as parents with children or as people who would be parents someday," until he watched his own children at play.[32] Often it is the birth of a child which makes the vet realize that, after all, the Viet Cong were not just "gooks," but human beings too.

In addition, since children in Vietnam were often used to carry hand grenades and other explosives or were used as ploys to trap vets, the vet may have learned to fear children. In a few isolated instances, children have not only been physically abused, but actually killed by their veteran father or stepfather because he allegedly mistook them for or responded to them as if they were Vietnamese children booby trapped or otherwise attacking.

If, in addition, the veteran actually killed children in Vietnam, his difficulties in relating to children, especially his own, are obvious. "Veterans who . . . feared or killed women and children during combat may find it difficult to make the transition to the roles of husband, protector, and nurturing parent," writes Haley.[33] In addition, Department of Veterans Affairs psychiatrist H. Glover has found that some vets who killed women and children in Vietnam suffer from auditory hallucinations which "manifest themselves as the anguished cries of women and children killed by the veteran. At times the vet may see the face of a Vietnamese woman or child while he is relating to a family member.[34]

Another source of the veteran's ambivalence and anger toward his children, which most vets admit is irrational, is that in protecting and guiding their own children, they are reminded of times they felt unprotected, or were misguided, in Vietnam. "I'm jealous of my own kids," admits Harry, who, through therapy, has realized that when he feels restrictive or punitive toward his children he is often angry about not being protected (parented) in Vietnam. "Why didn't someone tell me about Vietnam before I went? Why was I such a fool as to enlist?" he often asks.

Harry went to Vietnam thinking he would help to save lives as doctors did in World War II—in safely placed hospitals in demilitarized zones. He was totally unprepared for rocket and other attacks on his hospital, as well as for the volume of casualties and the horrible types of disfiguring injuries caused by guerilla warfare tactics. Furthermore, medical school had not taught Harry how to decide who would be helped to live vs. who would have to be allowed to die, decisions which he was forced to make due to limited medical supplies and services.

Harry's children receive the best medical care, but Harry cannot take them to the doctor. Just walking into a pediatrician's office fills him with an irrational rage. He can't help but compare the excellent care his children receive for relatively minor medical problems with what he saw in Vietnam—not only young Americans, but young Vietnamese children dying of napalm and various forms of hideous, deforming injuries. In addition, when Harry observes his children's innocence he is reminded of the innocence he lost in Vietnam. Since this is painful for him, he often avoids his children.

Military experience can also carry over into the veteran's attitude toward child discipline. Approximately 40% of the Vet Center counselors polled indicated that the Vietnam vet with PTSD tends to underdiscipline his children. However, an almost equal number reported that vets with PTSD tend to overdiscipline. In some cases, vets expect strict obedience from their children, treating their children as if they were small soldiers. For example, Tom and his two sisters must be constantly "on guard" or "at attention" when their father is at home. But the minute Dad leaves, the children become extremely unruly and undisciplined, taking out all their rebellious feelings and repressed anger at being ordered around on their mother, and on one another. Then their mother, Beth, is berated by her husband for not being able to "control" the children. Yet she feels powerless to counteract her children's normal reaction to being overregulated by their father.

Beth, like many Vietnam wives, sometimes hides her children's misbehavior from her husband. She fears that her husband might overly punish the children or call them derogatory names. Sometimes Beth becomes trapped, when, for example, one of the children imitates the father by "trashing" a piece of furniture. "If Dad can do it, why can't I?" Under such circumstances, Beth must either quickly replace the broken furniture and cover up the expenditure with a lie or else turn her children over to her husband for disciplinary measures.

In some homes, the veteran's need to control the children is disguised as a form of discipline. "My husband watches every move Tom makes," explains Beth. "He actually counts how many times Tom goes to the refrigerator. If Tom goes too often, my husband jumps all over him."

In some instances, the vet enforces certain home rules with great vigor, but seems relatively unconcerned when the children have disciplinary difficulties in school. According to Vet Center counselor Ellen Salom, such inconsistences in discipline are not uncommon and create confusion for the child who may often fail to understand different levels of "right and wrong."[35]

Still other veterans are not disciplinarians at all, but may become exceptionally harsh in response to their children's aggressiveness. When vets see their children being cruel to a pet or to a new baby, it may "reawaken (for them) the painful effects of combat aggression and sadism."[36] If a vet committed atrocities in Vietnam, he may react by being superstrict with his children, especially his sons, and may not allow even normal aggressiveness. Some vets even feel that their sadism and aggressiveness is being passed on to their children genetically.

Veterans may distance themselves from their sons when their sons approach the age that they were sent to war, and from their daughters as their daughters approach the ages of girls or women with whom they had traumatic encounters in Vietnam. Veterans who witnessed or participated in the sexual assault, maiming, or killing of young girls or women in Vietnam may, in some cases, experience a resurgence of their war memories when their daughters, nieces, or other females in their lives reach the ages of the girls and women whom they saw injured or killed during the war. The veteran's traumatic memories related to women may also be activated by media accounts of rapes and other forms of violence against women or by actual assaults on female relatives or friends.

For example, when James was in Vietnam, he saw one of his friends rape a thirteen-year-old girl. The girl screamed pitifully during the attack and bled profusely afterwards. James had considered trying to help the girl, but figured it was "none of his business." When the soldier subsequently shot the girl "for crying too loud," James looked the other way.

James had forgotten about the incident until his daughter turned 13. Suddenly, after several years of relative emotional stability, James became both suicidal and homicidal.

His daughter's thirteenth birthday triggered memories of the incident and intense feelings of guilt, shame, and horror. During the war, James had been in such a state of numbing, he was not affected by the abuse of the Vietnamese girl. But now, 20 years later, he felt like a moral coward for not having intervened on her behalf. Furthermore, it was not just this isolated instance which left James with a deep sense of moral shame, but many other instances involving the torture and death of Vietnamese, both soldiers and civilians alike.

James's therapist tried to explain to him that psychic numbing was almost automatic in combat and that if he had tried to protect the girl, he might have been attacked by his comrade. At the very minimum, he would have been considered an oddball of sorts and ostracized on some level. In war, being ostracized is lethal, given that one's life depends on the support of others. Therefore, the therapist argued, James's not helping the Vietnamese girl (and other Vietnamese later on) was not a sign of his moral deficiency, but a sign of his will to survive.

On an intellectual level, James agreed with the therapist's reasoning. But on an emotional and spiritual level, James damned himself and was certain God was going to damn him too. Ironically, James no longer believed in God, yet he was certain that God was going to punish him for what happened to the Vietnamese girl and other civilians by allowing his daughter to be raped and killed.

James immediately purchased firearms and was ready to shoot the first male who looked at his precious daughter the wrong way. When alone, James contemplated suicide. Far better that he die to pay for the Vietnamese girl's death than for his daughter to be the sacrifice.

When James' daughter developed a crush on one of her classmates, James began having chest pains and forbade her to have contact with the young boy. Even phone calls with him were off-limits. James' daughter defied her father as often as she could. She sneaked out of the home to call her young man and go on long walks with him. When James learned of her behavior, he called her a "whore" and told her that "all men were dogs" and that her crush would certainly rape and kill her someday. He further stated that if she so much as spoke with any young man without his approval, he would throw her into the streets, where she would surely be raped and murdered.

His daughter began to moan and cry and begged her father to please be reasonable. His daughter's moaning and begging, however, only reminded James of the Vietnamese girl's pleading with her rapist. Consequently, instead of becoming more rational, James entered the world of his trauma and became less able to think and reason.

James's wife then entered the scene and defended her daughter. How dare James ruin his daughter's entry into womanhood by calling her a whore? And how dare he tarnish their daughter's first innocent puppy love with talk of violent sex? Their daughter deserved a social life, and if James threw their daughter out because she was a normal teenage girl with normal teenage interests and hormones, then he would lose not only his daughter but his wife. For she would divorce him in a minute and take all their children and her paycheck with her.

James's response was to dissociate and withdraw from the family. James's daughter, however, experienced her father's withdrawal as a rejection both of her as a person and of her emerging womanhood. She began to hate her budding sexuality because she felt it had cost her her father's love and attention and because it had started a fight between her parents where they talked about divorce. Also her father's statement about rape and murder reinforced her own fears about becoming a woman in a society full of violence against women.

As a result, part of her wanted to be a little girl again. She began sucking her thumb, wetting the bed, and exhibiting other regressive behavior.

Mother's Helper

In homes where the mother is exceptionally stressed, as well as lonely, she may, in desperation, turn to one of her children for excessive emotional or other forms of support. Generally, women more often turn to daughters than sons for help with housework or child care, which in turn sets the stage for talking and emotional sharing.

Harry and Nelda's family is typical of this excessive use of a child for emotional support. Nelda had a fourth child, whose birth precipitated a panic attack in Harry, who found himself having flashbacks and periods of being unable to concentrate during surgery. He resigned from his position as a surgeon at a major urban hospital and found a job writing medical reports. However, the pay was less and since his depression had worsened, he was unable to stay focused on intellectual tasks, despite his brilliance. As a result, Nelda had to help him with his report writing, even though she had also had to assume a full-time job to make up for Harry's lower salary. Meanwhile, her fourth child was still an infant.

"It started when I found Mom crying in the kitchen, saying 'God help me. I can't do it all. I just can't do it all,'" says Joleen.

"'I'll help you Mommy,' I said, and from that day on I helped with all the dishwashing and dinner preparation and cleanup. I felt proud to be able to help my Mom, and when the new baby got old enough for me to hold, I took over being Mom to him too.

"I didn't mind not being able to watch T.V. after school, but I did mind having to quit Girl Scouts. But Mom needed me more and more and I had to help her so she could help Daddy so our family wouldn't be poor and have to move."

However, it was not Nelda's turning to Joleen for household help that was destructive, but rather Nelda's sharing of her marital secrets and emotional pain with her daughter. As Nelda instructed her daughter in certain chores, or as they did them together, Nelda would often graphically describe to Joleen how Harry verbally denigrated her and how disappointed she was with her marriage. She also warned Joleen never to marry a Vietnam veteran, or any kind of veteran.

At the age of seven, Joleen was unprepared to hear her mother's secrets about her father. Yet Joleen also felt privileged that her mother would turn to her. Since her father was usually emotionally distant from her and had often disappointed her, Joleen quickly sided with her mother. Yet, as any child, she still wanted and needed to believe that her father was a good man.

Surely her Daddy wasn't that bad. And if he was so horrible, didn't that make her, as his daughter, horrible too? Also, Joleen felt disloyal listening to her mother talk against her father. But how, at age seven, could she tell her poor victimized Mommy to stop?

As a child, Joleen had few defenses against her mother's feelings. She was easily overpowered by them and they became a part of her personality. Instead of developing along her own lines and having her own feelings, Joleen took on her mother's personality and emotions. Joleen became "enmeshed" with her mother.

For example, she would feel her mother's pain and sorrow as if they were her own and intuitively knew when her mother would be sad or unhappy. Often she would spend her allowance to buy her mother perfume or flowers, saying, "Someday Daddy will love you again and buy you presents. Meanwhile, you have me."

Starved for love and affection, Nelda accepted the gifts. By the age of 10, Joleen was not only buying her mother gifts, but giving her mother pep talks and advice on how to handle her husband and the other children. She could not imagine life without her mother and processed life through her mother's eyes. Furthermore, she dared not to be different from her mother, lest her mother crumble.

Needless to say, Joleen's peer relationships suffered. In addition, at the age of eleven or twelve, when children normally begin to separate from their parents, Joleen's natural separation process was stunted.

When Joleen, at age 13, developed an ulcer, Nelda went for help. "I know it wasn't fair of me to put Joleen between her father and myself," Nelda told the group. "But before this group, I had no one to turn to. My parents were far away and the only women I knew were the wives of other doctors. I couldn't talk to them because it would have ruined Harry's reputation. Besides, they would have never understood. All of their husbands were successful and none were having problems like Harry. Of course, none of their husbands had served in Vietnam either.

"I was so alone and afraid. Without Joleen I might have never been able to keep my sanity. And I needed her, I really needed her help. But I should have never had her take emotional care of me."

In order to reverse the dangerous trend which had begun in Joleen, Nelda ceased talking to her about her marital problems, asked Harry and Harry Jr. to assume some of Joleen's chores, even if they did balk at doing "women's work," and put Joleen in therapy.

According to Joleen's therapist, Joleen suffered from depression, as well as nightmares due to repressed anger and fears surrounding her enmeshment with her mother. In one recurring nightmare, her mother's hairbrush and one of her father's guns from Vietnam fly together from one room of the house to another, sometimes clashing into each other, sometimes chasing Joleen, and sometimes destroying furniture along the way. The hairbrush was interpreted as symbolizing her mother's anger, the gun, her father's. The dream shows that Joleen was afraid of her parents' arguing—as symbolized by the hairbrush and knife clashing into each other and destroying property—as well as her mother and father's individual anger toward her—as symbolized by both the hairbrush and the knife chasing Joleen. Joleen sincerely felt that if she did not help and comfort mother enough, mother would be mad. On the other hand, by sympathizing with her mother, Joleen was afraid of incurring the wrath of her father.

In another dream, Joleen envisioned herself as a mummy glued to her mother's leg. She asked her mother to release her, but her mother said, "No." This dream depicts the symbiotic nature of the mother-daughter relationship and Joleen's desire to be her own person, not someone attached to her mother. It also represents Joleen's awareness that if she remained an obedient "mother's helper" and caretaker, she would never become an individual. Instead she would remain a reflection of her mother's emotions and problems.

Joleen's progress in therapy was impeded by her brother Harry's teenage rebellion. Harry Jr. was now not only daring to talk back to his father, but deliberately defying his many rules, not completing his chores or homework, or staying out late. He even wanted to date an Asian girl! There were numerous father-son disputes, with Nelda threatening to commit suicide unless Harry and Harry Jr. came to terms.

Joleen was tempted to enter the fights as family peacemaker and to give her mother emotional support. In addition, she wanted to be an even more obedient and passive child in the family in order to compensate for her brother's rebellion. Joleen's therapist, however, advised her to detach from the family disputes as much as possible. Although Joleen could not help but have an emotional reaction to the family turmoil, she could stay in her room while the others argued. Also, Joleen was encouraged to continue being assertive about her need for time off from household duties in order to participate in some sports and social activities for herself.

Depression and conflicts such as Joleen's are not unique to Vietnam veteran families. In many families in which the mother is overwrought or dysfunctional, it is not uncommon for one of the daughters to become a little adult or to take emotional care of the mother or father. The resulting depression has also been observed among daughters of refugee camp survivors.[37]

There are many Joleens in the world. As they mature into young women, they may keep their "good girl" role of mother's helper and caring daughter, or they may become "bad girls" and abuse alcohol, drugs, and sex, all as a means of showing disregard for parental needs and rules. In the cases observed thus far, children who during their early years tried to "help" either mother or father may have discontinued this role at puberty or during the teen years. Some began rebelling against this role as soon as their bodies began to develop. Others were physiologically mature for several years before they made the break from their old family role.

Hence girls as young as 11 rebel against parental concerns by sexually acting out in front of their parents; other girls, only after they are

16 or 17, run away from home, bear children out of wedlock, or develop severe addictions. In a few cases adolescent boys (and girls) have chosen sexual partners whom they know either their mother or father would dislike (e.g., an Asian or someone from another racial or religious group one of the parents has stated he or she categorically dislikes).

While it is difficult to make global generalizations, in some cases adolescent sexual and other behavior can be an angry defiant act against one or both parents or against an overparentified role in the family. The same interpretation may also hold for reckless behavior in that it may be a means of expressing anger toward the parent (or parents) to whom the child was formerly tightly bonded in a helper capacity.

When Adolescents Express Anger

Adolescence is a time in life when children try to establish an identity of their own—apart from their parents' expectations of them. This process of separation and personal growth is called individuation. The tendency of adolescents to rebel against parental and other authority figures is, to some extent, a part of their effort to find out who they are.

In homes where the father suffers from PTSD, normal adolescent tendencies toward separation and rebellion can combine with the children's need to distance themselves from the veteran's agony or anger. Problems arise when the children's need for distance or self-assertion takes the form of rejection or disregard for the veteran.

The adolescents' negative attitude toward their father might be their way of defending themselves against feeling overwhelmed by the father's emotions or feeling helpless to help or "save" the father. Yet the veteran in the midst of a painful PTSD episode may not interpret his son's or daughter's rejection or indifference to him in such an objective or insightful manner. Quite to the contrary, the hurting veteran is likely to perceive his child's negative attitude toward him as a form of "friendly fire."

Imagine how a combat vet feels when his 15-year-old son or 18-year-old daughter snickers at him or ignores him at the very moment he is feeling most vulnerable or out of control (such as when he is angry, numb, confused, or weeping due to a PTSD-related flashback, nightmare, depression, or anxiety attack)? From the veteran's point of view, his own children are now mistreating him in the very same way his country did upon his return—with ridicule, rejection, and indifference.

Being spat upon by strangers is one thing, but being symbolically spat upon with sarcastic looks and words by one's own children is quite another. Such behavior on the part of adolescents can deepen the veteran's depression and sense of isolation, as well as ignite his rage. The stage is then set for an ugly family fight where no one wins. The only casualties in this fight are the people who probably love and need each other the most—the family members themselves.

More than one Vietnam wife's heart has been broken as she has seen her husband and teenage children snarl at each other and perhaps even come to blows. It is difficult for her to stand by and do nothing, no matter how adept she is at detachment. Yet when she attempts to intervene, she may be considered a "traitor" by all. Both her husband and children expect her to be on their side and their side only.

During such awful moments, the Vietnam wife has no one to turn to and no one to help her. She too, can feel helpless, powerless, and angry as the family life she has tried so hard to create is torn asunder. All her sacrifices and efforts seem to be being blown to bits, not by enemy fire, but by some kind of emotional time bomb planted within the hearts of her family members by a war fought in ride paddies long ago.

"It's so sad," comments Margaret, who has seen her husband and teenage children "go at it" dozens of times. "The children have felt unloved and criticized by their dad all their lives. When they were young, they accepted the way he treated them. No questions asked.

"Now that they're older, they know better. They know most dads don't spend most of their time in the basement and they're angry that other kids have dads who go to school events and take them places and their dad doesn't—or can't.

"When they were little, they were too afraid to tell their dad how angry they were. But no more. Last night my daughter said she'd get pregnant with a Vietnamese boy if my husband yelled at her one more time. Then my 18-year-old son said he'd forget about college and join the Marines so he could go crazy . . . just like dad.

"I try and get my husband and kids to talk it out peacefully, but they're all too raw to talk. One of them always says the wrong thing and that starts the civil war all over again.

"All any of them want is love. All my husband wants is to think his kids care about him. All they want from him is to hear him say, 'I love you. I wish I didn't have these problems from Vietnam, but I'm going to love you anyway—best I can.'

"And if my kids could just say, 'Dad, we love you. We missed you all those times you were in the basement. We thought you didn't like us and when we needed you we were scared to ask you for help. We might be growing up, but we still need a dad. Please come be with us,' my husband would probably start crying like a baby.

"But talking like that is impossible in my family. My husband is too angry and too proud. And now the kids are just like him—angry and proud. So all they do is fight and pop one smart remark after the next.

"When I try to intervene, they tell me it's none of my business. But how can it not be my business? They're my family."

Secondary Traumatization

One type of family which is considered dysfunctional is the enmeshed family. Joleen and her mother illustrate a case of mother-daughter enmeshment. Such enmeshment can also occur when one of the children becomes traumatized by the veteran's war experiences. This process, called "secondary traumatization," has been found not only among children of Vietnam veterans, but also among children of World War II veterans with PTSD, and among children of the survivors of the Nazi Holocaust.[38]

In secondary traumatization, the child, in some manner, relives his father's traumatic war experiences or becomes obsessed with the war-related issues which trouble and concern the veteran. The child may even manifest symptoms similar to the veteran's. The child may have nightmares about Vietnam, or combat, or worry a great deal about death and injury. Vet Center counselors report that, in some cases, children as young as three or four years old have learned to imitate their fathers and hide under their beds when an airplane or helicopter flies overhead. Whether or not these children actually experience fear or are simply imitating Daddy is not known.

In families of World War II veterans where there was secondary traumatization, R. Rosenheck also found that "for some of the veteran's offspring, their father was, by far, the most important person in their lives. It is as if they were constantly together, constantly embroiled in a shared emotional cauldron. For these children, life seems to have been a series of anticipation of, and reactions to, their father's moods, impulses, and obsessions."[39]

In another study, Rosenheck cites the case of Alan, the ten-year-old son of a Vietnam combat vet who, although he did not have nightmares, had great difficulty sleeping because he "worried about being killed or kidnapped. His main fear was that he, his father, or both would be shot 'like in the war.' In many of his (Alan's) fantasies, it was as if he was living in one of his father's flashbacks rather than in his own reality."[40] In the Vet Center study, about 65% of the counselors polled observed symptoms similar to the veteran's in his children. This does not mean that 65% of the children of Vietnam veterans evidence symptoms similar to their father's, but rather that 65% of the counselors said that they had witnessed this phenomenon in some children of vets.

I have observed only one child evidencing secondary traumatization. Like the ten-year-old described by Rosenheck, Ben was obsessed with power and violence. He was constantly playing war games and reading war comics, and only wanted war toys for Christmas. It was impossible to have a conversation with Ben without his mentioning Vietnam and his father's various heroic feats. Despite his superior I.Q., he had trouble concentrating in school and was in frequent fights. His participation in sports was intense, and, he admitted, a way to prove to his father that he was as strong and brave as any Vietnam veteran. Ben would also attack his sisters and the neighbors with plastic swords, hurling anti-Vietnamese epithets.

Children who suffer from secondary traumatization may or may not assume a "rescuer" role in relation to their fathers. The rescuer role may be assumed by another child in the family who takes it upon himself to help make the father happy.[41] Ben did assume the rescuer role and, when he wasn't playing sports or war games, spent an inordinate amount of time with his father, who was not only his father, but his best, if not only, friend.

At the age of 14, however, Ben, due to the natural changes of adolescence, began to want to separate from his father. Also, he became interested in girls, most of whom frowned on his interest in violence. Yet Ben felt guilty about experiencing the normal adolescent process of separating and becoming an individual, as if in growing up he was abandoning his father.

At the same time, Ben's father was experiencing his son's growing up—and away—as yet another loss, rekindling feelings of betrayal and abandonment associated with his war experience. In an effort to hold on to his son (who had been not only a son, but an admiring companion), Ben's father began to impose unnecessary restrictions on Ben's activities and to criticize Ben for minor imperfections, leading to further conflict between father and son, and more guilt on Ben's part.

Ben's father needed counseling to see that punishments and remarks were not bringing his son closer to him, but driving him farther away. Ben's father needed to be told repeatedly by his therapist, as well as by his friends who were parents, that losing children in their own lives is a normal part of parenthood, not a personal rejection.

Yet it still felt like a rejection to Ben's father and for a while he considered emotionally divorcing himself from his son and not interacting with him at all. "You don't have to disappear from your son's life. You only have to recede gradually," his therapist advised him.

"Your son still needs you and will continue to need you for the rest of your life. You are no longer in the forefront of his life as you were when he was younger, but this doesn't mean he doesn't love you. You need to learn to let go a little bit at a time."

The therapist's advice sounded easy, but Ben's father had difficulty tolerating the wrenching pain involved with allowing his son to develop his own interests and activities. Losing people is hard for anyone, but especially for Vietnam vets because they have already experienced many losses and because it threatens their sense of control. It highlights their powerlessness over other people, even their own children.

Yet this veteran was able to see that, by not being so demanding of his son's attention and by not creating friction over minor matters, Ben talked with him more and showed him more respect. The ultimate compliment came when, after a week of watching what he said, Ben's father heard Ben say, "Gee, Dad, you haven't bugged me for a whole week. That makes me feel real good. Like I have a real Dad."

On a day-to-day basis, however, it was usually difficult for Ben's father not to be jealous when his son rushed through dinner and then left to be with his friends. The pain of realizing that his son was growing up, and in small but real ways, progressively leaving him, filled him with anger and despair.

"What my son is doing is all so normal," he told his therapist. "Why can't I adjust?"

"Turn the situation around and look at the positive. Isn't your son's growth beautiful? Didn't you play a part in producing such a mentally and physically healthy child? Would you really want your son to have no friends and be glued to you all the time? What if all your son did was hang around with you? Then you really would have a problem."

There were still times when Ben's father had trouble accepting that his son was growing up. But with help, he was able to accept feelings of loss as part of living and to relate to his son in a more constructive manner.

Jim presents another case of secondary traumatization. Like Ben, Jim listened to his father's war stories but, more importantly, was present while his father grieved and expressed great remorse for having been involved in the killing of women and children. Some of these women and children were warriors in disguise; some were innocents. Jim took on his father's guilt, as well as his sorrow, and at age 15 began drinking heavily. While there were various reasons for his drinking problem, the internalization of his father's anguish and guilt was a major cause.

Jim was hospitalized several times for alcoholism. After each hospitalization he attended AA meetings and other recovery groups.

However, all his dedication to recovery did not seem to help him sustain sobriety.

Jim achieved sobriety only after the age of 25, when he met and married an impoverished Vietnamese refugee woman who had been brutalized during the war. He adopted not only her children, but her three siblings, one of whom had lost both legs during the war.

"I've never been happier," says Jim. "And alcohol no longer calls my name. There are four people who need me now. I can't afford to drink."

Advanced training in psychology is not needed to see that in caring for the traumatized Vietnamese refugees, Jim not only found a purpose for staying sober, but a means of making restitution for the actions over which his father carried such tremendous guilt, grief, and shame.

When the Veteran Overprotects and Overvalues His Children

While withdrawal from both wife and children is the most common pattern, there are instances where a veteran is able to maintain closeness with one or more of his children, but not his wife.[42] Even if a veteran is not particularly emotionally close to his children, however, he may still be extremely protective of them, triple checking their seat belts, carefully screening their friends and activities, or in general restricting their mobility.[43]

In addition to overprotection of children, overvaluation of children may occur. Overvaluing a child does not mean loving a child too much, for there are no real bounds to parental love. Rather, overvaluing a child means that the child becomes the parent's major, if not only, reason for living or that the child functions as a symbol or as a form of restitution for what the parent has lost.[44] This results in tremendous pressure on the child to fulfill the parent's need for a purpose in life or to achieve goals which the parent was unable to fulfill due to the war.

For example, a vet who lost his arm in Vietnam deeply desired that his son become a musician, which had been his career choice prior to his war injury. He gave his son music lessons, took him to concerts, and in many other ways encouraged his son to develop his musical talents. Upon reaching adolescence, however, the son abandoned his interest in music. Initially the veteran argued with him. Yet he eventually realized that he could not force his son into a musical career. As a result, the vet had to once again suffer his grief about his lost arm and musical career, a sorrow which the hope that his son would be a musician had eased substantially for many years.

Issues surrounding grief become more prominent as the veteran approaches midlife and wants to leave a legacy to the next generation. If
his children, whom he values so much, turn out different than he
hoped, or, for some reason, fail to idealize him as a parent, the veteran's
resulting despair may be great.[45]

For Vietnam veterans, a child's birth may symbolize the rebirth of
a dead buddy or of a dead Vietnamese girlfriend.[46] Even if the child does
not have a symbolic identity for the veteran, the child may provide the
veteran with his only real reason for living. Harry, for example, for all
his ambivalence toward his children, has frequently stated (both in
group and in front of his family) that if it weren't for his children, he
would have killed himself long ago. With his professional skills and ambitions at a standstill due to PTSD, and with his marriage now devoid
of love and passion, without his children there "would be no point in
living."

When Harry became suicidal, he pasted pictures of his children on
his car dashboard so as to resist his temptation to drive his car off the
road. His children, particularly Joleen and Harry Jr., were aware of the
pictures and experienced their importance to their father as an awesome
sense of responsibility for his well-being and for his very life. As a result,
Joleen and Harry Jr. became extremely anxious about not pleasing their
father. If they were delayed somewhere, they were frantic about finding
a phone to let him know they were safe; otherwise they were afraid he
would think the worst and try to kill himself. On the surface the children's anxiety was not apparent. It manifested itself in a decreased ability to enjoy themselves and a mental preoccupation with their father's
well-being.

Even after Harry's suicidal periods became less frequent and less intense, his children showed considerable concern for him and felt it was
their role to help take care of him. When Nelda would mention wanting to leave Harry, the children would protest. "You can't do that.
Daddy will kill himself," they said.

Today, however, some five years after Harry's last serious suicidal depression, Harry Jr. seems relatively free of excess concern about his father. Joleen, however, still worries about him and sometimes restricts
her activities so that she can stay home and protect her father from
himself. Even though she has been repeatedly told by her therapist, her
mother, and Harry himself that he is no longer actively suicidal and that
she is not responsible for his well-being, the old notion that she must
protect her father still exists in her mind.

Violence in the Family

Mark was referred for psychological testing due to poor school performance. He was also in frequent fights with his schoolmates and enjoyed disrupting the classroom. Talking with Mark revealed that his father began to beat him and his mother soon after returning from Vietnam. Despite his above average I.Q., Mark often could not concentrate on his schoolwork because he never knew in what condition he would find his mother after school or whether he would be abused himself. His aggression toward his peers and teachers was, to some extent, a displacement of his angry feelings toward his father, whom he was too small and weak to oppose.

When Mark was told that punching his peers and knocking them to the ground was wrong, he was surprised. He felt that hitting was okay. He had learned that violence was permissible from his father, who felt it was every man's right to beat his wife or girlfriend. Furthermore, the police usually supported Mark's father in this notion. When Mark's mother would call for help, sometimes the police would not even come. While the traditional police policy of "no arrest, get out fast, protect yourself," is slowly on its way out in some areas, it was still in effect in Mark's middle-class suburban neighborhood where, despite the new antibattering legislation, men could get by with almost murdering their wives.

One factor in the police's attitude may have been the fact that the largest percentage of police fatalities (some 23%) and some 40% of police injuries occur while intervening in family disputes. Training bulletins in some police departments explicitly warn officers of the danger to their lives if they arrest husbands, who are apt to turn on police to save face.[47] Among the police in Mark's neighborhood, it was well-known that Mark's father was a former combat Marine. Perhaps this awareness contributed to their avoidance of Mark's mother's calls and to their usually blaming the abuse on her. Other Vietnam wives whose husbands' fighting skills are known in the community have had similar problems with police response.

The root of Mark's father's violence was his low self-esteem. Even though he left Vietnam decorated as a hero and was now the manager of an electronics communication firm, Mark's father did not feel like a hero at all. He expended much of his psychic energy hiding his self-doubts, not only from others, but from himself as well. Battering was his means of coping not only with his present life frustrations, but with many of his unresolved feelings about Vietnam.

Family violence is often multigenerational—it tends to be passed down from one generation to the next.[48] Therefore, it followed that Mark would pattern himself after his father and use hitting and other forms of physical aggression as a means of feeling important, of coping with daily living, and of dealing with feelings. For example, if Mark felt slighted by another child, he would instantly hit the child rather than feel the pain of being rejected. Or if a teacher gave Mark a low grade, she could expect to be insulted or to have her property vandalized.

While Mark admired his powerful father, Mark also hated him. When Mark was in kindergarten, Mark used to pray that his father would get drunk and pass out. That way he would not have to feel helpless and impotent as he heard his mother scream. Many times Mark tried to protect his mother—only to be slammed against the wall and further emasculated by his father's taunts of "punk," "wimp," or "sissy."

In many abusive homes, often one child is singled out to be abused and he or she becomes the family's battered child. But in Mark's home, both Mark and his younger brother were beaten. The sisters were spared. Research shows that while girls are more often the recipients of sexual assault within the family, boys are more often the targets of severe physical battering.[49] "Boys are tough; they can take it. Girls can't," the thinking goes. Often the physical battering of boys is rationalized as a means of preparing them for the rigors of manhood.

Ostensibly in order to "toughen up" his sons, Mark's father did not allow them to cry or show pain. If they did they were beaten even harder. On some level, Mark felt responsible for his own abuse. If only he was more lovable, smarter, or better, then his father would not beat him so.

Psychological testing revealed that Mark's chronic internal guilt and poor self-image began at the age of four in his mother's kitchen. There Mark saw his father cut his mother's arms three times as a punishment for Mark's poor table manners. Obviously Mark's table manners were but a pretext for the abuse. However, given the egocentric thinking of children, after this incident, Mark began to take responsibility for the parental fights and kept trying to be perfect in hopes of keeping battering incidents to a minimum.

Mark harbored considerable hostility toward his father. Yet, he also loved him very much. After all, his father was not an inhuman monster, but an individual with many strengths and admirable qualities. Mark's father could be exceptionally charming, loving, and playful. When not being brutish, he would take Mark and his brother on camping trips and overseas vacations and lavish them with the special attention every child craves from his father.

Furthermore, the three-stage battering cycle which applied to

Mark's father and mother also applied to Mark and his father. Battering tends to occur in a three-stage cycle. During stage one, the tension rising stage, tensions rise between the couple, leading to stage two, the acute battering incident. Following the violence, however, comes stage three, the honeymoon stage, where the abuser repents and promises never again to hurt the woman he so loves. Usually this stage is accompanied by a profusion of gifts and ardent lovemaking, during which the woman's hopes for love and romance are renewed. Therefore she forgives and stays.

While this pattern of arguing and making up is common to many relationships, the distinctive feature of the battering cycle is that it involves what psychologist Lenore Walker calls a "sense of overkill."[50] The batterer is extreme, not only in his physical cruelty, but in his loving repentant behavior. Mark's father, for example, once tried to cut off his wife's hair, while also punching her. When she tried to phone the police, he ripped the phone off the wall. She finally escaped to her bedroom, where she locked herself up for 12 hours and contemplated suicide. When her husband returned from work that evening, he gave her a 12-stone ruby ring, which he had purchased for her in Thailand during R&R and had been saving to give to her at "just the right moment." He begged his wife's forgiveness. This time he was truly sorry. Surely it would never happen again. Just to prove it, he would go to church on Sunday.

This honeymoon period lasted three weeks. After the next incident, Mark's father came home with a gold-plated hairbrush and a bouquet of orchids.

The same battering cycle applied to Mark and his father, who would come home with carloads of gifts for his sons following particularly severe beatings. Other times he took them out to dinner or to a ball game, shared "top-secret" Vietnam war stories with them, or in other ways was the most wonderful father imaginable. During these brief times, Mark's spirits soared. His dreams of having a "real father" were kindled and he was determined to be the best boy imaginable so his father would continue to love him. But when his father would become abusive again, as he always would, Mark's self-confidence would crash.

Starved for his father's affection and approval, Mark was determined to join the Marines when he came of age. There he would volunteer for the most difficult assignments. Mark hoped that our country would be involved in another Vietnam war by then, so he could prove his manhood to his father, as well as to himself. Meanwhile he would content himself with wearing Vietnam combat fatigues and harassing the Vietnamese clerks at the local drugstore.

Although Mark presented a tough-guy image, in reality he was frightened not only of the world, but of the monsters on his inside. He had panic attacks which he never shared with anyone. In the course of therapy, it was discovered that the monsters he feared were his own feelings, specifically his murderous, vengeful impulses, not only toward his father, but toward his mother as well.

Mark saw his mother as a victim, but he valued strength and despised his mother for being weak. Fundamentally, he was furious with her for accepting the abuse and for failing to protect him from the father. It did not help that Mark's father often blamed his wife for his abusiveness. "I'm only hitting you because your mother did . . . ," or "Your mother makes me hit you." Sometimes Mark's father would even claim that his wife had beaten herself up, even though Mark himself had witnessed the beating.

Mark did not know what to believe, his eyes or his father's lies. In addition, he was exposed to so much verbal denigration of his mother by his father that he lost most of his respect for his mother despite his love for her.

Mark also resented his mother when she put his father first, as she often had to, to keep the peace, and consequently had little time for him. In general, depending on the level of abuse, battered Vietnam wives often struggle to fulfill their maternal role. They usually have to spend so much of their time placating the veteran, avoiding beatings, or recovering from them, they sometimes have little energy left over for nurturing their children. At times, they may even wish they were childless so they could run away from home with ease.

Mark's mother was a very dedicated mother. Yet, on some level, she resented Mark, as she did all her children, for it was her very dedication to them which prevented her from leaving her abusive veteran. On one occasion, unforgettable to Mark, she communicated the depth of her resentment.

Once, when Mark was six, his father came home drunk. That night the acute battering incident lasted six hours. Listening to his mother's cries and troubled by fantasies of hurting his father, Mark could not sleep.

The next morning, Mark's father left for work, cursing his wife and blaming her for making him drink and causing the beating. If she were not such an inept dumb-dumb, he would not have to discipline her to keep the family in order.

As soon as his father slammed the door, Mark felt sick to his stomach. When his mother stooped to help him, she winced with pain.

Three of her ribs were broken. But she was not going for medical treatment. She was forbidden to go to the family doctor. If she kept showing up at his office with injuries, he might become suspicious. Usually Mark's mother, like many abused women, went to the hospital emergency room.[51] Treatment was more impersonal there and lies such as "I fell off a ladder" were more readily believed. But Mark's father had to approve first.

Weeping over the toilet bowl, Mark's mother removed the ruby ring from her finger and threw it down the toilet.

Mark was horrified. "Dad will kill you for that."

She just glared at him, grabbed the gold-plated hairbrush and tried to flush it down the toilet too.

"Stop, Mom!"

"You stop!" she growled back. "I wish I could flush you down the toilet. You, your brother, and all your sisters and Vietnam too. If it weren't for you kids and that . . . war, I'd have been out of here long ago. Now I'm trapped, a slave in my own home."

The woman then became hysterical. "Don't you ever cross me, Mark. Or I'll whip you with this hairbrush."

Mark's mother never used the gold-plated hairbrush, or any other physical force, on her children. Other parents, however, have used hairbrushes and other weapons on their children, sometimes with deep, long-term effects.

To date, there are no formal studies of children from abusive Vietnam veteran homes. In general, our knowledge of children from violent homes is limited. Preliminary studies, however, show that these children often do not achieve at their grade level and evidence various emotional immaturities.[52] Some of these children cling to stuffed animals, their blankets, or other security symbols long after their peers have abandoned such objects. In school, they may have reading or math problems, even though they do not have a learning disability. Mark's brother, for example, also performed below-average in school. In fact, he was considered almost mentally retarded by school officials until psychological testing revealed that he had an average I.Q. His school performance was stymied by the violence at home, which rendered him passive, rather than aggressive like Mark. Like his brother, this child was also involved in school fights, but of a different nature. He did not attack other children. Rather, whenever he saw other children fighting, he would intervene to help protect the weaker one.

According to Walker, in a paper presented to the American Psychological Association, existing studies also show that a disproportionate number of children from violent homes become runaways, alcoholics, drug addicts, prostitutes, and pimps. For many, life on the streets seems more benevolent than life at home, where the two people they love and need the most are tearing each other apart.[53] Some children side with the victim (the mother); others identify with the aggressor (the father) and eventually come to imitate him by abusing the mother and perhaps other family members as well. Most children, however, feel some loyalty toward both parents and become split down the middle emotionally. They also tend to have ambivalent feelings toward both parents loving them, yet also hating them for all the fighting. "If they really loved me, they wouldn't fight," explains Mark.

Like combat vets, children from violent homes can learn to "tune out" and deny the violence. They can just continue watching T.V. or listening to the radio. Even when their mother emerges black and blue, or bleeding, they may act as if nothing happened. As they grow older, these children may turn to alcohol, food, or drugs as a way of furthering the pattern of denial and emotional numbing.[54]

Vietnam veterans who were also battered as children sometimes have two sets of PTSD: one from the Vietnam war and another from their childhood. They have flashbacks not only about the Viet Cong, but about their angry fathers. After issues regarding Vietnam are dealt with, vets who were battered as children often need to examine yet another level of trauma—that of being abused by a parent.

According to the Vet Center study, some 10% of Vietnam wives seen report that their husband is physically abusive to one or more of their children. This does not mean that 10% of Vietnam veterans are child abusers, but rather that at the Vet Centers polled, counselors found approximately 10% of wives seeking help complaining about this problem. Child abuse is a widespread social problem affecting all social groups, not just Vietnam veterans with PTSD. In 1985, for example, there were 1,928,000 reported cases of child abuse and neglect. Some 40%–43% of these cases were substantiated.[55] Other surveys, however, suggest that the actual rates of physical abuse of children are higher than official reports show.[56] A recent report found that in 1986 approximately 1,300 children were killed by their parents. This represents a 23% increase from 1985.[57]

Studies of family violence show that once violence is introduced into a home, it not only escalates over time but has the potential of spreading to more than one family member. While there is no in-depth study specifically on the dynamics of family violence in Vietnam veteran homes, it can only be assumed that the phenomenon observed in other homes where there is physical abuse of the wife may also hold true in violent PTSD-afflicted homes. Further research, however, would be needed to clarify this point.

In general, however, it has been found that there is a greater probability that children will be injured in a home where there is wife abuse than in a home where the mother is not being violated. In homes where there is physical abuse of the mother, the children may be injured simply because they are in the way; because they, like Mark, try to protect their mother; or because their mother uses them as a shield against the veteran.

Furthermore, if a veteran is in the hitting habit, when his wife is not available as a victim, he may extend his violence to his children.

When child abuse occurs in a Vietnam home, it is more likely to be committed by the veteran than by his wife. According to the Vet Center study, only approximately 3% of Vietnam wives who seek help report having abused their children. This finding supports my observation that the majority of the women who have attended the Vet Center group have proven to be extremely dedicated mothers. They work hard to provide their children not only with the necessities of life, but also with needed psychotherapy, medical attention, or educational help. Most of the mothers who are single now continually put their children's needs above their own. Free evenings are not spent at parties or the spa, but driving children to therapy, doctor's appointments, or to Al-A-Teen meetings.

Yet there have been instances where women have been under so much stress for such an extended period of time that they have succumbed to physically assaulting one of their children. Some of the incidents did border on child abuse. In each case, the assault was a one-time occurrence, reflecting the woman's extreme state of physical and psychological exhaustion. In addition, each assault also involved displaced anger toward the veteran. Afraid to talk back to, or confront, her husband for fear that he would strike her or "go crazy" some other way, the woman would discharge her frustrations and pent up anger toward her veteran on a relatively safe, available target—her child.

Needless to say, the guilt and loss of self-esteem experienced by the mother who has hurt her child are enormous, in some instances precipitating a suicide attempt on her part. Her guilt also usually prevents her from giving herself much-needed rest or "time out" from her many duties, both inside and outside the home, or from seeking help.

It cannot be overemphasized that no woman who has attended group thus far could be classified as a child abuser and that those who have committed even a single act of physical child abuse number less than 4%. Almost all of them function as their children's major caretaker, emotional support system, and protector from the veteran's indifference and inconsistencies toward his children or his emotional or physical abuse of them.

Yet, among the battered Vietnam wives, there have been instances where the woman has put her husband before her children, sometimes due to her real fear of her husband, but sometimes due to her intense psychological attachment to him. In several cases, adolescent and even preadolescent children of battered Vietnam wives have run away from home to avoid being beaten by their veteran father. In other instances, children have run away from home to protest the beating of their mother, even though they themselves were not abused.

In cases where the abused Vietnam wife has allowed her child to be abused in order to appease her batterer, the knowledge that she has sacrificed her child to her veteran's anger diminishes her already low self-esteem and confirms her batterer's image of herself as a worthless person and "no good" mother. Hence when her child leaves her or verbally chastises her, she feels she deserves it and increasingly sinks into a state of helpless passivity and personal despair. While the beating of one of her children has often precipitated the battered woman's flight from her home, some abused Vietnam wives have not had the economic means to escape or their self-esteem has become so eroded that they lack the will and self-confidence to make the break.

Children and Alcoholism

"I grew up in a little Vietnam," says a child of an alcoholic. "I didn't know why I was there. I didn't really know who the enemy was."[58]

Like children from violent homes, children from alcoholic homes also suffer from living in the emotional crossfire between the parents. Often they learn to suppress their feelings—especially their anger—and their emotional needs. Many erroneously feel that they are the cause of their father's drinking. Girls especially may adopt a caretaker role toward the alcoholic or toward the mother.

Also like children from violent homes, children from alcoholic homes frequently suffer from low self-esteem and guilt. With approximately 90% of child abuse cases involving alcohol, children of alcoholic homes may also develop some of the symptoms of PTSD.[59]

These patterns, however, are common to many alcoholic homes, not only to homes where there is both PTSD and alcoholism. Yet, when the alcoholic also has PTSD, these patterns become intensified for there are now two powerful forces which keep children emotionally stifled and feeling guilty about their father's condition. For example, Lisa's father is a vet who became addicted to alcohol only after his tour of duty and who used alcohol in order to deal with his PTSD. While he was drinking, there was no clue that Vietnam haunted his present life. Before he joined A.A., all Lisa had to worry about was whether or not her father would be too drunk to help her with her homework or drive her to her piano lessons.

After her father joined A.A., however, his PTSD clearly emerged. Before, he was waking up in the middle of the night to drink. Now he was waking up to search out Viet Cong. In both situations, Lisa felt protective of her father but it was more embarrassing for her to have a father who thought himself in the jungles than one who drank too much. At least alcoholism was something her friends had heard of. Alcoholism was bad but it wasn't "crazy," like PTSD. Who had heard of PTSD?

Stepchildren

Some Vietnam veterans are jealous of their children. The birth of a child and the many demands of parenting (especially during the early years) usually divert the wife's attention away from the veteran to her child. Young children interrupt not only lovemaking, but the quiet and privacy which the PTSD-afflicted veteran might feel he needs in order to recover from his war experiences.

If a vet has cause to resent his own children, how much more so those of another man? While no research has yet been completed on stepchildren of Vietnam veterans, in my experience some of the most severe cases of child abuse have occurred in families where there are stepchildren. In each instance, however, the veteran was not in treatment or was attending therapy irregularly.

While child abuse has certainly not occurred in each family where there are stepchildren, the majority of women with children from former marriages report that their vet frequently resents the time and money they spend on these children. Such jealousy, however, is not uncommon among blended families. In a few extreme cases, the veteran insisted that the wife send her children by her former marriage to their father or to another relative.

The Pros and Cons of Disclosing the Trauma

At the 1994 convention of the International Society for Traumatic Stress Studies, a panel of experts in the area of trauma discussed the effects of parental trauma on children. While most of the discussion centered around the children of Holocaust or incest survivors, many parallels can be drawn between these children and children of Vietnam veterans.[60]

The panel emphasized that the relationship between parental trauma and the child's emotional and mental development is highly complex. In the first place, traumatized parents, such as combat veterans, are not all the same and each individual reacts to his or her trauma in his own way. Secondly, parental trauma is not the only factor affecting a child. Thirdly, parents vary in the ways in which and degrees to which they disclose aspects of their traumatic pasts. Fourthly, parents vary in their motives for such disclosure.

Furthermore, the effects of trauma do not go just from parent to child, but also from child to parent. Kathi Nader, for example, points out that trauma does not just go up and down, from the older generation to the younger, but back and forth, from the younger to the older and vice versa.

Nader gives an example of a World War II veteran who lost his hair after his son was sent to Vietnam. After his son returned, the father's hair grew back. This is an instance of how a child entering a situation which was traumatic for the parent can greatly affect the parent.

In my experience, numerous Vietnam veterans sought help for their combat stress only after their sons or daughters were sent overseas or were in danger of being called to serve in the Persian Gulf conflict. Some of these veterans had experienced PTSD symptoms during and after their tour in Vietnam. But their symptoms had never debilitated them sufficiently so that they felt they needed to seek help until one of their children was sent overseas to the Persian Gulf.

The panel also pointed out that a child's growth could activate a combat veteran's trauma. Children's aggressive feelings, especially when directed toward the veteran or other family members and the child's emerging sexuality, can also activate strong feelings in the veteran. The veteran may try to hide his reactions from his children, but children cannot help but observe their father's increased distress or symptoms.

As a result, children may come to feel that their normal growth processes, feelings of aggression, or evolving sexuality are threatening or troublesome for their parent. Children can then feel guilty, as if they are wounding an already hurting parent. At the same time, children can resent having to feeling guilty, as well as angry for not being allowed to grow up and "be normal" like other children.

As the panel cited above concluded, in homes where the father is a combat veteran, the effect of war experiences on his children is not a simple one, for the child is not a blank slate upon which the parent's trauma is written. Children have their own issues and conflicts which interact with their knowledge of, or fantasies about, their father's war trauma.

In homes where the veteran is obviously suffering, but there is no talk of Vietnam or why father is so sad, so angry, or so confused, the child is exposed to the father's pain and depression with little understanding as to why the father is so tormented. Children then have to come up with their own explanations. On the most simple level, they may feel as if they are at fault. "If only I were a more lovable, more obedient, or more [something] child, my father would not be so unhappy," they may think. Or they may fantasize a reason (e.g., if their father has a physical disability or scars from combat, the children may surmise that their father is very ill and perhaps dying). Yet they don't know if their thoughts are true and hence may be confused.

If children are told nothing about their father's war experiences, yet know their father was a combat veteran, they may fantasize about their father's trauma or mix fantasy in with whatever partial knowledge they have about the Vietnam war. Their knowledge may be from the media and other non-familial sources, from relatives who may inadvertently drop small bits of information about their father or the war in general, or from overheard conversations between their parents or between one of the parents and other adults.

For example, a child may have heard from the media or friends that soldiers in Vietnam were "babykillers." Even though the father may not have hurt civilians and has never discussed his killer role in Vietnam, the child may fantasize or wonder if father did hurt children. If, at the same time, children are struggling with jealous feelings toward a younger sibling, step-siblings, or other new members of the family, the fantasies of the father's aggression can fuse with their own fantasies about hurting the young rival for attention in the family. As a result, the guilt a child might feel about wishing harm to a newborn brother or sister, niece or nephew, or grandchild is intensified by any guilt the child might be carrying regarding the father's actions in Vietnam.

The affected child may be young or an adolescent. For example, Susan, age 18, is the youngest of three children born to Charles, a Vietnam combat vet. As the youngest and only daughter, she was feted over by her parents, aunts, and uncles. However, when Susan's oldest brother married and had a baby girl, the new baby became the center of the family's attention and replaced Susan as the family's "little darling."

Susan felt she was too old to be jealous, yet she resented her young niece. When Susan babysat her niece, she was distressed to find herself fantasizing slitting the child's throat, as she imagined her father had done to Vietnamese infants. Imprinted in her mind were photographs of the My Lai massacre which she had seen in a magazine at her school library.

"Your father was there, wasn't he?" a schoolmate had taunted her.

Charles had not been at My Lai. Nor had he killed any children in Vietnam. But Susan did not know that. All she knew was that her father didn't talk about Vietnam and refused to answer any of her questions about what he did or did not do there. He refrained from discussing Vietnam with his children in order to protect them from being traumatized, but the lack of discussion left many questions in Susan's mind about what her father did or did not do. Due to her classmate's and other's assumption that all Vietnam veterans committed atrocities, Susan began to feel guilt over what her father might have done as a combat vet. This guilt, combined with her own guilt over her own murderous wishes toward her baby niece, became an enormous burden. Yet she could not tell anyone of her thoughts about her father or her niece. She was certain she would be seen as an evil person if she talked about her jealousy toward her niece and as a disloyal daughter if she expressed concerns about her father's combat role.

Another problem area for Susan, as for other children of combat veterans, especially adolescents, is their father's wartime sexual behavior. As children read newspaper accounts of the rape and mistreatment of women and girls in present wars, they almost cannot help but wonder if their father saw or was involved in such behavior himself. They may also wonder if their father frequented prostitutes in Vietnam or coerced any Vietnamese girls or women into sexual acts with him.

These questions take on special importance if the veteran was already married to their mother while in Vietnam. If children feel that their father had sexual relations while in Vietnam, in addition to any feelings they might have regarding their father as a sexual being, they might also feel their father betrayed and belittled their mother by his behavior.

If such questions appear while the child is entering adolescence or struggling with his or her own sexual issues, the child's sexual identity and values may be affected. On the other hand, open communication between parent and child on the issue of the father's relations to Vietnamese women (or other women) during his military career is extremely difficult. Not only is sex a relatively taboo topic in many families, but the subject may have traumatic memories for the father.

In addition, quite justifiably, a veteran may feel his wife and children can not handle the truth about his sexual behavior in Vietnam. If a veteran told his wife or children that he raped women in Vietnam or that he had sex with preadolescent prostitutes there, he may fear he might destroy his marriage, as well as his children's faith in him. Also, he may have trouble remembering or accepting such behavior himself and therefore be unable to talk about it at all, even with his therapist, much less with his family members.

On the other hand, the child's fantasies about the father's behavior might be much worse than the father's actual actions. For example, children might wonder if their father left children in Vietnam. Such a question may have been sparked by the publicity given to the plight of Amerasian children in the early 1990s and the publicized attempts of some Vietnam veterans to try and locate former girlfriends and children they had left in Vietnam. The 1990s also saw the emergence of news-clips and movies on the subject, as well as books and articles by Vietnamese women about their experiences with American soldiers.

Children may feel disappointed in their fathers if they somehow suspect he had children in Vietnam, then left them there. Children may then reason that if their father abandoned his Vietnamese child, he might also abandon them. On the other hand, they might feel relieved that they do not have to contend with a half-Asian step-sibling in the home.

In a few cases where the veteran and his wife adopted a Vietnamese or Asian child, the veteran's natural child may wonder if the Asian half-sibling is a substitute for a child left in Vietnam. The truth may be, however, that the father did not abandon his Vietnamese child, but that the child and/or its mother were killed or lost in the confusion of war.

Research in the area of the effects of exposure to a father's combat trauma on children is extremely limited. However, it appears to me that caring parents are in a double bind. If the veteran and his wife tell the children nothing about the father's war experiences, the child is left to imagine what happened or didn't happen. The child's fantasies, along with whatever information or misinformation about the war presented by the media or obtained from family members, can dominate the child's perceptions about the father's experiences.[61]

On the other hand, to talk about combat and other traumatic experiences associated with combat may overwhelm the child. Ideally, the information is presented to the child in an age-appropriate manner and the child's reactions to the information are processed and discussed with the child sufficiently. In general, partial knowledge or sharing traumatic stories with a child without also giving that child the opportunity to process the information and support in coping with the information has the potential of complicating the child's development. In other words, partial knowing or incompletely processed knowing has the potential for creating as much emotional conflict and pain in the child as not knowing at all.

While parents may wonder what is the right thing to do, there is no single answer. Some children might be relieved to hear the truth because the truth is much more benign than their fantasies. On the other hand, when told the truth, some children may feel intruded upon and angry. The knowledge of trauma given to them may create negative self-esteem and the children may come to feel as scarred, unlovable, tainted or "abnormal" as their PTSD-afflicted father.

The problem with trauma is that it just doesn't go away. Whether the veteran talks about it or not, whether traumatic material is shared with the children or not, trauma makes its impact. The crucial ingredient is how the trauma is discussed in the family and the supports available to those who were traumatized or who live with someone who was. It is also crucial, yet very difficult, for veterans and their families to be able to identify whether it is the trauma or its aftermath which is upsetting their lives. When they can draw a connection between a family problem and the trauma they can be spared the self-defeating conclusion that the family problem is a sign of someone's personal or moral failure, unlovableness, or incompetence.

Helping Children Cope With PTSD

Based on his studies of children of World War II veterans and Vietnam veterans with PTSD, Robert Rosenheck suggests that children who are extensively and repeatedly exposed to detailed descriptions of their father's traumatic war experiences are more likely to develop secondary traumatization than children who are given little or no information about their father's war experiences. He notes that secondary traumatization did not occur in those World War II families where the father deliberately kept his war experiences a secret so as not to negatively affect his children.[62]

This finding, however, should not imply that Vietnam cannot be openly discussed in the family. There is a profound difference between excessively exposing a child to descriptions of traumatic events and giving that child certain basic information about the nature of the Vietnam war and the potentially devastating effect of war on the human psyche. Furthermore, children from homes in which there are "no talk" rules often hunger to understand their father. In addition, if they are educated about PTSD and its effects on the family, they are less likely to blame themselves for their father's problems. They will also feel less alienated from him.

While it is difficult, if not impossible, for young children to understand the nature of their father's war experiences, or to comprehend the meaning of these experiences to their father, even children as young as four or five can understand some of the father's basic feelings about his war experiences. While a young child will certainly not profit from gory descriptions of combat, he or she usually can understand sadness or anger: "Daddy is sad (or mad) because somebody he loved died (or got lost, sick) in the war." Perhaps an analogy could be made between the father's feelings and the child's feelings upon having a bike stolen or watching a pet die.

In addition, mothers can acknowledge to their children when their father is behaving unusually or inappropriately. While the mother need not denigrate or ridicule her husband, she can make factual statements about his behavior which may help the child to understand. A mother can say, "In the war, Daddy learned that noises meant danger. That is why he jumps when you drop something"; "In the war, Daddy learned to be afraid of strangers and new places. That is why he likes to sit near the door"; or, "Daddy walks around the house at night because he can't stop thinking about sad and scary things that happened in the war."

Often children, especially young children, cannot identify their feelings, especially when they are coping with several emotions at the same time. A mother can help her children become in touch with their various emotions by asking, "How do you feel when Daddy and Mommy argue so much?"; "when Daddy drinks so much?"; or "when Daddy makes a hole in the wall?"

If the children cannot articulate their feelings, the mother can suggest feelings to them. She can say, "If I were a little girl (or boy) and my Mommy and Daddy argued, I would be scared that they would start hitting each other and forget about taking care of me. I would be mad at them too. I would also be mixed up because I wouldn't know who was right and who was wrong. I would want both of them to be right because they are my Mom and Dad. I would want to stop the fight but I would feel sad because I wouldn't know how to make them stop. Do you ever feel any of these ways?"

Instead of pretending that her husband's absence or sudden departure from the home doesn't matter or shouldn't be talked about, a mother can acknowledge the reality of the father's absence and say, "When Daddy leaves like that, I worry about him. I wonder if he is safe and am scared that he might be hurt. But I'm also mad at him for leaving without saying where he is going. Sometimes I get so mad at him I wish he would never come back. But then I'm sorry for thinking like that. It sounds funny, but I can be mad at him and love him at the same time too. Do you ever feel like me?" or "How do you feel when Daddy is gone?"

Or, "When Daddy yells at me, I feel scared and angry. I feel as if it was my fault that he yelled even though I know it wasn't."

Depending on the particular family situation, a mother can encourage her children to share their feelings about their family life with her and with their father, if she judges her husband as being able to tolerate and accept the children's honesty. In addition, unacceptable behavior must not be denied or minimized. If there is violence in the home, it is important that it be stated that violence is wrong, and dangerous. Similarly, if the veteran has an alcohol or drug problem, it is important that the problem be acknowledged.

Regardless of their ages, children need to be told repeatedly that they are not the cause of their father's or their mother's turmoil. According to Ellen Salom, who has conducted groups for adolescent children of Vietnam veterans, adolescents can profit greatly from direct instruction about PTSD and its potential effects on family life.[63] In her groups, children hear lectures and see films about Vietnam and are encouraged to identify the particular symptoms their father exhibits. The ways in which their father's specific symptoms affect them and what they can do to cope are also discussed.

Salom also assists children in seeing that they probably have little to do with the veteran's emotions or actions, but that there are ways in which they can deal with their father's behavior. Children also receive help in recognizing "what they can control and what they cannot, what they are and are not responsible for."[64] In addition, children are assisted in developing their self-esteem. To date, an estimated 14% of Vet Centers offer programs for children.

Self-mutilating children, depressed or suicidal children, or children who manifest other psychological symptoms need help beyond a Vet Center children's group. A private psychologist, psychiatrist, or social worker must be consulted since most Vet Centers do not employ child specialists.

In addition, physical or sexual abuse of children cannot be tolerated. The children's physical safety must be a top priority, regardless of the circumstances. Either the abuser, or the children, must be removed from the home and appropriate help sought for each. Child abuse is not only a moral offense, but a crime. All states have mandatory child abuse reporting laws for professionals and others who come into contact with children. In some states, however, the mandatory child abuse reporting laws apply to all persons, including other family members. Therefore, a mother may be in violation of the child abuse laws of her state if she permits her children to be abused without reporting the abuser.

Summary

In homes where the veteran suffers from PTSD, the children are affected. Low self-esteem and self-blame for their father's unhappiness are the two most common problems seen so far. Some children will show symptoms similar to the father's.

If the vet tends to withdraw from his children because he cannot handle the pressures of parenting or because he had bad combat experiences with children, the children tend to feel unwanted, unloved, and inadequate. In some cases, they blame the mother for their father's PTSD and in other cases, they cling excessively to her.

Vietnam wives often feel as if they are single parents with the burden of their children's emotional and physical well-being on their shoulders alone. They often try to compensate for their husband's distancing behavior, alcoholism, or violence by being supermothers.

In some homes, the financial and emotional pressures on the parents sometimes lead to child abuse, by either the veteran or his wife. More common than physical abuse is verbal criticism of the children. While some vets distance themselves and avoid disciplining their children, others are deeply involved in excessively critical reviews of their children's behavior. In many instances, the Vietnam wife is a buffer between her children and her husband, finding herself unappreciated and misunderstood by both sides.

Children from PTSD-afflicted homes often suffer from mixed feelings about their parents and mixed loyalties. Their feelings of being different because of their father's PTSD is only compounded if he is also an alcoholic or violent. As a Vet Center counselor who works with these children suggests, "It is quite possible that the future will see self-help groups for Adult Children of Vietnam Veterans similar to contemporary groups for Adult Children of Alcoholics."

11

Suicide and the Vietnam Veteran Family

I was crazy about him. He was crazy about me. But why we were so attracted to each other, I'll probably never understand. I am beginning to understand, however, why Joel killed himself.

I met Joel about seven years after he got out of the service. His face was all scarred, but it wasn't just from Vietnam. It was from his youth in the slums of New Orleans too. Because of his childhood and Vietnam, he looked tough, but he was really very kind. He just didn't believe in himself, no matter what I said or did. He didn't believe in my love for him either.

For no particular reason, one day he woke up and said he was leaving me. He had to head up north where he could be free.

I thought there was something wrong with me, but I never asked. In those days, I never asked men questions, I just accepted what they said.

For a year and a half I wrote him in Wisconsin, where he was working on a farm. The first few months, he'd send me a postcard once a month. Then the postcards started getting shorter and shorter and fewer and fewer. When I called for his birthday, he refused the call. Then my letters started coming back to me unopened.

I gave up then and started dating other men. Eventually I married. About a month later, I received a letter from Joel's landlady. Joel had committed himself to a psychiatric hospital, then escaped his ward and thrown himself in front of a bus.

The landlady had seen my letters. No one else wrote Joel. She thought I would want to know.

My first reaction was to blame myself. Was it something I had said or done? Could I have possibly prevented this? Was it my fault for marrying another man?

But Joel hadn't even known I was engaged, much less married. And after all, he had rejected me, not the other way around. But still, I felt guilty.

Bits and pieces of our conversations came back to me. Sometimes he'd make jokes about 'Nam . . . about how his first day there he saw some guy blow his brains out and what color the brains were . . . about some village and some mother and child . . . about seeing heads mounted in the sand . . . about how even living in the slums hadn't prepared him for Vietnam. But he was always so funny about it that nobody realized he had a problem, not even he.

After the news of his death, I went to a counselor. She told me to detach from the situation—not to blame myself and to try not to let Joel's suicide upset me and my new marriage. But how can you detach from someone you loved? From someone you've slept with and given yourself to in so many ways?

At least if I could have attended his funeral, I could have mourned him. But I couldn't go and there was nowhere else to mourn him either until I came to group. To so many people, Joel was just a "shiftless, crazy" Vietnam vet. But I know there was more to him than that and that his death was something more than one guy's failure to cope.

—Joel's girlfriend, Brenda, now a volunteer at a Vietnam Veteran
Outreach Center

On June first, when Harry (the brain surgeon we met in Chapter 10) mentioned suicide, Nelda went into denial. His statement of suicidal intent raised her anxiety level to such a degree that she shoved it out of her mind. When Harry made subsequent remarks about wishing to die in a car accident or hoping that God would take him away, Nelda would tremble. She didn't know what to say and felt helpless. "Come off it," "Stop joking," or "Let's talk about something pleasant," she would say, or in other ways dismiss Harry's remarks.

Yet she was uneasy. Recent newspaper articles on suicide had warned that all suicidal statements should be taken seriously. Nelda had also read that the "person who most frequently commits suicide in the U.S. is a white Protestant male in his 40s or 50s on a downwardly mobile social course, who has suffered a severe interpersonal loss in a relationship with wife or girlfriend, and who has used a gun to kill himself."[1] Physicians were also reported to have high suicide rates.[2]

While Harry did not have a gun and still had a marriage, he was a white Protestant physician approaching 50 and definitely on a downwardly mobile social and occupational course. When Nelda suggested having a small gathering in honor of his 49th birthday, Harry stormed out of the house. "I'm almost fifty now. Half my life is over and I've never truly lived. Don't talk to me about birthday parties. I need a death day party."

Harry then tore up a copy of his birth certificate.

Nelda obviously had cause for concern. However, the possibility that her husband would actually kill himself was so threatening to her, she preferred to hope that if Harry's suicidal wishes were not talked about they would magically disappear.

In addition, although Nelda would dare not admit it to herself, Harry's suicidal statements made her furious. How dare he talk about suicide! Didn't she have enough to deal with—children, teenagers, job, a financial crisis, and PTSD—without him becoming suicidal too? After all, Harry was supposed to be the man in the family, and now he was falling apart on her.

"You'll feel better after you eat breakfast," Nelda would tell Harry when he'd wake up saying he was profoundly sad to still be alive.

On October first, Harry announced to Nelda that if things didn't get better, he would kill himself on New Year's Eve. There were other signs also: Harry stopped attending group at the Vet Center and, although he had always been withdrawn from the family, he was now more withdrawn than ever. Sometimes he would spend the entire weekend in his bedroom. He had little, if any, interest in sex.

It was Harry's brother, John, however, who finally shattered Nelda's denial. Harry had given John a birthday present in advance, saying he would probably not be alive for his brother's birthday. He had also asked John to help take care of Nelda and the children after he killed himself with an overdose of certain medications. Since Harry was a physician, he could easily obtain any medications he wanted and knew perfectly well how many pills to take, and in what combinations, to die.

Nelda went into shock. She was finally facing the reality of Harry's suicide threats. Despite her anger at Harry, she did love him. She also felt guilty. Hadn't she been a good wife? Where had she failed him? Why hadn't she picked up on the obvious signs before? She was angry too. Didn't he want to live—for her?

"No, no, it can't be true," she sobbed in group. "But it is true. What do I do now?"

Nelda's first step was to talk to Harry openly about his suicidal plans and to contact his therapist at the local Vet Center. In cases of impending suicide—not vague suicidal wishes or suicidal thoughts—therapists sometimes decide to break the bonds of confidentiality and inform family members that their loved one is planning to kill themselves. Similarly, if a Vietnam wife determines that her husband shows definite signs of suicidal intent, she should not hesitate to call her husband's therapist, his minister, or other authorities. Depending on the circumstances, she may even decide to inform her husband's family, friends, or other persons who she feels could be helpful.

Also, the Vietnam wife need not hide her actions from her husband. Nelda told Harry, "I don't care whether you object or not, I'm letting your therapist and your parents know. You can go kill yourself if you want to, but you're going to have to fight us first."

In some cases, if the veteran is capable of violence or extreme paranoia, the actions suggested above may not be advisable. It is strongly suggested that the Vietnam wife discuss the particulars of her situation with a qualified mental health professional.

In general, suicidal persons usually welcome such action—and the subsequent attention. In many cases, they want someone else to take over. If they were 100% intent on killing themselves, they would have already done so. Instead, they chose to live and send out signals to others, hoping that someone would take care of them, give them hope, and affirm the worth of living.

Like Nelda, the Vietnam wife whose husband has been or is suicidal or who has suicidal periods lives under immense pressure. Even more than other wives, she refrains from expressing her anger and is careful about her speech and behavior toward her husband. In addition, she often searches for ways to minimize the stresses in her husband's life so as to avert a possible tragedy. Nelda, for example, found herself carefully monitoring not only her own actions, but those of her children. "Don't do that! Don't do this!" she'd say. "We can't let your father feel bad." She also tried to make life easier for Harry by not pressuring him to attend certain social and family functions. At first she was willing to go alone, despite the embarrassment. Eventually, however, she stopped going at all and became reclusive—like Harry. Only after Harry had made noticeable progress in his therapy and began to socialize again did Nelda realize how detrimental the isolation had been to her mental health.

Even after the acute suicidal crisis has subsided, the Vietnam wife needs to be aware that suicide can occur several weeks or months after her husband appears calmer and more elevated in mood. Sometimes the veteran's seeming improvement is the result of his inner decision to commit suicide at some future time and thereby terminate what he perceives as an unbearably painful or hopeless existence.[3]

The veteran's suicidal state, or statements, can also spill over to his children, conveying to them the message that life is not worth living. In several instances, children of veterans who have threatened or attempted suicide have threatened or attempted suicide themselves, children as young as 13.

This association between parental suicidal behavior and suicidal behavior in children is not unique to Vietnam veterans. As research has shown, suicide in the family is a significant risk factor for suicide in the other family members. In fact, it used to be believed that suicide was hereditary.[4] Although the genetic basis for suicide has not been scientifically substantiated, when a father commits suicide, or even talks about it, he provides a suicidal model for his child. The child can also acquire a sense of hopelessness and powerlessness. "If Father, who is bigger and stronger than me, a warrior even, cannot handle life, how can I, who am so much smaller and less experienced, ever hope to do so?" The child can also develop PTSD symptoms and a sense of guilt that can last a lifetime, especially if it is the child who discovers the body of the suicide victim.

In some cases, the veteran's threats of suicide may seem manipulative in that they occur in some predictable fashion—on a monthly basis, when his wife disagrees with him, when she refuses him sex, or whatever. After several such threats, sometimes wives begin to laugh. "There he goes again—talking suicide—just to get me to do what he wants," they may say. Despite their laughter, however, the women are afraid. "My worst fear," says one wife, "is that someday I'll come home from work and find that he's shot himself with one of his 'Nam guns."

This woman's husband has threatened suicide at least a dozen times. Although she has learned not to panic at every suicide note, she knows enough about suicidal behavior not to be led into a false sense of complacency. Just because her husband has made several suicidal gestures, as well as a few unsuccessful attempts, does not mean that he lacks the potential to complete a suicide. Even if his suicide threats are generally manipulative, someday, somewhere, given the right amount of stress, he may, in fact, self-destruct.[5] According to some researchers, approximately one-tenth of those who threaten suicide actually do follow through to completion.[6] Furthermore, some 35%-40% of those who commit suicide have been found to have made previous suicide attempts.[7] Some researchers contend that 80% of those who die had at least one prior suicide attempt.[8]

Veterans with combat stress tend to be more vulnerable to suicide during anniversary dates or periods of their most significant war traumas, following the death or suicide of a Vietnam buddy, or after the suicide or attempted suicide of a Vietnam veteran they do not know personally, but who receives media coverage.

In several instances, vets have threatened suicide upon learning of their wife's or girlfriend's decision to separate. The woman is often confused, not knowing whether the threat is serious or merely a means of coercing her into staying. "He might just be trying to scare me, but I also believe that if I leave, he might do it," says Susan, whose husband, with few friends and no support system, is at a high risk for suicide. In addition, he has suffered from depression ever since Vietnam and has refused to have children due to possible contamination from Agent Orange. Since he is also dissatisfied with his job, should Susan leave, he feels he has nothing to live for. To compound the problem, he has amassed a variety of medications, not only from his tour of duty in Vietnam, but from subsequent hospitalizations for war injuries. These medications are hidden throughout the home, along with at least two weapons, one from Vietnam and one purchased since.

Susan decided to stay with her husband until he sought help. When she suggested therapy, she expected him to resist the idea. But he did not. Like many suicidal persons, male and female, young and old, Susan's husband was ambivalent about whether to live or die and was looking for someone else to save him.

After he made noticeable progress in therapy and began to develop a support system, Susan left, confident that should her husband become suicidal again he would have a therapist and friends to lean on. Susan, however, is an exception. In my experience, more typically, the unhappily married Vietnam wife whose husband has threatened suicide feels compelled to stay in a marriage she no longer desires in order to preserve her husband's life. Even though she may be miserable, she does not want the guilt of her husband's death on her conscience. If there are children in the family and the veteran has stated to her, in front of the children, "If you leave me, I'll kill myself," or has made an overt suicide attempt, the pressure on the woman to stay is obvious.

"If you divorce Dad, he'll die," or "Don't let my Dad die," children have told their already guilt-ridden mothers, in some instances foreclosing the possibility that the woman will pursue separation or divorce. Even though the veteran's suicidal behavior is the veteran's responsibility, not his wife's, some wives have been told by the veteran's parents, siblings, or war buddies, "If you leave and he kills himself, it'll be all your fault."

As children grow older, their arguments against separation may become more elaborate and may become confused with their own life issues. In some cases, however, a child or teenager may argue for separation, rather than against it. "Go ahead. Leave him and let him kill himself like he says he will. He's so miserable he's better off dead. He wants to die anyway," a teenage boy told his mother.

Among the physically abused Vietnam wives who have attended group, a pattern has been noted. Upon deciding to leave her abuser, the battered Vietnam wife typically reports that he has threatened to kill either her or himself. In some cases, the veteran actually does make a suicidal gesture or attempt suicide. In my experience, however, to date, no abusive veteran has clearly committed suicide under the circumstance of his wife's departure or statement of intent to leave. Some abusers have, however, checked themselves into psychiatric units at V.A. or other hospitals. Still others have gone to live with their mothers or other relatives, where they have sunk into deep depressions, often asking the woman to come back in order to "save" them.

Despite the guilt heaped upon them by the veteran's suicidal messages or behavior, some women have nevertheless managed to leave abusive or otherwise undesirable marriages.

Suicide is the ninth leading cause of death in the United States among the general population.[9] In general, there are 10-12 suicides per 100,000 Americans per year.[10] There are no statistics on suicide among wives and children of Vietnam veterans and the statistics on suicide among Vietnam veterans themselves are presently an area of considerable debate. In 1975 the Public Health Service Center found that the suicide rate among Vietnam veterans was 23% higher than among other veterans in the same age group. However, this study has not been duplicated. In addition, the studies that do exist on suicide among Vietnam veterans are not only few in number, but highly controversial in nature.[11]

In some instances the suicide is masked. For example, one-car collisions and other vehicular accidents may sometimes be deemed as suicidal. However, it is impossible to interview the victim to determine whether the cause of death was a driving error or a sincere wish to die. The same problem arises regarding certain poisonings or drug overdoses. Were they accidental or suicidal? Along these lines, alcohol and drug abuse, as well as other forms of self-destructive behavior, can be seen as mini-suicides, which, for some individuals, ultimately lead to death.

Such deaths, however, are typically not included in suicide statistics.

In the case of the Vietnam veteran, the question arises as to whether veterans who pursue life-threatening vocations or avocations are motivated, in part, by suicidal wishes. For example, is the veteran who works in law enforcement or on dangerous construction suicidal or not? What about veterans who volunteer to handle contaminated radioactive wastes or ask to be assigned to the most risky tasks on their particular job?

Similarly, if the veteran's hobbies include boating in shark-infested waters when he cannot swim, wine-tasting, gourmet cooking, or cake-baking when he is diabetic, sky diving, or high speed motorcycle racing, is the veteran seeking death, consciously or unconsciously? While he may not be overtly suicidal, his lifestyle may lead to death. Such a death, however, will not be recorded as a suicide.

Similarly, if a vet provokes another person—his wife, the police, a drunken or armed stranger or attacker, or a violent known enemy—into killing him, his death will probably be listed as murder, not suicide. As M. E. Wolfgang noted in his famous study of spouse murders, some murders are "victim-precipitated." In these murders the victim is a "direct positive precipitator in the crime."[12] "This does not mean that the victim merely quarreled with or insulted the offender. It means that the victim was the first to use physical force, to show and use a weapon, or to strike a blow."[13]

"A lot of things Ted did made me feel he wanted to die," explains Elaine. "Yet he always laughed at men, especially Vietnam vets, who killed themselves. 'Sissies,' he always called them. Just to prove he wasn't a 'wimp' he'd drive fast down icy hills and eat wild mushrooms without checking to see if they were poisonous."

The biggest risk Ted took was standing up to two muggers. "I gave them my purse immediately," said Elaine, "but Ted refused to give up his wallet. When they pounced on him, I was certain it was the end."

Luckily a police car passed by just at the right moment. But there was no police car in Elaine's kitchen when Ted threatened to scald her with boiling water. This threat climaxed a Memorial Day weekend of physical abuse and threats on the life of Elaine's mother, whom Ted was certain was trying to convince Elaine to leave him.

Elaine tried to calm him down but he only punched her harder and began to boil water. "You ungrateful bitch," he shouted. "I'm going to scar your face so that nobody else will ever want you. That way, you'll never leave me." At this point, Elaine grabbed a kitchen knife and killed him.

Elaine's story illustrates what Wolfgang found to be true in his study of mate slayings: that a "higher proportion of husbands than wives provoked their mates into killing them, that is, first struck their mates and changed the level of social interaction from that of verbalizing to assaulting."[14] On the basis of his findings, Wolfgang theorizes that men who view suicide as unmasculine or passive, but who nevertheless harbor serious suicidal wishes, may achieve their death wish not by killing themselves directly, but by placing themselves in dangerous situations where they invite another person's attack.[15]

Some Vietnam wives incarcerated for the murder or attempted murder of their veteran describe their husbands as "begging to die." In one instance the veteran beat his wife with the butt of a rifle to the point where she required hospitalization. He not only refused to take her to the hospital, but handed her the rifle and dared her to shoot him. "I saw plenty of death in Vietnam," he said. "I'm not afraid to die."

She vowed to take him up on his dare should he hit her again. When he tried to attack her with a broken dish, she shot him. Was his death homicide, suicide, or both?

The first major study of suicide among Vietnam veterans completed by N. Hearst, T. Newman, and S. Hulley examined death records of California and Pennsylvania men who were involved in the lottery draft system between 1974 and 1983.[16] On the basis of their results, these researchers concluded that motor vehicle accident and suicide rates were higher among those who served in Vietnam than among those who did not.

The second study sampled several thousand vets and nonvets and found that "total mortality among Vietnam veterans was 17% higher than for other veterans." The excess deaths occurred "mainly in the first five years after discharge . . . and . . . involved primarily motor vehicle accidents, suicide, homicide, and accidental poisonings."[17]

Even though several other studies have been completed on suicide and suicidality among Vietnam veterans, the results have been inconclusive. Some studies show that suicide rates are substantially higher among combat veterans than other groups, but some do not.[18]

Daniel Pollock and others, for example, question the idea that having PTSD predisposes a veteran toward suicide. Pollock, along with others, contends that while the suicide rate among veterans is somewhat higher than that of other same-age men, it is at most only 1.54 times higher, not six times higher, as has been alleged by other reports.[19]

Other studies do not attempt to tabulate the rates of suicide among Vietnam veterans as a group, but rather try to identify those aspects of the Vietnam experience which might predispose a veteran toward suicidal feelings or suicide attempts. To date these studies have found that

Vietnam veterans who have survivor guilt, guilt about having killed others (especially civilians, women, or children) are more likely to suffer from intense feelings of wanting to die and are more likely to have attempted suicide than other veterans. These studies, however, were completed on veterans still alive in the 1980s, not on those who already killed themselves prior to that time.[20]

There are several factors which may put the PTSD afflicted veteran at special risk for suicide:

1. His depression or alcohol or drug abuse;
2. His social isolation;
3. His familiarity with, and often possession of, firearms or other weapons;
4. The hopelessness which he may experience as part of his PTSD;
5. Unresolved guilt over participation in killing or atrocities in Vietnam;
6. The death of a child or other family member when the veteran perceives that he is, to some extent, responsible for that death or where he feels that if he had behaved differently, the death might have been averted;
7. The lack of a support system or a major loss within in the veteran's support system (e.g., the loss or a wife or parent, the loss of a support group, expulsion from a group where there was prior affiliation);
8. The sudden, non-medically monitored stopping of taking medications for depression, anxiety or other symptoms of PTSD; and
9. Significant increases in physical pain, especially when combined with little hope of relief or cure, or chronic, unremitting physical pain due to war injuries or to newly-developed physical problems.

Among some PTSD-afflicted veterans, there may also be a mindset which views violence, even violence toward himself, as a viable solution to life's problems.

The Vietnam wife must be alert to signals, not only from her husband, but from her son or daughter, that suicide is on their minds. She must also take seriously any wishes on her part to end her own life.

Most suicides do not happen without warning. The suicidal veteran, like other suicidal persons, will often give clues regarding his intentions.[21] The Vietnam wife must not think, "No, it could never happen in my family," as if suicide were a moral disgrace or a phenomenon limited to the mentally deranged or the lower socioeconomic classes. In the United States suicide occurs proportionally among all levels of society, among the well-educated as well as the uneducated, and among mentally healthy persons who are, nevertheless, extremely unhappy.[22]

For example, Richard came from a family of high achievers. His father, an immigrant, had worked two jobs during the Depression, rising from dishwasher to restaurant owner in less than 10 years. While Richard's father prided himself on being the best gourmet chef in Pittsburgh, he wanted more for his children than that.

"I want you all to be professors, doctors, lawyers," he repeatedly told his children, echoing the words of countless immigrants before him. Richard's siblings did what their father wanted; they became doctors, lawyers, and teachers. Richard, however, dropped out of college to go to Vietnam.

His parents' feelings were mixed. In their country of origin, only desperate people joined the military. Richard's grandfathers had dressed as girls in order to avoid conscription. On the other hand, Richard's parents shared their son's patriotic fervor. By serving his country, Richard was making the entire family "real" Americans. They were certain that if only Richard returned alive, he would resume his plans to become a famous biologist.

In Vietnam, Richard was given the job of pulling bodies out of rivers and trying to identify them. Some of the bodies were decomposing or half eaten by fish. Some were American, others were Vietnamese. Often he had to salvage bodies from "no man's land," where he was constantly subject to attack.

When Richard returned home, he was given a hero's welcome by his ethnic community. Yet he did not feel like a hero. Sure, he had been shot at many times, but he had never valiantly saved lives or conquered the enemy. Why, he hadn't even had the courage to stand up for himself whenever he was falsely blamed for errors in the body counts.

Under pressure from his parents, Richard returned to the University of Pittsburgh, but his heart wasn't in it. A depression was growing in him which he did not want to face. He was also starting to experience flashbacks. For example, whenever his class had to go to a river or lake to obtain plant specimens, Richard saw arms, legs, and dismembered bodies in the water. In his dreams, these arms and legs reached out to him.

"Just forget about it. You'll snap out of it soon," he would tell himself in the mornings. But he did not snap out of it and began using alcohol in order to cope. He also married April, the girl next door, hoping that marriage might help solve his problem.

But neither April's beauty nor her love could stop his nightmares. Nor did sex cure his insomnia. Yet Richard continued to suffer in silence. Like his father, he felt that seeking help outside the family was a disgrace and that "real" men solved their problems on their own.

By the time Richard finished graduate school, he was not only a father, but a weekend drinker. He functioned fine during the week, but on weekends his life belonged to the bottle. All during graduate school, April attributed Richard's drinking and his emotional withdrawal to the pressures of his studies. Once he began working, however, she blamed his drinking on his authoritarian section chief, Dr. G.

Richard was one of the research firm's most brilliant biologists. Although Dr. G. was often critical of Richard, he also valued Richard highly and assigned him to top priority experiments. With the help of alcohol, Richard was able to veil his war memories and work diligently on all his assignments. One time, though, he made a serious mistake. He forgot to set the correct temperature on a certain specimen and ruined the experiment. Unfortunately, the experiment was part of a $1 million project.

Richard was willing to duplicate the experiment by working overtime without pay, but Dr. G wouldn't hear of it. For some reason, Dr. G. became rigidly irrational and chose to use this incident to try to get Richard fired. He even went so far as to examine Richard's college records and, on the grounds of some minor technicality, tried to prove that Richard did not really have a graduate degree.

Richard fantasized about burning down Dr. G.'s home and other aggressive acts. His alternate fantasy was of suicide. April had never seen her husband so angry or so depressed. Sometimes when he read newspaper accounts of murder/suicides, he would say, "That's the way out—I'll kill him, then myself." These words were so horrifying to April that she refused to really hear them.

The path Richard eventually chose, however, was not aggressive at all; he simply resigned from his job. He was afraid that if he tried to stand up for himself and lost, the sense of failure would be too bitter. He also feared that, in revenge, he might attack Dr. G., set explosives to his home, or do something else of a very violent nature. Rather than risk failure, or an act of aggression, Richard quelled his anger with alcohol and gave up. He felt he did not have the patience to go through the formal procedures and investigations which would have been necessary for him to save his job. In leaving without a fight, however, Richard confirmed his Vietnam view of himself as a weak, inept coward.

He then began working in his father's restaurant. "It should be a snap," he thought. The pressures, however, came to feel enormous, which only deepened his sense of inadequacy.

Among other problems, Richard had great difficulty managing the personnel beneath him. While he did not want to be authoritarian like some of his military commanders (and like Dr. G.), he could not tolerate "insubordination" either. Furthermore, the food in boiling pots sometimes reminded him of the bodies in the rivers in Vietnam and working with fish gave him migraines. The intense heat in the kitchen didn't help either.

His drinking increased, as did his absences from home. April began to wonder if Richard was cheating on her and hired a private detective to follow him. But Richard was not visiting other women, only the local bars and the local Vietnam memorial. Some times he sat by the memorial for hours.

By now Richard wasn't just a weekend drinker, but a full-fledged, everyday alcoholic. His sexual interest and abilities waned, leaving April with virtually no contact with him at all. She resorted to masturbation, which she tried to keep a secret from him. Once he caught her.

"He didn't say much," April related. "But I knew that it destroyed him.

"I thought of saying, 'Well, isn't this better than me having an affair?' but thank God, I didn't. Then he asked me how long I had been doing it. I lied to spare his feelings, but he knew I was lying. After that, he hardly ever touched me."

Next Richard quit his restaurant job and floated from one odd job to the next. April was now almost totally emotionally and sexually abandoned. And financially insecure as well. Feeling as if she no longer had a husband, she moved in with her parents.

"I can't live without you. I need you. You are my whole life," Richard pleaded. Yet when she would phone him, he usually wouldn't talk with her.

April was disgusted but she was willing to consider returning to Richard, provided he mend his ways.

Richard, however, felt there was no hope for him. He turned over all his assets to his wife, then left town to go work as a cab driver in Scranton. Once in a while he would drive to Pittsburgh to see his parents and son, but basically he was detached from his entire family. Each time he returned, he was more withdrawn and more depressed.

When his brother, a successful lawyer, received yet another big promotion, Richard didn't even attend the family's celebration party. In fact, the last time Richard visited Pittsburgh was to go to his son's birthday party. He hadn't wanted to attend, but his favorite cousin talked him into it. All during the party, Richard sat in the corner, staring into space, saying nothing. Every now and then, he would mutter, "I wish I didn't have a son so I wouldn't have to leave him behind."

Nobody, not even April, picked up the clues. Even when Richard mailed the rest of his belongings to April and other members of his family, nobody suspected the depth of his misery.

Within weeks, Richard mailed a suicide note to his mother, then drove his cab into the Susquehanna River.

As Richard's story illustrates, suicide is not restricted to any particular social class. In fact, there is no one type of suicidal veteran, or Vietnam wife, or teenager, or child. However, the following characteristics have been found to correlate with suicide:

1. A family history of suicide or depression, or, a recent suicide of a friend, relative, or war buddy;
2. A prior suicide attempt;
3. Lack of strong affiliative bonds to another person or group of persons, or feelings of not belonging to anyone or to any human group;
4. Social isolation—lack of a support system or inability to use available supports;
5. Alcohol or drug use;
6. Reckless behavior;
7. Conflicts with authority (for vets, conflicts with employers, the law, or government agencies; for teens, expulsion from school, for example);
8. Depression, with possible irritability or agitation;
9. Feelings of being trapped, stuck, or sinful;
10. Feelings of hopelessness, helplessness, worthlessness, or humiliation;
11. Suppressed rage or free-floating hostility;
12. Negative thinking: negative view of past, present and future, black and white thinking, irrational beliefs.[23]

Signals that suicide is possible include:

1. Announcements of suicidal thoughts or intentions, such as, "I'm going to kill myself," "I won't be here for Christmas," "You won't have to worry about me anymore," "This might be the last time you see me," or "This is my last day";
2. Suicidal writings or drawings, or notes written as if already dead;
3. Termination behaviors (giving away prized possessions, writing a will, cleaning up unfinished business, saying goodbye to friends and relatives, purchasing a burial plot, writing one's own eulogy, designing one's tombstone, purchasing a one-way ticket to a potential suicide location);
4. Noticeable withdrawal from family or friends or from previously attended therapy;
5. Any dramatic change in mood or emotional state;

6. Changes in eating habits that result in significant weight gain or weight loss;

7. Changes in sleeping habits (increased sleeping, fitful sleep, insomnia);

8. Loss of interest in friends and formerly pleasurable activities such as sex, music, or sports;

9. Difficulties with concentration;

10. Recent interpersonal loss (death in the family, rejection by a significant other);

11. Increased alcohol or drug usage;

12. Decreased functioning at work or in school;

13. Preoccupation with fanatical or cult material;

14. Outbursts of violent or rebellious behavior (especially if out of character);

15. Psychomotor retardation—slumped posture, slow movements, repetitious behavior and statements;

16. Any evidence of loss of touch with reality;

17. Excessive or inappropriate guilt.[24]

While the Vietnam wife should not try to assess her husband's suicidal potential on her own, she needs to be aware of the factors which increase the likelihood of suicide and share information about her husband's suicidal intentions with an appropriate mental health professional, clergyman, or other authority, such as the police.

Upon the mere mention of the word "suicide" or upon the emergence of any of the suicidal indicators listed above, the veteran should be encouraged to seek professional help. Even if he is only thinking suicidal thoughts and has no definite plan, his suicidal thoughts need to be openly discussed. If the vet is already in treatment, he needs to be encouraged to share his suicidal thoughts with his therapist. Left unaired, the negative thoughts can feed upon themselves and develop into a full-blown suicide crisis.

In general, the probability of suicide is increased if the veteran has a well thought out, definite plan for killing himself rather than a vague wish to die. For example, the veteran who says he is planning to kill himself with an overdose of pills, but does not know what pills he would take or in what quantities and does not have a specific date established for his suicide, is probably less likely to kill himself than the veteran who has spent two weeks in the library researching various types of medication, has already purchased the pills, and has a definite date in mind. Similarly, the veteran who says he will shoot himself, but does not own a gun and has no plans to purchase a gun, is less likely to kill himself than the veteran who has one or more guns at his immediate disposal and who spends much of his spare time at rifle ranges.

This does not mean that the vet who talks about suicide but does not have a plan is not capable of suicide. He is, and his suicidal wishes need to be acknowledged and openly discussed.

A sign that suicide is imminent is if the vet feels compelled to act on his impulse to self-destruct.[25] Statements such as "I'm afraid to be alone," "I don't know if I can stop myself," "There's a voice in my head that says, 'Do it! Do it, now!'" or "Hide the rat poison. I'm afraid I'll take some" warrant an immediate response. Even if the veteran has several powerful deterrents to his suicidal plans, such as a strong commitment to his job, family, or certain friends or strong religious beliefs against suicide, if he is evidencing any signs that he is unable to control his impulses, he should not be left alone. He may need hospitalization, or at least the intervention of a therapist or clergyperson. If the veteran states that God, voices, or some force outside himself is "ordering him" to kill himself, psychiatric hospitalization is almost always needed.

Another important clue that suicide is imminent is if the veteran, after having communicated in some way that he is planning to kill himself, is unable to talk to anyone about his suicidal wishes or plans. As long as he can talk about his suicidal feelings and maintain an emotional connection with at least one person, whether it be his wife, a relative, a friend, or a therapist, there is hope.

Basically, the Vietnam wife can ask her husband the following questions:

- Do you want to kill yourself?
- Do you have a plan?
- What is your plan?
- On a scale of one to 20, what is the probability you will put your plan into effect? Or, How much do you want to die? How much do you want to live?
- Do you have a particular date in mind?
- Do you feel you must kill yourself?
- Do you feel there is someone trying to kill you? (For vets with paranoid tendencies.)
- Is there someone, or something, telling you to kill yourself? (For vets with histories of psychoses or paranoia.)
- Are you willing to give me the pills, the gun, the keys to the car (or whatever is the designated means of suicide)?

• Can you promise me you won't kill yourself until you talk to a therapist (the family doctor, a clergyman, or some other trained professional)?[26]

The veteran's responses to these questions can help the Vietnam wife identify the possibility that her husband might hurt himself. If he has a plan and a date, is unwilling to relinquish the means of self-destruction, or is unable to commit to not killing himself for a short period of time, the wife must not hesitate to act. In addition to any observable signs or disturbing answers to the above questions, the Vietnam wife must also trust her own gut reaction.

If, for any reason, she feels that her husband might possibly hurt himself or is not in control of himself, she must attempt to get control over whatever the veteran has identified as his means of self-destruction and seek outside help immediately. She can call the local Vet Center, Department of Veterans Affairs Medical Center, or any local suicide crisis hotline for help. The police or rescue squad could also be called for information and assistance. In an emergency, the suicidal Vietnam veteran can also be taken to the emergency room of any local hospital offering psychiatric care.

If there are signs of impending suicide and the wife must leave, a relative, family friend, or neighbor can be called to be home with the veteran. While some vets have welcomed the protective presence of another human being, others have yelled at their wives that they don't need "babysitters." Similarly, in situations where suicide seems imminent and the wife insists on finding help, sometimes the vet resists her efforts.

When the wife meets with such resistance, she can firmly say, "I am afraid. You just indicated to me that you are thinking about killing yourself. I care about you too much to take the chance that you might act on your impulse. Even if the chances of your killing yourself are one in a million, you mean too much for me to give you the opportunity to end your life. I would rather be safe than sorry."

In several instances, when the wife has been firm about initiating responsible action, the veteran has not only agreed to let a relative or friend be with him, but consented to go for help. In other instances, however, the veteran's resistance has only escalated. Some vets have even become extremely hostile or verbally abusive toward their wives. Yet, it is not uncommon for some suicidal persons (whether they are Vietnam veterans or not) to become angry or abusive at the very persons from whom they are seeking help. Many times, the hostility a suicidal person displays toward his or her helper is a reflection of the anger he or she harbors toward some other person.

The wife should not take her husband's anger personally, nor allow it to deter her from protecting her husband from his own impulses. However, if her husband begins to threaten violence—whether toward himself, toward her, or toward someone else—the woman must reconsider her strategy.

In my experience, there have been several instances where suicidal veterans have seriously threatened to kill themselves if their wives dared to call for help. In a few dramatic cases, vets have barricaded themselves in their homes, with their wives and children and sometimes with one or more weapons. "If you call the police, I'll kill myself first," "If the police come, I'll fire at them and let them kill me," or "Anyone you call near this house, even if it's my sister, is history! I don't care if I go to jail. There's no reason to live anymore anyway."

Other vets have threatened to jump into their cars and speed to certain death if their wives so much as touched the phone. Some wives have not even been allowed to talk to the veteran or to be in the same room with him. In one case the veteran threatened to harm his wife should she attempt to call for help.

More typically, however, when the veteran is resistant to help, the wife is cowed into not calling for outside assistance by his anger or threats to divorce her or otherwise abandon her or hurt her.

Although it is not generally advisable for the Vietnam wife to try to handle the suicidal veteran on her own, in some instances she may be forced to do so. Even though she is not a trained therapist, there may be times she needs to act like one. Through her talking, she might buy time and convince her husband to seek help and give life a chance.

She can discuss the subject of suicide with her husband directly. Many wives are afraid to mention the subject, thinking that this might precipitate a suicide attempt. However, suicidal persons generally experience great relief when afforded the opportunity to talk openly about their suicidal thoughts. Often they have not shared their suicidal feelings with others for fear of disapproval and rejection.

The suicidal veteran needs to be told, "When you say you want to kill yourself, I believe you," not "Oh, you can't mean it," "You'll get over it soon enough," or "Nothing is that bad." The latter responses can convey to the veteran one or more of the following messages:

1. Suicide is so socially unacceptable or morally repugnant to me, I don't want to discuss it;

2. There's something wrong with you if you are talking that way;
3. You aren't entitled to feel that bad;
4. I'm sick and tired of hearing you complain; or
5. I don't care enough about you to listen.

Most wives do care, however, deeply so. Yet even they, at least initially, may shrug off their husband's suicidal statements and discourage him from sharing freely. The subject of suicide may create considerable anxiety in the Vietnam wife. She may have a great fear of death or she may be struggling with her own suicidal thoughts. Furthermore, she may feel inadequate to handle the situation. "I can't cope with this suicide talk. Therefore, it can't be true," she may wish. Or perhaps she feels she cannot discuss the topic of suicide without blurting out, "And what's supposed to happen to me and the kids if you go kill yourself?"

Some Vietnam wives assume that if their husband is in treatment at a Vet Center, then there is no risk of suicide. This is not the case. True, suicidal feelings do sometimes force vets to seek help initially. However, being in individual or group therapy does not necessarily eliminate the veteran's negative thinking and sense of hopelessness. While suicidal thoughts and plans are often discussed in therapy, in some cases, it is to his wife or another family member, rather than to his therapist or therapy group, that the veteran first reveals his suicidal desires.

Furthermore, even after a vet has received help with and successfully overcome an acute suicidal crisis or protracted suicidal period, suicidal thoughts can return, for being in therapy does not spare the veteran (or anyone else) from life's agonies. Although it is not true that once a person is suicidal he is suicidal forever, if the veteran's response to pain, frustration, or life's many dilemmas was suicidal at one point in time, he may respond in like manner once again at some future time.[27]

The Vietnam wife with a suicidal husband often finds herself mentally preparing for the possibility by thinking about the family's financial situation. She wonders if she will need to go back to work or find a higher paying job. She also thinks about such things as child care, transportation, and bills. Yet she cannot discuss her needs, or her plans, with her husband lest she reinforce his suicidal feelings. Furthermore, she usually hesitates to concretely pursue any jobs or training programs for fear of arousing his suspicions. Special problems come up when the Vietnam wife has no training and must go back to school before she can find work. She may be reluctant to go through the admissions procedures, pay the fees, and commit herself to a job program unless her husband actually does kill himself, by which time she may be too late to get the training she needs.

"At least if I knew when he was going to do it, I could make plans," one wife explains, half-jokingly. "But I'm in limbo. I'm also stuck at home. Sometimes I feel I just can't do anything." Like other wives of suicidal veterans, this wife suffers from an extreme form of social isolation. She fears leaving her husband alone. Even if he insists that she go out alone, she stays home—just in case. Her children's social lives are also restricted. In essence, the family's entire life has slowly become tied up with the veteran's problems.

This wife, like others, also serves as the buffer between her husband and the world. She explains to relatives why he cannot be stressed or why he cannot attend family functions. At the same time, she feels guilty about talking about her husband's problems with others. "He would kill me if he knew I told his mother why he doesn't come to visit. But what am I supposed to do? She can tell when I'm lying."

The possibility of a husband committing suicide can create both anger and alienation, as well as emotional exhaustion. Yet there may be times when the wife is called upon to ignore her anger and help pull her husband through not one, but several, suicide crises. For example, when Nelda managed to shove Harry back into therapy, she thought she was finished acting as his counselor, but there were still many times when she had to help him deal with his suicidal feelings. In these discussions, she has the same approach and many of the same arguments against suicide as she did the first time, when she convinced Harry to flush his pills down the toilet.

The first step Nelda took in talking to her husband was to ask, "Why do you want to kill yourself?" or "What has changed in your life that you now want to die?"

While a suicidal condition is the result of many factors, not just one incident, there may be a single incident or a future imagined event or stress which precipitates a suicidal crisis. It is not the incident itself, but the meaning of the incident, which creates the overwhelming pain. In talking to a suicidal veteran, or to any other suicidal person, it is important not to mock their reasons for wanting to commit suicide, regardless of how insignificant the reasons might seem. It is also important to probe beneath the specific incident to discover its meaning to the individual.

For example, Harry's suicidal crisis was precipitated by his chief at work calling him "stupid" and making derogatory statements about his work performance. Instead of saying, "There you go again, overreacting to everything as usual" or "That's a dumb reason for wanting to commit suicide," Nelda empathized: "For someone like you, Harry, whose identity is so wrapped up in his work and in being intelligent, being called stupid must have been a devastating experience." Nelda then tried to move Harry away from the specific incident to the general issues which the incident symbolized. For Harry, his chief's remarks had highlighted the fact that ever since Vietnam, he had begun to lose confidence in his professional abilities. All of his life, being called "stupid" was one of his greatest fears. Now he had been called that by a man whom he respected.

Harry also felt like a failure as a husband and father. He knew he was not meeting his family's emotional needs. He also felt guilty because, due to his change in job status from a practicing surgeon to a medical report writer, Nelda had to work. He was certain that Nelda greatly resented him and was now staying with him only out of duty, not out of love.

He was also positive that his daughter Joleen's depression was all his fault and that Harry Jr., his pride and joy, was now rebelling against him at every turn because he was an inadequate father. Caught in the negative thinking which characterizes depressed persons, Harry was positive that Joleen would never improve, that he would never again be close to Harry Jr., that he and Nelda could never recapture their old romance.

Last but not least, the derogatory comments made by Harry's superior at work had reminded Harry of all the times he had failed to save lives or felt incompetent in Vietnam.

"But killing yourself now won't bring back the dead," Nelda shouted. "And would those boys you saw die want you to kill yourself, or would they want you to go on and live and do something positive in this world? Can you decide to go on living—for them?"

"I'm crazy, I'm crazy, I don't deserve to live," Harry replied.

"You're not crazy! You're a victim of trauma. Stop beating yourself up! You can't help it. You were caught in a war situation where there were limited medical supplies and personnel, but an abundance of confusion and exhaustion."

The same logic can be applied in talking to the suicidal combat vet, who may be chastising himself for his cowardice or mistakes (perceived or real) in Vietnam. If a vet is truly remorseful, he can be told that the best way he can make it up to those who are gone is to go on living and make a contribution to surviving Vietnam veterans or to society in general. However, if he kills himself, he will only be throwing away his intelligence, insight, or whatever other talents or skills he might have.

If the veteran has a belief in a higher being or God, the Vietnam wife is lucky. She can then use all the theological arguments against suicide and stress to the veteran that God's plan for him does not include self-destruction. Harry, however, hated God. Yet Nelda was still able to tell him that his life had a purpose.

"The reasons for your existence may not be clear to you at the moment, Harry," she said. "And they may not become apparent to you for quite some time, but you are here on this earth for a reason. In the past, you've helped a lot of people as a surgeon. Even in Vietnam, you saved lives, although you tend to remember only those who died on your table. Even if you never get better, just writing those medical reports serves a purpose.

"I know you wanted to be a famous doctor, Harry, but you don't have to be famous to matter to me or the kids. We love you. If you kill yourself, we'll be devastated."

"I'm a mess, Nelda, and frankly, those kids would be better off without me. Harry Jr. wishes me dead all the time!"

"He doesn't mean it, Harry, and even a messed-up father is better than no father at all. If you think you're a bad father now, I say that if you kill yourself, you really will be a bad father. Even if you have the most legitimate reasons in the world for ending your life, our kids won't understand. All they'll know is that Daddy didn't care enough about them to stay alive. If you kill yourself, their emotional problems won't get better; they'll only get worse because they'll feel abandoned and betrayed by you."

Nelda then began to list Harry's various strengths and talents, in a sincere, not superficial, manner. At first, Harry did not want to listen, for he did not quite believe that there was much positive about him. Yet, it did him good to hear Nelda enumerate the various times he had shown kindness and love to others, integrity on the job, and other qualities.

"You're so down on yourself, you feel worthless," Nelda continued. "But you're important to lots of people besides me and the kids." Nelda then listed these people one by one.

In his depressed state, Harry needed to be reminded that he mattered to others, that if he died, he would be missed. Furthermore, he would be teaching his children that life was not worth living.

"Well, that's the truth. Life isn't worth living," Harry insisted.

It would have made no sense for Nelda to argue with Harry that life could be joyous, unless she also empathized with his pain and depression.

"I know life seems black to you now, Harry, and with good reason. I wish I could say that I truly understand, but I can't. I never went to Vietnam, have never struggled with PTSD or been demoted on my job, or had many of the problems you've had which have led you to feel so terrible.

"Perhaps if I were you, right now, I'd want to kill myself too. But I also know that feelings aren't facts and that very few situations are utterly hopeless. This is not to say that what you went through in Vietnam wasn't horrible, horrible beyond belief. Part of your suicidal feeling has to do with your rage and sense of powerlessness over events in Vietnam. But part is also due to feeling powerless over your life today."

With a good therapist, Nelda suggested, Harry could make changes in his life in the present that would make his life more fulfilling and bearable.

"No situation is hopeless," Nelda kept repeating, "not even your PTSD. You could get more therapy, antidepressant medication, and other help. You could even go to a PTSD inpatient program. There's no reason for you to feel so bad all the time."

"Nothing can help," Harry insisted.

"That's your depression talking, not you! How do you know nothing can help unless you try? You walked out of therapy before you even finished dealing with your feelings. Give therapy another try. If it doesn't help after a few weeks or months, you can always kill yourself later."

"We can't afford any more help for me," Harry replied.

"What's cheaper, therapy bills or funeral expenses?" A typical funeral, Nelda estimated, cost at least $4,000, the price of about a year's worth of private sessions. Furthermore, if Harry killed himself Nelda was certain she would get so depressed she would have to go to therapy at least twice a week, for at least 10 years, which would cost about $80,000. The children would probably have to all go for therapy too. "So you see," Nelda concluded, "it's really cheaper for you to get help. Besides, the Vet Center is free."

Nelda then pointed out that right now, Harry was evaluating everything in terms of mistakes made in the past and problems coming up in the future. Also, as part of his depression, he was negatively projecting into the future. "How do you know Joleen isn't going to get better? She's already made progress. And how do you know that, a year from now, Harry Jr. and you won't be closer than you are today?

"A year from now, two years from now, you might even be doing surgery again. Who do you think you are, Harry, to predict the future, some kind of God?"

Despite Nelda's eloquence, Harry kept insisting that life was hopeless and not worth living. Furthermore, he would greatly appreciate it if Nelda would keep her Pollyanna logic to herself. His feelings were not a matter of logic, life was not a matter of logic. No words could talk him out of his misery.

"Even the Jews in the Nazi concentration camps and prisoners of war in Vietnam, Korea, and World War II wanted to live," Nelda said. "Sure, some of them died from giving up, but some of them carried on, hoping against hope that they would survive."

"Fools! They should all have committed suicide," Harry retorted.

"Life is hard," Nelda replied. "No one is happy all the time. Most of us live for moments, a few brief moments when we feel at peace with ourselves, when we see something beautiful, or when we feel close to someone. Some of those prisoners kept on living just to see a bird or the sun in the morning, or to show a small kindness to a fellow prisoner.

"I'm not bringing up the concentration camp victims to make you feel guilty, Harry, or to make you feel like you have no right to feel miserable. But your situation, as terrible as it is, isn't as hopeless as theirs."

Nelda then brought in examples of how friends of theirs, immigrants from Lithuania, had endured various struggles and persecutions. "They could have given up, many times, but they didn't. We all have an urge to live, Harry, you too, even though it's buried under your depression right now. A part of you does want to die, but a part of you wants to live also, or else you would already have killed yourself."

Nelda then also drew examples from some of Harry's Vietnam veteran friends, some of whom were missing arms and legs. "Would you tell your quadriplegic friend to go die because he lost all his limbs?"

Just as Nelda needed to address Harry's hopelessness, she needed to address his black and white thinking and irrational beliefs. For example, just because Harry and Harry Jr. were arguing did not mean that they were enemies or that Harry Jr. didn't love him anymore. Harry Jr. was going through the typical adolescent process of separation from the parents. His rebelliousness would not last forever. Also, just because she and Harry were having marital problems didn't mean she didn't love him.

"Are you angry at me, Harry?" Nelda asked. "They say that sometimes people kill themselves out of suppressed rage, as a form of vengeance on others. If you're angry at me, say so. I'd rather you yell at me and throw things all around the house than kill yourself."

Yes, Harry was angry at Nelda, but he was even angrier at one of his colleagues, in whom he had confided about his post-Vietnam psychological problems. Harry was certain that this colleague had informed the chief of the department about his PTSD, which had resulted in the chief's derogatory comments. Furthermore, this betrayal had activated for Harry all his feelings of betrayal surrounding his Vietnam experience.

"Maybe you think that if you kill yourself, you'll be punishing this so-called friend of yours," Nelda said. "Do you picture him at your funeral, overcome with remorse for how he mistreated you? Maybe he will drip with guilt, but I guarantee you, a week later, he'll be at a party having a wonderful time, and not think about you at all.

"Do you think that if you kill yourself, you'll be getting back at me and the kids for the ways we've let you down? If you kill yourself, we certainly will be sorry for all the times we hurt your feelings or were mad at you. We'll miss you a lot too.

"But we will go on to enjoy whatever there is that's enjoyable in this life. If you kill yourself, the main person you'll be hurting is yourself."

If the veteran is seeking vengeance on "the system" through his suicide, he needs to be reminded that "the system" will not be harmed one bit by his death. In fact, if he kills himself, he is letting "the system" win. While his death might create some commotion and perhaps even some guilt on the part of officials, the commotion and the guilt will be temporary. If the vet has tremendous rage toward "the system," he is better off learning how to channel that rage into positive action than in destroying himself.

Basically, the suicidal veteran needs to be told that suicide is not a rational solution to his problems. As David Burns points out, "suicide is unnecessary," as there are many other ways of solving problems.[28] The veteran can also be asked to identify his reasons for living. These deterrents to suicide can be mentioned to him as often as needed.

He can also be asked to go back in time and remember when he felt loved, competent, successful, and needed. However, the severely depressed veteran may have great difficulty remembering this. He may become even more depressed realizing that he can't even remember what happiness and self-satisfaction ever felt like. At this point, it is important to assure him that, although it may be a struggle, he can and will get better.

If he fears he is "insane" or "crazy" because he has suicidal thoughts, he needs to be assured that many persons have suicidal thoughts, even supposedly normal persons. In time, and with help, the thoughts can lessen in frequency and intensity. The veteran can eventually learn to cope with his other symptoms. In sum, the suicidal vet needs to see his depression and hopelessness, as well as his other symptoms, as parts of his psychological stress disorder, not as permanent features of his personality. He can also be helped to look forward to a future where he has a greater sense of mastery over himself and his environment, and where life will not be as painful.

In talking to her suicidal husband, the Vietnam wife should not limit herself to the suggestions presented in this chapter. She should not hesitate to use whatever arguments she feels would be encouraging to her husband and to ask those who know and love him for help. Even if her husband is in treatment, she should not hesitate to speak up. In our culture, there tends to be an overreliance on professionals. Women often feel inadequate in approaching their suicidal husband. Yet, a woman may have much wisdom and can support her husband on a day-to-day basis with a depth of heart and commitment which far exceeds what may be found in a therapist's office. Furthermore, she should discard any ideas presented in this chapter which she feels would not be effective with her particular husband.

Suicidal Thoughts in Children

Not only the Vietnam veteran but his wife or child can become suicidal. A number of children have not only talked about suicide, but have made suicide attempts, usually requiring subsequent hospitalization. In each case so far, the child, or teen, gave one or more clear warning signs.

If she recognizes one or more of the suicide warning signs listed in this chapter in either herself or her child, the Vietnam wife should seek professional help as soon as possible. Young children are in special danger because they are not always aware of how final their actions can be. Also, they, like teenagers, tend to be more impulsive than adults, hence even more attention needs to be given to any indication that suicide is on their minds. Children and teens are also more likely to view life's problems as permanent, rather than temporary. They may react intensely to events that to adults may seem trivial. For instance, a teenage boy may want to kill himself because his girlfriend began to date another boy; a teenage girl, because she binged and gained three pounds.

However, it is strongly recommended that a child's or adolescent's concerns, regardless of how insignificant they may seem, not be dismissed as "trivial." They must be talked about. Just as wives have hoped that their husband's suicidal intentions would disappear if they were not talked about, they have also hoped that their children's talk of suicide would also magically go away if left undiscussed.

This is not the case. The Vietnam wife needs to address the subject of suicide as openly with her child or teen as she would with her husband. Some of the suggestions offered in this chapter for questioning and talking to the suicidal veteran can also be used with appropriate modifications in approaching the suicidal young person.

In asking her child questions about his or her plans to commit suicide, the Vietnam wife need not fear that she will spark a suicide attempt. In fact, her inquiry and concern may save her child's life, especially if she can convince her child to talk to someone—the family physician, a therapist, a minister, or a counselor. She should not allow her fears of not saying or doing the "right thing" or her guilt about the fact that her child has expressed suicidal wishes paralyze her from speaking to her child from her heart.

Even if her child is in therapy, she cannot necessarily rely on the therapist to detect all the signs and to provide all the support and action the child needs. In a few instances, mothers did inform therapists or school officials about their child's suicidal intentions, and these authorities either did nothing, minimized the possibility of suicide, or indicated that the child's suicidal state was not their responsibility, but the responsibility of some other professional or authority.

Ultimately, it is up to the parents to provide proper care for their suicidal child and to support that child in the absence of responsible outside help and when the child is in therapy. After all, no professional cares as much about the child as his or her mother. The Vietnam wife must communicate her love in as many ways as she knows how and let her child know that she is behind him or her 100%—for example, by being available to listen any time of the day or night. The child can also be told that even more help is available—inpatient hospitalization, intensive outpatient psychotherapy, medication.

If the family has financial difficulties and the child might feel guilty about the cost of therapy or other such help, the mother can stress that such help is a necessity, not a luxury. "You don't know how sad it makes me to see you so unhappy that you want to die. No amount of money is important compared to having you safe and happy," a mother told a suicidal daughter who was greatly concerned about the cost of her therapy. The daughter needed to be told that her life was worth more than any amount of money.

In addition, the Vietnam wife can give her child the phone number of the local suicide crisis center or hotline or other resources and urge him or her to use any of these resources in case of an emergency. She can also post these numbers, along with phone numbers of concerned relatives and friends, near the phone. As an added precaution, she can remove firearms or dangerous medications from the home, or keep them under lock and key. If the child becomes overtly suicidal, he or she can be hospitalized involuntarily.

Suicidal Thoughts in the Vietnam Wife

The Vietnam wife must also attend to her own suicidal impulses. When her thoughts begin to shift from simply thinking about suicide to planning the date and fantasizing about the funeral, she should run for help. Even if she is not serious about committing suicide, recurring or persistent suicidal thoughts betray a profound despair or sorrow or a suppressed rage which merit professional consultation. If she becomes too afraid of herself, hospitalization may be necessary.

A number of women who have attended group have contemplated suicide. A few have made suicide attempts. However, no woman has actually killed herself. Most of the women who have contemplated suicide have been prevented from carrying out their plans primarily due to a deep sense of responsibility and dedication to their children.

In the cases observed, two types of women have contemplated or attempted suicide—battered or formerly battered women and women sexually abused as children. Not all the abused women or incest survivors were suicidal, however—only those married to an abusive veteran who was not in treatment or who was in treatment only sporadically, dropping in and out of treatment programs as he desired.

Among all the suicidal women, three dynamics were present: active self-hate; suppressed or only partially recognized anger toward at least one, usually more than one, abusive male; and feelings of psychological bondage to an emotionally ungiving, and often outright emotionally abusive, veteran.

The suicidal battered and formerly battered women hated themselves for allowing themselves to be abused by their husbands or for permitting their veterans to abuse their children. They felt they were "crazy" or that there was something inherently wrong with them because they had chosen to marry or had been sexually or emotionally attracted to an abusive man. Some of the women were almost entirely out of touch with their anger toward their abusers, denying that they had any anger at all. Some were aware of their anger toward their batterer, but had never fully expressed it, or felt confused because they still had loving feelings toward him.

Like the battered woman, women who were incest survivors also had feelings of worthlessness and self-condemnation. Some had never dealt with their incest experience or had dealt with it incompletely or only superficially.

Based on my observations, in combination with the frustrations of marriage to a PTSD-afflicted Vietnam veteran who has not benefited from treatment, the Vietnam wife who is also an incest survivor or a battered or formerly battered woman may be at high risk for suicide. In a recent study, some 84% of female incest survivors had attempted suicide.[29] The suicide rate for battered women is also abnormally high.[30]

Summary

The Vietnam wife whose husband is at a high risk for suicide is living under immense pressure. On some level she may feel that she is both the source of, and the solution to, her husband's suicidal wishes. Her children may feel likewise. On another level, even if she knows she is blameless, she may still feel responsible for the veteran's death wish, or at the very least for preventing him from actually killing himself.

Once the veteran has talked of suicide, the wife typically watches her speech and behavior and trains her children to do the same. She also may take on additional responsibilities to try to make things as easy for her husband as possible.

In some cases, the Vietnam wife may sense that her husband's threats are manipulative. Yet even if so, she may hesitate to confront him or to leave him for fear that he will actually carry out his threat.

12

"I Believe In Love"— The Hope of Therapy

Before my husband began PTSD therapy, neither of us knew what was wrong with him. He blamed society for all his problems and I blamed him for all of mine. It took a year of individual and group therapy for him to unload his war stories and come to accept himself for what he did or didn't do during Vietnam. Then came the even bigger job of trying to live life with all its ups and downs.

When we were having our rough times, my parents and friends kept urging me to leave him. But I had faith in him and felt that counseling could help. And it has. We still have problems, though. PTSD counseling hasn't gotten rid of my husband's old-fashioned ideas about the woman's role or given me back the years I spent emotionally and financially supporting a man whose inner life was one raging storm after another. Counseling hasn't even gotten rid of all Stu's symptoms. But it has made them much more manageable.

Stu still gets depressed and angry, but not as often and not for so long. His nightmares are almost gone and so is all that hate he was carrying around. We even talk now. Before all we did was yell at each other. Believe it or not, now we make "appointments" to talk about things. If we find we can't communicate at home, we make a marriage counseling appointment for a "marriage tune-up."

By talking to other Vietnam wives, I've learned not to take it personally when Stu goes off. I just go and do something else. I've also learned not to blame my husband for all my problems. I have issues with my parents and things in my past that have nothing to do with him and I have to work them out myself.

But Stu had to get help and get on his feet before I felt free to take a look at myself. When he was into his depressions and his drinking, I didn't have the luxury of taking care of my emotional needs.

He's much better now, but that doesn't mean I am. I still don't feel comfortable asserting myself, though I'm not as afraid as I used to be. I still panic when I go against what other people want me to do. After all those years of being a people pleaser and doing everything for everybody else, it's hard to shift gears.

As a result of his therapy, Stu doesn't need me as much as he used to. I'm glad, but it leaves me at a loss. Frankly, I'm so used to one crisis after another that sometimes I don't know how to handle all this peace. I also don't know what to do with all the resentments I've built up over the years.

I find it impossible to forget some of my grievances. Yet I don't want to ruin the progress Stu and I have made by making a big deal about things that happened years ago.

The miracle is that, despite everything, the love we had long ago isn't all gone. Don't ask me why or how, but it survived. There must be something strong between us, otherwise we would have been history a long time ago.

—Wife of a combat vet

Today popular songs often call love an illusion and many books are devoted to finding pathologies in love relationships. Often a woman's dedication to her husband or lover is described as a "love addiction" or "co-dependency," or as an expression of one or more of her neurotic needs. Nevertheless, somehow, somewhere, despite all the disappointments and strains, many Vietnam wives still believe in love.

"Why would I put up with him if I didn't love him?" more than one woman has stated. "I know he has a bad case of PTSD, but how often do you fall in love?" asks Rita.

Despite her love, however, Rita, like many of the wives, seriously questions whether she can continue to remain in a marriage which is often not functional for her. Her major hope is that therapy will make the continuation of her marriage possible.

When Rita first came to group, she came looking for ways to help her husband. Although she wished her husband would seek counseling,

secretly she hoped to heal him herself. Wasn't her love and understanding enough? Hadn't she read numerous books on Vietnam and
PTSD? And, as the adult child of an alcoholic, wasn't she an expert caretaker? The problem was, however, that her husband would not open up
to her. In his view, her desire to be helpful was intrusive. "You can't understand. You weren't there," was his standard reply to her carefully
worded questions.

Rita's next hope was that medication would help free her husband
of his PTSD. In recent years, a number of psychiatric drugs have proven
effective in relieving some of the symptoms of PTSD—anxiety, depression, and paranoia, and in suppressing REM stage dreams and the startle response.[1] There is no one drug which has been used for all vets with
PTSD.[2] Since PTSD expresses itself differently in each veteran and since
some veterans suffer from problems in addition to PTSD, medication is
usually aimed at the symptoms which are most disabling to him.

While drugs are useful, drugs do not treat PTSD, but only the symptoms associated with PTSD.[3] By reducing the severity of the symptoms,
medication can increase the veteran's ability to function and his ability
to deal with the roots of his PTSD.

However, sometimes psychotropic medication can interfere with
therapy.[4] Furthermore, medication must be taken as prescribed and
monitored often. In some cases, vets are noncompliant, taking medication only when they "feel bad" and refusing to return for medication
check-ups. Other complications arise if the veteran is suicidal or if he is
abusing alcohol or drugs.[5] Medication alone is not the total answer.
While a useful adjunct to therapy, medication should never be used as
a substitute for therapy.

Vietnam veterans with PTSD are not all the same. Some have psychological stressors in addition to their PTSD. Because there are so many
things to consider, therapy must always be individualized. We can make
some generalizations, however.

In order for a veteran to overcome the paralyzing and destructive
effects of his war experiences, he needs to reconsider his Vietnam experience on three levels: the cognitive or mental, the emotional, and
the moral or spiritual. Group therapy with other Vietnam veterans, led
by a qualified, caring therapist knowledgeable about PTSD and the nature of the Vietnam war, is often recommended.[6]

Being in group helps the veteran emerge from his social isolation
and allows him to practice his often rusty social skills. The group can
help resocialize the veteran, while simultaneously providing him with
a community of support, as well as with a realistic perspective on his
war experiences. He may also receive honest and valuable feedback

about himself, feedback which he might be willing to accept only from people who were there.

For some vets, war experiences are only partially remembered. For others, they are almost totally repressed. The veteran's traumatic memories are not repressed because he is or was neurotic, but because, by definition, a trauma is an event which so overwhelms an individual that he cannot accept it as happening to him.

In order for healing to begin, the Vietnam veteran needs to "uncover the trauma."[7] The specific events which were traumatic to him need to be brought out of repression and into his conscious awareness, then shared in group or individual therapy. There he can be helped to understand the meaning of these events in his life. Often these events involve incidents when the veteran's action, or inaction, led to the injury or death of another human being.[8] The veteran does not need to remember all of his traumas. However, he needs to remember enough of his past so that he can make sense of his symptoms and understand his emotional and other reactions to current reminders of the trauma and other aspects of his life today.

In most cases, combat was the setting for such traumatic events, but there were other sites also. For example, like many medics and other medical personnel, some rear support personnel with PTSD feel that their errors in judgment (real or perceived) may have cost American or Vietnamese civilian lives. Similarly, some technical repair troops have suffered because they felt responsible for certain machinery breakdowns that resulted in casualties.

While there are veterans who have killed and felt no guilt, in many cases, the veteran's memories are "distorted in the direction of unreasonable guilt."[9] Such veterans often fail to acknowledge how the complex and ambiguous nature of combat or of the entire war situation may have contributed to their behavior.[10] The therapist and other veterans can help the vet evaluate the incident more objectively and relieve him of "long held guilt."[11]

In group, the vet may come to realize that perhaps he was not such a coward after all or perhaps his friends would have been killed anyway. If indeed his cowardice or viciousness resulted in an irreversible tragedy, the vet must feel the pain of his guilt directly, rather than run from it. With the help of the group, he can try to learn to forgive himself. "The message is," writes Williams, that many veterans ". . . did the best job in the situation that could have been done considering the circumstances and the resources available in the situation."[12]

In addition to reformulating the trauma mentally, the veteran needs to take steps toward feeling the feelings associated with the traumatic event(s), as well as with other war events, feelings which were not felt at the time the event(s) occurred. Repressed grief and repressed anger are usually the two major emotions which emerge. As the veteran's rage rises to the surface, he can be helped in learning how to direct the powerful energy of his rage into constructive, rather than destructive, channels. Often, at this point the veteran may begin to make associations between past and present and see how his war experiences and his reactions to them have negatively influenced his life and relationships since the war. He may also come to appreciate any positive aspects of his military experience.

For some vets, recovery from PTSD necessitates a spiritual or moral healing, as well as an emotional one. Spiritually, some vets seek absolution for their actions.

For some vets, group therapy is the route to self-forgiveness. For others, the assistance of a clergyman or minister is needed. The need for absolution may also result in the veteran becoming involved in various "survivor missions" (such as helping other Vietnam veterans or Vietnamese refugees) or in other charitable works.[13]

Many wives have been extremely tolerant of the time, energy, and money their recovering husbands have devoted to helping fellow veterans or other persons in need. As they see their husbands break out of their isolation, they rejoice. However, wives also feel resentful when their husbands seem to be giving more time and love to others than to their marriages and children.

In sum, therapy can help reduce the veteran's sense of guilt, teach him how to control his anger, and enable him to become aware of his various emotions and to be able to express them more effectively. Furthermore, therapy, especially group therapy, can help reduce the stigma associated with being a Vietnam veteran, build the veteran's pride in his honorable and dutiful actions, remove his "fear of mental illness," and help him "clarify (his) identity" and values.[14] This applies only to groups conducted by qualified therapists, not to informal or unstructured groups where veterans might be confronted in a destructive, rather than a constructive, manner.

If a veteran is abusing drugs or alcohol it is important for the therapist to determine if the veteran is a chronic substance abuser or if he is using drugs or alcohol as a form of self-medication for the symptoms of PTSD.[15]

If a veteran is given a primary diagnosis of alcohol or drug abuse with a secondary diagnosis of PTSD, usually it will be recommended, if not required, that he complete an alcohol or drug rehabilitation program before entering counseling for PTSD. If the veteran's primary diagnosis is PTSD and his secondary diagnosis is substance abuse, he will usually be asked to refrain from drinking or drugging for the duration of the therapy. Simply put, a veteran needs to be sober and drug-free before he can deal with his Vietnam issues.[16]

In the past, PTSD was largely unrecognized by the mental health community.[17] Even today, despite the large numbers of "competent research projects that validate PTSD," some psychiatrists, psychologists, and social workers still "doubt the validity of PTSD or consider it a very rare phenomenon."[18] Instead, they look to "predisposing factors" to account for the veteran's problems, almost totally ignoring or minimizing the trauma of war. As a result many vets with PTSD were, and in some instances, still are, misdiagnosed as being neurotic or psychotic or having various character disorders.[19]

Today, however, an opposite danger may also exist. As M. J. Jelinek and Tom Williams (both veteran therapists) point out, with increased recognition of PTSD, it is possible that therapists, especially veteran therapists "see PTSD in every veteran . . . and . . . elevate the importance of that disorder and minimize or neglect additional psychopathology."[20]

Furthermore, while perhaps too many veterans with PTSD have been misdiagnosed as being character disordered or psychotic, there are veterans with PTSD who are also character disordered, schizophrenic, paranoid, or who have personality problems beyond PTSD.[21] In many instances, previous personality problems or traumas only served to complicate and intensify the veteran's reaction to the Vietnam war.

These vets need help both with PTSD and their other problems. They can be helped. However, the full range of their problems must be acknowledged.

Wives are often disappointed when therapy doesn't "fix" their husbands as rapidly as they desire. Women who have waited 10 or 15 years for their husbands to finally seek help often are dismayed to discover that the healing process can be painfully slow. Children, too, may be anxious for their father to improve. Recovery takes a long time—at least a year, usually two or three years. Depending on the individual and the severity of his traumatization, it may take even longer. Furthermore, healing requires that the veteran attend sessions regularly, not sporadically or only when in crisis, as is the pattern with some vets.

Family members need to remember that the war occurred many years ago. Meanwhile, their veteran has been practicing certain coping mechanisms for many years. His coping mechanisms may be firmly entrenched. Considerable time may be needed for healing to occur. In addition, he may have been retraumatized since the war by a work-related or vehicular accident, by criminal assault, or by personal losses of other types.

Family members sometimes hope that after their veteran undergoes therapy they will never hear the word "Vietnam" again or that they will no longer have to be saddened by the veteran's sadness or plagued by his negativity or bitterness. While therapy can help restore a man to his pre-Vietnam level of functioning, no therapy can remove Vietnam from the veteran's memory. Just as rape victims cannot "forget" the rape, or battered women their abuse, Vietnam will be with some veterans until the day they die.

That the trauma of war can leave permanent physical and psychological scars has been well-documented.[22] The veteran's sadness, anger, or other feelings about the war are bound to return. Being well, for the Vietnam veteran, lies not in "feeling better all the time," or in "never thinking or hurting about Vietnam again," but rather in being reintegrated into society and in being able to function in a family or career.[23] For the veteran, as for any human being, therapy cannot promise the absence of pain, or rage, but only a closer emotional connectedness to oneself and others. A prerequisite for this is gaining increased understanding of one's "trigger" events and situations and learning ways of coping with traumatic reminders that do not include, or at least minimize, rage reactions, severe withdrawal, or self-destructive behaviors, such as substance abuse or self-mutilation.

Nevertheless, with help, the veteran can grow past much of his Vietnam experience and learn to put more energy into his present life. While he may still suffer from intrusive thoughts, they will be less frequent and hopefully less intense. Similarly, there may still be periods of numbing, rage, or grief. But these periods will be shorter in duration, better understood, and less feared by the veteran and his wife.[24] Rita explains:

> It took three years of therapy—his therapy, my therapy, couples therapy, the works—for our relationship to improve. Frankly, I never thought our marriage would make it. But today he's less angry. That's a miracle. Also, when he gets angry about Vietnam, he can now say, "Rita, I'm having a PTSD attack. Leave me alone." That's a miracle too.
>
> But even if he doesn't warn me, I've learned to walk out of the room and not take his anger or coolness so personally. Talking to other Vietnam wives helped me with that too.

While Rita's husband can never forget Vietnam, he, like many vets who have sought help, has experienced considerable relief from some of the symptoms of PTSD. In addition, he is able to deal with reality more constructively, is more flexible, and has found "creative and constructive outlets" for his anger and his pain.[25] For example, after his two sons left home for college, to help assuage his sense of loss, he became a Big Brother to an inner-city youth and became actively involved in an anti-smoking campaign in his community.

While wives can usually understand why therapy for PTSD can take time, it may still be difficult for them to wait for their husband's healing to manifest itself. Many a wife has held back expressing her grievances toward her husband while he was in therapy for fear of overloading him. "He can't deal with me and Vietnam," they often say. Some of these women have also been advised by their husband's therapist not to bring up marital problems until their husband has resolved many of his Vietnam issues.

In cases where the veteran's PTSD is so severe that the veteran is severely regressed, almost totally noncommunicative, or extremely rigid or violent, the wife's decision to refrain from voicing her various concerns may be prudent. On the other hand, she cannot be silent forever, nor can she always wait until her husband is substantially healed to discuss certain matters. Often there are issues, especially regarding children, that cannot wait. Furthermore, an improved relationship with his wife and children and an increased capacity to deal with present realities are a part of the veteran's recovery. The veteran cannot be protected forever from knowledge about how his behavior is stressing his family.

For example, Marsha had to confront her husband, Kevin, about certain issues because she had to make a decision about their son's school placement. He was achieving beyond his grade level and had been recommended for the gifted and talented program. However, for him to be part of this program he would have to be bused to a school far from his home and in a less desirable neighborhood.

Marsha knew that Kevin had many fears about vehicular accidents and crime. When he was seven, one of his friends had died in a school bus accident. Once, before entering PTSD therapy, he had had an anxiety attack and had nearly run into a school bus himself. Several car accidents, combined with his Vietnam experience, intensified his concerns about his family's safety.

Usually Marsha didn't bring up problems that might make Kevin "hyper" but on this issue she needed to get Kevin's views. Also, if their son was to be enrolled, she needed Kevin's written consent. When she brought the subject up, Kevin refused to deal with it.

"Don't pressure me. You know I can't take pressure. Let me get more counseling under my belt before bringing up things like that."

"But if we don't make up our minds, our son is going to lose his chance," Marsha reminded him.

"It'll have to wait."

"But we can't wait."

"I said, it'll have to wait."

A few days later, Marsha brought the subject up again. Kevin still refused to discuss the issue, saying he had to get himself together first. Marsha pressed the issue and Kevin accused her of being willing to endanger their son's life. Marsha, in turn, accused Kevin of letting his "irrational fears" stunt their child's development. Then Kevin started on Marsha's weight and Marsha let loose on the subject of how Kevin and his "stupid war" had made her not only fat but a nervous wreck.

As the argument escalated, the original subject of discussion was lost. Marsha forgot to mention her own fears about busing and Kevin forgot about his pride in his son's abilities and his deep desire to help the child do well.

Meanwhile, the child, who was supposed to be sleeping, tried to stop the fight. "Don't fight because of me. I don't want to go to that new school anyhow. All I want to do is grow up and be a soldier like Daddy and get wounded in a war," he said.

"See what you've done! You've warped his mind," shrieked Marsha.

Kevin yelled back and the argument finally ended with Kevin frozen in anger for days.

At a total loss, Marsha went to Kevin's counselor and asked for his assistance. He suggested an emergency couples counseling session limited to the school issue only. During the session, Kevin and Marsha were able to give up the arguing and look at the school problem objectively. They found out that they basically agreed. They wanted every advantage for their son but were afraid of the busing and the poor neighborhood.

The counselor suggested that they look at programs in other counties, perhaps even move to an area with a gifted and talented program nearer home. Or they could make arrangements to drive their son to school or have a cab take him.

As Marsha's case illustrates, a consultation with the veteran's therapist may be needed to help a woman decide whether or not to confront her husband, and on what issues and to assist her in resolving certain issues which cannot wait. In this regard, couples counseling may also be helpful. However, couples counseling is usually advised only after the veteran has made noticeable progress in his PTSD treatment.

When vets are in treatment, their wives or girlfriends often find it helpful to attend a women's support group. There they can air grievances which they sometimes feel they must keep to themselves at home. If a woman decides to remain silent on all but the most urgent matters until her husband has achieved a certain level of recovery, her decision needs to be respected. She can, however, commit to the group, and to herself, that she will speak up at some future point in time.

If a woman cannot wait, however, the group can give her encouragement and support for her decision, as well as help in prioritizing her marital concerns so as to not bombard her vet with all her complaints at once.

Many of wives have exercised tremendous patience in waiting for their husbands to reach the point where they can tolerate, and profit from, feedback from a woman. Wives have also endured their husband's therapeutic process where, in many cases, "it gets worse before it gets better." As Rita explains to newcomers:

When your husband goes into therapy, you think, "Hurrah! The problems are finally over with." Well, guess what? There are more nightmares, more holes in the wall, more anger at you.

In therapy all the feelings your husband has bottled up for years start coming out, in group of course, but on you too. My husband even started drinking more—blaming it all on me, as usual. It got so bad, I started wondering why I ever begged him to go for help in the first place.

Then, when the group started teaching him how to be assertive, rather than passive or aggressive, which were his usual styles, I got mad. Here I was, holding in everything for years and not being assertive so he wouldn't get upset and quit therapy, and here he was, practicing his group's assertiveness training on me. Then, when I objected, he accused me of undercutting his therapy.

Now things have evened out between us. Thanks to the other Vietnam wives I've talked to, I've learned how to be more assertive too and, thanks to the men's group, my husband can take it. But it took us three years of counseling, not to mention a lot of yelling and a lot of tears and heartache on my part.

But it was worth it. At least I have a marriage now. Before I had nothing.

Not just wives, but clinicians have noted that therapy may bring about increased thinking and dreaming about Vietnam, as well as more emotionality.[26] If the therapy is working, many of the veteran's long-buried emotions and memories will begin to surface. As they surface, the veteran will experience more inner turmoil, more restlessness, and more pain. Experiencing these feelings may make him temporarily inefficient in terms of work and more vulnerable psychologically. In some cases, as a defense against his increased feelings of personal vulnerability, the veteran may become more hostile, or domineering, toward his wife and others.

While the wife need not tolerate violence, she can expect her husband to be not only angrier, but sadder, and perhaps more openly afraid. She may need to assure him frequently that he is not falling apart and that the feelings, although intense, will not destroy him. Neither will they last forever. The vet may also need to be reminded that although feeling his feelings can be a very painful and disorienting process, in the long run he will only be strengthened by facing his feelings rather running from them.

Rita's husband, for example, sat in group for six months before he shared his Vietnam experiences. "That night," Rita says, "he went out drinking. The next night, he cried on my lap all night long, just like a baby. Then he cried for almost a whole week afterward too. He couldn't even go to work.

"'Am I going crazy?' he'd ask me.

"'No, honey, you're just feeling your pain.'"

Rita's husband is a well paid, highly functional professional. His PTSD never expressed itself in job problems. Rather, his major difficulty was depression and an inability to relate to others. Upon starting group, he became more depressed, but eventually he began the grieving process. He needed to go through the grieving process not just once, but several times, before he could free himself of certain memories.

As a result, he is now closer to his wife, can read bedtime stories to his children without becoming excessively annoyed, and is even able to take Rita on vacations without criticizing her.

While Rita was overjoyed at her husband's progress, at first she didn't know how to act around him. "I'm not used to him being normal," she says. It was a new feeling for her not to have to think four times before she said something to him. Furthermore, although she felt relieved that her husband was finally able to participate more in family life, she felt somewhat disoriented giving up her old role of managing almost everything all by herself. Also, she was somewhat frightened of the demands her husband might make of her emotionally and sexually.

When my husband finished therapy, it was like starting all over again, not only in terms of renegotiating who was going to do what, but in terms of our entire relationship.

After Vietnam, my husband and I got into this pattern where he shut me out and I, in my own way, shut him out too. I learned not to expect much from him emotionally and sometimes, even when he did want to be close, I rejected him. I guess I was angry at having to be the stable one while he was allowed to be moody and unpredictable.

Our entire relationship became centered around money and the children. We stopped going out and having fun together, like we used to, before Viet-

nam. We even forgot how to talk to each other like husband and wife, or even like friends. All our talk was about the house and the kids, me complaining about him, or him about me.

Now he wants to have a "real" relationship with me. But I've forgotten how to be relaxed around him. I'm a whiz at anticipating his moods and appeasing him, but now he wants to know me as an individual.

What a joke! After all these years of functioning, functioning, functioning, am I still an individual? Somewhere, in the midst of just trying to survive and keep the family, and myself, from going under, I lost myself.

It's been five years since I've read a book. I haven't done anything else interesting either. Is my husband now going to find me boring? Now that he's better, will he still want me?

Like Rita, other wives sometimes voice feelings of personal insecurity as they watch their husbands become stronger. Since their previous relationships with their husbands were often based on being their caretakers, the women fear that they will be abandoned now that they are not so intensely needed. In my experience, however, very few veterans have abandoned their wives following successful treatment for PTSD. The women who have been deserted are those whose husbands did not seek help or who came for help only intermittently.

According to the Vet Center study, 91% of the counselors polled indicate that Vietnam wives who seek help often complain of feeling as if they have lost their personal identity in constantly responding to the veteran's needs and the many family crises. In some instances, the veteran's recovery poses an identity crisis for his wife, who must now deal with herself and her own feelings, which in the past were put on hold because of her husband's PTSD. As Candice Williams notes, "Total sacrifice of the woman is characteristic in dysfunctional combat veteran family systems . . ."[27] One of the group members, Marsha, was typical of wives who face this kind of identity crisis.

I was a girl when I married. Now I sometimes feel like I'm an old lady, even though I have yet to hit the big "5-0". My husband is fine, or almost fine, but I'm not, even though everybody expects me to be. Worse, I expect me to be. But just because he's got his PTSD under fair control doesn't mean that I'm over my pain and anger.

Nowadays I even get hugs without asking for them. You'd think I'd be overjoyed. But I keep remembering all the times I was dying for a little love and never got a crumb.

Sometimes I think about telling my husband how I feel, but I don't want to ruin the progress he's made by bring up all my past resentments. Yet he senses my feelings and asks me why I'm so cold.

I never know what to say.

"Don't dare look back," I tell myself. "If you start thinking about all you sacrificed for him, you'll start putting holes in the wall and tearing up the furniture like he used to."

Usually I try to cast out my resentments as soon as they crop up, but it doesn't always work. I guess all those years of supporting him before therapy and then during the stress of therapy have drained me. Sometimes I feel a great emptiness and hollowness inside, as if I've lost all my blood and have no more strength or love to give.

I want to get back to who I was before Vietnam came into my life. In my head, I know there's a wonderful future out there for me, but there's this bitter, angry woman standing in my way. That's me. She's a tired woman too, who has spoiled not only her husband, but her children, and her in-laws too.

I'm in a rut and I know it, but I can't seem to get out of it. My husband isn't stopping me as much as he used to, although he still gets in my way. My main problem is that I don't know where to begin. There's got to be more to life than working and having a family. But what?

Marsha is in the midst of her own midlife crisis. Sometimes she thinks about taking a course or pursuing a hobby but it seems like too much effort for her. Yet she knows that doing something small, just for herself, is the first step toward getting more satisfaction out of life.

She also suffers from what she calls "PTSD, or Vietnam wife, burnout." After having spent years focused on her husband and his postwar problems, she is at a loss in establishing goals for herself. While her husband's progress has freed her somewhat, she is hindered in taking a look at herself by the emotional and physical exhaustion accumulated over the years. Or perhaps depression has eroded her ability to concentrate and her self-confidence to such a degree that she now doubts she will be able to complete any project she starts.

In some cases, the Vietnam wife is impeded in her development by a husband who, although he has made substantial progress, is still reluctant to assume major responsibilities with the children or the housework. Even though the Vietnam wife in this situation may no longer have to deal with constant crises, she will still have little time and energy to pursue her individual goals aside from earning a living and taking care of a family.

It is often suggested to Vietnam wives that they begin where they left off—that they examine their pre-Vietnam or premarital years and try to remember things which used to spark their interest. They also need encouragement in asking for what they need from their husbands. One wife remembered that she had enjoyed painting before her marriage. She has since taken an art course and is thinking about starting a small hand-painted card business. It all began, however, with her signing up for a two-hour art workshop which she almost didn't go to because her 15-year-old son needed a last-minute ride to a basketball game.

Gathering together all her assertive skills, she told her son that in the future he would have to give her advance notice about his games or find his own ride. In addition, she insisted that this time her husband do the chauffeuring. After years of feeling as if she was living in her husband's shadow, and the shadow of the Vietnam war, it was now time for her. What's more, she felt she had earned it.

Getting Help

Today both Vet Centers and Department of Veterans Affairs Medical Centers offer counseling and other help for Vietnam veterans. Often individual, group, and marriage counseling can be obtained through the psychiatric, psychological, or social work services, or through the medical center's outpatient mental hygiene clinic. In addition, several VA hospitals sponsor PTSD inpatient units. Inquiry about these PTSD units, as well as about help in the private sector, can be made at Vet Centers or at VA Medical Centers.

A veteran may be reluctant to seek help because it violates his sense of masculinity or his vow to have as little to do with the government as possible. Or perhaps he learned to mistrust mental health professionals, as he did clergymen, because of certain negative experiences with such professionals during the war. During the war, some vets saw psychiatrists, psychologists, and other mental health professionals as being in collusion with the military.[28] Or perhaps the veteran avoids therapy because he fears he will be misdiagnosed or misunderstood.

A veteran may also feel embarrassed to admit to still being bothered by events that occurred some years ago. Perhaps he feels he should be over Vietnam by now and wonders if he is abnormal for still thinking or dreaming about the war. Or perhaps he envisions therapy as a form of entrapment.

Some vets do seek help on their own, but others are shoved into treatment by wives or other family members, or by employers.

Perhaps the most frequently asked question by wives is, "How do I get my husband into treatment?"

Each woman is an expert on her own husband. Often she, more than anyone else, knows which approach will be most effective with him. In general, reluctant vets need to be told, either by their wives, another family member, or another veteran, that having PTSD is not shameful or unmanly and that seeking help is an act of courage and honesty, not a sign of weakness. The vet can also be reminded that other veterans have sought help and benefited immensely.

As Williams points out, some vets feel they do not deserve treatment because their problems are not as severe as those of other veterans, because they were not as seriously wounded as others, or because they did not see as much combat.[29] In such cases, the vet needs to be reminded that trauma is trauma and that PTSD is a normal human response to extraordinary stress. Even American civilians who were in Vietnam developed PTSD.

If the veteran has a negative attitude toward the VAMC or the Vet Center program, he can be encouraged to give the VAMC and the Vet Centers a chance. What does he have to lose by attending a few sessions? If he does not benefit, he can always quit.

Generally, telling a veteran that he is "crazy" and listing his character defects will not motivate him to seek help. Empathy works far better. Rita, for example, was able to convince her husband to go to a Vet Center by saying, "Haven't you suffered enough? Don't you deserve a little help? You're always complaining about how the government ripped you off. Well, here's a way the government can pay you back."

David Harrington, who conducts groups for Vietnam veterans in 12 two-hour sessions, tells resistant vets, "You owe yourself 24 hours of help—that's one day out of your life. Is that too much for all the suffering you've been through?"[30]

Williams asks, "What good has it done keeping all this inside of yourself for so long? You might want to try something else, such as sharing with men who have had similar experiences and can understand."[31] Other arguments that might be used are, "You're paying for these services, you might as well use them" or "How do you know it won't help until you've tried it?'"

A woman can let her husband know that help is available by giving him the phone number of the Vet Center or VAMC and literature about PTSD. She can also indicate her willingness to be supportive. However, many women fear, and justifiably so, that if they push too hard, their husbands will become even more resistant to the idea of treatment. Some women dare not mention the idea to their husbands, knowing that the idea will be immediately rejected if it comes from them. In desperation, some women have called the VAMC or the Vet Center asking for a Vietnam veteran who has undergone therapy to please come by the home posing as a repairman and "casually" mention treatment to her husband.

While Vet Centers and VAMCs cannot provide such services, vets who have undergone therapy are often willing to talk to veterans who are hesitant about seeking help. Often another veteran or a concerned relative or family friend may be able to discuss the need for therapy with a veteran more effectively than his wife.

In some circumstances, however, the woman does not have the luxury of waiting for her husband to seek treatment. When her husband becomes so regressed, so violent, so self-destructive, or so disoriented that he cannot take care of himself or becomes a danger to himself or others, the woman may need to explore the possibility of strongly urging him to seek help and, in certain extreme circumstances, of committing him against his will. Department of Veterans Affairs Medical Centers do not accept involuntary patients; however, they may have information on state or county commitment procedures. Such information may also be available at local courthouses or police stations.

In some communities, emergency crisis teams are available to come to the home to evaluate the veteran. If these crisis teams include police, the veteran must be informed in advance that police are coming and that they are coming to help him, not assault him. Also, the crisis team needs to be advised that they are dealing with a Vietnam veteran whose anxiety level may be aroused by seeing uniformed personnel.

Some women feel guilty about calling in rescue squads or literally driving their husbands to Department of Veterans Affairs Medical Centers, Vet Centers, or alcohol or drug treatment centers for help. They feel they are wrong or doing their husband a disservice. However, when a man is severely impaired by PTSD, alcoholism, or a drug addiction, the woman is not betraying him, but saving his life by forcing him to seek help. When the husband is unable to think and act rationally, he must no longer be seen as head of the household, but as a family member who needs help. The woman must take control of the situation, as she would if her husband were a child who needed help. The first step can be to contact the nearest Vet Center or Department of Veterans Affairs Medical Center or a community service agency.

Summary

PTSD therapy involves several steps: helping the veteran uncover the specific events in the war which he has been attempting to deny or which he has been unable to accept; supporting him as he feels the feelings associated with these traumatic events; helping him acquire a greater understanding of how his war experiences have affected his life in the present; and helping the veteran find constructive uses for his Vietnam experience.

Healing is not an absolute. It does not mean a total disappearance of symptoms, but rather a reduction in their frequency and intensity. Once the symptoms are under control, the veteran will be able to enjoy a more satisfying life. Most likely he will think about Vietnam many times but his war experiences will no longer paralyze him or be the focus of his mental and emotional life. As he puts the war in perspective, he learns that he is not alone in his feelings. He will move from hopelessness and helplessness toward an attitude of gratitude that he is alive and can be useful to his family and society.

Healing is a lifelong process. The initial investment of time in a counseling effort, however, may take many months. Some time may pass before any gains are evident. During those initial months, therapy can create its own stresses on the veteran and his family. He may be retraumatized by what he remembers, by the intensity of his own emotions, or, if he is in a group setting, by the stories and emotions of other veterans.

This disruption affects not only the veteran, but also his wife, who can expect to witness some of the veteran's previously suppressed emotions. Furthermore, PTSD therapy does not necessarily solve all of the veteran's problems. Nor does it automatically heal his marriage. Usually, both the veteran and his wife need to learn how to stop scapegoating each other and improve their communication skills. Couples counseling is often useful to help them discuss problems left unresolved due to the veteran's PTSD and issues involving parenting, division of labor in the home, and other such concerns. Couples counseling is most beneficial, however, when the veteran is psychologically ready to deal with marital problems and when the therapist is sex fair.

One of the most common feelings experienced by Vietnam wives who have nursed their husbands first through PTSD and then through PTSD therapy is the feeling of burnout. Once the vet is finally on the path to recovery, his wife may find herself aware of many months and years of stored up anger and resentment. She must then deal with the dilemma of what to do with this pile of grievances. On the one hand, she may want to confront her husband directly. On the other hand, she may want to enjoy the vet's improved emotional state and to keep the family peace.

In many cases, the veteran's emotional progress frees the Vietnam wife to focus on her own goals. However, if her vet still adheres to traditional views of the woman's role or is unwilling to consistently assume various child care or housekeeping functions, the vet may continue to pose a formidable obstacle to her personal development. Even when the veteran is supportive, the Vietnam wife may experience difficulties grappling with the challenge of establishing her own identity and interests. In many cases, emotional and physical fatigue, as well as years of focusing on the veteran rather than herself, have depleted the woman's emotional, intellectual, and creative resources. Often a recuperation period is necessary before the woman can begin working on her own issues.

As a result of counseling, many couples have renewed their commitment to one another and can relate to each other on a deep and meaningful level. Not only in their marriage, but in their personal lives, they are able to make positive use of the frustrations, pain, and anger they experienced in the past.

13

Stay or Go?

Should I stay or should I go? The question haunts me. I keep praying for the right answer, but no answer seems right. I don't want to end my marriage; I just want to stop hurting so much.

Some days I make a definite decision to go. But when I think of my children, pangs of guilt seize me. "What will happen to them if I leave? Won't they hate me for taking them away from their father and disrupting the only life they've ever known? Doesn't divorce damage children emotionally? Can't I stick it out for their sakes?"

Soon they'll be grown and gone, but won't they hate me anyway—for leaving their poor disabled dad?

On the other hand, I feel I am doing myself and my children no favor by staying in a marriage where I am so miserable. But isn't some of that unhappiness my fault? Maybe I just expect too much.

I'm in a rut and I know it. The rut feels hellish at times, but at least its familiar. All my life I've been taught that a woman needs a man and that she can't possibly survive in the cold, cruel world without one.

If I leave my husband, who will I have? I now feel so unattractive and undesirable as a woman that I can't conceive of any other man ever wanting me. Isn't it better to have my husband than to have no one at all?

Sometimes when I sleep with him, I feel both love and hate, and I can't tell which is stronger. When I see his missing toes and fingers, my feelings are all mixed up. I pity him and want to take care of him, yet a growing part of me is tired of all that. I want more for me.

I'm stuck in indecision. Hopefully in the next year or two, I'll finally make a choice. I'm really scared though, for this may well be the most difficult choice of my whole life. But at least I'm willing to deal with my options, rather than run from them the way I used to.

—Wife of a veteran

Some women come for counseling with their minds already made up—they are leaving their veteran tomorrow. For example, Trudy came for help only once and then only because her husband had pleaded with her to find out more about PTSD and the Vietnam war before saying goodbye. But Trudy wasn't interested in hearing any more about Vietnam or PTSD. She had heard enough already. "I'm Vietnamed out," she said. "Now I want out."

She was not interested in couples counseling or in the women's group either. She felt her husband's problems were deeper than Vietnam and she was tired of his using Vietnam as an excuse. He had been in PTSD counseling for three years now, but, according to Trudy, nothing had changed. True, his nightmares and other symptoms had diminished and he had given up alcohol, but he still was unable to give her the emotional warmth and closeness she desired. Therefore, she was leaving—the sooner the better.

In contrast to Trudy, most of the women who come for counseling are in a state of confusion about whether to stay with their veteran or not. Fran has been thinking of leaving her husband for four years. Her first statement to the group was, "I've thought about it and thought about it. But I still can't make up my mind."

Like some of the other women, Fran vacillates between wanting to make her marriage work and feeling exhausted. "I've tried and tried with him, with no success. I feel like giving up. Yet I just can't say, 'The heck with him,' either. Many times I ask myself, 'Do I still love him?' only to come up with the sorry conclusion that after 10 years of marriage, I honestly don't know."

While Fran no longer hopes for a storybook romance with her husband, in the back of her mind she fantasizes that someday he will reduce his verbal abuses, stay sober, and show her more affection and appreciation. Yet Jerry, who served two tours of duty in Vietnam, has never sought help. In fact, whenever Fran suggests that he might do well to drop by the Vet Center or attend an A.A. meeting, he laughs. In his view, the marital problems are all Fran's fault.

When Fran decided to join the women's group, Jerry rejoiced. He thought the women's group would help Fran be more understanding toward him, help "straighten her out," and turn her into a better wife and mother. Jerry was dismayed when he realized that while Fran did learn about PTSD in group, she also learned that she had options other than staying in a marriage that did not meet her needs. Furthermore, she was not responsible for his PTSD or his alcoholism. Although Fran came to acknowledge that she had brought several of her own problems into the marriage, she also came to realize that she was not 95% to blame for the marital difficulties, which was her belief in the early years of her marriage.

When Fran began to be more assertive at home, Jerry wanted her to quit the women's group. But Fran was no longer taking orders from him, like she used to. She had hardened her heart toward Jerry's negative comments and various accusations. Today when he chastises or criticizes her, she no longer shudders with fear, guilt, or shame. She doesn't even become defensive. Instead, she stares at him blankly, calls a friend, or simply leaves the room. "You're full of baloney," she might even say.

Nevertheless, years of being blamed and criticized have served to erode Fran's self-esteem and to demoralize and immobilize her to the point where she has difficulty taking action in many spheres of her life. For instance, she has abandoned some of her career interests and hobbies, as well as some of her friendships, not only because Jerry was and is so often jealous of such involvements, but because she is too fatigued and too preoccupied with the state of her marriage to invest her energies elsewhere.

Years of living with criticism and rejection have also resulted in Fran's feeling unattractive as a woman, even though she is a graceful, lovely woman. "If I leave him, will I be able to find another man?" she wonders. Even if she could, she feels too worn out to start all over again with a new man. "This is my second marriage," she explains. "I really want to make it work this time. Besides, by now I'm used to Jerry. It isn't great with him, but at least I know what to expect. There's a certain security in that. On the other hand, I don't want to spend the rest of my life like this either."

Many times Fran has planned to leave Jerry, then she changes her mind. She then berates herself for staying in a marriage where she feels emotionally deprived while at the same time physically and emotionally overextended. Fran frequently states that the main reason she stays with Jerry is for her children, whom she feels would be devastated by a marital breakup. Furthermore, it is difficult to leave a man with whom one has shared many years.

Also, Fran is confused about who her husband truly is. In her view, he has at least two different personalities. "There's the PTSD Jerry and the non-PTSD Jerry. The sober Jerry and the drinking one. If he was all bad all the time, it would be easy to make up my mind. But he can be so charming, so loving, so sensitive, so good when he's good. It gives me hope."

What Fran is reluctant to admit, however, either to herself or to the group, is the extent to which she has become emotionally dependent on Jerry. Fran is not alone with this problem. Many of the wives who have attended group are, for a variety of reasons, emotionally dependent on their husbands. In some cases, this emotional dependence is the result of the social isolation and restrictions which the veteran has imposed or required. For Jerry's sake, Fran severed many important family and social ties, depriving herself of many sources of feedback and positive regard. Consequently, over the years, Fran's self-esteem has become closely tied to Jerry's reactions and views of her.

Jerry is also her only source of affection since by now Fran has become distant from her parents, her siblings, and many of her former friends. Should Fran leave Jerry, she does not feel she would have a family or social network to turn to for support. She is afraid she would find herself literally almost entirely alone in the world. Although she could turn to certain persons for help, after having minimized her relationships with these persons for so many years, she is hesitant to do so.

Not all Vietnam wives are as socially isolated as Fran. Yet, in my experience, those who are generally find it more difficult to leave their veteran when the relationship deteriorates than do those wives who have a supportive extended family or a network of friends.

The irony is that prior to meeting Jerry, Fran, like many wives, was a very independent woman, managing both her personal and work life on her own. In fact, Fran is certain that one reason Jerry was drawn to her initially was that she was so self-sufficient and autonomous. "But he's destroyed the very qualities in me that attracted him in the first place," she sadly admits.

Other Vietnam wives have the same lament. However, unlike Fran, some women have not even embraced the possibility of ending their marriage with their veteran. This is especially the case with women who have strong religious convictions or moral scruples against divorce. Yet even these women begin to consider the idea of separation or divorce once they reach the breaking point of endurance.

In my experience, only a small percentage of women seeking help have actively pursued a separation or divorce. This observation is inconsistent with statistics that show a relatively high divorce rate for Vietnam veterans, at least upon initial return from Vietnam and as late as 1979. According to the President's Commission on Mental Health (1978), "approximately 38% of the marriages of Vietnam veterans broke up within six months of their return from Southeast Asia."[1]

Furthermore, according to the largest study of Vietnam veterans completed thus far, the National Vietnam Veteran Research Study of 1988, almost one-fourth of Vietnam veterans were separated, 70% were divorced (35% two or more times); 49% had high levels of intimacy problems with their wives or girlfriends; and 55% reported significant parenting difficulties.[2] Clinical experience has shown that "nonmarital relationships involving . . . veterans have shown the same trend toward instability."[3]

Perhaps this inconsistency between the relatively high divorce rates for Vietnam veterans and the tendency of women seeking help to stay with their marriages can be explained by the possibility that women on the brink of divorce or separation are not generally those who seek counseling at VA facilities. Rather, VA counseling programs most likely attract women who are still seeking ways of improving or saving their relationships with their veteran. Furthermore, Vietnam wives in the process of divorce may be furious with their veteran and may want to divest themselves of everything and anything having to do with him, including Vietnam. Therefore, they are not likely to appear at the Vet Center or VA Medical Centers inquiring about PTSD.

Vietnam wives who stay in marriages that are extremely stressful and painful for them stay for a variety of reasons. They fear the loneliness, the financial hardship, or the stigma associated with being separated or divorced. Many women interpret divorce as an admission that they have failed at marriage. While both men and women tend to experience a sense of failure and shame upon the breakup of their marriage, research has shown that these feelings are deeper and tend to persist for a longer period of time in women.[4] The Vietnam wife may also stay with her veteran because she feels sorry for him. She may pity him because he has PTSD, war injuries, or other scars from the war. Or perhaps he had a physically or sexually abusive childhood. If her children have left home she may feel her marriage is all she has left.

On a very personal level, the Vietnam wife may experience the collective guilt many Americans feel regarding the U.S. involvement in Vietnam and the subsequent shunning of Vietnam veterans. Most likely she is well aware that her veteran has felt profoundly betrayed and abandoned by the U.S. government, by U.S. society, and, in some instances, by his family and community as well. She may have stood in long lines and made many phone calls to help her veteran obtain certain financial or medical benefits. Or perhaps she has spent hours waiting with him at doctors' offices or educating his family, her family, their neighbors, and their clergy about PTSD in hopes of creating a more understanding and sympathetic environment for him and for their children.

Consequently she may have difficulty even contemplating leaving the veteran because, on some level, she does not want to add to his feeling of being betrayed and abandoned by deserting him also. This is especially the case when the veteran has war-related medical problems or when he has begun counseling for PTSD. Some Vietnam wives want to wait and see if their husband is going to recover from his back condition (his skin condition, his Agent Orange tumors, or some other condition acquired in Vietnam) before they decide to leave him. Others want to see if counseling will help.

Yet even these women sometimes angrily say, "I don't feel sorry for him anymore. The only person I feel sorry for is me!" and vehemently announce that they no longer want to be "living sacrifices" for men who, for a host of reasons, may be not only trampling on their affections, but squandering their money on alcohol, drugs, or, in few cases, other women.

The sense of guilt which the Vietnam wife might feel about leaving her veteran is compounded in those cases where the Vietnam veteran is exceptionally emotionally or financially dependent on her and where she is aware of that dependency. "He has nobody but me. What will happen to him if I go?" women say. Or "I don't love him like I used to, but I don't want to see him crack up or on the streets either." Some women fear the veteran will commit suicide if they leave.

Rose, Daniel's third wife, greatly fears what would happen to Daniel should she leave. Daniel lost many friends in Vietnam. Upon returning from the war, he found that his wife had taken a lover. She promptly divorced him, taking with her their infant son. Six months later she and the infant were killed in an automobile accident. Almost immediately, Daniel married another woman who, after five years of marriage, also became adulterous and fled the state with their young child.

Rose does not think her husband can handle another loss, which he would interpret as yet another betrayal. Although Daniel has never been violent with Rose and has never even threatened to hurt her, Rose senses the tremendous amount of rage he harbors within and his intense loneliness. "He says I'm the only one he trusts in the world. His whole life revolves around me and our three daughters," she says. "I'm afraid of what would happen to him—and possibly to me—if I go."

For Rose, as for a few others, the sense of fear and guilt about leaving the veteran is combined with feelings of fear and guilt regarding prior experiences of disappointing a father or father figure. For example, Rose's father greatly disapproved of her marriage to Daniel due to religious differences. Soon after the wedding, Rose's father had a heart attack and the entire family blamed Rose. Despite the irrationality of their accusation, Rose believed she had caused, or at least significantly contributed to, her father's illness. Now, thoughts of leaving her husband bring to the surface all of Rose's old fears surrounding "deserting" her father at the time of her marriage to Daniel.

Today Rose is in crisis. Daniel wants to move to an isolated rural area. As a result of his experiences in Vietnam, he has a low tolerance for noise and for other people, except Rose and the girls. Rose, however, likes city life and other people.

"Just because you want to be a hermit doesn't mean the kids and I have to go be hermits too. And what about our girls? Do you think two teenage girls are going to stay home on the farm? First chance they get, they'll leave. We'll lose our kids if we move," she argues in marriage counseling.

Yet Daniel is certain that living in the country would eliminate his depression. Perhaps he would be less grouchy and more affectionate to Rose if they moved.

Rose, however, feels she would literally die all alone on a mountain top, with just Daniel and the children. Yet, if Daniel insists on moving, she will follow. "If it'll help him, I can't say no," she says. "After all he's been through in Vietnam and since, he deserves to spend the rest of the years the way he wants. Besides, the girls have to leave home sometime anyway."

Other couples are like Rose and Daniel, with the veteran wanting to relocate to a relatively secluded area and his wife not wanting to give up her present lifestyle. Not all wives are like Rose, however. Many refuse to relocate. Sometimes the veteran leaves his wife in favor of living in an isolated locale. Other times the couple becomes stalemated on the issue.

"If you loved me enough, you would do what is best for me," the veteran may say. On the other hand, his wife may feel that what the veteran perceives as being best for him would be a form of emotional and intellectual death for her and detrimental to their children.

Some wives, like Rose, feel they must go along with their husbands in order to prove their loyalty and dedication. However, for many of them, this sense of loyalty coexists with a host of fears about venturing forth into the world as a woman alone. Some of these fears stem from the woman's personal insecurities. Some, however, stem from having learned as children that women are too weak to make it on their own, without a man to protect and support them. Traditionally, society has also taught many women to seek love and approval from men, rather than from themselves or from other women. Unless she has had a nontraditional upbringing, the Vietnam wife may not be able to feel like a worthwhile, competent person without male approval or companionship.

Women are also taught that if they are "good" they will be rewarded by having a strong man to love and support them. Consequently many women are "often ill-prepared, psychologically or educationally, to sustain themselves without a husband." Furthermore, most women have few role models for independent living. Making the break may mean "an incredibly complex and difficult journey into territory that has never been mapped for them by society or by other women in their families or social groups."[5] Or, if the woman has already undergone a separation or divorce prior to her relationship with the veteran, she may remember the hurt, anxiety, and stress involved and may not want to reexperience such pain ever again.

Women in midlife or older may stay because they feel their chances for remarriage or finding a new love relationship are slim because of their age or because they feel so scarred inside. Midlife and older women may also be suffering from low-grade depressions (or worse) due to years of living in a stressful marriage. Hence they may be suffering the classical symptoms of depression, which include low self-esteem, helplessness, hopelessness, and fatigue.

Such symptoms make daily living difficult and far-reaching decision-making nearly impossible. To quote many a woman, "It's enough to put one foot in front of the other and do what I have to do for that day without trying to contemplate the future too." Yet the fact that the years are passing and she is not taking charge of her life may only further lower the Vietnam wife's low self-esteem and sense of helplessness. In such a demoralized state, she is hardly in a position to make a major decision, such as whether or not to leave her husband.

Last but not least, some Vietnam wives stay because, on some level, they feel responsible for their husband's PTSD. Even though "C-C-C" (you didn't Cause it, you can't Control it, you can't Cure it) is continually emphasized in group, some women have not overcome the cultural conditioning which has taught them, as women, to take responsibility for the peace and harmony of the family and for their husband's emotional and physical well-being. They still hope that if only they change or improve themselves enough, that their husband's PTSD and other sources of marital unhappiness will significantly diminish.

In a few cases, this cultural conditioning has been reinforced by certain religious ideas, such as the belief that the husband is the God-ordained head of the household to whom the woman should always be submissive and subservient. Along these lines, some women feel that their marital problems are trials sent by God which they must suffer and endure. A few even feel that their husband's objectionable behavior is God's punishment to them for certain sins and that their husband's abusiveness is God's means of chastising them and developing their moral character.

While some women are trapped by sex role conditioning, or by various religious ideologies, others are trapped by sheer economics. Leaving would mean financial hardship, if not outright destitution. Some women have handed over their property to their husbands, allowing them to retain the family's assets in the husband's name only, or have otherwise lost control of their property. Some women were coerced into surrendering their property through violence; others, through the veteran's pleading and cajoling. In several instances, however, women relinquished control of their assets as a matter of course, simply because they were brought up in an era where the man, not the woman, was supposed to take care of the finances. They unthinkingly gave their houses, their bank accounts, and other material possessions to their husband in good faith, not realizing that someday they might want to separate.

Vietnam wives in such financial situations would have to begin their new lives with practically nothing. Or they may even be unable to consider a new life because they cannot afford an attorney or legal costs. Lack of funds is a crucial problem in instances where the veteran has threatened to contest the divorce, keep most of the marital property for himself, or fight for custody of the children. The Vietnam wife who does not have the economic power to fight for her rights in court may decide to stay rather than lose her children or her assets.

Financial reasons for staying are especially prevalent among Vietnam wives who are being physically abused. A common pattern in homes where there is wife abuse is for the abuser to have tight control over the family's finances, even if the wife is an outside wage earner.[6] In addition, should the abused Vietnam wife decide to leave, she will have to contend with police or legal systems which are only beginning to respond to the needs of battered women. Often, abused Vietnam wives have been discouraged from seeking a formal separation or divorce because of the lengthy and complicated legal procedures involved in domestic violence cases. These women are especially discouraged when they are called names or not believed by police or by various court officials, when they are blamed for the abuse, when they are required to produce evidence or eyewitnesses for abuses which have largely occurred behind closed doors, or when they are considered "just another battered woman" who is cluttering up the court dockets and who will probably "kiss and make up" with her batterer after filing for a divorce.

Nevertheless, due to recent legislation and improved attitudes toward abused women, many forms of legal and police protection and help are available to battered women today which were not available 10 years ago. Numerous legal and police obstacles can still exist, however, significantly impeding the woman's attempt to obtain an equitable separation or divorce.[7] If the legal and financial obstacles are too great, then she may give up trying to obtain her independence and decide to stay with her abuser instead.

She will be especially tempted to stay if her husband has threatened to retaliate against her, their children, or other family members should she leave. Under such circumstances, the woman may reason that it is safer for her to stay at home. As Suzanne Schechter, author of "The Future of the Battered Woman's Movement," points out, "So it does not surprise me that battered women sometimes choose to stay with their abusers and know where they are, rather than wait to be hunted down. The illusion of control that comes from knowing where he is can be easier to live with than the more explicit terror of uncertainty."[8]

For some battered Vietnam wives, ending their marriages has necessitated disguising their identity and fleeing to other states. The costs, however, have been high. Not only have these women had to leave their jobs, their communities, their families, and their familiar surroundings, but they have had to uproot their children, interrupt their schooling, disrupt their friendships, and in other ways significantly alter their lives.

Not all women can have such courage and fortitude. Furthermore, during the "honeymoon" stage of the battering cycle, the abuser can be so loving and repentant that it is easy for the woman to forgive him one more time and to give the relationship yet another chance.

"How many of his problems are due to Vietnam and PTSD and how many are due to his basic personality, his family background, or other factors?" women ask. They also wonder about their own role in the relationship difficulties: "Who's to blame? Him, me, Vietnam, the U.S. government, my childhood, his childhood, or what?"

Younger women or women who do not yet have children, that is, women who have less time and energy invested in their veteran and who can thus more easily envision a future without him, especially want answers to these questions. Often they say, "If I could be sure that most of his problems have to do with Vietnam, I'd stay with him until he finishes therapy. But if his problems are deeper than that, I want out now, while I'm still young and without children."

While some women urgently want answers, there are no simple replies to their questions. In most cases, understanding the dynamics of a relationship and predicting its future is a far more complex matter than simply assigning blame to one partner, the government, or society at large. Furthermore, the concept of PTSD was only officially accepted in 1980 and is still being researched and in the process of being understood.

In addition, it is being increasingly recognized that a veteran can be suffering from other psychological syndromes in addition to PTSD. This area is still being explored and debated by researchers and therapists. Once again, there are no clear lines of demarcation between veterans who suffer "only" from PTSD and those who suffer from PTSD in addition to other problems. However, some rough guidelines do exist.

Some possible differences between the veteran who uses alcohol as a form of self-medication for PTSD and the veteran who is truly a problem drinker, or an alcoholic, have already been discussed. In addition, there are some ways to differentiate between a veteran who suffers primarily from PTSD and one who suffers primarily from a character disorder in addition to PTSD.

The primarily PTSD-afflicted veteran is characterized by excessive self-blame and survivor guilt. As James Newman says in *PTSD: A Handbook for Clinicians*, veterans with a primary diagnosis of PTSD are aware of their maladaptive behavior, "generally accept responsibility for (it) and are genuinely distressed by it. Although they view their PTSD symptoms as irrational, they tend to blame themselves for being the way they are."[9] In contrast, the primarily character-disordered veteran uses PTSD to justify his actions and may use his disorder to take advantage of others.

The PTSD-afflicted veteran's major fear is loss of control, that is, being overwhelmed by pain, helplessness, or rage. Even though he may have infrequent outbursts of temper, in general much of his psychic energy is directed toward controlling his aggressive impulses. When his internal tensions mount to the bursting point, however, his internal controls may fail him and he may erupt. Subsequently, he usually experiences remorse over his outburst and may expend even more energy trying to suppress his aggressiveness. Hence, he may become increasingly socially and emotionally withdrawn following an angry outburst.

In contrast, the character-disordered veteran expresses his anger not only more frequently than the primarily PTSD-afflicted veteran, but with little remorse.

A final difference is that the primarily PTSD-afflicted veteran often has a strong aversion to social contact and may be excessively withdrawn. In contrast, the primarily character-disordered veteran may fear being alone.[10]

Vietnam wives whose husbands were alcoholic, drug addicted, or violent prior to the war, whose husbands show definite signs of being character-disordered in addition to having PTSD, and whose husbands are determined never ever to seek help have a much clearer picture of their veteran's psychological state than women whose husbands pursue therapy or alcohol or drug rehabilitation inconsistently, or who seem to be involved in a therapeutic program only halfheartedly. According to some of the wives, their husbands seek some form of counseling only when in crisis or only when so depressed or distraught that they absolutely must talk to someone.

"But the minute he feels better, he starts canceling his appointments and says he doesn't need help anymore," says Carol, whose husband has been in and out of therapy for many months. Like many women who are married or involved with veterans who display this pattern of attendance at counseling sessions, Carol has postponed deciding about whether to stay with her husband or leave him because she hopes that if her husband would only follow through on his counseling program, he might overcome his PTSD and be able to give more to the marriage.

"He's always so much better after he sees his counselor," says Carol. "In fact, for one or two weeks afterward, he's wonderful to me. Then he starts to crash again. When he hits bottom, he goes running back to the Vet Center.

"I keep telling him that he should keep all his appointments and go for counseling even when he feels good. He says he doesn't want to take up some other guy's time. But I think that's just an excuse.

"If I knew that it would always be like this, some good times, followed by more bad times, I'd probably pack my bags tomorrow. But when I see how well he does, even after just a one hour session, I can't help but hope that if he really stuck with the counseling, our marriage would be a good one."

"Tell him you'll leave him if he doesn't stick with the counseling," another Vietnam wife suggests to Carol. Women frequently make this suggestion to one another. Some women, however, are unable to present such ultimatums to their husbands, primarily because they are not prepared to follow through. They are not willing to actually leave should the veteran fail to pursue a counseling or alcohol or drug rehabilitation program.

Some women do insist that the veteran get help—or else lose the wives. The results have been mixed. Some veterans have sought help and benefited greatly.

Most vets can recover. Recovery, however, depends on the degree of exposure to combat: the greater the exposure to death, the greater the therapeutic task before the veteran. In some cases, recovery is limited. The veteran is able to take care of himself and his family. He is able to keep a job and abstain from substance abuse, but he still functions emotionally as if he were in Vietnam, to one degree or another.

His wife is then faced with the dilemma of whether or not to accept this degree of progress as enough. "I hate to leave him now that he's finally standing on his own two feet. He's come so far and had to work so hard to get where he is. But I had hoped for more." Yet this wife is the envy of wives whose husbands have not yet reached this degree of recovery and of wives who are still trying to figure out the veteran's reasons for going into counseling and whether or not there will be any permanent changes as a result of that counseling.

Veronica, for example, wonders if her husband is sincere about dealing with his PTSD or other problems or if he is only pretending to be interested in therapy, or in improving, in order to prevent her from leaving.

I don't know what to think. This is the second time I've insisted he seek help. The first time he went to group for two months, then quit. During that time, he'd cancel appointments a lot—but when I'd remind him that I would leave unless he went back to counseling, he'd keep a couple of appointments, then stop going again.

This time he's not only attending his Vet Center group regularly, but also is going to his A.A. meetings twice a week.

Yet I'm scared. Is he only doing this to get me to stay? And, once he knows that I'm not going to leave him, will he go back to his old ways?

Veronica, like many wives, is in emotional limbo, waiting to see what the outcome of her husband's present involvement in therapeutic programs will be. Other wives have already separated from their veterans but are willing to return upon signs of marked improvement in specific areas. However, like Veronica, they wonder if their veteran is only faking good behavior in order to get them back or not. They very much want to believe that their husband is sincere and that his progress is real and permanent.

Some questions a Vietnam wife might ask in order to assess her husband's progress are as follows:

1. Does he attend sessions or A.A. or N.A. meetings regularly? Regular attendance is a positive sign. However, it is not a guarantee that the veteran is truly working on himself.

2. What is his attitude toward his counseling? Has he been able to establish a trusting relationship with his therapist, counselor, or group leader? If he is in group, has he been able to identify with, and make friends with, some of the other veterans? Or is he almost always negative and contemptuous of the counseling program, the therapist, or the other veterans?

If the veteran is able to maintain an open-minded, trusting attitude toward treatment and is able to emerge from his social and emotional isolation by forming some sort of emotional bond, either with the therapist or with the other veterans in group, this is another positive sign. Recovery from PTSD does not mean forgetting about Vietnam as much as it means being reintegrated into society and being able to emotionally connect and trust others again. For some vets, this process begins in group or individual therapy when the veteran forms ties with the therapist or other group members.

3. Are there any consistent signs of positive change, either in behavior or in attitude, however small?

The important word here is "consistent." Most people can display good behavior for a short time, but the changes need to be long lasting and able to endure the inevitable stresses in life.

As stated in Chapter 11, changes in the veteran due to treatment may not be evident for many months. It is possible for some veterans to attend individual or group therapy, A.A. meetings, or other treatment programs for six to eight months without any dramatic signs of change. Yet there may be small indications that the veteran is coming to understand and accept himself, and to blame others less. There may be less anger displayed at others, increased contemplativeness, as well as increased emotional pain. Certain activities—overworking, compulsive sex, compulsive exercising, gambling—which may have served "escapist" functions may diminish in frequency, although they might not disappear entirely.

In addition, the veteran may seem more discontented and confused about who he is, what he feels, and what he wants out of life after going into treatment. These, however, can be positive, not negative, signs. Increased inner turmoil and self-questioning suggest that the veteran may be beginning to deal with some of the deep issues and long buried feelings underlying his symptoms. In fact, if a person is in treatment and does not show some signs of increased anxiety, emotional pain, or confusion, this may be an indication that he is not taking the therapy seriously or not working hard in therapy. Almost always, personal growth entails some degree of emotional pain and periods of self-questioning and self-doubt.

4. Is he beginning to assume responsibility for his moods, his emotions, and his behavior or is he still blaming others?

The veteran who is showing increased awareness of his PTSD or who is making progress in therapy will have increased recognition of his emotional, physical, or other needs and have less need to blame others. He may say, "Something happened today at work that reminded me about Vietnam. I didn't think it would bother me, but apparently it did. That makes me feel like not being with you and the kids tonight. Usually I would start a fight with you just so I could get to be alone. But maybe this time I can just tell you that I need to be by myself."

Or he may say, "You picked a terrible time to ask me for help. I feel awful, but it's not your fault. I'm just really angry tonight about . . . Maybe I'll feel better in a few hours."

5. If the veteran previously could not talk about Vietnam, is he now able to discuss some aspects of experience, at least in part? Or, if the veteran was previously obsessed with Vietnam, has his preoccupation with Vietnam lessened somewhat?

A "yes" to any of these questions indicates some movement toward resolving Vietnam issues. One wife, for example, was certain that her husband was making progress when he was able to see cooked rice without becoming upset. Rice was a forbidden food in their home due to its association with Vietnam. Talk about Vietnam was also forbidden.

"How long do I wait and how many signs of change do I have to see before I can be sure that he is really going to improve and stay improved?" women often ask. Once again, there are no pat answers to such questions. In all cases, these questions must be addressed on an individual basis, taking into account the full complexity of the veteran's personality and the entire family system.

In some cases, veterans have shown remarkable improvement over a short period of time. They have given up alcohol or drugs, or battering, or some other problem behavior almost entirely after just a few weeks of help. Upon seeing such changes, some women are tempted to give up their skepticism about the future of their marriage, or, if they have already left, they may be tempted to return.

Mary's husband, Les, suffered from both PTSD and alcoholism.

With the aid of her in-laws, but at considerable financial expense to herself, Mary shoved her husband into a private alcohol rehabilitation program. He left treatment with the best of intentions, but resumed drinking almost immediately.

"The next time he hits bottom, I'm not going to be around," Mary vowed to the group. That night she gave Les her final ultimatum: Get help or get out!

Les admitted himself to the alcohol ward at the local Department of Veterans Affairs Medical Center and promised to attend group therapy at the local Vet Center after completing alcohol treatment. After discharge, he wanted to come back home. Just to prove he was sincere, he attended follow-up sessions at the hospital and A.A. meetings faithfully. He even got a sponsor and brought gifts when he visited. When he thanked Mary for all she had sacrificed for him and showered love and attention on their nine-year-old daughter, Mary's heart melted—almost.

Mary could see the happiness in her daughter's eyes when her Daddy was around. Yet Mary did not want to open her heart to Les, only to have it broken again. More importantly, she did not want to give their daughter, Merle, any false hopes. At 10, Merle was well over 140 pounds. According to the child's therapist, Merle was using excess food to cope with her feelings, especially her anger and her grief. She was angry with both parents for arguing, but she was especially angry at her father for his inconsistencies and failures to keep his word with her. Time after time she had waited for him to show up as he had promised and time after time he didn't come. Despite all her disappointments, she missed him and ate to hide her feelings of abandonment.

Even though Les had disappointed the family many times, this time it appeared he was truly turning over a new leaf. He had stayed sober for over six weeks. When Merle pleaded with her mother to let Les return, Mary couldn't say no.

The family then went on a wonderful vacation. Mary felt as if she were on her second honeymoon and Merle lost 10 pounds. Within months, however, Les stopped attending A.A. meetings. In addition, he failed to pursue PTSD therapy as he had promised. Apparently when he gave up drinking, his PTSD symptoms began to manifest themselves more forcefully and he turned again to alcohol for relief.

As before, Les began to stay away from home and make promises to his daughter that he didn't keep. Merle's weight skyrocketed.

Mary grieved for her own disappointment, but she grieved even more for her daughter. "How can you explain this to a child? Now she's not only lost faith in her father, but in me for telling her that her daddy was 'okay' or almost okay."

Not only for herself, but for her children, a waiting period has always proved important for the Vietnam wife to make sure the vet has really changed. A "pink cloud" phenomenon often accompanies the start of treatment. Individuals often show drastic initial improvements and excitedly announce that their problems are finally over. Yet for this initial alleviation of symptoms and rush of good feelings to become permanent usually requires some close self-examination and emotional work.

It is at this point—the point of confrontation of previously hidden feelings and conflicts—that many people quit treatment despite the initial positive results and their initial surge of enthusiasm. Therefore, it is prudent for a woman to assume the role of observer when her husband first enters treatment and to see if he is willing to do the hard work which self-knowledge and personal growth entails.

The decision-making process is even more complex and more difficult for two special groups of Vietnam wives: those who are obese and those who were sexually or physically abused as children. Often the obese wife feels trapped in her marriage by her weight, saying, "As fat as I am, what other man would want me?"

While the obese Vietnam wife feels ugly on the outside, the wife who was sexually or physically abused by a parent or caretaker as a child may feel ugly on the inside, especially if she has yet to deal with her childhood experiences. The low self-esteem which usually results from having been abused, combined with other factors associated with the abuse, often serve to keep the formerly abused Vietnam wife in her marriage.

"How can I leave Ralph? His love was the first love I ever knew," explains Phyllis, who was physically battered by both parents and sexually molested not only by her father, but by her brother too. Thrown out of her home at 18, she met Ralph, who was on his way to Vietnam. When he returned, they married. At the time, Ralph's PTSD was dormant. He was supportive of Phyllis, not only financially, but emotionally.

Later, when his PTSD began to manifest itself, when Phyllis was ill, sometimes Ralph would ignore her. But many times he was helpful and protective, fulfilling Phyllis's deep wish to finally have someone take care of her.

As a child she had had no parent to lean on and very little nurturing; in fact her parents leaned on her. While it is difficult to make a general statement about such a diverse group as abusive parents, usually they have been found to be emotionally immature and unreliable in meeting their family responsibilities. They are also often impulsive, have a low frustration level tolerance and act out their frustrations and needs through verbal and physical abuse or sexual molestation of their children. They have also been found to be overdemanding, highly critical, and often extremely punishing of the child who does not fulfill their expectations.[11]

The child is forced to meet the parent's needs, not the other way around. In essence, the child becomes the abusive parent's caretaker as well as the parent's victim.[12] In cases of incest, for example, the daughter is sometimes expected to fulfill the father's emotional and sexual needs.[13]

As a result, the Vietnam wife who, like Phyllis, comes from an abusive past may find her husband's mood swings, his impulsive or unpredictable behavior, his low frustration level tolerance, and his periods of irresponsibility familiar. Due to her background, she is used to living with an adult who can be emotionally immature, overly demanding, excessively critical, abusive, and at the same time, emotionally dependent on her. She has also had many years of practice at being a caretaker.

Therefore, she may be more tolerant of her husband's verbal or physical assaults and his excessive emotional and financial dependence on her. She is also more liable to accept the social isolation and other restrictions her husband may place on her. The Vietnam wife may stay in the marriage because, compared to other Vietnam wives, she may be more tolerant of her husband's ambivalence toward her. A common complaint of Vietnam wives is that they receive double messages from their husbands. "I need you . . . stay away." While some women get furious at receiving both rejection and affection from the same man, the Vietnam wife who was abused as a child may be more accepting of this behavior. In her past, she may have lived with such double messages and the experience of receiving both pain and love from the same person on a daily basis.

On the other hand, if the Vietnam wife is sufficiently aware of what went on in her childhood, she may be infuriated at having to once again live with double messages and be considerably less tolerant of her husband's mixed messages than other wives. In addition, when she is angry at her husband, she may be experiencing double anger: first, anger toward her husband and second, anger toward the parent who gave her double messages in the past. At times she may be confused about with whom she feels most angry. Phyllis explains, "Sometimes when I think about leaving my husband, I wonder if I really want to leave him or whether I am really trying to leave my father. It's not fair to put the anger I have toward my parents onto my husband but sometimes that's what I do." Because of her past, it is often difficult for Phyllis and wives like her to form an objective picture of her husband and his PTSD and to view him as separate from other persons in her life.

Mental health professionals who work with Vietnam wives need to inquire about any history of childhood abuse and help the Vietnam wife who is a child abuse or incest survivor identify how her past experiences are influencing her marriage and her decision to stay with, or leave, her veteran. If the Vietnam wife has yet to deal with being victimized as a child, therapy that is oriented toward helping her understand and resolve her traumatization by a qualified mental health professional is recommended.

Theoretically, mental health professionals are supposed to be entirely objective, encouraging a couple neither to stay together nor to split apart. Yet, in reality, sometimes the counselor's personal beliefs about marriage and the family may emerge. Responsible therapists need to be aware of their values and attempt not to force their beliefs on their clients.

Vietnam wives in the process of deciding whether to stay or go should not allow themselves to be unduly influenced by the therapist's biases or by the therapist's own marital status. The therapist may be married, divorced, or single. But the marital status which is right for the therapist may not be right for the Vietnam wife. Furthermore, if the Vietnam wife senses that the therapist is trying to push her either into staying with the veteran or into leaving him, she should ask the therapist to adopt a more neutral attitude.

Some wives report being told by therapists to "leave immediately" or to "go home and give more." Candice Williams, in *Post-Traumatic Stress Disorders: A Handbook for Clinicians,* cites an instance of a "woman who was crying out for help . . . a well-meaning counselor told her she should be more patient and show greater compassion and understanding for her veteran husband. However, this woman was on the verge of collapse. She had given and given and had nothing left. Yet she was supposed to give more. The woman had no way out; there was no recognition that she had her own problems. Following intervention through the women's group, she was able to see herself as important. Rather than focusing on her failure to keep her husband, she was better able to take care of herself. As a result, she was better able to give support of a positive nature."[14]

Almost every Vietnam wife has many options other than staying with her veteran. If she does not recognize her options, she may feel trapped. This feeling of entrapment is dangerous. It can lead not only to extreme emotional numbing, depression, or a general sense of paralysis and desperation about life, but to suicidal thoughts or suicide attempts, or to eating disorders, substance abuse, phobias, and a host of other problems.

It is important for every Vietnam wife, even if she wants to stay with her veteran, to recognize her options. Even women who are firmly committed to their marriages need to affirm that they are with their veteran by choice and that, should the relationship substantially deteriorate or become unendurable for other reasons, they have a way out other than suicide or numbing.

"I would never leave my husband," one wife says, "But it's good to know that I could, if I wanted to. This makes me take responsibility for myself in the marriage. Until now I've been using numbing as my way of coping. But I also realize that numbing is a way of punishing him too. The only problem is that my numbing affects my children, and where does it stop? Already I've been turning down invitations and avoiding my friends. Maybe someday I'll be almost totally isolated if this keeps up.

"Now that I realize that I'm not bound to my husband, like a serf to a lord, I have to take some action on myself."

Often I ask women to write a list of all their fears; both their emotional fears and their financial fears about both staying with the veteran and about leaving him. While a paper and pencil exercise may seem like a superficial means of dealing with such a profound issue as the fate of one's love relationship, often listing emotions and fears on paper can be helpful. At the very least, it can be a starting point to clearer thinking, the beginning of examining options other than accepting things the way they are.

With her list in hand, the Vietnam wife can match her fears with reality. For example, if she carefully assesses her finances and writes out a budget, she may realize that she can make it on her own, without the veteran's financial support. Of course, this may mean forsaking certain luxuries. For some women, financial discomfort may be a small price to pay for freedom from excessive criticism, physical abuse, or other forms of bondage.

Some women are willing to accept the reduced standard of living that might accompany a separation or divorce for themselves, but they are reluctant to deprive their children of the material advantages to which they are accustomed. Yet children will not crumble without certain luxuries, and it may be more important for mother to make the break and begin to take control of her life than for the children to have a new T.V. set or an annual vacation.

Nevertheless, as previously mentioned, there are some women who, for a variety of reasons, are, or feel, literally trapped into their marriages by financial pressures, threats of violence, or other constraints. Yet even in some of these cases, the constraints are temporary. With sufficient brainstorming and research, and with the help of others, the woman may be able to see a way out. Even if she cannot separate for a year or two years, or longer, she can make long-range plans to leave, if, and only if, this is her choice.

The Vietnam wife may also be surprised to discover that she has more financial options than she previously realized. Perhaps there is a family member or friend who can lend her the money she needs to start a new life. Perhaps she can even overcome her pride and ask for help, realizing that even if she has been alienated from certain friends or family members, these persons may still care about her and would be glad to be of assistance.

In addition, some women are shortsighted, looking at only their immediate assets or their immediate salaries. They tend to forget that in the years or even the months to come, they may be promoted or able to find better jobs. Furthermore, there is always the possibility of resuming one's education or job training and of searching out scholarships and loans to do so. All these possibilities entail hard work, of course, as well as the risks of trying something new. This can be extremely frightening to women, especially if their self-confidence has been eroded in their marriage. Women's centers and returning women's programs at local universities or colleges can help women, not only with vocational and educational planning, but by providing support services for women who are suffering a crisis of confidence.

Many women feel that the only options they have are either staying with the veteran and accepting things the way they are or leaving him entirely. In reality, however, a woman has several other choices. The Vietnam wife can negotiate for a trial separation, or she can make her staying contingent on the veteran seeking help for PTSD or any substance abuse problem. She can also require that the veteran not only attend therapy but that he show noticeable improvement in some areas or be drug or alcohol free for a certain length of time before she commits the rest of her life to him. In cases where the veteran has been physically abusive, the woman can make the continuation of the relationship contingent on the vet seeking help for his battering and on an end to violence in the home.

If the Vietnam wife is making the relationship contingent on certain changes on the part of the veteran, she needs to clarify for herself as specifically as possible what changes she is requiring. For example, she needs to ask herself, "What behaviors will I tolerate and which ones are totally unacceptable to me?"

Some wives want their husband to stop drinking entirely. Others, however, would be content if the drinking binges were reduced to twice a month, rather than being weekly occurrences. Still others have indicated a willingness to stay with the veteran if he would only switch from hard liquor to beer or from hard drugs to marijuana. Other wives will tolerate no form of alcohol, but can tolerate marijuana smoking, providing the veteran does not smoke himself into a semi-coma.

A major area of confusion is the issue of "slips." While some men manage to maintain almost perfect abstinence from alcohol or drugs after joining a substance abuse program, it is not uncommon even for the best intentioned man to slip back on occasion. However, these slips do not necessarily mean that the veteran is in total irreversible relapse or that he is not in recovery.

Only the Vietnam wife can decide how many slips she will tolerate. However, for a greater understanding of her husband's slips, she may want to discuss his behavior with his therapist or a qualified counselor. There are several questions she needs to consider.

Does her husband admit to the slips or does he try to hide them? After a slip, does he attempt to resume his efforts to get help? Over time, are the slips shorter in duration and do they involve less and less of the particular substance being abused? Or do the slips get longer every time, involving larger and larger quantities of alcohol or drugs?

Other desired changes may pertain to household and child care responsibilities. The Vietnam wife who wants her veteran to be more active in these areas needs to spell out her expectations as specifically and concretely as possible. For example, does she want her husband to take over certain chores entirely? Is she expecting him to take care of the children a certain number of hours a week so she can have some time for herself?

Perhaps she is seeking a change in attitude instead. Many wives have stated that they don't care if their husband never scrubs a toilet bowl or takes the children out on the weekend. What they want is for him to be less irritable around the children and to show some interest in their activities and homework.

Other wives would be content with even less. Some women feel that their marriages would be tolerable if only the veteran could bring in a reliable income, however small, if he could stop "trashing" the house or if, in other ways, he could "turn off his volcano."

The woman who is trying to decide whether she should stay or go can also set a time limit for herself. The deadline needs to be flexible, however. For example, a woman may decide to make up her mind after a year's trial separation. However, if after the year is past, the woman is still not certain, she has every right to extend her deadline. In fact, the deadline can be extended as often as is necessary for the woman to gather the information she needs about her veteran and for her to sort our her feelings about him.

Many women pressure themselves to make up their minds quickly, often chastising themselves for being "wishy washy," that is, wanting to leave their husband one day and being madly in love with or forgiving toward him the next. A standard joke in the group is "I was going to leave him on Saturday, but . . ."

The "but" usually begins a description of how, upon learning of his wife's intention to leave, the veteran became his most romantic, sexual, giving, and loving self and how, in displaying his strengths and many good qualities, convinced his wife to stay. It is the veteran who puts the woman on such an emotional yo-yo, yet it is the woman who berates herself for not being able to make up her mind and for having such strong conflicting feelings toward the same man.

Women who are ambivalent need to give themselves credit for taking the time and emotional energy to consider the future of their relationship seriously and for not acting impulsively. The Vietnam wife needs to appreciate that her decision is a very complex one, involving consideration of many factors. She may need many months, or even years, to come to a decision which is right for her. She needs to give herself permission to take as much time as she needs to decide.

There is no shame in waiting to be relatively sure that all the tender feelings are gone, or in waiting to be relatively certain that the veteran will never change. On the other hand, once the love affair is over, or, the veteran's behavior becomes totally unacceptable, there is no shame in her making a definite and quick decision to leave or to make him leave.

For example, Marcia's husband had been through both outpatient PTSD therapy and an inpatient alcohol treatment program. For many months afterward, he was not only sober but free from nightmares. After he began working, however, he began smoking marijuana, arguing to Marcia that compared to alcohol, the drug was relatively harmless. The marijuana led to some light drinking, which turned into heavy drinking.

When Marcia filed for divorce, her husband begged for another chance. He was on a waiting list to be admitted to a Department of Veterans Affairs Medical Center inpatient PTSD program. Couldn't Marcia wait until he had completed this program before she made her final decision?

"He's already eaten up three years of my life," Marcia told the group. "I'm afraid that if I don't get out now, I'll never get out. Maybe I'm wrong. Maybe this time he's really going to get better. But I just can't take the chance."

In making her decision, the Vietnam wife needs to be assured that there are seldom any right or wrong answers. Neither is there any way she can predict the future. A veteran may show all the signs of making significant changes and then, a few years later, revert to his old self-destructive patterns. On the other hand, some veterans have shunned treatment and all forms of help, only to conquer many of their symptoms on their own and to become extremely dedicated, supportive husbands.

In a few cases, veterans have pressured their wives to move to another city or town, or to a rural area, thinking that a geographical change, or a more isolated environment, would effect a personality change or help them give up alcohol or drugs. Generally, geographical cures do not work. However, in a few cases, they did. The veteran not only gave up his addiction, but also made significant progress in other areas of life.

Both the path of staying and the path of leaving are fraught not only with risks, but with pain. For the wife who decides to stay with her veteran, even if he does not meet her needs, there is pain in realizing that she is settling for much less than what she hoped for in a love relationship. Her pain is increased when she compares herself with women who have dissolved unfulfilling relationships, women whom she tends to perceive as stronger, braver, and having more self-respect than herself. On the other hand, the wife who decides to leave may deluge herself with the "what ifs." "What if I had waited just a little longer?" "What if it was just his job pressures, his mother's death, not his personality, that caused the problems?"

Furthermore, many women, even women who are almost totally alienated from their veteran at the time of separation, may experience a sense of loss when they finally end the relationship. Along with the relief of being "finally free," there may also be mourning for the positive aspects of the relationship and, at the very least, for the broken dreams and hopes. Furthermore, if there are children involved, the woman may become aware of her children's pain at the marital breakup and their grief at being separated from the father.

A common fear of Vietnam wives is that divorce is mentally unhealthy for children. Undoubtedly children suffer anger, grief, and pain when a divorce occurs. However, this does not mean that children will suffer irrevocable emotional scars. Children are often resilient and may ultimately find it easier to cope with the breakup of the family than to live in a household full of tension and unhappiness or with a depressed mother. In addition, a marital breakup does not mean that the children will not continue to have a relationship with their father. Especially in this age of joint custody, there are many flexible custody arrangements available to divorcing couples; children of divorce are no longer the oddity they were some 10 to 20 years ago.

On the other hand, the stress of a divorce on children should not be minimized. Some may need outside professional help during the transition period.

In a few cases, Vietnam wives have sought a separation or divorce, not because the veteran failed to seek help with his PTSD or because he was reluctant to make certain changes, but because they realized that even if the veteran totally recovered from his war experiences and met all their requirements, they no longer loved him. "He did beautifully in his PTSD group and he's making every effort to do what I want him to do, but—and I don't know why—the love is gone." Some of these women realize that they married the veteran for the wrong reasons. Perhaps they married young, due to social or family pressures to be married before a certain age. Other wives have simply discovered that their needs at age 40 or 45 are quite different from their needs at 19, 20, or 24 when they first married.

Whether a Vietnam wife decides to stay with her husband or to leave him, it is important that she attempt to consciously focus on her own needs and her personal goals for her life. Simply leaving the veteran will not guarantee that she will grow in the future. In her next relationship, she may continue to defer to her partner and neglect herself. The Vietnam wife who decides to stay with her veteran, or who feels trapped in her marriage for one reason or the other, needs to seek as many ways of taking care of herself within the constraints of her marriage as possible.

She can attempt to put into her life as much emotional support and self-expression as possible. While she may not be able to change the veteran or to change her marital status, she may be able to pursue activities or friendships which bring her at least some measure of joy and fulfillment. Or she may begin to work on some of her own problem areas. For example, several women who struggle with obesity, bulimia, or anorexia nervosa have decided to stay married. Yet they have committed themselves to obtaining help for their eating disorders by consulting a nutritionist, by participating in eating disorders counseling, or by beginning an exercise program.

A number of wives have felt that much of their discontent with their marriage was their fault in that they were overextending themselves as the veteran's caretaker. They hoped that the marriage could be saved if they began to allocate more of their energies for themselves and if the veteran could tolerate their personal growth. Some wives began to refuse to make appointments for the veteran, stopped paying his debts, or running his errands, and set limits on the amount of "therapy" and comforting they would give him when he was depressed about Vietnam or other issues. The ways in which these women focused on themselves were manifold. Some took up swimming or other sports. Others resumed certain hobbies or went back to school. Some simply hired babysitters so they could have time to themselves. In cases where the veteran was excessively threatened or otherwise could not tolerate the woman's self-development, or where the woman outgrew the veteran emotionally or intellectually, the marriages sometimes dissolved.

While some women leave their marriages with sufficient alimony, property, or child support so that they do not have to struggle financially and have children who adjust beautifully and instantly to the changes in the family, this has not been the reality for any of the Vietnam wives I have seen. For most of the women, separation or divorce has necessitated a host of adjustments: financial, emotional, social, and sexual.

Even though the Vietnam wife may have been an outside wage earner and felt like a single parent while married, the veteran usually provided some financial help, as well as some help with such things as the children, the housework, the car, and the finances. There is now a qualitative difference in her feeling of being responsible for everything. She now knows, in a new way, that the entire burden of the home, the family's finances, and the children's needs are on her, and on her alone. Unless, of course, the veteran continues to provide help or one of the children is an adult who can offer a substantial financial or emotional contribution.

In most cases, however, the separated or divorced Vietnam wife has even more multiple roles to contend with than she did before. While she is now released from the time-consuming, energy-absorbing role of wife, she may not have that much more time for herself because she now may have to work harder to meet her bills. She may find herself having to work full-time instead of part-time, or taking on a part-time job in addition to a full-time job. Or, if she was a homemaker prior to the separation or divorce, she may find herself thrust into the world of work, which in itself requires numerous adjustments. Furthermore, she may be competing in the labor force with single persons and with men who generally have more time and energy to devote to their careers. In addition, if she is a mother, the separated or divorced Vietnam wife also has to deal with her children's reaction to the family breakup. The reaction of a child is a highly individual matter, depending not only on the age of the child, but on his or her relationship to each parent, and the availability of emotional supports. While children may adjust eventually, they do not necessarily do so immediately. Almost always there is anger at one parent, or perhaps at both, as well as fear of abandonment and the discomfort of having to adjust to a lower standard of living. Some children may withdraw, become aggressive, develop psychosomatic problems, or become depressed.

It is not uncommon, for example, for previously quiet children to suddenly erupt with emotion several months after the family breakup. If the veteran and his wife engaged in emotional numbing as a defense during their marriage, one or more of their children may have learned to do likewise. Or perhaps the child learned to be quiet during any parental arguments, feeling that being quiet and repressing his or her own emotions was the safest thing to do. After the separation or divorce, however, children may feel more free to express their feelings.

Children need to be encouraged to talk. Supportive counseling, or at least access to a caring friend, family member, or minister, may be needed. Children often need assurance that their feelings of pain, anger, fear, and confusion are normal to children in the midst of a family breakup or that they are simply undergoing the grieving process for the family life that was and for the idealized family life that never will be.

For example, at first Jo-Allison's daughter hated her mother for "making Daddy leave" and said so frequently. Jo-Allison's son, however, said nothing. But at age 10, he began to wet the bed. Meanwhile Jo-Allison was trying to learn how to fix cars and broken water heaters in order to save on repair bills and was adjusting in other ways to the massive strains of being a single parent. She was also coping with her own sense of bereavement at losing her primary role in society, that of wife. It was hard for her to deal with her children's anger, grief, and their many emotional needs, which were intensified by the divorce, while at the same time coping with her own emotional pain.

Understandably, she felt overwhelmed. Yet she often berated herself for not being able to handle everything at once, even though she was doing the work of at least two people.

It's hard, it's just too hard. It was hard living with Albert and his moods —with a man who, although he had a good heart, was simply not there for me emotionally, financially, sexually, or spiritually. But divorce is no picnic either.

It's painful to be all alone, to have only myself to lean on, and not to have a buffer between me and the world. I never realized how vulnerable a woman could feel without a man beside her.

But still, I'm not sorry I left. Albert never abused me, but our marriage was going nowhere and I was going downhill fast. I was just too lonely in that marriage.

But it's lonely outside of marriage too. Whenever I see couples walk by hand in hand, it hurts, it hurts bad.

And I'm so sensitive now. At work, my feelings get hurt so easily. I even worry about what my friends think of me. Maybe it's because I don't have someone at home who loves me.

Even with his PTSD, Albert, in his own way, loved me. He really did, even though he couldn't show it very often. Sure my kids and my Mom love me, but it's not the same, not like a man loving you.

What if I get sick or hurt in a car accident? Who will take care of me?

Albert could never take my being ill. When I had my miscarriage, I had to drive myself to the hospital. But at least he was there, somewhere, and I knew he'd come around to help me eventually.

Now there's no one to help me with anything. It's all on me—the house, the kids, the car, the bills, and the stupid water heater too. I know I used to manage almost everything when I was married, so it really isn't that different. But it sure feels different. At least Albert was around, sometimes. And he did help, a little, and even that little bit helped.

I get very anxious sometimes, and afraid, even when there's nothing to be anxious or afraid about. Maybe it's just this sense that now I'm all alone in the world and that I, and only I, am responsible for the future of my life and for my own happiness. Before there was always Albert to blame for my misery, and to take up my time. But now he's gone.

Jo-Allison wishes that she had more self-assurance and self-confidence and frequently says she hates herself for not being "stronger" or "more definite." Not only does she fail to give herself credit for all the strengths she does have, but she fails to appreciate that the process of reformulating a personal identity and life goals after a divorce is difficult, painful, and frightening for both men and women, but especially for women who have spent years taking care of their husbands and children and not themselves.

While Jo-Allison's loneliness is real, it is also an expression of many of her unresolved feelings toward Albert, specifically her anger, if not rage, at his frequent rejections of her. Her loneliness lessened somewhat after she commenced the grieving process, which entailed the five stages of grief: denial, anger, bargaining, depression, and acceptance or forgiveness. Her feelings did not progress in cookbook fashion from one step to the other. Sometimes, she went back and forth between stages and sometimes she was at several stages simultaneously. Beginning to resolve the grieving, however, helped free her to go on to meet new men and to engage in new activities. Yet her mourning continued over several years, as old memories about her marriage were released from repression into conscious awareness.

In addition to dealing with her own grieving process and her children's reactions to the divorce, Jo-Allison had to contend with the reactions of her ex-husband's family. Her ex-mother-in-law, for example, frequently chastises Jo-Allison for "deserting" her deserving son.

"My mother-in-law and I used to be so close, but now she calls me names in front of my own children," Jo-Allison says. "Yet, I don't forbid my children to see her, because I know they need all the emotional support and sense of family they can get."

Despite the problems with her ex-mother-in-law, Jo-Allison considers herself fortunate in that she has considerable emotional and even some financial support from her own parents. Hence she tends to feel less alone and vulnerable than women whose parents are dead, rejecting, or otherwise unavailable. However, the increased contact with her mother and other members of her family after the divorce did bring to the surface some of Jo-Allison's unresolved issues with her family. "Here I was, dealing with all my feelings about separating from my husband, while at the same time having to deal with all the feelings my Mom and Dad had. I truly thought I was going nuts," Jo-Allison explains.

Another problem was that one of Jo-Allison's cousins felt she was a "sinner" for "breaking up a happy home." "It was never a happy home," Jo-Allison tried to explain, but her cousin was not interested in listening. Like Jo-Allison, many separated and divorced Vietnam wives are surprised and hurt to discover that they become the object of criticism and speculation by women in their families or in their circle of friends. These women do not approve of divorce, or secretly desire to divorce their own husbands but are too afraid to do so. Special problems arise when the Vietnam wife's mother or father is against divorce or when they remind her, "I told you so." In addition, the divorced or separated Vietnam wife may be perceived as a sexual threat by both single and married women. As a result, she may feel alienated from, and actually be excluded from, certain natural sources of support.

In general, separation and divorce tend to be easiest, both financially and emotionally, for women who are childless. The Vietnam wife who has no children can make a relatively clean break from her veteran. Not only does she never have to see him again unless she chooses to, but she is free to relocate, to move back to her hometown, or near her relatives. The Vietnam wife who is a mother, however, may be constrained by court injunction or by the needs of her children to see their father to remain in a certain geographical area.

In addition, she may find herself embroiled in a prolonged, expensive, and, perhaps, humiliating custody battle where she is accused of being a poor mother or of having been an inadequate wife. There may be social service and other investigations by mental health professionals who are less than sympathetic, who know little or nothing about PTSD, or who have a "blame-the-mother" perspective. Furthermore, considerable mudslinging can occur during court proceedings, which only compounds the Vietnam wife's loss of self-esteem at being divorced and which only exacerbates any bitterness she may harbor toward her veteran.

One wife explains, "After all those years I cared for my husband, nursed his war injuries, put up with his moods and his relatives, had sex with him when I didn't want to, then he tears me down in court and accuses me of things I never did.

"The lies, the accusations—they cut me in half. Is this my thanks? Being degraded in a courtroom in front of strangers by the man to whom I gave so much of my life!"

Wives who have to undergo prolonged and degrading court proceedings sometimes develop panic attacks, rage reactions, or certain phobic reactions, like the dry heaves or vomiting. They are understandably intimidated by the court proceedings and consequently are easily tempted to give in to the opposition and surrender certain rights rather than have to endure any more legal, financial, and emotional pressures. It is highly recommended that the Vietnam wife who finds herself in the midst of difficult court proceedings give herself permission to lean on others and to borrow their courage and strength. If possible, she needs to try to stand firm in requesting the child support and other financial help to which she and her children are entitled and in requesting the type of visitation schedule or custody arrangements which she feels are in the best interest of her children.

In general, only a handful of Vietnam veterans have been vindictive or have dragged their former wives and children through prolonged court procedures. Some vets have settled quietly and generously. Others have left town and made few, or only intermittent, attempts to see their children. In such cases, the child usually feels abandoned and goes into mourning for the lost parent. The child may even idealize the lost parent and may, like Jo-Allison's daughter, become angry at the mother for leaving the father. It has often been difficult for Vietnam wives who have their own feelings of being abandoned by the veteran to become the object of their child's anger, while at the same time trying to help their child with his or her grieving process.

While many women have been successful in obtaining child support in legal proceedings, very few have received any alimony. Furthermore, there are sometimes problems receiving the child support on schedule or in the full amount. In some cases, the ex-husband desires special favors in return for his prompt and full payment—meals, a place to stay, affection, extra visitation, even sex. Some Vietnam wives have had to expend considerable energy setting limits on their former husbands and defending themselves against the veteran's attempts to get them to act, once again, like wives or caretakers.

The Vietnam wife who is a mother may never be totally free of the veteran and may need continued support in handling the many times she must come into contact with him or otherwise have to deal with him. There may be problems when he picks up the children for visitation. He may engage in verbal or physical abuse, or perhaps attempt to manipulate her.

However, even if the veteran is a saint when he comes for the children, his sheer physical presence can arouse in the woman all the old feelings, both the love and the anger, and put her in a state of excruciating pain. Many women feel that once they are separated or divorced they will no longer have any tender feelings toward their former spouse. This is not the case. It is perfectly normal for a woman to still have feelings of love for her former husband, even if she feels she can no longer live with him or even if she is enraged at him. One cannot love a man for years and then suddenly and completely kill all the loving feelings one had for him.

Lest the above description of the transition period seem too negative and grim, it must be emphasized that the transition period does not last forever. The woman, like her children, can slowly make all the necessary adjustments. However, the process can be extremely difficult and taxing.

Nevertheless, out of the pain and the mess, a new woman can be born—one who will eventually be able to enjoy her freedom and autonomy. She can spend her free time and her money as she chooses without having to account to anyone. While there may always be loneliness, the fear of growing old alone, and sexual frustration, there are the opportunities which being alone can bring in terms of friendships, creative pursuits, or other interests.

It is highly recommended that the separated or divorced Vietnam wife who does not have a natural or already established support system avail herself of the services of a therapist or otherwise establish a support system for herself. Even though she may feel she does not have the time for friendships or a support group, she needs to be kind to herself and not try to handle all the adjustments alone, without some form of support.

There are books that contain many positive suggestions for coping with separation and loss, and with living alone. However, while taking some of the positive actions suggested in these books can be helpful, no amount of action or self-will can eliminate the suffering which is part of the mourning process. Neither is the process of letting go ever total or complete, especially if the marriage has been a long one. Some wives dream of their husbands years after the divorce. This does not mean that these women are neurotically clinging to the past, but rather that the effects of having been deeply attached to a man, of having slept with him and sacrificed hundreds of times, can never be 100% eliminated. Just as the Vietnam veteran cannot simply "forget about" Vietnam, the Vietnam wife may not be able to forget about a man she cared deeply about at one time in her life. Neither can a former Vietnam wife forget the trauma she experienced—the abuse, fear, and embarrassment.

Hence, the Vietnam wife must be prepared for recurring and sometimes unexpected times of sadness, anger, and pain regarding the breakup of her marriage. She should not immediately assume that these feelings are signs of getting stuck in the past. They may be legitimate feelings of mourning.

In addition, the Vietnam wife who is embarking on a new life as a woman alone must also be prepared for times of self-doubt, insecurity, fear, and tension. Once again, these are not indications that she is not strong, or overly dependent, or that she has a Wendy, a Cinderella, or some other complex. These moments are inevitable when leaving the security of the old role of wife and forging a new identity in a society that is just beginning to accept single and divorced women as normal and complete human beings.

Summary

For many Vietnam wives, the issue of whether to stay or go is fraught with indecision. Even if the Vietnam wife is unhappy, after having invested so heavily in her marriage, she may be reluctant to give up on her veteran, especially if he has yet to seek help or if he has serious war injuries. The woman's fear of the unknown and of loneliness also play a role, as do any fears surrounding the emotional and financial hardships involved in being on her own.

The Vietnam wife may also wonder if her decision will result in negative psychological effects for her husband and children. If her husband is suicidal or extremely dependent on her, she may worry that he will significantly deteriorate without her. If he has been violent, she may fear that he will be destructive to either her or her children.

Some women want to leave but cannot afford to do so financially. Others are, or feel, trapped by their obesity or some other source of personal inadequacy. Women who were abused as children are often influenced to stay because of patterns learned as children.

The Vietnam wife who is seriously considering the possibility of a separation or divorce should take as long as she needs to make a decision and feel free to change her mind as often as she needs to.

In making her decision, she should try for the most objective picture possible of her husband's condition and its effect on her and their children. She needs to keep in mind that, untreated, PTSD, alcoholism, and drug addiction usually get worse. If she decides to stay with a veteran who refuses help, she should try to build a support system for herself so that her husband's problems do not overwhelm her.

Both staying with the veteran and leaving him can involve risk and pain. Only the Vietnam wife herself can decide which path to choose.

Epilogue

The fighting in Vietnam may be over, but the war still lives, not only in the hearts and minds of Vietnam veterans and their families, but in the consciousness of our nation.

The Wall and many other memorials to Vietnam veterans are now part of our landscape and movies and television programs about the Vietnam war are still being produced.

Today our government is on relatively good terms with Vietnam, its former enemy, and in many areas Vietnamese refugees and immigrants have become naturalized American citizens. Some have become successful businessmen and scholars, while others have joined gangs and become criminals.

How does the Vietnam veteran feel when he views such changes? No surveys have been conducted on the Vietnam veteran's attitude about our nation's foreign policy toward Vietnam or toward Vietnamese immigrants. However, it may be safe to assume that those Vietnam veterans who feel they have failed to receive full compensation for their war injuries or other readjustment difficulties may feel even more embittered and betrayed. Quite possibly, their wives may feel the same way.

Some vets still proudly refuse to seek government help, but others are still waiting for their compensation claims to be processed. In addition, since the war some vets have developed new physical and psychological problems which they feel are war-related. For example, some veterans have had flashbacks which resulted in vehicular accidents and subsequent injuries to their emotional and physical health. Although they will not be compensated for damages due to such accidents, some vets feel they should be compensated because the accidents were, in truth, war-related.

In other instances, problems that were relatively minor upon discharge from the military have become major. For example, Anna's husband, Tony, left Vietnam with a red spot on his chest. Like many vets who served in the field, Tony suffered from rashes during his tour of duty. In his case, as in others, the rashes were quickly treated with available ointments and were not noted on the record. Today, a horrible rash covers Tony's arms and feet. Due to the lack of documentation, however, Tony does not know if he can prove that his rash is war-related.

Tony freely admits that his rash is exacerbated by his PTSD or other stresses. For example, whenever he sees war movies or has problems at home or at work, his rash flares up. Yet he feels that the physical origin of the rash, as well as the origin of his mental stress, lie in his war experiences and that therefore he should be compensated. When he takes time off work to receive medical treatment or to process compensation papers, his wife must work overtime to make ends meet. Both she and Tony become enraged when they read in the papers that Vietnamese officials are toning down the anti-American propaganda and talking about "two hundred years of friendship and only ten years of war."[1]

Today, Tony and Anna's sons, like the sons and daughters of other Vietnam families, are nearly of military age. To what extent will the vet or his wife promote or oppose their son's or daughter's participation in the military? While some Vietnam veterans and Vietnam wives are firm supporters of the military, others are totally against it. Still others feel that their support of the military is dependent on the nature of the military's current involvement. "If our country was invaded or there was another Hitler on the scene, I would gladly send my son to go die for his country," explains one wife. But she would never encourage her boy to go fight for another Vietnam.

Her husband, a much-decorated war hero and an extremely patriotic individual, agrees with her completely. They, like other Americans, are concerned that some of the current conflicts may evolve into "new

Vietnams" and that our country will once again be embroiled in the moral crisis and political and military controversies which fractured our nation during the 1960s.

This book is but a peek into the lives of a limited group of PTSD-afflicted Vietnam veterans and their families. Since PTSD has only been recognized as a significant psychological disorder since 1980, researchers are still in the process of gathering information about how trauma can affect an individual, our knowledge of the full impact of PTSD is limited. Consequently, it is difficult to make any accurate, long-range predictions about how PTSD may affect Vietnam families in the future. In some cases, the problems will simply continue, but in other cases, they will only escalate over time, especially if the vet has medical problems or has PTSD but has not sought assistance.

Yet even vets who have received readjustment counseling may continue to suffer. Tony, for example, still sees the faces of men who died in Vietnam. "I have a Ph.D. in psychology and have been through two years of PTSD therapy, but I still can't get over this thing," he says. Like many vets who have undergone therapy, Tony feels that therapy has helped him to better understand and get a handle on his PTSD, but there are still times when the numbing overcomes him or when he breaks down in tears. As Tony's case illustrates, trauma victims may never make the trauma go away. What they can do, however, is to enlarge their capacity to deal with the trauma.

"I can deal with only so much stress," Tony explains. "Vietnam raped my mind and my heart. If today I'm having trouble coping with my job, which is only a job, how am I going to handle it when something big happens, like somebody in my family dies or one of my children becomes terminally ill?"

To date, we have no data on whether or not PTSD-afflicted Vietnam veterans, like Tony, who experienced trauma and major losses in their late adolescence or early adulthood, will be more, or less, able to cope with the many personal losses that attend midlife and aging. The midlife crisis and the inevitable physical and psychological changes associated with growing older are difficult for most persons to accept. However, they may pose special challenges for both the veteran with PTSD and his wife.

The new wounds may reawaken the old ones. Or, if the vet has never allowed himself to feel, then the indisputable losses of midlife (the departure of children, the loss of a youthful appearance, the loss of certain career and social opportunities) and the even more obvious losses of aging (decreased physical abilities, increased medical problems, the death of friends) may shatter the vet's denial and force him to deal not only with his present life situation, but with his Vietnam memories as well.

Midlife and aging may also be especially difficult for vets who suffer from war injuries. In some cases, growing older may put stress on the war injuries, creating increased physical pain or other medical complications. The vet's physical and mental health will especially suffer if he develops a new medical condition like diabetes, lower back pain, or heart disease.

Even though the Vietnam wife does not have PTSD and war injuries, the midlife and aging years may be especially difficult for her too. It is at midlife that she may fully come to appreciate the heavy dues she has paid for keeping her marriage together. "Where's the reward?" she may ask. In some cases, she may have neglected herself, physically, emotionally, or spiritually, and is now paying the price for her lack of self-care. For example, she may have delayed seeking medical or psychological assistance, putting her husband's and children's needs before her own. She may also have postponed developing her career, her avocations, and certain friendships in order to serve her family.

While she may be proud of having been a faithful and dedicated wife and mother, her self-appreciation may be colored by sadness and grief regarding the opportunities she missed during her younger years due to her husband's PTSD and her family's pressing needs. She may also experience jealousy and anger toward women who appear to have had easier lives.

The Vietnam wife's attempts to accept her life are not helped by the fact that our society holds a double standard of aging—one for men and one for women. While many prejudices and misconceptions surround the aging process for both sexes, as a group women have been found to suffer more depression, anxiety, and role confusion than men when they begin to lose their youthful appearances or in other ways show that they are indeed aging.[2]

Traditionally, physical beauty has been one of the major sources of women's personal power and sense of self-esteem. In contrast, men have derived their sense of power and self-worth more from job and career achievements. Hence aging is more of a stigma for women than for men and can result in self-rejection, an identity crisis, or a flare-up of any pre-existing psychological problems. If, in addition, the Vietnam wife is obese, her feelings of valuelessness may be enormous, especially if she does not have a strong appreciation of her emotional and spiritual strengths.

For those Vietnam wives who are mothers, the aging process is especially painful because it includes the slow demise and eventual termination of the mother role. As women who grew up in the 1950s, most Vietnam wives were socialized to make their children their chief concern. In fact, some Vietnam wives have spent years functioning as virtual single parents, overextending themselves time and time again for the sake of their children's well-being.

However, as children naturally begin to separate, society expects women to suddenly drop the mother role. The lessening of the mother role, culminating in the "empty nest," represents a difficult transition for most women, but especially for the Vietnam wife who has often made her children the focus of her life.

As both the Vietnam wife and her husband approach the end of their lives, they will need more than ever to feel that their lives had meaning and purpose. In order to avoid stagnation and despair about their mortality, they will need to find sources of strength from within themselves and new directions in life and to extend themselves to others. This will be difficult, however, if the veteran is still emotionally stuck in Vietnam and his wife is emotionally trapped in an extreme caretaker role or, alternatively, in a multitude of unresolved resentments toward her husband.

Another danger is that, over time, the vet and his wife may to one degree or another succumb to the "learned helplessness syndrome," or the tendency of human beings to generalize defeat in one area of life to other areas of their life. For example, if the vet feels defeated in overcoming his PTSD or like a failure because he has not achieved vocationally or financially to the extent of his peers who did not go to Vietnam, his sense of failure regarding his work role may spill over into his evaluation of himself as a father, husband, or son.

Similarly, the Vietnam wife may allow her feelings about her wife role to generalize to her other roles. For example, it is not uncommon for the Vietnam wife to feel deficient as a wife. Even though she may be an excellent wife by many people's standards, because she is not receiving validation, encouragement, or sexual or emotional fulfillment from her husband, she may conclude that she has failed in her role as wife. She may allow this negative self-evaluation of her role as wife to spill over into her view of herself as a worker, mother, or other roles at which she may be obviously quite competent and successful. Her sense of failure will only be exacerbated if her children, to one degree or another, have made her the scapegoat for the family's problems or have imitated their father's patterns of emotional withdrawal or noncommunicativeness.

Not only the Vietnam wife but also her husband and children can be helped by realizing that, for most people, life is not a progression from one success to the other, one pleasure to the next. Even though the media often present normal life as being relatively pain-free, the reality is that most humans do suffer various failures, disappointments, and emotional heartaches on this earth. Even in our relatively affluent country, the stress-free existence so frequently portrayed on T.V. is, for many people, a myth.

In reality, veterans and their families may suffer traumatization in the form of criminal assault, medical malpractice, family violence, or natural disaster, such as an earthquake, flood, or fire, at any time in their lives.

A question which is frequently asked is: Are veterans with PTSD more or less able to handle subsequent traumas and the stresses of midlife and aging than people who have never been traumatized or severely stressed?

On the one hand, it has been argued that veterans can handle subsequent trauma better than others precisely because of the endurance and other survivor skills they acquired by being in combat. Also, simply living with PTSD on a daily basis is a testimony to the survivor skills, courage, and fortitude of combat veterans. On the other hand, it has been argued that combat stress impairs people to such a degree that negative events that occur later in life only increase their depressions and decrease their abilities to cope.

To date, fewer than a dozen studies have addressed this question. The results are mixed. For example, mass casualty survivors have been found to be more resilient and less helpless in the face of new disaster than people who have never been traumatized or who have been traumatized only once. Mass casualty survivors have also been found to be more assertive, more self-disciplined, and more able to persist in pursuing their goals in the face of adversity. Such results would argue that multi-trauma survivors are in many ways strengthened by the adversities they have experienced.[3]

On the other hand, new traumas and stresses and the inherent stresses in midlife and aging can bring to the forefront unresolved issues pertaining to the Vietnam experience. Consequently the veteran may find himself coping with two sets of stressors—the ones at hand and the old ones from Vietnam. In the past, the veteran may have not had the time or ability to deal with his Vietnam issues. However, subsequent traumatization, the traumatization of one of his family members, and the stresses of aging may compel him to examine not only the present, but his experiences in Vietnam. Such events can also put him on emotional overload, hence reducing his capacity to handle any current dilemma as he might wish.

"Under ordinary conditions, most previously traumatized individuals can adjust psychologically and socially. . . . However, they do not respond to stress in the same ways as their non-traumatized peers . . ." writes Bessel van der Kolk, a psychiatrist who has studied trauma survivors for many years.[4]

Dr. van der Kolk's research has found that subsequent trauma can throw veterans (as well as other multi-trauma survivors) back into the emotional climate of the original trauma. For example, even though a veteran may know he is not in Vietnam, a trauma or severe stress in later life can make him feel and act as if he is back in the war zone. Almost automatically, his body and his mind zoom into a state of physiological hyperarousal or "emergency alert." This response, while essential in battle or in life-threatening emergencies, makes it difficult for the veteran to think clearly and handle the situation at hand.[5]

The hyperalert state can also trigger the PTSD cycle and increase the veteran's PTSD symptoms. Eventually the hyperalert state shrouds the veteran in much-loathed feelings of helplessness and numbing, which only add to his demoralization.

According to Dr. van der Kolk, when traumatized people are subjected to further trauma and stress, they often react with "social withdrawal or aggression." They may also find themselves increasingly reluctant to attempt new activities, go new places, or meet new people. Because of the unbearably high levels of fear and terror implanted in them by their traumatic experiences in the past, they cling to the familiar, even if the familiar is, to one degree or another, unhealthy for them or restrictive of their growth.[6]

Time does not heal all wounds, and the vet who wants to be whole and have a positive outlook on life must usually fight for his psychological well-being. Those vets who have sought help are fortunate. At least they have been exposed to the tools by which they can achieve some measure of inner peace and cope with the stresses of life. In contrast stand vets who have never sought help. It is believed by many professionals who work with Vietnam veterans that there are thousands of vets who suffer from PTSD who have yet to avail themselves of the services of a therapist or counselor. Since these men have been living with their PTSD without help for so many years, their defenses, their social isolation, and any maladaptive behaviors resulting from the PTSD are by now well-ingrained and, consequently, more resistant to change. If these vets ever seek help, the healing process may be not only longer, but harder for them than for those who sought help when they were younger. If they do not seek help, they may continue a lifestyle which promotes the denial of emotion. In some cases, this will entail alcohol and drug abuse. In other cases, there may be no addictive illness, but the vet may push away his wife and children and ultimately lose his family.

A not unfamiliar story is that of the high-achieving vet with no external signs of stress. Not wanting to be identified as a "vet with problems," he not only shows no signs of emotional distress, but becomes a financial or intellectual success. Perhaps he works 12-14 hours a day and is admired by his colleagues. But he is alienated from his family and, over time, his family emotionally divorces him or develops a lifestyle without him. Or perhaps his wife actually leaves with the children. When the vet eventually kills himself or simply just disappears, Vietnam may never be suspected as having played a role because he never talked about Vietnam or acted as if Vietnam ever troubled him. Even if he does not commit suicide directly, but indirectly, through alcohol or drugs, Vietnam may still never be suspected.

According to some Vet Center counselors, some vets never seek help at Vet Centers or VA Medical Centers, but attempt a form of self-therapy by frequenting Vietnam veteran memorials or engrossing themselves in books and films about Vietnam. Some frequent these memorials at night so nobody can see them. Still other vets are affected unknowingly. Because they function at work or are able to maintain relationships at home, they are unaware of the impact of PTSD on their lives.

When the vet has a severe and untreated case of PTSD, his wife may slowly abandon all hope and retreat into social isolation and depression, just like her husband. Some Vietnam wives tentatively plan to stay with their husbands only until their children graduate from high school or college. At that point, if their marriages have not improved, they may divorce.

During midlife or later, veterans and their wives, like many other people, may evaluate and review their life histories. Some therapists have written, and hoped, that combat veterans and their families can look back at their lives without undue despair and without the emotional states associated with despair, for example, meaninglessness, hopelessness, and depression. These therapists also speak of people in midlife needing to "embrace the past lovingly" rather than "angrily rejecting or denying it."

Yet for people who have borne many irreversible losses, such as many veterans and their wives, despair, disappointment, and negative feelings are daily realities. These people do not wish to have these negative feelings. The individuals I have talked with are angry that they have to suffer despair, depression, bitterness, and grief. Yet such emotions, undesirable and painful as they may be, seem to be part of the emotional heritage of having been deeply scarred by life.

Therefore, in my view, veterans, their wives, and other trauma survivors who still must experience the so-called "undesirable" feelings of anger, sorrow, and depression should not be considered personal or therapeutic failures. Rather, psychological or emotional "success" needs to be defined to include these feelings, as well as whatever progress has been made in growing beyond them.

For example, a combat veteran or his wife should consider themselves "victorious" if they:

1) are able to endure painful demoralizing feelings (such as grief, anger, bitterness, resentment, and hopelessness) without harming themselves or someone else because of these feelings;

2) are able to function at work and at home in spite of episodes of such feelings;

3) are able, at times, to pursue personal or social goals and maintain relationships in spite of these feelings and the losses which gave birth to these feelings;

4) have acquired an empathy for (rather than a disdain of or attitude or superiority toward) others who suffer, as a result of having suffered themselves.

Our youth-oriented society perceives both midlife and aging almost as the beginning of the end. However, according to Erikson's developmental theory, midlife and aging pose a challenge to all people—that of generating meaning in life despite the loss of youthful vigor and innocence, among other losses. Most certainly the process of regeneration is complicated and made more difficult by having been severely stressed in the past, especially if no help was received.

In midlife and later, Vietnam veterans and their wives need to recognize their losses and grieve them, as often and as deeply is necessary. Their challenge is to build an identity and a purpose out of the ashes of lost hopes and restricted abilities and opportunities. Of course, this is much easier said than done, but it is possible and the rewards can be enormous.

If the veteran and his wife are able to feel that they have an identity they can be proud of, regardless of how aware they may be of lost possibilities, then they have succeeded. If they have a role in society which is meaningful to them and others, no matter how small or seemingly insignificant, they are also successes. If in addition, they have relationships with others which matter, no matter how few those relationships are or how fraught with conflict, then they are victorious.

In addition to such victories, the veteran and his wife may also have periods of intense rage, numbing, grief, or hopelessness. Given their difficult lives, such periods are to be expected and do not detract from the accomplishment of staying alive, attempting to be good people, and coping with very trying circumstances without hurting themselves or others. It is hoped that they can see themselves as strong and courageous for having lived through horrendous physical or psychological hells, even if they feel that parts of their psyches or spirits are broken. It is also hoped that they can find more and better ways of soothing their pain and coping with their justifiable anger and legitimate grief, as well as new sources of joy, peace, and love.

And what of the children? At this point, we have more questions than answers. Based on our knowledge of adult children of alcoholics, as well as limited information about some children from PTSD-afflicted families, we can surmise that some children may be plagued by low self-esteem and difficulties with anger and intimacy. "Don't talk, don't feel, don't trust," the message often given in alcoholic homes, has also been found in some Vietnam homes. In addition, a childhood atmosphere of emotional repression in combination with family tensions and stress is usually implicated in the later development of depression or alcoholism, drug addiction, eating disorders, or other means of dealing with conflicting and unacceptable feelings.

Furthermore, the child growing up in a home stressed by PTSD (especially untreated PTSD) may have as a role model for a husband or wife one or both individuals characterized by emotional withdrawal and anger. Later in life, when that child becomes an adolescent or adult and attempts to establish meaningful relationships with others, he or she may have difficulties. If the parents do not demonstrate good communication or have inadequate means of resolving their conflicts, the child may have to learn basic communication or assertiveness skills as an adult. If, in addition, there is physical abuse in the home, the child's problems will only be multiplied.

Another set of problems attend those families where the vet, and perhaps one of his children, suffers from Agent Orange contamination or where such contamination is suspected. Although the vet may attempt to hide his skin tumors or other evidence of the chemical exposure, children cannot always be totally protected from their father's condition. Children in such homes often wonder when, and if, their father is going to die and if they too will die or have physical effects from the chemical. They also wonder if their children too might bear the scars of Agent Orange.

On the other hand, in those instances where the veteran has been able to accept his pain and grow from it, his loving feelings toward his wife and children are usually intensified. In such homes the vet takes pride in his work, but is not a workaholic. His family life is a priority and there is good communication, not only between him and his wife, but between him and his children, not only about the matters of daily living, but about deeper issues also. Children as young as seven or eight can become sensitized to a wide range of human emotions and attuned to the issues of war, poverty, and other political and social controversies. Their development has been helped, not hurt, by realizing that life entails losses and pain and that past events can affect their lives on a daily basis.

Hopefully this book has not promoted any simplistic or stereotypical thinking about Vietnam veterans and their families. As I have repeatedly stressed, each Vietnam veteran, wife, and child is unique. Our knowledge of trauma and its effects on survivors and their families is only beginning to unfold and I view my observations as preliminary and limited in nature. I offer them in hopes of assuring those who are troubled that they are not alone and that help is available.

The next section outlines some suggestions for seeking help.

Coping Techniques for the Vietnam Wife

Coping with Anger and Depression

Your high levels of stress and the many demands on your physical and emotional energies can easily cause you to become overwrought and overextended, leading to anger. Most of the Vietnam wives I have worked with have harbored considerable anger, not only toward their husbands, but toward themselves and their life in general. However, out of concern for their husband's psychological state or for their children's emotional well-being, they have often kept their anger bottled up inside.

Yet repressed anger can cause as many difficulties for you as for your husband. For example, in some cases repressed anger has contributed to the development of an alcohol, drug, or, more commonly, an eating problem, usually compulsive overeating. In other cases, repressed anger has played a role in perpetuating certain physical symptoms, ranging from chronic headaches and backaches to hyperventilation, hypertension, asthma, chest pains, and sugar diabetes.

These medical conditions may be related to psychological factors, such as the repression of anger or high levels of stress and anxiety. In many instances, medical symptoms were relieved when the woman was able to vocalize her anger and then go on to make concrete changes in her life. Within months, blood pressure and sugar levels dropped, chest pains abated, asthma attacks decreased in frequency, and headaches and backaches almost disappeared.

One of the most common results of suppressed anger is depression. There are several theories on depression: that depression is anger turned inward; that depression results from negative self-evaluations; and that depression stems from lack of reinforcement from the environment. Depression can also develop as a result of psychological and biochemical changes resulting from trauma or extreme or chronic stress. There is also evidence that tendencies toward clinical depression can be, in some cases, inherited.

More than one of these theories may apply in your case. Not only may you be stifling your anger at your husband, but at the same time you may be judging yourself as a failure due to the unhappiness in your home. You also bear more stress than the average wife and mother because you must deal with the effects of post-traumatic stress disorder on your husband, your children, and yourself. If in addition, you, like many women, are or were a victim of sexual or physical abuse or emotional mistreatment, the scars born of these experiences also make your life harder.

You may be experiencing your anger at the burdens imposed on you both in the present and the past, as well as anger at the lack of recognition and appreciation in your life, in the form of depression and pain. Some of the classic symptoms of depression are excessive or inappropriate guilt, tearfulness or crying, indecision, insomnia or hypersomnia (sleeping too much), low energy level or fatigue, and feelings of inadequacy, low self-esteem, and hopelessness. Other symptoms are noticeable changes in weight or in eating habits, social withdrawal, loss of interest or enjoyment in pleasurable activities, and an inability to respond with apparent pleasure to praise or rewards.

If you are experiencing some of these symptoms, you may want to seek individual or group counseling. In counseling you can explore the possibility that repressed anger may be contributing to your depression. It is critical that you recognize and deal with your anger directly rather than indirectly and constructively rather than destructively. If you are unaware of your anger, you may find yourself displacing that anger onto yourself. Or you may find yourself lashing out at your children or inappropriately attacking your husband.

Acknowledging anger may be an extremely difficult task for you. In order for you to feel angry, you must get past the idea that you are responsible for your husband's and children's well-being. To be angry implies that you have rights—that you are entitled to a certain amount of respect and consideration from others. But when push comes to shove, you may still put men's rights ahead of women's rights and feel that your husband's happiness is more important than your own.

You may have special difficulty feeling angry if your anger is mixed with guilt over any inappropriate or sarcastic remarks you might have made to your husband. Guilt over having been verbally vicious may inhibit your awareness of your true anger. In general, most of the Vietnam wives I have seen have tended to express anger toward their husbands primarily only under four conditions:

1. When they were certain that they were almost 100% "right" on a certain issue. If they were only 90% "right," they tended to deny the anger.

2. When their partner's behavior was injuring one of the children, either emotionally or physically.

3. When they found themselves displacing the anger they harbored toward their husbands onto their children in the form of extreme irritability, excessive scolding, or even verbal or physical abuse.

4. When they found themselves at an emotional, financial, or physical breaking point.

You need to give yourself permission to appreciate, rather than deny or minimize, the burden which your husband's PTSD or other readjustment difficulties have imposed upon you and your family. You also need to acknowledge the full range of feelings you might have about your husband's problems. In individual or group therapy, or in a 12-step program such as Al-Anon or Nar Anon, you can learn:

1. That it is perfectly possible (and perfectly normal) to feel both anger and compassion toward your husband at the same time;

2. That you are entitled to some happiness despite the enormity of your husband's pain;

3. That you are not responsible for your husband's angry responses, unless, perhaps, you deliberately provoked a fight or made cutting comments.

The concept of "detaching with love," borrowed from Al-Anon, is useful for many Vietnam wives. Detaching from the troubled veteran does not mean that you become coldly indifferent toward him, but rather that you no longer take responsibility for his distress or his recovery. Detachment does not mean that you will not share in his sufferings, for such sharing is essential to marital intimacy. Rather it means that, to the best of your ability, you do not allow the veteran's behavior to control your actions, your mood, or self-esteem. You can, for example, understand and be empathic toward your husband's PTSD, but do your best not to be victimized by it.

While the concept of detachment is easy to grasp philosophically, it is usually difficult to practice on a daily basis. Since most of us do not wear earplugs, blindfolds, or coats of armor at home, it is usually hard for us to be immune to our husbands' mood or behavior. However, the more you can detach from taking responsibility for your husband's problems and the more you can focus on your own emotions and life goals, the more manageable your life can become. Your stress and anger levels will also be reduced.

Individual or group counseling or other supports may be needed, however, to help you identify your personal needs and see your needs as being as important as the needs of your husband and children. You also need to learn how to meet more of your needs yourself, without relying on your husband, who may be emotionally unavailable to you. For some Vietnam wives, this may mean reducing work loads, scheduling recreational activities, returning to school or to long abandoned personal projects.

Pursuing personal objectives, however, usually requires setting limits on giving to others. Most of the Vietnam wives I have seen have had considerable difficulty setting such limits and sticking to them. You need to see that limit setting and pursuing personal objectives is neither selfish nor incompatible with being a responsible, caring wife and mother. If you sacrifice yourself totally for your husband or children, you may end up resentful or extremely depressed and perhaps endanger your physical health as well.

Since many Vietnam wives fear their anger, I emphasize that anger is a normal human emotion. Most people become angry several times a day. Anger is especially inevitable in intimate relationships, particularly when one partner is troubled. Extreme or persistent anger is also a signal that some basic needs are not being met and that change is needed. In that light, anger can be positive. Being angry can tell you that something is wrong and needs to be changed.

All your years of stored up anger need not be dealt with all at once. You can express your anger to your therapist, to other group members, or to your husband or other family members in small, manageable doses.

Acknowledging your anger does not necessarily mean that you have to act on it. All you have to do is feel it. You can decide later what to do about your anger, if anything. Some wives fear that admitting to anger will lead to separation or divorce. In fact, the opposite is true. It is the long-term repression of anger on the part of either you or your husband that more often leads to the end of your marriage or to suicidal thoughts or suicide attempts. If you find yourself thinking about suicide, especially if you are making specific plans to kill yourself, you need to seek professional help immediately.

Couples Communication and Couples Counseling

Most Vietnam wives prefer to select one or two issues to discuss with their husbands at a time, rather than overwhelm him with numerous grievances. This might be a good approach for you to follow too. It is a good idea to wait until the appropriate time and place to approach your husband. For example, it is not generally advisable to approach him when he has been drinking or is exhausted on the anniversary of the death date of a buddy, or after some difficulty at work. Some wives have found it helpful to make appointments with their husbands for such discussions, letting their husbands help choose the time and place. On the other hand, don't keep waiting indefinitely for that "perfect" time, place, or emotional mood. At some point, you may have to actually sit down and discuss things with your husband even if conditions are not exactly right.

If you are worried about how to handle this discussion, you can practice in group or in individual therapy. You can rehearse your statements to your husband while the other women in group or the therapist pretend to be your husband. Then you will be prepared for his possible resistance, his guilt evoking responses, his angry retorts, or his indifference.

When you start this discussion, remember to pay attention to your body language too. You can say "I'm angry" in a firm, calm voice, with your eyes looking right at your partner, not on the floor or the wall. A major problem for some of the women has been that they smile or laugh while discussing their hurts or angers, undercutting the seriousness of their communications. Don't do this. Keep in mind that you are an adult with the right to express your views and have them heard as the legitimate concerns of an adult.

You can communicate anger without hysterics or assaults on your husband's personality. If you find yourself becoming physically or psychologically abusive toward your husband, you can excuse yourself and postpone the discussion for a later time.

Couples counseling is often a useful forum for airing grievances and finding areas of agreement. A problem that can easily arise, however, is that the session becomes dominated by the veteran's unresolved war issues. Vietnam wives have reported politely listening to their husbands and the male therapist talk about Vietnam for practically the entire session. They have great difficulty interrupting, especially if their husband begins to weep or is in obvious pain or if the male therapist is a Vietnam veteran himself, which is often the case at Vet Centers. When this happens, the session can sometimes end without your issues being addressed at all.

Therapists, especially male therapists, can help you with this problem by giving you permission and the opportunity to voice your concerns. Otherwise, the counseling sessions may make you feel that your concerns are less important than your husband's. If you feel that way, tell the therapist and insist that something be done so that you feel that you have time to discuss the things bothering you.

No one party, male or female, should be allowed to dominate the session. The presence of a female therapist, provided she does not have negative attitudes toward men or women, often helps a wife be more assertive and feel less defensive about presenting her needs and issues.

Couples counseling is available at many Vet Centers and VA Medical Centers, as well as with private therapists. Wherever you seek help, be sure that the therapist will help both your husband and you.

Help in Selecting a Therapist

The following books and pamphlets offer guidelines to women in selecting therapists:

Women and Psychotherapy, A Consumer Handbook, National Coalition for Women's Mental Health, Women's Studies Program, Arizona State University, Tempe, AZ 85287.

Woman's Guide to Therapy, Friedman, S., Gams, L., Gottlieb, N., Nesselson, C., Prentice-Hall, 200 Old Toppen Road, Old Toppen, NJ 07656.

"If Sex Enters Into the Psychotherapy Relationship," Order Dept., American Psychological Association, Box 2710, Hyattsville, MD 20784.

You can also contact any of the following organizations to inquire whether a listing of feminist or nonsexist therapists has been compiled: local women's centers, rape crisis or women's medical centers, local chapters of NOW (National Organization for Women), local hospitals, mental health centers, university counseling centers, or university women's studies programs.

Many psychologists—both men and women—call themselves "feminist" or "nonsexist" but you need to decide for yourself whether they actually are. Remember that just because a therapist is a woman does not automatically make her a nonsexist therapist. You do not have to choose a woman therapist. There are many male therapists who are committed to nonsexist treatment and provide excellent counseling. In general, though, it takes a lot of effort for a man to be nonsexist and truly understand the influence of sex role stereotyping on a woman.

I would suggest that you interview potential therapists very carefully and make your decision based on how they relate to you, what they say, and their actions. You need to make an emotional match with your therapist. You must feel that you can trust him/her to guide you, to listen to you, and to be concerned about the things that concern you. If you have some special experiences that you need help with, such as incest, battering, or drug abuse, you will want to find out what view the prospective therapist holds. If the therapist believes that a young girl is "provocative" and partially responsible for an incestuous relationship, then this is not the right therapist for you (or anyone).

Different therapies have different purposes. However, in general, the purposes of therapy are to help build a person up, not tear that person down. A person is built up by recognizing and beginning to heal the wounds inflicted by trauma, abuse, or other forms of mistreatment; by recognizing areas of inner conflict and taking steps to resolve some of those inner conflicts; and by recognizing and slowly accepting the full range of human feelings and growing tolerance for some of the most horrendous feelings, such as grief, rage, anxiety, hate and jealousy. Therapy should also help to build an individual's strengths and bring out his or her inherent goodness, not to highlight his or her inadequacies.

Problem areas are not to be ignored in therapy and there may be times in which confrontation in therapy is helpful. Yet this is an art and should not be done by using negative sounding labels. In some instances, Vietnam wives report being openly called "crazy" by their therapist or having had various diagnoses thrown in their faces. "You have a borderline personality (or a schizoid one, a hysterical one, a narcissistic one, a passive aggressive one, an overly dependent one)," women have been told both kindly and unkindly.

In one case, the wife was told by her therapist that she was a masochist for having married a "crazy" Vietnam veteran and even more of a masochist for deciding to stay with him. The therapist also felt that this wife had "preborderline personality," as well as an "addiction to destructive relationships," and repeatedly reminded the wife of her "neurotic tendencies."

This did not encourage the wife to examine her patterns of relating to men. The wife just accepted her therapist's view of her as "sick." She concluded that she might as well keep her life as it was and give up any ideas of ever changing her marriage. After all, she probably deserved the treatment she was getting from her husband and certainly no other man would ever want her.

In group, it was necessary to help this Vietnam wife identify her therapist's negative view of her and help her get rid of the idea that she was a "hopeless case." The problem was made worse by the fact that her husband had also established himself as a judge of her personality.

This wife, like many women, needed help in freeing herself from outside authority figures. In our society, therapists are seen as authority figures and can have tremendous power over people, especially people who are vulnerable because they are in great emotional pain. If a therapist comes to a conclusion, even one that contradicts what a woman knows about herself, the woman may believe the therapist over her own self-knowledge. That is what happened to this wife.

A feminist view of this particular wife's problems would acknowledge that, to some extent, her low self-esteem, anxiety attacks, and crying spells were the logical results of the strains of being a full-time worker, having three children, and living with a man marred by PTSD. This does not mean that all her problems are due to these stresses, but that in counseling Vietnam wives, these stresses have to be taken into account.

A basic premise in feminist therapy is that every woman is an expert on her own life. The therapist's role is not to tell the woman what to do, but to help her get in touch with her past experiences and her true feelings about herself and her life so that she can make her own decisions.

You should not hesitate to confront your therapist if he or she uses psychologically degrading labels or if you leave your sessions feeling more defeated than ever, taking with you not greater self-understanding, but more negative feelings about yourself.

Therapists, male or female, should be avoided if they devalue women or any of women's roles in society or if they use their position of authority to control their clients, advance their careers at the client's expense, or use their position as a therapist to vent personal frustrations and ambivalence about the female sex role identity.

Also to be avoided are therapists who rigidly adhere to the idea that, consciously or unconsciously, you have chosen an emotionally distant veteran due to some need on your part. Such therapists may then insist that you are perpetuating your husband's PTSD by unconsciously or subtly discouraging his recovery due to your own need to keep your husband emotionally distant and emotionally dependent on you. Such an attitude blames you for your husband's problems and implies that you have somehow brought most of your problems upon yourself.

Blaming someone for his or her own pain seldom motivates that person to examine him- or herself and make any concrete changes in his or her life. Especially in the case of women, a blaming attitude on the part of the therapist usually reinforces the woman's low self-esteem and sense of powerlessness and hinders, rather than helps, her ability to clearly assess herself, her marriage, or any other personal difficulties.

Women's Groups

Some Vet Centers and VA Medical Centers provide individual or couples counseling or groups for significant others. However, it is usually required that your husband be registered in treatment at a VA facility before you can receive services at a Vet Center or VA Medical Center.

Groups held for wives and significant others run anywhere from eight to 24 weeks after which a new group is begun. Other groups are open-ended in that they terminate after the leader and the group decide that sufficient progress has been made. While almost all groups offer education about PTSD, some groups are more structured than others. Some allow the members to choose the topics of discussion. In others, the topics are almost always leader-selected. Some groups are conducted by female therapists or volunteers; others by male therapists. Some groups have leaders of both sexes.

For more specific information about available help, contact the local Vietnam Veteran's Outreach Center or VA Medical Center.

Some of the Vietnam wives who have sought help report being told by previous counselors to "go home and give more." They were hesitant to join a women's group or engage in therapy at a VA facility or Vet Center because they feared the staff would be rigidly pro-veteran and would chastise them for their discontent with their marriages. Women also voiced fears about being pressured to stay married to the veteran and be supportive of him at all costs. "I heard these women's groups are band-aid operations," one wife stated. "We come here once a week to feel better, but never go on to make any changes in our marriages or our lives."

A viable women's support group, however, needs to be more than a band-aid operation. It needs to be a forum where there is open sharing of a full range of feelings from love to hate and a place where positive changes can be made. The prime purpose of the group needs to be the promotion of your emotional and physical well-being, regardless of the outcome of your marriage.

Competent women's group leaders or individual psychotherapists do not pressure you to stay with your veteran, or to leave him, but rather help you identify your feelings and your options. Group or individual counseling can offer you a variety of perspectives on your situation and a supportive context in which you can make your own decisions about your life, not only with regard to your marriage, but with regard to your children, your career, and other matters.

A wide variety of women's groups can also be found through community service organizations or through private therapists. However, these groups are usually not focused on PTSD-related marital issues. Some of these groups have a general focus on women's issues. Other have more specific concerns—coping with sexual harassment, coping with midlife, or whatever. Unlike Vet Center groups, however, these groups usually have a fee.

Listings of women's groups can usually be found at local libraries, in local papers, or through local social work organizations, psychological/psychiatric clinics, or local mental health bureaus. In addition, in some areas there are private therapists with expertise in PTSD who offer couples counseling or couples group work for PTSD-afflicted families.

Coping with Multiple Roles

You can reduce your stress level by appreciating, examining, and making some concrete changes in your multiple-role lifestyle. The first step involves examining early sex role messages and myths and their effect on you. The "shoulds" which you typically carry with you are often the source of intense and recurrent guilt feelings as you try to make your own choices. Typically a woman has grown up learning about women in the most stereotyped, traditionally feminine, ways. Her image of what a woman ought to be, how she ought to feel, and what she ought to want often clashes with how she experiences herself and what reality demands of her, resulting in feelings of being "not O.K."

Typically, over time, the Vietnam wife finds herself doing more and more. The expectations for her personal capacity seem to increase as the tasks increase. Yet the recognition of the strengths necessary to perform the tasks tend to fade. Frequently, your self-esteem diminishes as you and others start to take your efforts for granted. Then you need to focus (or be focused by a therapist or counselor) on what you are accomplishing and on appreciating your positive qualities. I have provided you with several exercises to help you acknowledge your strengths.

In the midst of her profusion of activities, the working Vietnam wife tends to neglect herself. Among the women I have worked with, many have tended to postpone not only activities which are emotionally or spiritually fulfilling to them, but needed medical attention. The woman needs to "mother herself" as readily as she would (and probably has, numerous times) for her veteran or their children. "You wouldn't think twice about spending the money (or time) on your husband (or child), would you?" I point out. "Why do you think you deserve less?"

The importance of learning self-nurturing is critical. While you need to seek and gain external support, you must also be able to give to yourself. Quite often, people who accomplish a great deal come to be taken for granted and are not congratulated as often as they may need to be. Therefore, you need to learn to congratulate yourself, as well as to make time for activities which you enjoy which do not involve taking care of somebody else or completing a task. Some wives have found great solace in ceramics, music, sewing, writing, or other activities.

Most of the Vietnam wives I have counseled attempt to maintain their traditional roles intact. They often accept all family and domestic responsibilities as though they were full-time homemakers. Redefining roles in human rather than sex role terms is a vital part of the counseling process through which the woman and her partner or family come to see home care as a family matter. "Mothering" does not have to include laundering; "fathering" does not have to exclude it. Family care needs to be seen as a responsibility to be shared by all adult partners in the home.

In addition, outside support services can be utilized. You need to find and utilize support services such as child care, houseworkers, and tutoring.

You may also want to re-examine your career choice and job options. Traditionally, schools and counselors have not educated girls for careers. The assumptions about a woman's place have resulted in limited options being made available to women in their working lives. While visions of job or career choices have definitely expanded and are continuing to expand, the majority of women still work in traditionally female occupations. There may be career and educational options available to you now that were not available years ago. Some wives have sought out assertiveness training workshops, communication skills training, or specialized help in making educational and vocational decisions. You might want to explore doing the same kinds of things.

In group, women have found it useful to ask themselves what their career goals and job preferences would be (a) if they were not married to a PTSD-afflicted veteran or to a drug addicted or alcoholic PTSD-afflicted veteran; (b) if they were not married at all; or (c) if they did not have children. Separating your career goals from your family identity helps you select a new career goal.

Many a marriage has been saved by the wife forging ahead toward her goal, even in some small manner. In several cases, had the woman not pursued one of her vocational ambitions, she would have been strongly tempted to abandon her marriage. The sense of achievement, self-regard, and self-respect these women acquired by pursuing even one of their own goals gave them the strength to cope with husbands who had little to offer emotionally because of their PTSD.

The specific exercises listed below are based on the experiences Dr. Brenda Alpert Sigall and I used in developing programs for multiple-role women at the University of Maryland Counseling Center and the Washington, D.C. Department of Veterans Affairs Medical Center.

The Shoulds Exercise

Think of all the "shoulds" you learned regarding your role as a woman (in general) or as a wife, mother, daughter, worker, or professional woman (in particular). On a piece of paper draw three columns. In the first column, list as many shoulds as you can remember. Include those shoulds you heard as you were growing up as well as those which you hear now: from your parents, husband, children, neighbors, friends, employees, and the media.

In the second column, list the source of the should—where you learned it or who taught it to you. In the third column, describe what happened to you in the past when you did not live up to this particular should. For example, were you verbally chastised, rejected, hit, or made to feel ashamed?

Review your list, then ask yourself, How did it feel to list the shoulds? Which shoulds do you desire to keep? To alter? To discard? Do you see the shoulds as goals to be striven for or as measures of self-worth?

Other questions to be considered are: What happens inside you when you do not live up to the expectations of the shoulds? What do you say to yourself? How do you feel? How does this compare to what other people say to you?

What makes you feel okay when you diverge from the shoulds? What makes you feel not okay when you diverge? What can you do to help yourself feel better when you digress from the shoulds?

Writing Your Own Script: Tailoring Superwoman to Yourself

Almost every woman has an image of superwoman—the "ideal" woman who is all things to all people at all times with no wear and tear on the self and with a constant smile and loving heart to boot.

Brainstorm a list of adjectives describing the cultural ideal or stereotype of this super or "perfect" woman. Then brainstorm a list of personal costs and costs to others that attend the ideal image or the striving toward this ideal. For instance, I always think of the ideal woman as perfectly dressed. Some of the costs of this could be money or time to take care of the clothes or do the necessary shopping. The costs to others could include less money to spend on things for them.

Now write your own script, not a superwoman script, for one of your roles. (This exercise can be completed for additional roles also.)

Junk vs. Joy

Another version of "Writing Your Own Script" is the "Junk vs. Joy" exercise.

Think about what is truly important about being a mother, wife, or worker. Which of your qualities do you really want to share with your family? Your co-workers? What activities are really necessary in each role?

For example, what is it to be a Mom? Is there a difference between being loving and baking cupcakes? When do the cupcakes get in the way of the loving?

The point of this exercise is to identify the junk vs. the joy of the roles in order to have more of the joy and less of the junk. On a piece of paper, draw a line dividing the paper in half. One side of the paper is labeled "joy," the other "junk." Underneath, list the junk vs. the joy of your various roles as a woman.

The Little Nothings I Do List

In a sexist society, work and tasks that are allocated to women—for example, housework, child rearing, managing social events—are often considered inferior work, unimportant work, or no work. The credit for this exercise goes to a Vietnam wife who worked part-time and was constantly being accused, on the days when she did not work outside the home, of "doing nothing" in her traditional roles of homemaker, wife, chauffeur, and facilitator of her successful husband's numerous projects.

The problem began when she started to believe that she was doing nothing on her days off even though she was a very busy person and always short on time. For many years she believed that she was doing nothing until one day she got very smart. When her husband said, "Why can't you do this for me? You've had nothing to do all day," she decided to make a list of "all the little nothings I do."

Instructions: Make a list of all the little nothings you do, the essential tasks you perform to keep the house or human system you live in flowing, for which you get little or no credit, and which are virtually unrecognized by praise or money. You may be amazed at the number of things you actually do and how much time it takes to get them all done.

Personal Goals vs. Cultural Expectations

We rarely take the time to think about what kind of person we want to be in relation to others (our partner, mate, child, or colleague). Too often we try to meet the cultural stereotype for the role instead of being the person we want to be and can truly be.

Pick one person—your husband, a child, a parent, or a colleague—and think about what kind of person you want to be in relation to that person. Think about it quietly and alone for a while. Then try to think of things you can do to get you closer to being that person.

Visualizing Yourself as a Success

This exercise encourages thinking of yourself as a person who is capable and competent to learn new skills. It is especially helpful for women who often tend to see themselves as incapable of succeeding at something new.

Relax for a few minutes, then close your eyes.

1. Visualize a particular specific aspect of your work life in which

you feel inadequate or incompetent. Pick a definite and concrete instance in which you have not succeeded thus far and in which you feel you may never succeed (3–4 minutes).

2. Now visualize yourself as succeeding in this particular task (3–4 minutes).

Consider what steps you would need to take to make your success fantasy a reality and make a commitment to begin working for this success.

Give Yourself a Medal

For the next five minutes, get into yourself. Relax. Pretend you would like to give yourself a medal. What would it be for and what would be inscribed upon it?

Now write a two- or three-sentence statement about this medal.

Now write a two-- or three-sentence statement about the process of giving yourself a medal. Was it difficult or easy to give yourself a medal or otherwise see your admirable qualities? Have you ever done it before? If you told other people about your medal, what would they think?

Acknowledging Your Strengths

This exercise format is the same as the "Medals" exercise above, except that you are asked to list five to 10 of your strengths. Although this exercise seems very simple, it has usually proven extremely effective in helping women to acknowledge their strengths.

A variation of this exercise is to list five to 10 accomplishments. Women tend to remember incomplete tasks and ways in which they have not lived up to some ideal image of womanhood. This would help you focus on some of the things you have finished and done well.

Combine, Combine, Combine

Time is the working woman's scarcest commodity. In this exercise, list all chores and activities both at home and at work by the week (not the day). Then review the lists to see if there are any ways in which responsibilities or activities can be possibly combined so as to save time.

An important condition in combining activities is that combining the activities not interfere with the quality of the outcome. For example, sit-ups can be performed and nails painted while watching TV. Necessary phone calls can be made while cooking or cleaning up in the kitchen. But activities cannot be combined if one of the tasks requires all your concentration.

The second part of this exercise involves routing driving so that you do not make a series of separate trips, but plan stops and chores to be time-efficient.

Coping with Eating Disorders

Regardless of how oppressive or unrewarding your life situation may be, you must take responsibility for your eating disorder rather than blame it on your husband, children, or some other outside factor. Usually some form of food abuse has been a lifelong pattern for a woman, beginning before her marriage, although perhaps worsened by stresses in the marriage. Over half the obese and bulimic Vietnam wives I have seen were victims of child sexual abuse or child sexual assault. Compulsive overeating or bulimia were their admitted means of coping with their rage, self-hate, and sense of powerlessness at being abused by a parent.

Usually the obese or bulimic Vietnam wife needs and deserves help beyond the latest diet published in a woman's magazine. Her first step toward recovery involves consulting a medical doctor or dietician to obtain a nutritionally sound food plan. Strange as it may sound, dieting is fattening. Excessive dieting reduces the basal metabolic rate and calories are burned more slowly. Secondly, dieting leads to binging.

You need a food plan for living that meets your nutritional needs, not a crash diet. However, you need more than just a good diet. If losing weight and keeping it off was simply a matter of finding the right diet, then every person who desired to be thin would achieve his or her goal.

You also need a form of individual or group therapy that addresses the emotional issues underlying your excessive eating (or bulimia). For the compulsive overeater or bulimic, losing weight usually requires dealing with feelings she finds unacceptable (anger, rage, and sexual desire) or extremely painful (sorrow and disappointment). You must also learn to develop a sense of self-worth that is based on more than cosmetic external appearance and includes a deeply internalized sense of self-respect and personal integrity.

Losing weight also requires that you learn to love yourself, all of yourself, including your fat or bulimic self. You must learn to see your eating disordered self not as bad or immoral, but as a representation of your emotional needs for more love and support.

Compulsive overeating and bulimia are cunning, baffling, and often lifelong problems. You will need a tremendous amount of support and encouragement in learning how to face life without the crutch of excess food. I recommend that you find a therapist knowledgeable about eating disorders or get involved in a self-help group, such as Overeaters Anonymous (O.A.). The therapy should help you identify your feelings and help you with diet management and other behavioral techniques for weight control.

You should have a complete medical examination, especially if you are bulimic. Women with bulimia need to have their iron and potassium levels checked regularly. Bulimia often results in an abnormally low potassium concentration as well as electrolyte imbalance. Physical checkups are especially essential when you suffer general ill health as a result of your eating disorder.

An exercise program is also a good idea. Not only can it help you lose weight but it can be a means of expressing pent-up frustrations and anger.

About O.A. (Overeaters Anonymous)

O.A. is not a diet or calories club. It is a 12-step program similar to A.A. (Alcoholics Anonymous) and N.A. (Narcotics Anonymous) which views compulsive overeating (and bulimia) as a problem in living, rather than as just a food or weight problem. The focus of O.A. is not on weight loss alone, but on emotional and spiritual recovery as well.

There are thousands of O.A. meetings taking place throughout the world every week. Members do not sign up for meetings. They simply attend as often as they feel the need. Many attend meetings more than once a week, especially during times of stress. There are no coercive techniques, no dues or fees, and no humiliating "weigh-ins." Like A.A. and N.A., O.A. is an anonymous program. Members reveal their first names only.

In addition to meetings, the O.A. program offers members the advantage of sponsors—supportive individuals who achieved some measurable degree of recovery from their compulsive overeating or bulimia—who are willing to help other overeaters or bulimics cope with their feelings and their life difficulties without the buffer of excess food.

O.A. is not a substitute for psychotherapy. In fact, O.A. encourages the use of medical doctors, dieticians, and knowledgeable psychotherapists. O.A., however, provides a readily available support group for those who desire to stop eating compulsively and to not abuse themselves with food. In many areas, special meetings are oriented toward bulimics.

So far, O.A. boasts a comparable, if not higher, recovery rate for compulsive overeaters as compared to commercial weight loss programs and weight loss programs conducted by mental health professionals. If recovery is defined as long-term maintenance, not just losing excess weight but keeping it off for two years, the recovery rate for O.A. is close to 22%. The recovery rate for commercial and mental health administered weight loss programs and all other therapies combined is usually much lower.

O.A. can be found in most major metropolitan cities, as well as in some outlying areas. For further information contact O.A. World Service Office.

Suggested Readings

Overeaters Anonymous, Overeaters Anonymous Inc., Torrance, CA, 1980, available from O.A. World Service, 6075 Zenith Ct. N.E., Rio Rancho, NM 87124-6462.

The Nutritional Ages of Women: A Lifelong Guide to Eating Right for Health, Beauty and Well-Being by Patricia Long, Macmillan Publishing Co., New York, 1986.

Fat is a Family Affair by Judith Hollis, Harper and Row, San Francisco, 1985.

Fat and Furious: Women and Food Obsession by Judith Hollis, Ballantine Books, New York, 1988.

Feeding The Hungry Heart, The Experience of Compulsive Overeating, Bobbs-Merrill, Indianapolis, IN, 1982.

Shadow On a Tightrope: Writings By Women on Fat Oppression edited by Lisa Shoenfielder and Barb Wieser, Aunt Lute Book Company, Iowa City Women's Press, Iowa City, Iowa, 1983.

Reversing the Weight Gain Spiral by Merlene Miller and David Miller, Ballantine Books, New York, 1994.

Pamphlets available from Hazelden Press, Educational Materials, Box 176, Pleasant Valley Road, Center City, MN 55012-0176, or call toll free (800) 328-9000:

"Think Before You Eat"

"Sexuality and Compulsive Eating"

"Enough is a Feast"

"Learn about Eating Disorders"

"Anorexia"

"Bulimia: The Binge Eating and Purging Syndrome"
"Please Don't Give Me Chocolates"
"What is OA?"
"Killing Ourselves with Kindness"
"Accepting Powerlessness"
Hope for Compulsive Overeaters (Cassettes)
(Additional books and materials on eating disorders are listed in the "Reading List" at the end of this book.)

These are some of the ways you can start to take better care of yourself. I urge you to take that first step. Call a Vet Center, contact O.A., reach out in whatever way you can. You can get better control of your life, but only if you can take that first step. Many Vietnam wives have and so can you.

Resource Guide

Where to Get Help for Wife Abuse

IN THE MILITARY

Family Advocacy officers or representatives exist on every Army, Navy, Air Force, Marine Corps, and Coast Guard installation. They can usually be contacted directly or through a family service or family support center. Abused wives may also contact the chaplain, the medical department, the Staff Judge Advocate, the social worker, the nearest Women's Advocacy office (if available), their husband's commanding officer, or anyone in his chain of command.

Help can also be obtained from civilian sources listed in the following section, sources such as courts, social service agencies, churches, libraries, hospitals, and battered women's shelters. Even wives living on bases under exclusive federal jurisdiction may seek help from civilian resources.

CIVILIAN WIVES

You can get help from the courts, from the police, and through local organizations such as battered women's shelters, city or county social service agencies, churches, or community hot lines. Local universities, colleges, and community colleges also have hot lines and women's associations which may be of assistance. Check your Yellow Pages telephone book or call your local police station, library, or hospital for direct assistance or for the location of helping agencies and groups. Vet

Centers (some times called Outreach or Readjustment Counseling Centers) or the Psychology Service, Social Work Service, Psychiatry Service, or Mental Health Clinic of your nearest Department of Veterans Affairs Medical Center may also have listings of local abused persons programs and agencies.

A national directory of resources with information such as hospitals, crisis centers, support groups, and other domestic violence programs is maintained by the *Family Violence and Sexual Assault Institute*, 1310 Clinic Drive, Tyler, TX 75701, (903) 595-6600.

Where to Get Help for Child Abuse

Parents Anonymous is a self-help group for parents who are abusive or fear they might become abusive. Chapters are located in most states and offer free local support groups to parents who would like to learn more effective ways of parenting and coping with stress. For more information or the location of the nearest chapter, contact the *National Organization for Parents Anonymous*, 675 W. Foothill Blvd., Suite 220, Claremont, CA 91711, (909) 621-6184. You can also check your local telephone directory, library, or hospital or call a nearby abused persons or battered women's shelter for assistance.

Due to child-abuse reporting laws, most mental health and other health care professionals have listings of resources for both abusing parents and abused children. State or county social service offices, local police stations, courthouses, hospitals, as well as private physicians and mental health professionals, will also have listings for local helping agencies both for abusive parents and abused children.

Help for Problems with Alcohol or Drug Abuse

Information about A.A., Al-Anon, ACOA, N.A., and Nar Anon meetings can be obtained from the local telephone directory, local A.A. or N.A. meetings, or local libraries or hospitals. Many mental health facilities and clinics hold such meetings in their offices or have information about such meetings.

Each of these programs has a national headquarters, whose current address and phone number can be obtained from a local meeting representative or a referral source, such as a library, hospital, or mental health worker. You can write the national headquarters for information about meetings and about the programs, as well as for a listing of program related pamphlets, books, and other literature.

The following is a listing of some of these organizations and their current phone number as of the writing of this book:

Alcoholics Anonymous World Services: (212) 870-3400

Families Anonymous World Services (for family members and friends of alcohol or drug-addicted persons): (818) 989-7841

Narcotics Anonymous World Service, Inc., (818) 773-9999

Numerous books, pamphlets, and audiotapes on alcoholism and drug addiction both for addicted people and their family members are available from Hazelden Educational Materials, Box 176, Center City, MN 55012-0176, or toll free: (800) 328-9000. A catalog can be requested.

Organizations Helping Veterans and Their Families

Numerous organizations exist that help veterans and their families. They vary greatly in the types of services offered. However, in general, the services range from claims assistance and information and referrals for health, education, tutoring, jobs, and legal assistance to help in obtaining medical care, discharge review, Agent Orange compensation, and other forms of compensation. Some of these organizations are listed below. For the current listing of the address and phone number of these organizations, consult your local telephone directory.

If the organization you are interested in does not have a chapter in your area and is not listed in your local telephone directory, the phone number of the nearest office of the organization can possibly be obtained from another local veterans organization or from the Department of Veterans Affairs Medical Center (VAMC) or Veterans Outreach Center (Vet Center) nearest you. Information on how to contact the VAMC or Vet Center will be provided below.

In addition, your local library should have a listing of veterans organizations, as well as the address and phone numbers of the national headquarters of various veterans organizations.

Veterans of the Vietnam War
Headquarters: Wilkes-Barre, PA

Vietnam Veterans of America
Headquarters: Washington, D.C.
Many local and state chapters

American Legion
Headquarters: Washington, D.C.
Many local and state chapters
Provides help in obtaining employment, Department of Veterans Affairs benefits, medical care, discharge review, and Agent Orange.

Veterans Educational Project (VEP)
Headquarters: Washington, D.C.
VEP has a National Referral Directory which lists the network of organizations, attorneys, doctors, and others who offer assistance to veterans. Contact VEP for listings in your state specifying the type of referral needed and the type of professional organization you are seeking. There may be a fee for the computer search.

American Veterans of World War II, Korea, and Vietnam (AMVETS)
Headquarters: Lanham, Maryland

Blinded Veteran's Association
Headquarters: Washington, D.C.
Offers information and referrals for health, education, tutoring, jobs and legal assistance to blinded veterans and their families.

Disabled American Veterans
Headquarters: Washington, D.C.
The DAV serves as a catalyst to obtain needed services for disabled veterans and their families.

Marine Corps League
Headquarters: Arlington, Virginia
The Marine Corps League offers employment counseling and job placement assistance along with referral data, helps Marines get VA and service connected benefits, and helps handicapped Marines with their rehabilitation.

Military Order of the Purple Heart
Headquarters: Springfield, Virginia
National Service Office: Washington, D.C.

Readjustment Counseling Service
National Veterans Outreach Program
Headquarters: Washington, D.C.

Non-Commissioned Officers Association (NCOA)
Veterans Employment Assistance Program
Headquarters: Alexandria, Virginia

Paralyzed Veterans of America
Headquarters: Washington, D.C.

United States Office of Personnel Management
Federal Job Information Center
National Office: Washington, D.C.
Offers federal job information to vets, including information on veterans' preference in appointments, credit for military service, jobs for preference eligibles only, special appointing authorities for disabled veterans and Vietnam-era veterans, as well as other services.

Veterans of Foreign Wars of the United States
National Headquarters: Washington, D.C.
The VFW has a national program of veteran's assistance regarding claims and employment referrals as well as other services.

In some areas the American Red Cross offers limited financial and other services to veterans. Check with the local office of the American Red Cross for further information.

Local universities and colleges and local and state or country employment commissions, personnel departments, or labor departments sometimes have special offers for veterans. Check in a local directory or call the nearest Vet Center for more information.

Department of Veterans Affairs Medical Centers (VAMCs) and Veterans Outreach Centers (Vet Centers)
There are Department of Veterans Affairs Medical Centers and Vet Centers in every state. Department of Veterans Affairs Medical Centers (DVAMCs), formerly known as VA Hospitals, offer both medical and psychiatric care.

Some medical centers also have specialized teams, called PTSD teams, or in some places PCT teams, designed to assist veterans with combat stress on an outpatient basis. Other VAMCs specialized inpatient units for veterans with PTSD or addiction problems.

If you are interested in help for combat stress, when you call the VAMC nearest you, inquire whether or not the hospital has an inpatient PTSD unit or an outpatient PCT or PTSD unit. You may ask the hospital operator for this information or you may ask to speak to an official in the outpatient Mental Health Clinic or in the hospital's Psychology, Psychiatry, or Social Work service. Such persons can also provide you with information about alcohol or drug rehabilitation programs within the VA and in the community.

You can find the phone number of the VAMC nearest you by consulting your local telephone directory, library, or local hospital. You can locate the Vet Center nearest you through the local telephone directory or by contacting the VAMC nearest you. Sometimes Vet Centers are called Outreach Centers, or Readjustment Counseling Centers, rather than Vet Centers.

Veterans Outreach Centers

Anchorage, AK 99508   4201 Tudor Centre Dr., Suite 115

Fairbanks, AK 99701   520 5th Ave., Suite 104

Kenai, AK 99611   P.O. Box 1883

Wasilla, AK 99654   851 E. Westpoint Ave., Suite 109

Birmingham, AL 35205   1425 S. 21st St., Suite 108

Mobile, AL 36604   951 Government St., Suite 122

North Little Rock, AR 72114   201 W. Broadway, Suite A

Phoenix, AZ 85004   141 E. Palm Ln., Suite 100

Prescott, AZ 86301   637 Hillside Ave., Suite A

Tuscon, AZ 85719   3055 N. 1st Ave.

Anaheim, CA 92805   859 S. Harbor Blvd.

Benicia, CA 94510   555 1st St., Suite 200

Burlingame, CA 94010   1234 Howard — San Mateo

Chico, CA 95926   109 Parmac Rd.

Commerce, CA 90040   5400 E. Olympic Blvd., #140

Concord, CA 94520   1899 Clayton Rd., Suite 140

Eureka, CA 95501   305 V St.

Fresno, CA 93726   3636 N. 1st St., Suite 112

Los Angeles, CA 90003   251 W. 85th Pl.

Los Angeles, CA 90025   2000 Westwood Blvd.

Marina, CA 93933   455 Reservation Rd., Suite E

Oakland, CA 94612   287 17th St.

Riverside, CA 92504   4954 Arlington Ave., Suite A

Rohnert Park, CA 94928   6225 State Farm Dr., Suite 101

Sacramento, CA 95825   1111 Howe Ave., Suite 390

San Diego, CA 92103   2900 6th Ave.

San Francisco, CA 94102   25 Van Ness Ave.

San Jose, CA 95112   278 N. 2nd St.

Santa Barbara, CA 93101   1300 Santa Barbara St.

Sepulveda, CA 91343   16126 Lassen St.

Upland, CA 91786   313 N. Mountain Ave.

Vista, CA 92083   1830 West Dr., Suite 103

Boulder, CO 80302   2128 Pearl St.

Colorado Springs, CO 80903   411 S. Tejon, Suite G

Denver, CO 80204   1815 Federal Blvd.

Hartford, CT 06120   370 Market St.

Norwich, CT 06360   100 Main St.

West Haven, CT 06516   141 Capt. Thomas Blvd.

Washington, D.C. 20003   801 Pennsylvania Ave., S.E.

Wilmington, DE 19805   1601 Kirkwood Hwy., VAMROC Bldg 2

Fort Lauderdale, FL 33301   315 N.E. 3rd Ave.

Jacksonville, FL 32202   255 Liberty St.

Lake Worth, FL 33461   2311 10th Ave., North #13 Palm Beach

Miami, FL 33129   2700 S.W. 3rd Ave., Suite 1A

Orlando, FL 32809   5001 S. Orange Ave., Suite A

Pensacola, FL 32501   202 W. Jackson

Sarasota, FL 34239   1800 Siesta Dr.

St. Petersburg, FL 33713   2837 1st Ave., N.

Tallahassee, FL 32303   249 E. 6th Ave.

Tampa, FL 33604   1507 W. Sligh Ave.

Atlanta, GA 30309   922 W. Peachtree St.

Savannah, GA 31406   8110 A White Bluff Rd.

Hilo, HI 96720   120 Keawe St., Suite 201

Honolulu, HI 96814   1680 Kapiolani Blvd., Suite F

Kailua-Kona, HI 96740   75-5995 Kuakini Hwy., #415

Lihue, HI 96766   3367 Kuhio Hwy., Suite 101-Kauai

Wailuku, HI 96793   Ting Bldg., 35 Lunalilo, Suite 101

Des Moines, IA 50310   2600 Harding Rd.

Sioux City, IA 51105   706 Jackson

Boise, ID 83706   1115 W. Boise Ave.

Pocatello, ID 83201   1975 S. 5th St.

Chicago, IL 60637   5505 S. Harper

Chicago Heights, IL 60411   1600 Halsted St.

East St. Louis, IL 62203   1269 N. 89th St., Suite 1

Evanston, IL 60202   565 Howard St.

Moline, IL 61265   1529 46th Ave., Room 6

Oak Park, IL 60302   155 S. Oak Park Ave.

Peoria, IL 61603   605 N.E. Monroe St.

Springfield, IL 62703   624 S. 4th St.

Evansville, IN 47711   311 N. Weinbach Ave.

Fort Wayne, IN 46802   528 West Berry St.

Gary, IN 46408   2236 West Ridge Rd.

Indianapolis, IN 46208   3833 N. Meridian, Suite 120

Wichita, KS 67211   413 S. Pattie

Lexington, KY 40503   1117 Limestone Rd.

Louisville, KY 40208   1355 S. 3rd St.

Bossier City, LA 71112   2103 Old Minden Rd.

New Orleans, LA 70116   1529 N. Claiborne Ave.

Shreveport, LA 71104   2620 Centenary Blvd., Bldg. 3, Suite 260

Boston, MA 02215   665 Beacon St.

Brockton, MA 02401   1041 L Pearl St.

Lawrence, MA 01840   45 Franklin St.

Lowell, MA 01852   73 East Merrimack St.

New Bedford, MA 02740   468 North St.

Springfield, MA 01103   1985 Main St., Northgate Plaza

Winchendon, MA 01475   Town Hall

Worcester, MA 01605   108 Grove St.

Baltimore, MD 21230   777 Washington Blvd.

Cambridge, MD 21613   5510 W. Shore Dr.

Elkton, MD 21921   7 Elkton Commercial Plaza, S. Bridge St.

Silver Spring, MD 20910   1015 Spring St., Suite 101

Bangor, ME 04401   352 Harlow St.

Caribou, ME 04736   228 Sweden St.

Lewiston, ME 04240   475 Pleasant St.

Portland, ME 04101   63 Preble St.

Sanford, ME 04073   441 Main St.

Grand Rapids, MI 49507   1940 Eastern Ave. S.E.

Lincoln Park, MI 48146   1766 Fort St.

Oak Park, MI 48237   20820 Greenfield Rd.

Duluth, MN 55802   405 E. Superior St.

St. Paul, MN 55114   2480 University Ave.

Kansas City, MO 64111   3931 Main St.

St. Louis, MO 63103   2345 Pine St.

Biloxi, MS 39531   2196 Pass Rd.

Jackson, MS 39206   4436 N. State St., Suite A3

Billings, MT 59102   1948 Grand Ave.

Missoula, MT 59802   500 N. Higgins Ave.

Charlotte, NC 28202   223 S. Brevard St., Suite 103

Fayetteville, NC 28301   4 Market Square

Greensboro, NC 27406   2009 Elm-Eugene St.

Greenville, NC 27834   150 Arlington Blvd., Suite B

Fargo, ND 58103   1322 Gateway Dr.

Minot, ND 58702   2041 3rd St. N.W.

Lincoln, NE 68508   920 L St.

Omaha, NE 68106   5123 Leavenworth St.

Manchester, NH 03104   103 Liberty St.

Jersey City, NJ 07302   115 Christopher Columbus Dr., Rm. 200

Linwood, NJ 08221   222 New Rd., Bldg. 2, Suite 405

Newark, NJ 07102   77 Halsey St.

Trenton, NJ 08611   171 Jersey St., Bldg. 36

Albuquerque, NM 87104   1600 Mountain Rd., N.W.

Farmington, NM 87402   4251 E. Main, Suite B

Santa Fe, NM 87505   1996 Warner St., Warner Plaza, Suite 5

Las Vegas, NV 89101   704 S. 6th St.

Reno, NV 89503   1155 W. 4th St., Suite 101

Albany, NY 12206   875 Central Ave.

Babylon, NY 11702   116 West Main St.

Bronx, NY 10458   226 East Fordham Rd., Rms. 216-217

Brooklyn, NY 11201   165 Cadman Plaza East

Buffalo, NY 14209   351 Linwood Ave.

New York, NY 10036   120 West 44th St., Suite 201

New York, NY 10027   55 W. 125th St.

Rochester, NY 14608   134 S. Fitzhugh St.

Staten Island, NY 10301   150 Richmond Terr.

Syracuse, NY 13203   210 North Townsend St.

White Plains, NY 10601   200 Hamilton Ave., White Plains Mall

Woodhaven, NY 11421   75-1OB 91st Ave.

Cincinnati, OH 45219   30 E. Hollister St.

Cleveland, OH 44111   11511 Lorain Ave.

Cleveland Heights, OH 44118   2134 Lee Rd.

Columbus, OH 43205   1054 E. Broad St.

Dayton, OH 45402   6 S. Patterson Blvd.

Oklahoma City, OK 73105   3033 N. Walnut, Suite 101W

Tulsa, OK 74101   1855 E. 15th St.

Eugene, OR 97403   1966 Garden Ave.

Grants Pass, OR 97526-3214   211 S.E. 10th St.

Portland, OR 97220   8383 N.E. Sandy Blvd., Suite 110

Salem, OR 97301   318 Church St., N.E.

Erie, PA 16501   G. Daniel Baldwin Bldg., 1000 State St.

Harrisburg, PA 17110   1007 N. Front St.

McKeesport, PA 15132   500 Walnut St.

Philadelphia, PA 19107   1026 Arch St.

Philadelphia, PA 19120   101 E. Olney Ave., Box C-7

Pittsburgh, PA 15222   954 Penn Ave.

Scranton, PA 18509   959 Wyoming Ave.

Arecibo, Puerto Rico 00612   52 Gonzalo Marin St.

Ponce, Puerto Rico 00731   35 Mayor St.

Rio Pedras, Puerto Rico 00921   Suite LC8A & LC9, La Riviera

Cranston, R.I. 02920   789 Park Ave.

Columbia, S.C. 29201   1313 Elmwood Ave.

Greenville, S.C. 29601   904 Pendleton St.

North Charleston, S.C. 29406   5603A Rivers Ave.

Rapid City, SD 57701   610 Kansas City St.

Sioux Falls, SD 57104   601 S. Cliff Ave., Suite C

Chattanooga, TN 37404   425 Cumberland St., Suite 140

Johnson City, TN 37601   703 S. Roan St.

Knoxville, TN 37914   2817 E. Magnolia Ave.

Memphis, TN 38104   1835 Union, Suite 100

Amarillo, TX 79106   3414 E. Olsen Blvd., Suite E

Austin, TX 78723   3401 Manor Rd., Suite 102

Corpus Christi, TX 78404   3166 Reid Dr., Suite 1

Dallas, TX 75244   5232 Forest Ln., Suite 111

El Paso, TX 79924   6500 Boeing, Suite L112

Fort Worth, TX 76104   1305 W. Magnolia, Suite B

Houston, TX 77004   4905A San Jacinto

Houston, TX 77007   8100 Washington Ave., Suite 120

Laredo, TX 78041   6020 McPherson Rd., #1

Lubbock, TX 79410   3208 34th St.

McAllen, TX 78501   1317 E. Hackberry St.

Midland, TX 79703   3404 W. Illinois, Suite 1

San Antonio, TX 78212   231 W. Cypress St.

Provo, UT 84601   750 North 200 West, Suite 105

Salt Lake City, UT 84106   1354 East 3300 South

Norfolk, VA 23517   2200 Colonial Ave., Suite 3

Richmond, VA 23230   3022 W. Clay St.

Roanoke, VA 24016   320 Mountain Ave., S.W.

Springfield, VA 22150   7024 Spring Garden Dr., Brookfield Plaza

St. Croix, Virgin Islands 00820   Village Mall, Barren Spot

St. Thomas, Virgin Islands 00801   Upper Havensight Mall

South Burlington, VT 05403   359 Dorset St.

White River Junction, VT 05001   Gilman Office Center, Bldg. 2, Holiday Inn Dr.

Seattle, WA 98121   2230 8th Ave.

Spokane, WA 99201   1708 W. Mission St.

Tacoma, WA 98409   4916 Center St., Suite E

Madison, WI 53703   147 S. Butler St.

Milwaukee, WI 53208   3400 Wisconsin

Beckley, WV 25801   101 Ellison Ave.

Charleston, WV 25312   512 Washington St. West

Huntington, WV 25701   1005 6th Ave.

Martinsburg, WV 25401   105 S. Spring St.
Morgantown, WV 26505   1191 Pineview Dr.
Princeton, WV 24740   905 Mercer St.
Wheeling, WV 26003   1070 Market St.
Casper, WY 82601   111 S. Jefferson, Suite 100
Cheyenne, WY 82001   3130 Henderson Dr.

Reading List

Chapter 1

Recommended Reading

Achilles in Vietnam, Jonathan Shay; Atheneum Press, 1994.

Back From the Brink: A Family Guide to Overcoming Traumatic Stress, Don R. Catherall; Brunner/Mazel Inc., New York, 1991.

Brothers in Arms, William Broyles; Knopf, New York, 1986.

For Self and Country, Rick Eilert; William Morrow & Company, New York, 1983.

"The Grief of Soldiers: Vietnam combat veteran's self-help movement," *American Journal of Orthopsychiatry*, 1973, 43(4): 640-653.

Long Time Passing: Viet Nam: The Haunted Generation, Myra MacPherson; Doubleday and Co., Inc., Garden City, NY, 1984.

Out of the Night, William P. Mahedy; Ballantine Books, New York, 1986.

Paco's Story, Larry Heinemann; Penguin Books, New York, 1987.

The Ravens, Christopher Robbins; Crown Publishers, Inc., New York, 1987.

"Readjustment Problems Among Vietnam Veterans: The Etiology of Combat-Related Post-Traumatic Stress Disorders," Jim Goodwin, Psy.D.; Available from the Disabled American Veterans, National Headquarters, P.O. Box 14301, Cincinnati, OH 45214.

Recovering From the War: A Woman's Guide to Helping Your Vietnam Vet, Your Family and Yourself; Patience H. C. Mason, Viking Penguin, New York, 1990.

"The Road to Hill Ten," William Broyles; *Atlantic*, April, 1985.

Shrapnel in the Heart, Laura Palmer; Random House, New York, 1987.

Soldier's Heart: Survivors' Views of Combat Trauma, Sarah Hansel, Ann Steidle, Grace Zaczek & Ron Zaczek; The Sidran Press, Lutherville, Maryland, 1995.

To Heal a Nation, Jan Scruggs & Joel Swerdlow; Harper and Row, New York, 1985.

Technical But Still Readable

The Forgotten Warrior Project, John P. Wilson; Disabled American Veterans, Cleveland, Ohio, 1978.

The Journal of Traumatic Stress, Plenum Press, 233 Spring Street, New York, N.Y. 10013-1578.

Legacies of Viet Nam: Comparative Adjustment of Veterans and Their Peers, The Center for Policy Research, Inc., New York City, March, 1981; A Study Completed for the Veterans Administration.

Vol. I: Summary of Findings; Principal Investigators: A. Egendorf; C. Kadushin; R. Laufer; G. Rothbart; L. Sloan.

Vol. II: Educational and Work Careers: Men in the Viet Nam Generation; Principal Investigators: G. Rothbart and L. Sloan.

Vol. III: Post War Trauma: Social and Psychological Problems of Viet Nam veterans in the Aftermath of the Viet Nam War; Principal Investigator: R. Laufer.

Vol. IV: Long Term Stress Reactions: Some causes, consequences and naturally occurring support systems; Principal Investigator: C. Kadushin.

Vol. V: Dealing with the War: A view based on the individual lives of Viet Nam veterans: Principal Investigator: A. Egendorf.

Post-Traumatic Stress Disorder and the War Veteran Patient, edited by William E. Kelley; Brunner/Mazel, New York, 1985.

Post-Traumatic Stress Disorder: Psychological and Biological Sequelae, Bessel

A. van der Kolk; American Psychiatric Press, Washington, D.C., 1984.

Post Traumatic Stress Disorders: A Handbook for Clinicians, T. Williams, Editor; Disabled American Veterans, Cincinnati, Ohio, 1987.

Strangers at Home: Vietnam Veterans since the War, C.R. Figley and Seymour Leventman, Eds.; Praeger, N.Y., 1980.

Stress Disorders Among Vietnam Veterans: Theory, Research and Treatment, C. R. Figley, Editor; New York, Brunner/Mazel, 1978.

Trauma and Its Wake: The Study and Treatment of Post-Traumatic Stress Disorder, Charles Figley, Editor; Brunner/Mazel, New York, 1985.

Trauma and Its Wake, Vol. II: Traumatic Stress Theory, Research, and Intervention, Charles Figley, Editor; Brunner/Mazel, New York, 1986

Trauma and Recovery, Judith Herman; Basic Books, New York, 1992.

Trauma and the Vietnam War Generation, Richard Kulka, et. al.; Brunner/Mazel, New York, 1990.

The Trauma of War: Stress and Recovery in Viet Nam Veterans, S. Sonnenberg, A. Blank & J. Talbott, Eds.; American Psychiatric Press, Inc., 1400 K. St., N.W. Washington, D.C., 20005.

Chapter 2

Recommended Reading

Beyond Grief: A Guide for Recovering from the Death of a Loved One, Carol Staudacher; New Harbinger Publications, Oakland, CA, 1987.

The Courage to Grieve, Jack Tatlebaum; Harper and Row, New York, 1980.

Fortunate Son, Lewis Puller; Bantam Books, New York, 1993.

Grief as a Family Process: A Developmental Approach to Clinical Practice, Ester R. Shapiro; Guilford Publications, New York, 1995.

Home-coming: When the Soldiers Returned From Vietnam, Robert Greene; G. P. Putnam's Sons, New York, 1989.

Men and Grief: A Guide for Men Surviving the Death of a Loved One, Carol Staudacher; New Harbinger Publications, Oakland, CA, 1991.

Where Light Is As Darkness, Kellan Kyllo; New Sweden Press, Minneapolis, MN, 1991.

Technical but Still Readable

"Legacies Of A War: Treatment Considerations with Viet Nam Veterans And Their Families," P. Brown; *Social Work,* July–Aug., 1984, pp. 372–379.

"The Veteran System with a Focus on Women Partners," C. M. Williams;

pp. 169–192, and "Family Therapy for Viet Nam veterans," by C. Williams and T. Williams, pp. 221–232 in *Post Traumatic Stress Disorders: A Handbook for Clinicians*, T. Williams, Ed., Disabled American Veterans, Cincinnati, Ohio, 1987.

Chapter 3

Recommended Reading

Dr. Ruth's Guide to Good Sex, Dr. Ruth Westheimer, Warner Books, New York, 1984.

Technical But Still Readable

Handbook of Sex Therapy, J. Lo Piccolo; Plenum, New York, 1978.

Human Sexual Inadequacy, W. Masters and V. Johnson; Little and Brown and Company, Boston, 1970.

The Pleasure Bond: A New Look at Sexuality and Commitment, J. Masters and V. Johnson; Little Brown and Company, Boston, 1970.

Principles and Practice of Sex Therapy, S. Leiblum and L. Pervin; The Guilford Press, New York, 1980.

The Psychology of Women, Judith Bardwick; Harper and Row, New York, 1971.

Psychology of Women: Behavior in a Biosocial Context, Juanita H. Williams; Second Edition, W. W. Norton, New York, 1983.

Survivors and Partners: Healing the Relationships of Sexual Abuse Survivor, Paul A. Hansen; Heron Hill Publishing Co., Longmont, CO, 1991

Chapter 4

Technical But Still Readable

"Fail: Bright Women," M. Homer; *Psychology Today*, 1969, 3(6), pp. 36–38, 62.

"The Measurement and Behavioral Implications of Fear of Success in Women," M. Horner in J. Atkinson and J. Raynor, (eds.,) *Motivation and Achievement*, New York, Wiley, 1974.

"Multiple Role Women," B. Sigall and A. Matsakis; *The Counseling Psychologist*, Counseling Women 111, Vol. 8, no. 1979, pp. 26–27.

Chapter 5

Recommended Reading

Addictive Drinking: The Road to Recovery for Problem Drinkers and Those Who Love Them, Clark Vaughan; Penguin Books, 40 W. 23rd St., New York, NY 10010.

Adult Children of Alcoholics, Janet Woititz; Health Communications, Deerfield Beach, FL, 1983.

The Big Book and *The Twelve Steps and Twelve Traditions*, Alcoholics Anonymous World Services, Box 459, Grand Central Station, New York, NY 10163.

Co-dependent No More, Melody Beatty, Hazelden Educational Materials, Box 176, Pleasant Valley Road, Center City, MN 55012-0176.

Dual Disorders: Counseling Clients With Chemical Dependency and Mental Illness, Dennis Daley, H. Moss, F. Campbell; Hazelden Foundation, Center City, MN, 1987.

"Facts About Alcohol and Alcoholism," "Alcohol: Some Questions and Answers," and other pamphlets on alcoholism, available from the National Clearinghouse for Alcohol Information, Box 2345, Rockville, Md. 20852.

From Chocolates to Morphine: Understanding Mind Active Drugs, by Andrew Weil and Winifred Doren, Houghton Mifflin, New York, 1983.

I'll Quit Tomorrow, Vernon E. Johnson; Harper and Row, New York, 1983.

Loving an Alcoholic: Help and Hope for Significant Others, Jack Mumey; Contemporary Books, 180 N. Michigan Avenue, Chicago, IL 60601.

Marty Mann Answers Your Questions About Drinking and Alcoholism, Marty Mann, Rev. Ed., Holt, Rinehart and Winston, New York, 1981.

Stress and Addiction, E. Gottheil, K. Druley, S. Pashko & S. Weinstein; Brunner/Mazel, New York, 1987.

A Time to Heal: The Road to Recovery for Adult Children of Alcoholics, Timmen Cermak; Avon Books, New York, 1988.

The Tranquilizing of America, Richard Hughes and Robert Brewin, New York Warner Books 1979.

Under the Influence: A Guide to the Myths and Realities of Alcoholism, James R. Milam & K. Ketchan; Bantam Books, New York, 1981.

Catalogues

Books, brochures and audio and video cassettes on all issues related to alcoholism, drug addiction and other forms of substance abuse are available through the following:

Al-Anon Family Group Headquarters
Box 862
Midtown Station
New York, N.Y. 10018-0862
212/302-7240.

Alcoholics Anonymous World Services
Box 459
Grand Central Station
New York, NY 10163
212/686-1100.

Comp-Care Publications
2415 Annapolis Lane
Minneapolis, MN 55441
800/328-3330.

Council on Alcoholism
1511 K St., NW
Washington, D.C. 20005
202/737-8122.

Hazelden Educational Materials
Box 176
Pleasant Valley Road
Center City, MN, 55012-0176
800/328-9000.

Chapter 6

Recommended Reading

The Angry Book, T. Rubin; Collier Books, Macmillan, New York, 1970.
Dr. Weisenger's Anger Work-Out Book, Hendrie Weisenger; Quill, New York, 1985.
Of Course You're Angry, Gayle Rosellini & Mark Worden; Harper/ Hazelden, San Francisco, CA, 1985
When Anger Hurts, Matthew Mc Kay, Peter Rogers & Judith McKay; New Harbinger Publications, Oakland, California, 1989.

Chapter 7

Recommended Reading

Battered Wives, Del Martin; Pocket Books, New York, 1976.

The Battered Woman, Lenore Walker; Harper and Row, New York, 1979.

Help for the Battered Woman, Lydia Savina, Bridge Publishing, Inc, S. Plainfield, New Jersey, 1987.

The Speaking Profits Us: Violence in the Lives of Women of Color, Center for the Prevention of Sexual and Domestic Violence, 1914 N. 34th St., #105, Seattle, WA 98103.

Wife-Beating: The Silent Crisis, Roger Langely and Richard Levy; E. P. Dutton, New York, 1977.

Technical But Still Readable

Battered Women: Issues of Public Policy: Consultation Sponsored by the U.S. Commission on Civil Rights, Jan., 1978, Washington, D.C.

Behind Closed Doors: Violence in the American Family, M. Strauss; R. Gelles; S. Steinmetz; Anchor Book, New York, 1970; M. Strauss; "Wife-Beating: How Common and Why?" *Victimology*, Vol. 2, No. 3–4, pp. 443–458, 1978.

Ending the Cycle of Violence: Community Responses to Children of Battered Women, Einat Peled, Peter Jaffe & Jeffrey Edeleson, Eds.; Sage Publications, Thousand Oaks, Calif., 1994.

It Could Happen to Anyone: Why Battered Women Stay, Ola W. Barnett; Sage Publications, Inc., Thousand Oaks, Calif., 1993.

Violence in the Family, Marie Borland (ed.); Atlantic Highlands, Manchester University Press, 1976.

The Violent Home, R. Gelles; London, Sage Publications, 1972.

Chapter 8

Recommended Reading

"The Battered (Military) Wife," Jane Sobie, *Ladycom* (present name, *Military Lifestyle*), August, 1980, pp. 43–46; 59–62.

Technical But Still Readable

Wife Abuse in the Armed Forces, A. West; W. Turner; E. Dunwoody; Center for Women Policy Studies, Washington, D.C., 1981.

Chapter 9

Suggested Readings: Books by African-American or African women discussing race and sex oppression.

The Color Purple, Alice Walker; Harbrace Paperback, San Diego, CA, 1982.

"Double Jeopardy: To Be Black and Female," by Frances Beal, in *Sisterhood is Powerful*, edited by Robin Morgan, Vintage Books, Random House, 1970, pp. 340–353.

The Joys of Motherhood, Buchi Emecheta; Braziler Press, New York, 1980.

A Question of Power, B. Head; Heinemann Educational Books, Portsmouth, New Hampshire, 1974.

The Salt Eaters, Toni Cade Bambara; Random House, New York, 1980.

Sassafras, Cypress, and Indigo, Ntozake Shange; St. Martin's Press, New York, 1982.

Their Eyes Were Watching God, Zora Neale Hurston; University of Illinois Press, Urbana and Chicago, 1978.

Suggested Readings: PTSD among African-American and Hispanic Vietnam Veterans

Bloods: An Oral History of the Vietnam War by Black Veterans, Wallace Terry; Ballantine Books, New York, 1984.

Technical But Still Readable

"Alcoholism in Black Vietnam Veterans: Symptoms of Post-traumatic Stress Disorder," James Carter; *Journal of the National Medical Association*, Vol. 74:7, 1982, pp. 655–660.

"Diagnosis and Treatment of Post-Traumatic Stress Disorder in Hispanic Viet Nam Veterans," Georgio Pina, 111, pp. 389–402, in *The Trauma of War: Stress and Recovery in Vietnam Veterans*, American Psychiatric Press, Inc., Washington, D.C.

Hispanic Psychology: Critical Issues in Theory and Research, Amado M. Padilla, Ed.; Sage Publications, Thousand Oaks, Calif., 1994.

"The Intercultural Setting: Encountering Black Vietnam Veterans," E.R. Parsons, in S. Sonnenberg; A. Blank; J. Talbott, *The Trauma of War: Stress and Recovery in Vietnam Veterans*, American Psychiatric Press, Inc., Washington, D.C., 1985, pp. 361–387.

"Post-Traumatic Stress Disorder Among Viet Nam Veterans," Irving Allen, *Hospital and Community Psychiatry*, Jan., 1986, Vol 37:1, pp. 55–60.

Chapter 10

Recommended Reading on Children and Family Violence and Child Abuse and Neglect

The Battered Woman, Lenore Walker; Harper and Row, New York, 1979.

"Catalogue of Materials," Clearinghouse on Child Abuse and Neglect Information, P.O. Box 1182, Washington, D.C., 22013, a listing of free and low cost pamphlets on child abuse and neglect.

Children of Trauma, Jane Middleton-Moz; Health Communications, Deerfield Beach, FL., 1989.

Help for the Battered Woman, Lydia Savina; Bridge Publishers, South Plainfield, New Jersey, 1987.

Manchild in the Promised Land, Claude Brown; MacMillan, New York, 1965.

The Other Side of the Family: A Book of Recovery from Abuse, Incest, and Neglect, Ellen Ratner; Health Communications, Deerfield, Beach, FL, 1990.

Victims No Longer: Men Recovering from Incest and Other Sexual Abuse, Mike Lew; Nevramont Publishing Co., New York, 1989.

When the Bough Breaks: A Helping Guide for Parents of Sexually Abused Children, Aphrodite Matsakis; New Harbinger Publications, Oakland, CA., 1991.

Recommended Reading on Child Sexual Assault and Incest

Kiss Daddy Goodnight, Louise Armstrong; Pocket Books, New York, 1978.

Voices in the Night, Toni McNaron and Yarrow Morgan, eds.; Cleis Press, Pittsburgh, PA, 1982.

Technical But Still Readable

The Battered Child, R. Helfer and C. Kempe; Second Edition, University of Chicago Press, Chicago, 1974.

Child Abuse and Neglect, The Family and the Community, R. Helfer and C. Kempe; Ballinger Publishing Company, Cambridge, MA, 1976.

Child Abuse Trauma: Theory and Treatment of the Lasting Effects, John Briere; Sage Publications, Thousand Oaks, Calif., 1992.

Child Sexual Abuse: New Theory and Research, David Finkelhor; Free Press, New York, 1984.

Father-Daughter Incest, Judith Herman; Harvard University Press, Cambridge, MA 1981.

Healing the Incest Wound, Christine Courtois; W. W. Norton & Co., New York, 1988.

Incest, K. Meiselman; Jossey-Bass,San Francisco, 1978.

PTSD and Children, Spencer Eth and Robert Pynoos; American Psychiatric Press, Inc., Washington, D.C., 1985.

Sexual Violence: The Unmentionable Sin, Marie Fortune; The Pilgrim Press, New York, 1983.

Sexually Abused Children, David Finkelhor; Free Press, New York, 1979.

Recommended Reading on Children and Alcoholism

Adult Children of Alcoholics, Janet Woititz; Health Communications, Pompano Beach, FL, 1983.

Guide to Recovery: A Book for Adult Children of Alcoholics, Herbert Gravitz and Julie Bowden; Learning Publications Inc., Holmes Beach, FL, 1985.

Technical But Still Readable

Children of Alcoholism, Judith Seixas and Geraldine Youcha, Harper and Row, New York, NY 10022.

"Effects of paternal exposure to prolonged stress on the mental health of the spouse and children," J.J. Sigal, *Canadian Psychiatric Association Journal*, Vol. 21, 1976, pp. 169–172.

"Impact of Post-traumatic Stress Disorder of World War II on the Next Generation," Robert Rosenheck, *The Journal of Nervous and Mental Disease*, Vol. 174:6, June, 1986, Serial No. 1243, pp. 319–327.

"Secondary traumatization in the children of Vietnam veterans with post-traumatic stress disorder," R. Rosenheck and P. Nathan; *Hospital and Community Psychiatry*, 36:5, May, 1985, pp. 538–539.

"The Viet Nam veteran and his preschool child: childrearing as a delayed stress in combat vets," Sarah Haley; *Journal of Contemporary Psychotherapy*, Vol. 14: 1, Spring/Summer, 1984, pp. 114–121.

Chapter 11

Recommended Reading

The Depression Workbook, Mary Ellen Copeland; New Harbinger Publications, Oakland, CA, 1992.

Feeling Good: The New Mood Therapy, David D. Burns; Signet Books, New American Collection, New York, 1980.

First Aid for Depression, Louis Presnall; Hazelden Educational Materials, Center City, MN, 1985.

Here Comes the Sun, Gail Rosellini and Mark Warden; Hazelden Educational Materials, Center City, MN, 1988.

Vietnam Veterans: The Road to Recovery, Joel O. Brende and Erwin R. Parson; Plenum Press, New York, 1985.
Waking Up Alive: The Descent, The Suicide Attempt and the Return to Life, Richard Heckler; Grosset Putnam Books, New York, NY, 1994.

Technical But Still Readable

Anxiety and Depression in Adults and Children, edited by Kenneth D. Craig and Keith S. Dobson; Sage Publications, Thousand Oaks, CA, 1994.
The Suicidal Patient, Victor Victoroff; Medical Economics Books, Cradell, NJ, 1983.
Suicide: Inside and Out, D.K. Reynolds and N.L. Farberow; University of California Press, Berkeley, CA, 1976.

Chapter 12

Recommended Reading

The Anxiety and Phobia Workbook, Edmund J. Bourne; New Harbinger Publications, Oakland, CA, 1990.
Chronic Pain Control Workbook, Harold Carson; New Harbinger Publications, Oakland, CA, 1987;
Farewell Darkness: A Veteran's Triumph Over Combat Trauma, Ronald Zaczek; The Naval Institute Press, Annapolis, MD, 1994
I Can't Get Over It: A Handbook for Trauma Survivors, Aphrodite Matsakis; New Harbinger Publications, Oakland, CA, 1992.
Long Time Passing: Vietnam and the Haunted Generation, M. MacPherson; Doubleday, Garden City, NJ, 1984.
The Relaxation and Stress Reduction Workbook, 3rd Edition, Martha Davis, Matthew McKay & Elizabeth Eshelman; New Harbinger Publications, Oakland, Calif., 1988.
Trauma and Recovery: The Aftermath of Violence—from Domestic Abuse to Political Terror, Judith Herman; Basic Books, New York, 1992.

Technical But Still Readable

"Individual Psychotherapy with Viet Nam Veterans," pp. 125–164 and "Rap Groups and Group Therapy for Viet Nam Veterans," pp. 165–192 by John R. Smith in *The Trauma of War: Stress and Recovery in Viet Nam Veterans*, ed. by S. Sonnenberg, A. Blank, and J. Talbott; American Psychiatric Press, Inc., Washington, D.C., 1985.
Post-Traumatic Stress Disorder: A Complete Treatment Guide, Aphrodite Matsakis; New Harbinger Publications, Oakland, California, 1994.

Post Traumatic Stress Disorders: A Handbook for Clinicians, T. Williams, Ed.; Disabled American Veterans, Cincinnati, Ohio, 1987.
"Stages of Treatment in PTSD," by Stephen T. Perconte, *VA Practitioner*, Feb. 1988, pp. 47–53.
Stress Disorders Among Vietnam Veterans: Theory, Research and Treatment, edited by Charles R. Figley; Brunner/Mazel, New York, 1978.

Chapter 13

Recommended Reading

Compassion and Self-Hate: An Alternative to Despair, T. Rubin, with Eleanor Rubin; Collier Books, Macmillan Publishing Company, New York, 1975.
The Courage to Heal: A Guide for Women Survivors of Child Sexual Abuse, Ellen Bass and Laura Davis, Harper and Row, New York, 1988.
Inner Joy: New Strategies for Adding Pleasure to Your Life, H. Bloomfield and R. Kory; a Jove Book, New York, 1985.
Living Alone and Liking It, L. Shahan; Warner Books, New York, 1981.
Necessary Losses, Judith Viorst; Fawcett Gold Medal Book, Ballantine Books, New York, 1986.
Why Do I Think I'm Nothing Without a Man?, Penelope Russianoff; Bantam Books, New York, 1965.

Help in Selecting a Therapist

Recommended Reading

Help for the Battered Woman, Part One, Chapters 13 & 17, L. Savina; Bridge Publishing Inc., S. Plainfield, NJ, 1987.
I Can't Get Over It: A Handbook for Trauma Survivors, Appendix A, Aphrodite Matsakis; New Harbinger Publications, Oakland, CA., 1993.
Notes of a Feminist Therapist, E. Williams; Praeger Publishers, New York, 1976, p. 20.
"Seeking Professional Help: Finding the Right Therapist and the Right Treatment," in *Back from the Brink: A Family Guide to Overcoming Traumatic Stress*, Don R. Catherall; Bantam, New York, 1992.
Women and Madness, Phyllis Chesler; Avon Books, New York, 1972.

Technical But Still Readable

"'Kinde, Kuche, Kirche' as Scientific Law: Psychology Constructs the Female," Naomi Weisstein; pp. 228–244 in *Sisterhood is Powerful*, Robin Morgan; Vintage Books, Random House, New York, 1970.

"Mother Blaming in Major Clinical Journals," P. Capland and I. Hall Mc-Corquodale; *American Journal of Orthopsychiatry*, 55 (3), July, 1985, pp. 345–353.

Towards a New Psychology of Women, Jean Baker Miller; Beacon Press, Boston, 1976.

Eating Disorders—General

Dying to Please: Anorexia Nervosa and Its Cure, Avis Rumney; McFarland, Jefferson, NC, 1983.

Fat and Furious: Women and Food Obsession, Judith Hollis; Ballantine Books, New York, 1993.

Fat is a Family Affair, Judith Hollis; Harper and Row, San Francisco, 1985.

The Nutritional Ages of Women: A Lifelong Guide to Eating Right for Health, Beauty and Well-Being, Patricia Long; MacMillan Publishing Co., New York, 1986.

Starving for Attention, Cherry Boone O'Neill; New York, Continuum Books, 1982.

A catalogue of pamphlets and books on food addiction is available from Hazelden Educational Materials, Box 176, Pleasant Valley Road, Center City, MN 55012-0176, (800) 328-9000.

See also books on eating disorders listed in the chapter entitled, "Coping Techniques for the Vietnam Wife."

Technical But Still Readable

Anorexia Nervosa: A Multidimensional Perspective, P. Garfinkel and D. Garner; Brunner/Mazel, New York, 1982.

Eating Disorders: Obesity, Anorexia Nervosa, and the Person Within, Hilda Bruch; Basic Books, New York, 1979.

The Golden Cage: The Enigma of Anorexia Nervosa, Hilda Bruch; New York, Random House, 1979.

Treating and Overcoming Anorexia Nervosa, Steven Levenkron; Scribner, New York, 1982.

Notes

Introduction

1. Anonymous, "The Best Years of Our Lives," Vet Center, Fort Wayne, Indiana, 1985.

2. Idem.

3. Lyons, Richard, D., "Vietnam Veterans Turn to Therapy," The New York Times, Nov. 13, 1964; Personal communication, Kerry Merback, National Readjustment Counseling Service, Feb. 1988.

4. Jennings, Ben, as cited in "Veteran Centers Offer Refuge To All Who Served in Vietnam," by Marcie Ritz, *The Montgomery Journal*, Nov. 10, 1986, p. A-8; Lyons, op. cit.; Houston Vietnam Veteran Leadership Program, "Vietnam Veteran Leadership Fact Sheet," compiled by Richard K. Kolb, Chairman, PO Box 77091, Houston, TX, March 20, 1985, pp. 3–4 (data taken from "Veterans in the U.S.: A Statistical Portrait," 1980 Census); Blank, Arthur S., "Irrational Reactions to Post-Traumatic Stress Disorder and Vietnam Veterans," pp. 69–98 in Sonnenberg, S.; Blank, A; Talbott, J., *The Trauma of War*, American Psychiatric Press, Inc., Washington, D.C., 1985; Harris L. and Associates, "Myths and realities: A Study of Attitudes Toward Vietnam Era Veterans," Submitted by the Veterans Admin-

istration to the Committee on Veterans Affairs, US Senate, Senate Committee Print No. 29, U.S. Government Printing Office, Washington, DC, 1980; Carter, J., "Message to Congress, Vietnam Era veterans" Oct. 10, 1978, Weekly Compilation, Presidential Documents 14, 1737–1742, 1978; Blank, A., "Discussion of Papers on the Psychological Problems of Vietnam Veterans," Annual Meeting of the American Psychiatric Association, San Francisco, 1980; Blank, A., "Vietnam Veterans—Operation Outreach," presented at the First Training Conference on Vietnam Veterans, St Louis, Missouri, 1979; Kulka, Richard, et al., *The National Vietnam Veteran Readjustment Study*, Research Triangle Park, North Carolina, November, 1988.

   5. Kulka, et al., op. cit.

CHAPTER ONE

   1. *Vietnam Veteran*, August 1980, as cited on p. 293 in Blank, Arthur S., Jr. "The Unconscious Flashback to the War in Vietnam Veterans: Clinical Mystery, Legal Defense and Community Problem," in *The Trauma of War: Stress and Recovery in Vietnam Veterans*, edited by Sonnenberg, S., Blank, A., Talbott, A., American Psychiatric Press, 1985, pp. 293–320.

   2. Sorenson, Gary, "Hinterlands are home, not a hideaway, for Vietnam veterans," *Vet Center Voice*, Vol. VI, No. 9, October, 1985, p. 1.

   3. *Diagnostic and Statistical Manual of Mental Disorders*, Third Edition, (DSM III-R), American Psychiatric Association, 1987, Washington, D.C., pp. 247–251; *Diagnostic and Statistical Manual of Mental Disorders*, Fourth Edition (DSM IV), American Psychiatric Association, 1995, Washington, D.C., pp. 424–432.

   4. Vercozzi, Carol, "The War that Refused to Die: Vietnam Again," unpublished paper, Department of Communications, Hartford, Massachusetts; p. 3, Silverman, Joel, "Post-Traumatic Stress Disorder," *Advanced Psychosomatic Medicine*, Vol. 16: 115–140, 1986.

   5. DSM III, op. cit., pp. 247–251; DSM IV, op. cit., pp. 424–432; Vercozzi, Carol, "The War That Refused to Die: Vietnam Again," unpublished paper, Department of Communications, Hartford, MA; Silverman, Joel, "Post-Traumatic Stress Disorder," *Advanced Psychosomatic Medicine*, Vol. 16, pp. 115–140, 1986. Gaines-Carter, Patrice, "Salvadoran Pupils Here Still at War," *The Washington Post*, Tuesday, Oct. 15, 1985, pp. 1, 8. Terr, Leonore C., "Chowchilla Revisited: Effects of psychic trauma four years after a school bus kidnapping," *American Journal of Psychiatry*, 1983, 140:1543–1550. Wilkinson, Charles B., "Aftermath of a Disaster: The Collapse of the Hyatt Regency Hotel Skywalks," *American Journal of Psychiatry*, 1983, 140:1134–1139. Green, Bonnie L.; Grace, Mary C., et al. "Levels of Functional Impairment Following a Civilian Disaster: The Beverly Hills Supper Club Fire," *Journal of Consulting and Clinical Psychology*, 1983, Vol. 51, No. 4, pp. 573–580. McFarlane, Alexander, C. "Post-traumatic Morbidity of a Disaster: A study of cases presenting for psychiatric treatment," *Journal of Nervous and Mental Disease*, 1986, Vol. 174: 1, pp. 4–11.

   6. Gaines-Carter, Patrice, "Salvadoran Pupils Here Still at War," *The Wash-

ington Post, Tuesday, Oct. 15, 1985, pp. 1, 8; Blake, Dudley; Albano, Anne & Keane, Terence, "Twenty Years of Trauma: Psychological Abstracts 1970 Through 1989," *Journal of Traumatic Stress*, 1992, Vol. 5, No. 3, pp. 477–484; Herman, Judith, "Complex PTSD: A Syndrome in Survivors of Prolonged and Repeated Trauma," *Journal of Traumatic Stress*, Vol. 5, No. 3, July, 1992, pp. 377–392.

7. *Diagnostic and Statistical Manual of Mental Disorders*, Third Edition, (DSM III), American Psychiatric Association, 1980, Washington, D.C., pp. 236–238; Herman, 1992, op. cit., p. 380.

8. Haley, Sarah, "I Feel A Little Sad: The Application of Object Relations Theory to the Hypnotherapy of Post Traumatic Stress Disorders in Vietnam Veterans," Society for Clinical and Experimental Hypnosis, San Antonio, Texas, October 25, 1984.

9. Williams, Candice, "Peace Time Combat," in *PTSD: A Handbook for Clinicians*, edited by Williams, T., Disabled American Veterans, Cincinnati, Ohio, 1987, pp. 267–293.

10. Green, Bonnie; Grace, M.; Glesser, G., "Identifying Survivors at Risk: Long Term Impairment Following the Beverly Hills Supper Club Fire," *Journal of Consulting and Clinical Psychology*, 1985, Vol. 53: no. 5, pp. 672–678; Modlin, J., "PTSD: No Longer Just For War Veterans," *Post Graduate Medicine*, Vol. 79:3, Feb. 15, 1986, pp. 26–44; Mc Farlane, Alexander, "Post Traumatic Morbidity of a Disaster," *Journal of Nervous and Mental Disease*, 1986, Vol. 174, no. 1, pp. 4–14.

11. Williams, Candice, op. cit., 1987, p. 267.

12. Bard, Morton, "Forward," in Williams, T., *PTSD: A Handbook for Clinicians*, op. cit., p.iii.

13. Gerdemen, Eric, Vet Center Program, Region II, Baltimore, Md., "PTSD and the Vietnam Veteran," unpublished paper, 1984.

14. The list of symptoms of PTSD is taken from a DAV (Disabled American Veterans Project) called "The Forgotten Warrior Project," conducted by Dr. John Wilson at Cleveland State University, and is cited in Rick Ritter's "Bringing the War Home: Vets Who Have Battered," Vet Center, Ft. Wayne, Indiana, 1984, p. 8.

15. Arnold, Arthur, "Diagnosis of Post-Traumatic Stress Disorder in Vietnam Veterans," in *The Trauma of War: Stress and Recovery in Vietnam Veterans*, edited by Sonnenberg, S.; Blank, A.; Talbott, A., American Psychiatric Press, 1985, p. 103.

16. Ziarowsky, Peter A. and Broida, Daniel C., "Therapeutic implications of nightmares of Vietnam combat veterans," *The V.A. Practitioner*, July, 1984, Vol. 1, No. 7, pp. 63, 67, 68.

17. Ziarowsky, et al., pp. 67–68

18. Arnold, op. cit., p. 104.

19. Blank, op. cit., p. 296.

20. Jaffe, R., "Dissociative phenomenon in former concentration camp inmates," *International Journal of Psychoanalysis*, 49: 310–312, 1968; Herman, 1994, op. cit.

21. Niederland, W.G., "Clinical observations on the survivor syndrome," *International Journal of Psychoanalysis*, 49: 313–315, 1968.

22. Grinker, R. R. and Spiegel, I. P., *Men Under Stress*, New York, McGraw, Hill, 1945.

23. Blank, op. cit., p. 297.

24. Blank, op. cit., p. 297.

25. Blank, op. cit., p. 297.

26. Blank, op. cit., pp. 295–296.

27. Blank, op. cit., p. 305.

28. Blank, op. cit., p. 104.

29. Arnold, op. cit., p. 104.

30. Vercozzi, op. cit., p. 3; Goodwin, Jim, Psy. D., *Continuing Readjustment Problems Among Vietnam Veterans: The Etiology of Combat Related Post-Traumatic Stress Disorders*, published by the Disabled American Veteran's National Headquarters, P.O. Box 14301, Cincinnati, Ohio, 45214, p. 6; Grinker, R. P. and Spiegel, J. P., *Men Under Stress*, McGraw Hill, New York, 1963, p. 28.

31. *Congressional Record*-Senate, S 10062–10072, July 15, 1987.

32. Goodwin, Jim, op. cit., p. 5; Lipton, Merril and Shaeffer, W., "PTSD in the Older Veteran," *Military Medicine*, Vol. 151, Oct. 1986, 522–526.

33. Glass, A.J., "Introduction," in P.G. Bourne (Ed.), *The Psychology and Physiology of Stress*, N. Y. Academic Press, 1969, xiv–xxx.

34. Bourne, P.G., *Men, Stress, and Vietnam*, Boston, Little & Brown, 1970.

35. Futterman, S. and Pumpian-Midlin E., "Traumatic war neuroses five years later," *American Journal of Psychiatry*, 195;, 108 (6): 401–408.

36. Thienes-Hontons, P., Watson, C., and Kucala T., "Stress disorder symptoms in Vietnam and Korean war veterans," *Journal of Consulting and Clinical Psychology*, 1982, 50, pp. 558–561; Caroll, Edward, "Stress Disorder Symptoms in Vietnam and Korean War Veterans: A commentary on Thienes-Hontos, Watson, and Kucala," *Journal of Consulting and Clinical Psychology*, 1983, Vol. 51:4, No. 4, 616–618; Thienes-Hontos, P., "Stress-Disorder Symptoms in Vietnam and Korean War Veterans: Still No Difference," *Journal of Consulting and Clinical Psychology*, 1983, Vol. 51:4, 619–620.

37. Streimer, J. H., "The Psychosocial Adjustment of Australian Vietnam Veterans," *American Journal of Psychiatry*, 142:5: May, 1985, 616–618.

38. Bowman, Bruce, et al., "Psychiatric Disturbances Among Australian Vietnam Veterans," *Military Medicine*, Vol. 150, 2: 77–79, Feb., 1985. Bowman, Bruce, "Post-traumatic Stress Disorder (Traumatic War Neurosis) and Concurrent Psychiatric Illness Among Australian Vietnam Veterans: A Controlled Study," *T.R. Army Medical Corps*, 1985, 131, pp. 128–138.

39. Solomon, Zahava, et al., "The 'Koach' Project for Treatment of Combat-Related PTSD: Rationale, Aims, and Methodology," *Journal of Traumatic Stress*, 1992, Vol. 5. No. 2, pp. 175–194.

40. La Guardian, R., et al., 1982, "Incidence of delayed stress among Vietnam era veterans: the effects of priming on response set," *American Journal of Orthopsychiatry*, 42 (3): 000–010; Frye, J. and Stockton, R., "Discriminant analysis of post-traumatic stress disorders among a group of Vietnam veterans," *American Journal of Psychiatry*, 1982, 139, pp. 52–56.

41. Harrington, David, "Who's Conning Whom?" *Veteran*, Washington, D.C., October, 1986, p. 22.

42. Houston Vietnam Veteran Leadership Program, "Vietnam Veteran Fact Sheet," compiled by Richard K. Kolb, Chairman, P.O. Box 77091, Houston, Texas, March 20, 1985, p. 4. (Data taken from "Veterans in the U.S.: A Statistical Portrait," 1980 Census.)

43. Kulka, R. A., Schlenger, William E., Fairbank, John A., Hough, Richard B., Jordan, Kathleen, Marmar, Charles R., and Weiss, Daniel, S., *National Vietnam Veterans Readjustment Study (NVVRS)*, Brunner/Mazel, New York, 1990.

44. *NVVRS*, op. cit.; Lyons, Richard, D., "Vietnam Veterans Turn to Therapy," *The New York Times*, Nov. 13, 1964, Houston Vietnam Veteran Leadership Program, op. cit., p. 3; Blank, Arthur S., "Irrational Reactions to Post-Traumatic Stress Disorder and Vietnam Veterans," pp.69–98 in Sonnenberg, et al., *The Trauma of War*, op. cit.; Harris, L. and Associates, "Myths and realities: A Study of attitudes toward Vietnam era veterans," Submitted by the Department of Veterans Affairs to the Committee on Veteran Affairs, U.S. Senate, Senate Committee Print No. 29, U.S. Government Printing Office, Washington, D.C., 1980; Carter, J. "Message to Congress, Vietnam era veterans," October 10, 1978, *Weekly Compilation, Presidential Documents* 14, 1737–1742, 1978; Blank, A., "Discussion of Papers on the Psychological Problems of Vietnam Veterans," Annual Meeting of the American Psychiatric Association, San Francisco, 1980; Blank, A., "Vietnam Veterans-Operation Outreach," presented at the First Training Conference on Vietnam Veterans, St. Louis, Mo., 1979. Walker, J. I., and Cavenar, J. O., "Vietnam Veterans: Their Problems Continue," *The Journal of Nervous and Mental Disease*, Vol. 170, No. 3, pp. 174–180, p. 176.

45. Jennings, Ben, as cited in "Veteran Centers Offer Refuge To All Who Served in Vietnam," by Marcie Ritz, *The Montgomery Journal*, Nov. 10, 1986, p. A-6.

46. "Integrity vs. Despair: Trauma, Grief, and the Older Adult," Audio Tape 73, International Society for Traumatic Stress Studies, 10th annual meeting, Chicago, Illinois, 1995.

47. Blank, Arthur, "Irrational Reactions to Post-Traumatic Stress Disorder and Vietnam Veterans," op. cit. in *The Trauma of War: Stress and Recovery in Vietnam Veterans*, edited by Sonnenberg, S. and Blank, A.

48. Walker, I., Cavenar, J. O., "Vietnam Veterans: Their Problems Continue," *The Journal of Nervous and Mental Disease*, Vol. 170, No. 3, p. 174–180, Figley, Charles, Ed. *Stress Disorders Among Vietnam Veterans*, Brunner Mazel, Publishers, N.Y., 1978; Yesavage, Jerome, "Dangerous Behavior by Vietnam Veterans with Schizophrenia," *American Journal of Psychiatry*, 140: 9, September, 1983, pp. 1180–1183.

49. Houston Vietnam Veteran Leadership Program, op. cit., p. 4.

50. Gerdeman, op. cit.

51. Kolb, Richard K. Chairman, Houston Vietnam Veteran Leadership Program, Inc., P. O. Box 77091, Houston, Texas, 77213, "Vietnam Veteran Statistics," March 20, 1985, p. 3.

52. Gerdeman, op. cit., Vercozzi, op. cit.

53. Wilson, John, as cited in "Vietnam Veterans Turn to Therapy" by Richard D. Lyons, *The New York Times*, Nov. 13, 1984, p. 5.

54. Gerdeman, op. cit.

55. Kolb, op. cit., p. 3.

56. Kolb, op. cit., p. 4.

57. Kolb, op. cit., p. 3.

58. Idem.

59. Wilson, op. cit., p. 4, p. 2.

60. Downs, Frederick, *The Killing Zone: My Life in the Vietnam War*, New York, W.W. Norton and Co., 1978, as cited in Blank, A., "Irrational Reactions," op. cit., pp. 72–73.

61. Vercozzi, op. cit., Blank, "Irrational Reactions," op. cit.

62. Frye, S. and Stockton, R., "Discriminant analysis of PTSD among a group of Vietnam veterans," *American Journal of Psychiatry*, Vol. 139: 1, January, 1982, pp. 52–56.

63. Figley, Charles, "Delayed Stress Response," *Journal of Marriage and Family Counseling*, 4(3): 53–60, 1978.

64. Laufer, Robert S., "War Trauma and Human Development, The Vietnam Experience," in Sonnenberg, et al., *The Trauma of War*, op. cit., pp. 31–67; Frye, op. cit.

65. Gault, W. B., "Some Remarks on Slaughter," *American Journal of Psychiatry*, 128:4, Oct., 1971, pp. 82–86.

66. Laufer, op. cit., p. 48.

67. Houston Vietnam Veteran Leadership Program, "Vietnam Veteran Fact Sheet," compiled by Richard K. Kolb, Chairman, P.O. Box 77091, Houston, Texas, March 20, 1985, p. 4. (Data taken from "Veterans in the U.S.: A Statistical Portrait," 1980 Census.)

68. Futterman, op. cit., p.402.

69. "Integrity vs. Despair," Audio Tape 73, op. cit.

70. As cited in Pentland, Bruce and Dwyer, James, "Incarcerated Vietnam Veterans," pp. 405–416, in Sonnenberg, et al., *The Trauma of War*, p. 405.

71. Cruden, John, "Veteran's spiritual needs arise in counseling sessions," *Vet Center Voice*, Vol. VI, No. 11, December, 1985, p. 6–9; Sorenson, Gary, "Veterans struggle to integrate war and values," *Vet Center Voice*, Vol. VI, No 11, December, 1985, p. 5–6; Devine, Patrick, Fr. "PTSD shadows moral/spiritual dimension," *Vet Center Voice*, Vol. VI, No. 6, July 1985, pp. 1, 9.

72. Melton, Roger, "Ideals, Death, Betrayal are central to PTSD Theme," Vet Center, Ft. Wayne, Indiana, 1969; Marin, Peter, *Psychology Today*, Nov., 1981, pp. 68–80.

73. Holloway, Harry C., Ursano, Robert J. "Vietnam Veterans On Active Duty: Adjustment in a Supportive Environment," pp. 323–338, in Sonnenberg, et al., *The Trauma of War*.

74. Leventman, Seymour, "Epilogue: Social and Historical Perspectives on the Vietnam Veteran," pp. 291–295 in Figley, C., Ed., *Stress Disorders Among Vietnam Veterans: Theory, Research and Treatment*, Brunner/Mazel, Publishers, New York, 1978, p. 295.

75. Herman, Judith, *The Aftermath of Violence—From Domestic Abuse to Political Terror*, Basic Books, New York, 1992.

76. van der Kolk, Bessel, *Psychological Trauma*, American Psychiatric Press,

Washington, D. C., 1987; van der Kolk, Bessel, "The drug treatment of PTSD," Journal of Affective Disorders, 13, pp. 203–213, 1987; van der Kolk, Bessel, "The Trauma Spectrum: The interaction of biological and social events in the genesis of the trauma response," *Journal of Traumatic Stress Studies*, 1: 273–290, 1988.

77. van der Kolk, Bessel, "The Compulsion to Repeat the Trauma," *Psychiatric Clinics of North America*, Vol. 12, No. 1, p. 389–409, 1989.

78. Herman, 1992, op. cit.

79. Matsakis, Aphrodite, *I Can't Get Over It—A Handbook for Trauma Survivors*, New Harbinger Publications, Oakland, California, 1994.

80. Kardiner, A., *The Traumatic Neuroses of War*, Hoeber, New York, 1941.

81. van der Kolk, op. cit., 1987.

82. Wilson, R.R., *Breaking the Panic Cycle: For People with Phobias*, Phobia Society of America (now called Anxiety Disorders Association), Rockville, Md., 1987.

CHAPTER TWO

1. Gerdeman, Eric, "PTSD and the Vietnam Veteran," unpublished paper, Vietnam Veteran Outreach Center, Silver Spring, Md. 20902, 1985, p. 1.

2. Idem.

3. Idem. p. 2.

4. Anonymous, "The Best Years of Our Lives," Vet Center, Fort Wayne, Indiana, 1985.

5. Walker, J. and Cavenar, O., op. cit., p. 174–180; Vercozzi, op. cit., Gerdeman, op. cit.

6. Santoli, 1981, as cited in Vercozzi, op. cit., p. 10.

7. Goodwin, Jim, "Readjustment Problems Among Vietnam Veterans," Disabled American Veterans, National Headquarters, PO Box 14301, Cincinnati, Ohio 45214. Wilson, John, *Identity, ideology, and crises: The Vietnam veteran in transition*, Pt. 2, Cincinnati, Ohio, Disabled American Veterans, 1978; Egendorf, A.; Kaduschin, C.; Laufer, R.; Rothbart, G.; Sloan, L.; *Legacies of Vietnam: Comparative adjustment of veterans and their peers*, 5 volumes, New York: Center for Policy Research, 1981; Egendorf, A.; Laufer, R.; Sloan, L., *Legacies of Vietnam: Comparative adjustment of veterans and their peers: Overview of the report*, Washington, D.C., U.S. Government Printing Office, 1981; Penk, W., et al., "Interpersonal problems of Vietnam combat veterans with symptoms of PTSD," *Journal of Abnormal Psychology*, 1982, Vol. 91:6, 444–450; Penk, W., et al., "Adjustment differences among male substance abusers varying in degrees of combat experience in Vietnam," *Journal of Consulting and Clinical Psychology*, 1981: 49:3, 426–437; Frye, T. S. and Stockton, R.A., "Discriminant analysis of PTSD among a group of Vietnam veterans," *American Journal of Psychiatry*, Vol. 139: 1, January 1982, pp. 52–56; Palmer, S. and Harris, D., "Supportive group therapy for women partners of Vietnam veterans," *Family Therapist*, 4(2), 3–11, 1983; Blank, Arthur S., "Psychological Aspects in the Vietnam War," in Charles A. Stenger (chair), *Vietnam Veterans: Traumatic effects and post war adjustment problems, treatment approaches*, symposium presented at the meeting of the American Psychological Association,

Montreal, Canada, Sept. 1980; Fairbank, John; Keane, T. M.; Malloy, P. "Some Preliminary Data on the Psychological Characteristics of Vietnam Veterans with Posttraumatic Stress Disorders," *Journal of Consulting and Clinical Psychology,* 1983, Vol. 51, No. 6: 912–919; Keane, T. M. and Fairbank, J.A., "A Survey analysis of combat-related stress disorders in Vietnam veterans," *American Journal of Psychiatry,* 1983, 140, 348–350; Carroll, Edward, et al. "Vietnam combat veterans with Post-traumatic Stress Disorder: Analysis of Marital and Cohabitating Adjustment," *Journal of Abnormal Psychology,* 1985: Vol. 94, No. 3, 329–337; Van Kampen, Melodie; Watson, Charles; Tilleskjor, Curt; Kucala, Teresa; Vassar, Patricia, "The Definition of Posttraumatic Stress Disorder in Alcoholic Vietnam Veterans," *The Journal of Nervous and Mental Disease,* Vol. 173:3, 1986, pp. 137–144.

8. Cruden, John, "Vet Center staff members analyze homeless situation," *Vet Center Voice,* Vol. 8: No. 2, 1987, pp. 3–7.

9. Flynn, Charles and Teguis, Alexandra, "Grief and the Treatment of PTSD," unpublished paper, Manchester Community College, 1985. Address all correspondence to Charles Flynn, Department of Sociology and Anthropology, Miami University, Oxford, Ohio, 45056.

10. Scaturo, Douglas and Hayman, Peter, "The Impact of Combat Trauma Across the Family Life Cycle: Clinical considerations," *Journal of Traumatic Stress Studies,* Vol. 5:2, April, 1990, pp. 273–288, p. 282.

11. Scaturo and Hayman, op. cit., p. 282.

12. Daniel, Yail, "As Survivors Age," *PTSD Quarterly,* Vol. 4:1, Winter, 1994, p. 1–7.

13. Rosenbeck, Robert, "The Role of Family Therapy in the Treatment of PTSD," Unpublished paper, presented at "Diagnosis and Management of Post-Traumatic Stress Disorders in the V.A.," V.A. Mid-Atlantic Regional Medical Education Center, Baltimore, Md., Aug. 21, 1985.

14. As cited in "The War That Has No Ending," by John Lagone, *Discover,* June, 1985, pp. 44–54.

CHAPTER THREE

1. Masters, William and Johnson, Virginia, *The Pleasure Bond: A New Look at Sexuality and Commitment,* Little, Brown and Company, Boston, 1970; Moustakas, Clark, E., *Loneliness,* Spectrum Book, Prentice-Hall, Inc., Detroit, 1961; Bardwick, J., *The Psychology of Women,* Harper and Row, New York, 1971; Williams, J., *The Psychology of Women: Behavior in a Biosocial Context,* Second Edition, W. W. Norton, New York, 1983.

2. Masters and Johnson, op. cit., p. 29.

3. Bardwick, op. cit.; Williams, op. cit.

4. Carroll, Edward M.; Rueger, Drue B.; Foy, David W.; Donahoe, Clyde P., "Vietnam Combat Veterans with Posttraumatic Stress Disorder: An Analysis of Marital and Cohabitating Adjustment," *Journal of Abnormal Psychology,* 1985, Vol. 94:3, pp. 329–337.

5. Egendorf, A.; Kadushin, C.; Laufer, R.; Rothbard, G.; Sloan, L., *Legacies of Vietnam: Comparative adjustment of veterans and their peers,* Vol. 3, Center for Pol-

icy Research, Inc., New York, March, 1981; Yaeger, T.; Laufer, R.; Gallops, M., "Some problems associated with war experience in men of the Vietnam generation," *Archives of General Psychiatry*, Vol. 41, April, 1984, pp. 327–333.

6. Modelin, H., "Post Traumatic Stress Disorder: No Longer Just for War Veterans," *Postgraduate Medicine*, Vol. 79, no. 3, Feb. 15, 1986, pp. 26–29, 32, 37.

7. Matsakis, Aphrodite "The Effects of PTSD on Family Life," Research Project, Psychology Service, Veterans Administration, Washington, D.C. 1988.

8. Klonoff, H.; Mc Dougall, G.; Clark, C.; Kramer, P.; Horgan, I., "The neuropsychological, psychiatric, and physical effects of prolonged and severe stress: 30 years later," *The Journal of Nervous and Mental Disease*, Vol. 163: No. 4, pp. 246, 252.

9. Masters and Johnson, op. cit., Bardwick, op. cit., Leiblum, Sandra R., and Pervin, Lawrence, A., Eds., *Principles and Practice of Sex Therapy*, The Guilford Press, New York, 1980.

10. Reich, Wilhelm, *The Function of the Orgasm: The Discovery of the Orgone*, The World Publishing Company, New York, 1971, pp. 138, 240.

11. Reich, op. cit., p. 240.

12. Reich, op. cit., describes the same masochistic thoughts in some of his patients, p. 81.

13. Kuhne, et al., as cited in "The Definition of Posttraumatic Stress Disorder in Alcoholic Vietnam Veterans," VanKampen, Melodie; Watson, Charles; Tilleskjor, Curt; Kucala, Theresa; Vassar, Patricia, *The Journal of Nervous and Mental Disease*, Vol. 174, no. 3; pp. 137–144, Kampen, et al., op. cit.

14. Vercozzi, op. cit., p. 8.

15. Reich, op. cit., p. 82.

16. Reich, op. cit., pp. 298–99.

17. Reich, op. cit.

18. Masters and Johnson, op. cit., Masters W. H. and Johnson, V.E., *Human Sexual Inadequacy*, Boston, Little, Brown & Company, 1970; O'Connor, J. F., *Sexual problems, therapy and prognostic factors*, in J.K. Meyer (Ed). *Clinical Management of Sexual Disorders*, Baltimore, Md., Williams and Wilkins, 1976; Leiblum and Pervin, op. cit.; Fischer, Joel and Gochros, Harvey, *Handbook of Behavior Therapy with Sexual Problems, Volumes 1&2*, Pergamon Press, New York, 1977.

19. Bardwick, op. cit., Masters and Johnson, *The Pleasure Bond*, op. cit.

20. Walker, Lenore, *The Battered Woman*, Harper and Row, N.Y., 1979.

21. Bardwick, op. cit., p. 69.

CHAPTER FOUR

1. Wyman, Elizabeth and McLaughlin, Mary E., "Traditional Wives and Mothers," *Counseling Women III, The Counseling Psychologist*, Vol. 8., No. 1, 1979, pp. 24–26.

2. Idem., Bardwick, Judith, *The Psychology of Women*, Harper and Row, New York, 1971.

3. "Twenty Facts on Women Workers," U.S. Department of Labor, Office of the Secretary, Women's Bureau, Washington, D. C., 1986.

4. Matsakis, A. and Sigall, B., "Multiple Role Women," *The Counseling Psychologist, Counseling Women III*, Vol. 8, no. 1979, pp. 26–27.

5. Matsakis and Sigall, op. cit., p. 26.

6. Idem.

7. Idem.

8. Idem.

9. Bardwick, Judith, *The Psychology of Women*, Harper and Row, New York, 1971.

10. Matsakis and Sigall, op. cit., p. 27; Horner, M. "Fail: Bright Women," *Psychology Today*, 1969 3(6), 36–38, 62, Horner, M., "The measurement and behavioral implications of fear of success in women," in J. Atkinson and J. Raynor (Eds.), *Motivation and Achievement*, New York, Wiley, 1974.

CHAPTER FIVE

1. Boscarino, Joseph, "Current Drug Involvement among Vietnam and non-Vietnam veterans," *American Journal of Drug and Alcohol Abuse*, 6(3), 1979, pp. 301–312. Nace, E. P.; O'Brien, C. P.; Mintz, I., et al., "Adjustment among Vietnam veteran drug users two years post service," in *Stress Disorders Among Vietnam veterans: Theory, research and treatment*, C. R. Figley (ed.) Brunner/Mazel, 1978, pp. 71–128.

2. Boscarino, 1979, op. cit., p. 302.

3. Nace, et al., op. cit.

4. Idem.

5. Robins, L.N., *The Vietnam Drug User Returns, Special Action Office Monograph*, Series A, No. 2, 1974, U S. Government Printing Office, Washington, D.C.; Robins, L.N., "Veterans' Drug Use Three Years After Vietnam," St. Louis, Department of Psychiatry, Washington University School of Medicine, 1974; Nace, et al., op. cit.; O'Donnell, J. A., Voss, H. J. H., Clayton, R. R., "Young Men and Drugs—A Nationwide Survey," Washington, D.C. U.S. Government Printing Office, 1976. Ray, M.B., "The cycle of abstinence and relapse among heroin addicts," Social Problems, 1961, pp. 132– 140; Waldorf., D., Careers in Dope, Prentice-Hall, Englewood Cliffs, New Jersey, 1973; O'Donnell, J., et al., op. cit.; Duvall, H. J.; Locke, B. Z.; Brill, L. "Follow up study of narcotic addicts five years after hospitalization," *Public Health Rep.* 78: 1963, pp. 185–193.

6. Lacoursiere, Roy and Coyne, L., "Comment on Roy's 'Alcohol Misuse and PTSD (Delayed): An Alternative Interpretation of the Data,'" *Journal of Studies on Alcohol*, Vol. 45:3, 1984, pp. 283–237; Boscarino, op. cit., 1980; Branchey, L., Davis, W., and Lieber, C., "Alcoholism in Vietnam and Korea Veterans: A Long Term Follow Up," *Alcoholism: Clinical and Experimental Research*, Vol. 8: No. 6, Nov./Dec., 1984, pp. 572– 575; Wish, E.; Robins, L.; Hesselbrock, M.; Heltzer, J.; "The course of alcohol problems in Vietnam veterans," in Seixas, F. (Ed); *Currents in Alcoholism*, Vol. 4, New York, Grune and Stratton, pp. 230–256; 1979; Robbins, L.; Hesselbrock, M.; Wish, E., "Polydrug and alcohol use by veterans and non-veterans," in Smith, D.E., Editor, *A Multicultural View of Drug Abuse*, Pro-

ceedings of the National Drug Abuse Conference, 1977, Cambridge, MA, GK Hall, 1978, pp. 74–90.

7. Sierles, Chen, McFarland, Taylor, op. cit.; Lindy, J.D.; Grace, M.C.; Green, B.J., "Building a conceptual bridge between civilian trauma and war trauma: Preliminary psychological findings from a clinical sample of Vietnam veterans" in B.A. Van Der Kolk (ed.), *Post-traumatic stress disorder: Psychological and Biological Sequelae*, pp. 43–58, Washington, D.C., American Psychiatric Press, Inc. 1984; Lacoursiere, et al., op. cit.; Schnitt, J., and Nocks, J., "Alcoholism Treatment of Vietnam Veterans with Post-Traumatic Stress Disorder," *Journal of Substance Abuse Treatment*, Vol. 1, pp. 179–189, 1984; Jelinek, I. M. and William, T., "Post-Traumatic Stress Disorder and Substance Abuse in Vietnam Combat Veterans: Treatment Problems, Strategies and Recommendations," *Journal of Substance Abuse Treatment*, Vol. 1, 87–97, 1984; Krystal, H. "Psychoanalytic view on human emotional damages," in B. A. van der Kolk (ed.), op. cit., pp. 1–28.

8. Robins, L. N., *The Vietnam Drug User Returns*, U.S. Government Printing Office, Washington, D.C., 1973; Nace, et al., op. cit.; Sanders, C. R., "Doper's wonderland: Functional drug use by military personnel in Vietnam," *J. Drug Issues* 3: 65–78, 1975; Boscarino, 1979, op. cit.

9. Holloway, H., and Ursano, R., in *Trauma of War*, op. cit., p. 324.

10. Jones, F.D. and Johnson, A.W., "Medical psychiatric treatment policy and practice in Vietnam," *Journal of Social Issues: Soldiers In and After Vietnam*, 1975, 31(4), 49–65.

11. Goodwin, Jim, "The Etiology of Combat-Related Post-Traumatic Stress Disorders," in *Post-Traumatic Stress Disorders of the Vietnam Veteran*, Tom Williams, ed., Disabled American Veterans, National Headquarters, P.O. Box 14301, Cincinnati, Ohio 45214, 1980, p. 9.

12. Holloway, op. cit., p. 324.

13. Idem.

14. Vercozzi, op. cit., Goodwin, op. cit.

15. Goodwin, op. cit., p. 9.

16. Schnitt, J. and Nocks, J., op. cit.; Lindy, Grace, and Taylor, op. cit.; Lacoursiere, Godfrey and Ruby, op. cit.

17. Milam, J. and Ketcham, K., *Under the Influence: A Guide to the Myths and Realities of Alcoholism*, Bantam Books, N.Y., 1981, p. 33.

18. *Drug Abuse Facts*, Nelson Taxel, 1971, Woodmere, N.Y., 11598.

19. De Fazio, Victor and Pascucci, N., "Return to Ithaca: A Perspective on Marriage and Love in Post Traumatic Stress Disorder," *Journal of Contemporary Pyschotherapy*, Vol. 14: No. 1, Spring/Summer, 1984.

20. "Confronting the Addict: When Families Draw the Line," Adams, Jane M., *The Washington Post*, Health Section, July 17, 1990, p. 12–15.

21. Adams, op. cit., p. 13.

22. Haley, Sarah, "The Vietnam Veteran and His Preschool Child, Childrearing as a Delayed Stress in Combat Vets," *Journal of Contemporary Psychotherapy*, Vol. 14:1, Spring/Summer, 1984, pp. 114–121.

CHAPTER SIX

1. Lagone, John, "The War That Has No Ending," *Discovery*, 6, pp. 44–47, 1985; Stein, Jeffrey, "Coming Home," *Progressive*, 45:10, April 1981; p. 10.

2. Wilson, J.P., *Identity, ideology and crises: The Vietnam veteran in transition*, (Pt. 2), Cincinnati, Ohio, Disabled American Veterans, 1978; Egendorf, A.; Kaduschin, C.; Laufer, R.; Rothbart, G.; Sloan, L., *Legacies of Vietnam: Comparative Adjustment of Veterans and their peers: Overview of the Report*, Washington, D.C., U.S. Government Printing Office, 1981; Penk, W., et al., "Interpersonal problem of Vietnam combat vets with symptoms of PTSD," *Journal of Abnormal Psychology*, 1982, Vol. 91:6, 444–450; Penk, W., et al., "Adjustment Differences among male substance abusers varying in degrees of combat experience in Vietnam," *Journal of Consulting and Clinical Psychology*, 1981; 49:3, 426–437; Carroll E., et al., "Vietnam veterans with Post-Traumatic Stress Disorder: Analysis of Marital and Cohabitating Adjustment," *Journal of Abnormal Psychology*, 1985, Vol. 94, No. 3, pp. 329–337.

3. Solursh, Lionel Paul, "Combat Addiction: Overview of Implications in Symptom Maintenance and Treatment Planning," *Journal of Traumatic Stress*, Vol. 2, No. 4, pp. 451–460, 1989.

4. Shay, Jonathan, *Achilles in Vietnam*, Atheneum Press, Maxwell Mac Millan, New York, 1994, p. 91–93

5. Shay, op. cit., p. 91–93.

6. Haley, Sarah, "When the patient reports atrocities," *Archives of General Psychiatry*, 30: 1974, pp. 191–194.

CHAPTER SEVEN

1. Walker, Lenore, *The Battered Woman*, New York, Harper and Row, 1979. Savina, Lydia, *Help for the Battered Woman*, S. Plainfield, New Jersey, Bridge Publishers Inc. (1987).

2. Walker, op. cit.; Savina, op. cit.; Borland, Marie (ed.), *Violence in the Family*, Atlantic Highlands, Manchester University Press, 1976; Gelles, Richard, T., *The Violent Home*, London, Sage Publications, 1972; Martin, Del, *Battered Wives*, New York, Pocket Books, 1976.

3. Walker, op. cit., Savina, op. cit., Borland, op. cit.

4. Strauss, Murray A., Gelles, Richard J., & Steinmetz, Suzanne K., *Behind Closed Doors: Violence in the American Family*, New York, Anchor Books, 1970; Langely, Roger and Levy, Richard, *Wife Beating: The Silent Crisis*, New York, E.P. Dutton, 1977; Strauss, Murray, "Wife Beating: How Common and Why?" *Victimology*, Vol. 2, No. 3–4, 1978, pp. 443–458; Jensvold, Margaret, "The Female Brain: The Intersection of Traumatic Experience and Hormonal Events in the Lives of Women," Presentation, "Trauma, Loss and Dissociation," The Foundation of 21st Century Traumatology, Radisson Plaza, Alexandria, Virginia, Feb., 1995.

5. Strauss, Gelles, and Steinmetz, op. cit., Strauss, op. cit., Walker, op. cit.,

Langely and Levy, op. cit., Gelles, op. cit., Del Martin, op. cit.; Savina, op. cit.; Borland, op. cit.; "Analysis of Official Army Reports of Spouse Abuse: 1982," Army Family Advocacy Program, U.S. Army Community and Family Support Center, Alexandria, V.A. 22331-0521; MacLennan, Beryce, W., U.S. General Accounting Office, "Problems in Estimating the Nature and Extent of Family Violence in the Armed Forces," Research report: National Security Management; National Defense University, Washington, D.C.; April, 1985; *Battered Women, Issues of Public Policy*, Consultation Sponsored by the U.S. Commission on Civil Rights, Jan, 1978, Washington, D.C.

6. *Response*, Jan./Feb., 1984, vol. 7.

7. Stark, Evan and Flitcraft, Anne, "Medical Therapy as Repression: The Case of the Battered Woman," *Health and Medicine*, Summer/Fall, 1979; *Programs for Battered Women: Data Summary Report*, Minnesota Dept. of Corrections, St. Paul, Minn., 1982; Stark Evan; Flitcraft, Anne; Frazier, William, "Medicine and Patriarchal Violence: The Social Construction of a 'Private' Event," *International Journal of Health Services*, 9:3, 1979.

8. Smith, William French, U.S. Attorney General, as cited in "Domestic Violence Fact Sheet," Southern California Coalition on Battered Women, 1986, Santa Monica, CA 90405.

9. Williams, C. M. "The 'veteran system' with a focus on women partners: Theoretical considerations, problems, and treatment strategies," in T. Williams (ed.), *Post-traumatic stress disorders of the Vietnam veteran*, Cincinnati, Ohio, Disabled American Veterans, 1980, pp. 73–124.

10. Ritter, Rick, "Bringing the War Home: Vets Who Have Battered," Vet Center, Fort Wayne, Indiana, 1980; Matsakis, Aphrodite, "The Effects of PTSD on Family Life," Research Project, Department of Veterans Affairs Medical Center, Washington, D.C., 1988.

11. Walker, op. cit.

12. Kaufki, Mark, as cited in "Anger dominates hostile, inappropriate social responses," by John Cruden, *Vet Center Voice*, Vol. 7: 10, 1986, p. 6.

13. Cruden, op. cit.

14. West, L., Turner, Wm.; Dunwoody, E., *Wife Abuse in the Armed Forces*, Center for Women Policy Studies, Washington, D.C., 1981.

15. West, et al., op. cit.; Savina, op. cit.; Arkin, W. and Dobrosfsky, L., "Military Socialization and Masculinity," *Journal of Social Issues*, 34 (1978): 150–167; Horowitz, J. and Solomon, George F., "A Prediction of Delayed Stress Response Syndrome in Vietnam veterans," *Journal of Social Issues*, 31:4, 1975.

16. Ritter, op. cit., p.1.

17. Ritter, op. cit., p. 9.

18. Bliss, Shepherd, "The Military, Masculinity and the Men's Movement" (Response to the film, "Between Men," United Documentary Film, P.O. Box 315, Franklin Lake, N.J., 07417), unpublished paper, available from Vet Center, Fort Wayne, Indiana, p. 6.

19. Savina, op. cit., p. 338.

20. Ritter, Rick and De Pew, Bobbie, "Masculinity and the Vietnam Vet,"

Fort Wayne Vet Center, Fort Wayne, Indiana, p. 5, as cited in Savina, op. cit., p. 338.

21. Ritter and De Pew, op. cit., p. 12, as cited in Savina, op. cit., p. 338.

22. Goodwin, op. cit.; Figley and Sprenkle, op. cit.

CHAPTER EIGHT

1. Sobie, Jane, "The Battered (Military) Wife," *Ladycom* (present name, *Military Lifestyle*), Aug., 1980, p. 43–46, 59–62. Beryce MacLennan, "Problems in estimating the nature and extent of family violence in the Armed Forces," U.S. General Accounting Office, 441 G St., N.W., Washington, D.C. 20543, National Defense University, Washington, D.C., 1985; West, A.; Turner, William; Dunwoody, Ellen, *Wife Abuse in the Armed Forces*, Center for Women Policy Studies, Washington, D.C., 1981; "Analysis of Official Army Reports of Spouse Abuse," Department of the Army, Family Advocacy Program, U.S. Army Community and Family Support Center, Alexandria, Virginia 22331, 1984; Warren, Ava, "An Investigation of United States Army Programs for Men Who Batter," Doctoral Dissertation, Catholic University of America, Washington, D.C., 1982; Orlander, CRD, E. A., "Amends: Abusive Men Exploring New Directions," *Military Chaplain Review*, Spring, 1986, Vol. 15: no. 2, pp. 43–53; Strauss, Murry; Gelles, Richard; Steinmetz, Susanne, *Behind Closed Doors: Violence in the American Family*, Anchor Books, New York, 1970.

2. "Analysis of Official Army Reports of Spouse Abuse," op. cit.

3. West, et al., op. cit.

4. MacLennan, op. cit., p. 8.

5. MacLennan, op. cit., West, et al., op. cit.; Warren, op. cit.

6. Army Family Advocacy Report, op. cit., p. 2.

7. MacLennan, op. cit., pp. 1–2.

8. Sobie, et al.

9. West, et al., op. cit.

10. MacLennan, op. cit., p. 7.

11. West, et al., op. cit.

12. Family advocacy program, Department of Defense Directive (No.: 6400.1), Washington, D.C., May 19, 1981; "Child sexual abuse action plan," Department of the Army, Advocacy Program, HGDA, 1986.

13. West, et al., op. cit.

14. Martin, Del, "Scope of the Problems," in *Battered Women: Issues of Public Policy: A Consultation*, sponsored by the U.S. Commission on Civil Rights, Washington, D.C., Jan, 30–31, 1978, p. 11.

CHAPTER NINE

1. Carter, James, "Alcoholism in Black Vietnam Veterans: Symptoms of Posttraumatic Stress Disorder," *Journal of the National Medical Association*, Vol. 74, No. 7, 1982, p. 655–660; Terry, op. cit.

2. Terry, Wallace, *Bloods: An Oral History of the Vietnam War by Black Veterans*, Ballantine Books, New York, 1984; Carter, op. cit.

3. Terry, op. cit.; Irving M. Allen, "Posttraumatic Stress Disorder Among Vietnam Veterans," *Hospital and Community Psychiatry*, January, 1986, Vol. 37:1, p, 55–60.

4. Allen, op. cit.

5. Goff, S.; Sanders, R.; Smith, C., *Black Soldiers in "The Nam,"* Harrisburg, PA., Stackpole, 1982 as cited in Allen, op. cit., p. 56.

6. Terry, op. cit., p. 39.

7. Allen, op. cit., p. 56.

8. Allen, op. cit., p. 55.

9. Terry, op. cit.

10. Allen, op. cit., p. 57; Baskir, L., Strauss, W., *Chance and Circumstance: the Draft, the War, and the Vietnam Generation*, New York, Vantage, 1981.

11. Allen, op. cit.

12. Allen, op. cit., p. 56.

13. Eisenhart, R., "You Can't Hack it, Little Girl," *Journal of Social Issues*, 30: 13–23, 1975; Allen, op. cit.

14. Allen, op. cit., Carter, op. cit., Parsons, Erwin, "The Intercultural Setting: Encountering Black Vietnam Veterans," in Sonnenberg, S.; Blank, A.; Talbott, J., *The Trauma of War: Stress and Recovery in Vietnam Veterans*, American Psychiatric Press, Inc., Washington, D.C., 1985, pp. 361–387.

15. Parsons, op. cit., Allen, op. cit.

16. Idem.

17. Parsons, op. cit., p. 366.

18. Allen, op. cit., p. 56; Parsons, E.R., as cited in "The gook identification syndrome and post-traumatic stress disorder in Black Vietnam veterans," *The Black Psychiatrists of America Quarterly*, 13:14–18, 1984.

19. Parsons, 1985, op. cit., Allen, et al., Carter, et al.; Yaeger, Thomas; Laufer, R.; Gallops, M., "Some Problems Associated with War Experience in Men of the Vietnam Generation," *Archives of General Psychiatry*, Vol. 41, April, 1984, pp. 327–333.

20. Parsons, 1985, op. cit., Terry, op. cit.

21. Idem.

22. Terry, op. cit., p. xv.

23. Beale, Frances, "Double Jeopardy: To Be Black and Female," in *Sisterhood Is Powerful*, edited by Robin Morgan, Vintage Books, Random House, 1970, pp. 340–353.

24. *Twenty Facts on Women Workers*, Fact Sheet No. 93-2, U.S. Department of Labor, Women's Bureau, June, 1993.

25. *Earnings Differences Between Women and Men: Facts on Working Women*, Fact Sheet No. 93-5, U.S. Department of Labor, Women's Bureau, December, 1993, p. 1–2.

26. The United Nations Decade for Women, 1976–1985, Employment in the U.S., *Report for The World Conference on the United Nations Decade for Women, 1976–1985*, U.S. Department of Labor, Office of the Secretary, Women's Bureau, July, 1985, p.13.

27. Helms, Janet, "Black Women," *Counseling Women III, The Counseling Psychologist*, Vol. 8, No. 1, 1979, pp. 40–41.

28. Beal, op. cit.

29. Helms, op. cit., p. 40; Beale, op. cit.

30. Terry, op. cit.

31. Parsons, op. cit.

32. Halpern, Florence, *Survival: Black/White*, New York, Pergamon Press, 1973, p. 126, as cited in Parsons, 1985, op. cit., p. 375.

33. Parsons, 1985, op. cit., p. 380.

34. Parsons, 1985, op. cit., p. 380.

35. Boyd, Julia, "Whose Reality?" *Aegis*, No. 42, 1987, pp. 40–42.

36. Escobar, Javier I., et al., "Post Traumatic Stress Disorder in Hispanic Vietnam Veterans," *The Journal of Nervous and Mental Disease*, Vol. 171, no. 10., Oct., 1983, pp. 585–596; Pina, G., "Diagnosis and Treatment of Post-Traumatic Stress Disorder in Hispanic Vietnam Veterans," pp. 389–402, in Sonnenberg, et al., *The Stress of War*, op. cit.

37. Harrington, David, "Healing in the Telling, Helping in the Listening," National Hispanic PTSD Conference, Chicago, Ill., Oct. 24, 1986, pp. 22–23.

38. Escobar, et al., op. cit.; Pina, op. cit.

39. *Twenty Facts*, op. cit.

40. Barajas, Lillian, as cited in Sorenson, G., "Educating spouses and partners plays important role," p. 7, *Vet Center Voice*, Vol. 8: No. 8, 1987, pp. 7–8.

41. Sorenson, op. cit., p. 7.

42. Sorenson, op. cit., p. 7.

43. Sorenson, op. cit., p. 8.

CHAPTER TEN

1. Anonymous, "Kid of a Vet," Handout #17, Vet Center, 528 West Berry St., Fort Wayne, Indiana, pp. 1–2.

2. Shovar, G. Phil, "Medical Professionals," pp. 145–159, in *PTSD: A Handbook for Clinicians*, edited by T.M. Williams, Disabled American Veterans, Cincinnati, Ohio, 1987.

3. Shovar, op. cit., p. 145.

4. Shovar, op. cit., p. 146.

5. Allen, Irving, "PTSD Among Black Vietnam Veterans," *Hospital and Community Psychiatry*, Jan., 1986, Vol 31: 1, pp. 55–60.

6. Williams, Candice, and Williams, T. "Family Therapy for Vietnam Veterans," pp. 195–209, in Sonnenberg, S.; Blank, S.; Talbott, J., *The Trauma of War: Stress and Recovery in Vietnam Veterans*, American Psychiatric Press, Washington, D.C., 1985, p. 198.

7. Williams, C. and Williams, T., "Family Therapy for Vietnam Veterans," p. 228, in *PTSD: A Handbook for Clinicians*, op. cit., pp. 221–232.

8. Reppucci, Christine, James, Thomas, "Intervention with Children of Viet-

nam Veterans," Community Outreach to Vietnam Era Returnees (COVER), Charlottesville, Virginia, p. 1.

9. Ibid.

10. Rosenheck, R. and Nathan P., "Secondary traumatization in the children of Vietnam veterans with posttraumatic stress disorder," *Hospital and Community Psychiatry*, 36:5, May, 1985, pp. 538–539.

11. Salom, Ellen, Vet Center North, 5601 N. Broad St., 2nd Floor, Philadelphia, PA., 19141, personal communication, May 15, 1987.

12. Van Der Kolk, Bessel, "Post-Traumatic Stress Disorder," in *Post-Traumatic Stress Disorder: Psychological and Biological Sequelae*, edited by Bessel A. Van Der Kolk, American Psychiatric Press, Inc., Washington, D.C., 1984; Silverman, Joel L., "Post-Traumatic Stress Disorder," *Advanced Psychosomatic Medicine*, Vol. 16, pp. 115–140, 1986; Rosenheck, Robert, "Impact of Posttraumatic Stress Disorder of World War II on the Next Generation," *The Journal of Nervous and Mental Disease*, Vol. 174, No. 6, June, 1986, Serial No. 1243, pp. 319–327; Sigal, John J.,"Effects of Paternal Exposure to Prolonged Stress on the Mental health of the Spouse and Children," *Canadian Psychiatric Association Journal*, Vol. 21, 1976, pp. 169–172; Barocas, Harvey and Barocas, Carol, "Manifestations of Concentration Camp Effects on the Second Generation," *American Journal of Psychiatry*, 130:7, July, 1973, pp. 820–821; Trossman, Bernard, "Adolescent Children of Concentration Camp Survivors," *Canadian Psychiatric Association Journal*, Vol. 13: 2, pp. 121–123; Sigal, John and Rakoff, Vivian, "Concentration Camp Survival, A Pilot Study of Effects on the Second Generation," *Canadian Psychiatric Association Journal*, Vol, 16, 1971, pp. 393–397.

13. Rosenheck, op. cit., 1986, p. 322.

14. Suhr, Melanie, "Trauma in Pediatric Populations," *Advanced Psychosomatic Medicine*, Vol. 16: 1986, pp. 31–47; Paulauska, S.; Ottaviano, C.; Campbell, S.; "Children of Divorce: Some Clinical Issues," Department of Psychology, Clinical Psychology Center, University of Pittsburgh, Pittsburgh, PA, 15260: Symposium presented at the Fifth Annual National Conference on Feminist Psychology, Pittsburgh, PA., March 2–5, 1978.

15. Suhr, op. cit., p. 36.

16. Paulaskas, et al., op. cit.

17. Rosenheck, 1986, op. cit.

18. Paulaskas, et al., op. cit., pp. 8–9.

19. Sigal, op. cit., Trossman, op. cit., Rosenheck, 1986, op. cit., Freyberg, J.T., "Difficulties in Separation and Individuation as experienced by offspring of Nazi Holocaust Survivors," *American Journal of Orthopsychiatry* 50: 87–95, 1980.

20. Conn, Lois, "Self-Mutilation: The Symptoms and Its Management," Treatment Trends: A Newsletter of Taylor Manor Hospital, Ellicott City, Maryland, Vol. 1:1, Sept., 1986, pp. 1–3.

21. Albeck, Joseph, "Intergenerational Consequences of Trauma: Reframing Traps in Treatment Theory—A Second Generation Perspective," p. 109 in *Handbook of Post-Traumatic Therapy*, Mary Beth Williams and John F. Sommer, Jr., Eds., Greenwood Press, Westport, Conn., 1994, pp. 106–128.

22. Albeck, op. cit.

23. Haley, Sarah, "The Vietnam Veteran and His Preschool Child: Childrearing as a Delayed Stress in Combat Vets," *Journal of Contemporary Psychotherapy*, Vol. 14:1, Spring/Summer, 1984, pp. 114–121, p. 117.

24. Haley, op. cit., p. 117.

25. Sigal and Rakoff, op. cit., p. 395.

26. Haley, Sarah, "Treatment Implications of Post-Combat Stress Response Syndrome for Mental Health Professionals," pp. 254–264, in *Stress Disorders Among Vietnam Veterans: Theory, Research and Treatment*, Charles Figley, ed., Brunner-Mazel Publishers, New York, 1978, p. 263.

27. Van der Kolk, B.; Boyd, H.; Krystal, J., et al., "PTSD as a Biologically Based Disorder: Implications of the Animal Model of Inescapable Stress," p. 123–134 in Van Der Kolk, op. cit.

28. Shovar, op. cit., p. 153.

29. Haley, op. cit.

30. Williams T., "Therapeutic Alliance and Goal Setting in the Treatment of the Vietnam Veteran," pp. 25–34 in *Post Traumatic Stress Disorders of the Vietnam Veteran*, Disabled American Veterans, 1980, Cincinnati, Ohio.

31. Harrington, D. and Jay, J., "Beyond the Family: Value Issues in the Treatment of Vietnam Veterans," *Family Therapy Networker*, May/June, Vol. 6:3, 1982, pp. 13–15, pp. 44–45, p. 45.

32. Haley, op. cit., p. 117.

33. Haley, op. cit., p. 115.

34. Glover, H., "Guilt and Aggression in Vietnam Veterans," *The American Journal of Social Psychiatry*, Vol. 1, Winter, 1985, pp. 15–18.

35. Ellen Salom, Vet Center North, 5601 N. Broad St., 2nd Floor, Philadelphia, PA, 19141, Personal Communication, May 15, 1987.

36. Haley, op. cit., p. 116.

37. Sigal, op. cit., p. 171.

38. Rosenheck, 1985, op. cit.; Rosenheck, 1986, op. cit.; Silverman, op. cit.; Sigal, op. cit.; Epstein, H., *Children of the Holocaust*, New York, Putnam's, 1979.

39. Idem.

40. Rosenheck, 1985, op. cit., p. 538.

41. Rosenheck, 1985, op. cit.; Rosenheck, 1986, op. cit.

42. Williams and Williams, 1985, op. cit., p. 198.

43. Salom, op. cit.

44. Trossman, op. cit., Silverman, op. cit., Barocas and Barocas, op. cit.

45. Teguis, Alexandra, Presentation at The Vietnam Experience, conference sponsored by the Springfield, Virginia, Vet Center, Disabled American Veterans, Washington, D.C., April 3–4, 1987.

46. Rosenheck, Robert, "The Role of Family Therapy in Treatment of PTSD," unpublished paper, presented at "Diagnosis and Management of Post-Traumatic Stress Disorders in the V.A.," V.A. Mid-Atlantic Regional Medical Education Center, Baltimore, Md., Aug. 21, 1985.

47. *Battered Women, Issues of Public Policy: A Consultation*, sponsored by the U.S. Commission on Civil Rights, Jan., 1978, Washington, D.C.

48. Strauss, Murray, "Ordinary Violence, Child Abuse, and Wife Beating: What Do They Have in Common," in *The Dark Side of Families*, ed., David Finkelhor, et al., Beverly Hills, CA: Sage Publications, 1983; Walker, Lenore, *The Battered Woman*, Harper and Row, New York, 1979.

49. Savina, Lydia, *Help for the Battered Woman*, Bridge Publishers, South Plainfield, New Jersey, 1987.

50. Walker, op. cit., p. 37.

51. Walker, op. cit.

52. Walker, Lenore, "Children as Victims: Prostitution and Pornography: Children as Victims of Violence," Battered Women's Research Center, Colorado Women's College, Symposium presented at the American Psychological Association. New York, NY, Sept., 1979.

53. Idem.

54. Idem.

55. Highlights of the Official Child Abuse and Neglect Reporting, 1985, American Association for the Protection of Children, American Humane Association, Denver, Colorado.

56. Strauss, Murray; Gelles, Richard; Steinmetz, Suzanne, *Behind Closed Doors: Violence in the American Family*, Garden City, NY, Anchor Press, 1980.

57. Life Magazine, Jan., 1988, p. 121, "Outrage-The Death of an Innocent Exposes a Grim Reality: Child Abuse."

58. Corbett, Ann, "The Alcoholics' Legacy," *The Washington Post*, April 6, 1987, p. C5.

59. Idem.

60. Albeck, J., Armsworth, M., Auerhaln, N., Figley, C., Kudler, H., Lamb, D., Nader, K., Pearlman, L., James, K., and Fitzgerald, "The Intergenerational Effects of Trauma," Audio Tapes 12, 13, 14, and 15, Trauma, Memory and Dissociation, International Society for Traumatic Stress Studies, Annual Convention, Chicago, Illinois, Nov., 1994.

61. Albeck, J., Armsworth, N., et al., op. cit.

62. Rosenheck, 1985, 1986, op. cit.

63. Salom, op. cit.

64. Salom, op. cit.

CHAPTER ELEVEN

1. Reynolds, D.; Kalish, R.; Farberow, N., "A Cross Ethnic Study of Suicide Attitudes and Expectations in the U.S.," p. 36 in Farberow N., (Ed.), *Suicide in Different Cultures*, op. cit., pp. 35–50.

2. Victoroff, V.M., *The Suicidal Patient: Recognition, Intervention, Management*, Medical Economics Books, Oradell, New Jersey, 1983; Berman, A. L., "Suicide," Staff Development Seminar, Counseling Center, University of Maryland, College Park, MD, April 17, 1987.

3. Reynolds, D.K. and Farberow, N.L., *Suicide Inside and Out*, University of California Press, Berkeley, California, 1976.

4. Victoroff, op. cit.

5. Smith, C. W. and Bope, E. T., "The Suicidal Patient: The Primary-Care Physician's Role in Evaluation and Treatment," *Postgraduate Medicine*, Vol. 79: 8, June, 1986, pp. 195–199, 202; Reynolds, op. cit., Reynolds, D.K. and Farberow, N.L., *Endangered Hope—Experiences in Psychiatric Aftercare Facilities*, University of California Press, Berkeley, California, 1977.

6. Carney, C., also Salganik, A. "Teenage Suicide: The Despair, the Doubts, And the Haunting 'Why?'" *The Washington Post*, March 24, 1982; Victoroff, op. cit.

7. Berman, op. cit.

8. Smith and Bope, op. cit.

9. Bhatia, S., Khan, M., Sharma, A., "Suicide Risk: Evaluation and Management," *American Family Physician*, 34 (3), Sept. 1986, pp. 167–174.

10. Bhatia, et al., op. cit.

11. Stein, Jefferey, "Coming Home," *Progressive*, 45:10, April, 1981, p. 10.

12. Wolfgang, Martin E. "Husband-Wife Homicides," *Journal of Social Therapy*, 1956, pp. 263–271.

13. Savina, Lydia, *Help For the Battered Woman*, Bridge Publishing Inc., South Plainfield, NJ, 1987.

14. Wolfgang, Martin E., "Husband-Wife Homicides," *Journal of Social Therapy*, 1956, pp. 263–271.

15. Wolfgang, M. E., "Who Kills Whom?" *Psychology Today*, Vol. 3, 1969, p. 55, 56, 72, 74.

16. Hearst, N.; Newman, T.; Hulley, S., "Delayed Effects of the Military Draft on Mortality," *The New England Journal of Medicine*, Vol. 314:10, March, 1986, pp. 620–624.

17. The Centers for Disease Control Vietnam Experience Study, "Postservice Mortality Among Vietnam Veterans," *Journal of the American Medical Association*, Feb. 13, 1987, Vol. 257, No. 6, pp. 790–795, p. 790.

18. Polluck, Daniel A., "PTSD and the Risk of Suicide," *American Journal of Psychiatry*, Vol. 140 (1), Jan., 1992, pp. 142–143; Farberow, Norman; Han, Kang; Bullman, Tim, "Combat experience and post-service psychosocial status as predictors of suicide in Vietnam veterans," *Journal of Nervous and Mental Disease*, Vol. 178 (1), Jan, 1990, p. 32–37; Polluck, Daniel A,; Rhodes, Philip; Boyle, Coleen; Decoufle, Pierre, et al., "Estimating the Number of Suicides among Vietnam Veterans," *American Journal of Psychiatry*, Vol. 147 (6), June, 1990, pp. 772–776; Hearst, Norman; Newman, Thomas; and Hulley, Stephen B., "Post-discharge mortality from suicide and motor vehicle injuries among Vietnam-era veterans: Response," Vol 317 (8), Aug., 1987, p. 507.

19. Polluck, op. cit., 1992; Polluck, et al., op. cit., 1990; Farberow, et al., op. cit., 1990.

20. Hendlin, Herbert; Haas, Anne, "Suicide and guilt as manifestations of PTSD in Vietnam combat veterans," *American Journal of Psychiatry*, Vol. 148 (5), May 1991, p. 586–591; Hendlin, Herbert, "PTSD and the Risk of Suicide: Reply," *American Journal of Psychiatry*, Vol. 149 (1), Jan., 1991, p. 143.

21. Berman, op. cit., Victoroff, op. cit., Bhatia, et al., op. cit., Smith and Bope, op. cit.

22. Burns, op. cit., Iga, M. and Tatai, K., "Characteristics of Suicides and Attitudes toward Suicide in Japan," pp. 255-280, in *Suicide in Different Cultures*, Edited by Farberow, N.L., University Park Press, Baltimore, MD, 1975.

23. Berman, op. cit., Victoroff, op. cit., Smith and Bope, op. cit., Burns, op. cit., Bhatia, et al., op. cit.

24. Berman, op. cit., Smith and Bope, op. cit., O'Neill, op. cit., Reynolds and Farberow, 1977, op. cit.

25. Berman, op. cit., Burns, op. cit., Schutz, Ben, "The Suicidal Patient," Staff Development Seminar, Department of Veterans Affairs Medical Center, Washington, D.C., May 12, 1982.

26. Berman, op. cit., Schutz, op. cit., "Suicide," op. cit.

27. Schutz, op. cit., "Suicide," op. cit.

28. Burns, op. cit., p. 337.

29. Fisher, Kathy, "Sexual abuse victims suffer into adulthood," *APA Monitor*, Vol. 18:6, June 1987, p. 25.

30. Savina, op. cit.

CHAPTER 12

1. Silverman, Joel, "Post-Traumatic Stress Disorder," *Advanced Psychosomatic Medicine*, Vol. 16: 115-140, 1986; Yost, John, "The Psychopharmacologic Treatment of the Delayed Stress Syndrome in Vietnam Veterans," pp. 125-133, in *Post Traumatic Stress Disorders of the Vietnam Veteran*, edited by Tom Williams, Disabled American Veterans, Cincinnati, Ohio, 1980; Yost, J., "The Psychopharmacologic Management of Post-Traumatic Stress Disorder (PTSD) in Vietnam Veterans and in Civilian Situations," pp. 93-102 in *Post Traumatic Stress Disorders: A Handbook for Clinicians*, Williams, T., ed., Disabled American Veterans, Cincinnati, Ohio, 1987; Lipton, Merrill and Schaffer, W., "Post-Traumatic Stress Disorder in the Older Veteran," *Military Medicine*, Vol. 151: 10, Oct., 1986, pp. 522-524; Falcon, Spencer, "Psychopharmacology and PTSD: Sharing a Perspective," Presentation at Diagnosis and Management of Post Traumatic Stress Disordes in the V.A., Aug. 21-23, 1985, Baltimore, MD.

2. Allen, Irvin, "PTSD Among Black Vietnam Veterans," *Hospital and Community Psychiatry*, Vol. 371, Jan., 1986, pp. 55-60.

3. Falcon, op. cit.; Yost, 1980, 1987, op. cit.

4. Falcon, op. cit.

5. Falcon, op. cit., Yost, 1980, 1987, op. cit., Allen, op. cit.

6. Harrington, David, "Healing in the Telling, Healing in the Listening," Paper presented at the National Hispanic PTSD Conference, Chicago, Illinois, Oct., 1986; Williams, T., "A Preferred Model for Development of Interventions for Pyschological Readjustment of Vietnam Veterans," pp. 37-48 in *Post-Traumatic Stress Disorders of the Vietnam Veteran*, edited by T. Williams, op. cit.; Lifton, R.J., "Advocacy and Corruption in the Healing Profession," pp. 209-230 in *Stress Disorders Among Vietnam Veterans*, C. Figley, ed., Brunner-Mazel Publishers, New York, 1978; Smith, J.R., "Rap Groups and Group Therapy for Vietnam Veterans," pp. 165-191, in Sonnenberg, S.; Blank, A.; Talbott, J., *The Trauma of War: Stress*

and Recovery in Vietnam Veterans, American Psychiatric Press, Washington, D.C., 20005, 1985.

7. Smith, John R., "Rap groups and Group Therapy for Vietnam Veterans," op. cit., p. 182.

8. Smith, John R., "Individual Psychotherapy with Vietnam Veterans," op. cit.; Smith, John R., "Rap Groups and Group Therapy for Vietnam Veterans," op. cit.; Lifton and Schaffer, op. cit.; Lifton, op. cit.

9. Gault., W.B., "Some Remarks on Slaughter," *American Journal of Psychiatry*, 128:4, Oct. 1971, pp. 450–454.

10. Lifton and Schaffer, op. cit., p. 522.

11. Idem.

12. Williams, Tom, "Diagnosis and Treatment of Survivor Guilt," pp. 75–92, in *Post-Traumatic Stress Disorders: A Handbook for Clinicians*, T. Williams, ed., Disabled American Veterans, Cincinnati, Ohio, 1987, p. 86.

13. Haley, op. cit., Lifton, op. cit., Smith, a, b, op. cit., Williams, T., 1987, op. cit.

14. Williams, 1980, op. cit., p. 40.

15. Newman, James, "Differential Diagnosis in Post Traumatic Stress Disorder: Implications for Treatment," pp. 19–34, in *Post Traumatic Stress Disorders: A Handbook for Clinicians*, op. cit.; Harrington, op. cit.; Jelinek, M. J. and Williams, T., "Post Traumatic Stress Disorders and Substance Abuse: Treatment Problems, Strategies and Recommendations," pp. 103–118, in *Post Traumatic Stress Disorders: A Handbook for Clinicians,* op. cit.; Jelinek, M. J. and Williams, T., "PTSD and Substance Abuse in Vietnam Combat Veterans: Treatment Strategies and Recommendations," *Journal of Substance Abuse Treatment*, Vol 1, pp. 87–97, 1984; Schnitt J. and Nocks, J., "Alcoholism Treatment of Vietnam Veterans with PTSD," *Journal of Substance Abuse Treatment*, Vol. 1, 1984, pp. 179–189.

16. Newman, op. cit.; Schnitt, J. and Nocks, J., op. cit.; Jelinek and Williams, 1984, op. cit., Harrington, op. cit.

17. Jelinek and Williams, 1987, op. cit., p. 105.

18. Blank, Arnold, "Irrational Reactions to PTSD and the Vietnam Veteran," pp. 99–124 in *The Trauma of War,* op. cit., Jelinek and Williams, 1987, op. cit.

19. Jelinek and Williams, 1984, 1987, op. cit., Newman, op. cit., Walker, J., Cavenar, J. "Vietnam Veterans: Their Problems Continue," *Journal of Nervous and Mental Disease*, Vol. 170:3, 1982, pp. 174–180.

20. Jelinek and Williams, 1987, op. cit., pp. 105–106.

21. Jelinek and Williams, 1987, op. cit., Newman, op. cit., Walker and Cavenar, op. cit.

22. Langer, R., "PTSD in Former P.O.W.'s," p. 3550 in *Post Traumatic Stress Disorders: A Handbook for Clinicians,* op. cit.; Lifton, op. cit.; Smith, a, b, op. cit.; Lipton and Schaeffer, op. cit.; Ursano, R.J., "Vietnam Era Prisoners of War: Studies of U.S. Air Force Prisoners of War," pp. 339–358 in *The Trauma of War,* op. cit.; van der Kolk, Bessel, ed., *Post-Traumatic Stress Disorder: Psychological and Biological Sequelae*, American Psychiatric Press, Inc., Washington, D.C., 1984.

23. Harrington, op. cit.; Harrington, D., "Group Therapy with Vietnam Veterans," Presentation, The Vietnam Experience, conference sponsored by the Vet

Center, Springfield, Virginia, Disabled American Veterans, April 3–4, 1987, Washington, D.C.; Gerdemen, Eric, Presentation, Vet Center, Silver Spring, MD, Oct., 1982.

24. Gerdemen, op. cit.

25. Menninger, Wm., as cited by Rick Ritter in *DMZ Vet Center*, Vol.3:2, p. 1, Vet Center, Fort Wayne, Indiana, March, 1985.

26. Lipton and Schaeffer, op. cit., Smith, op. cit., Bowman, B., "Early Experiential Environment, Maternal Bonding and the Susceptibility to Post-traumatic Stress Disorder," *Military Medicine*, 151, 10:528, 1986.

27. Williams, Candice and Williams, Tom, "Family Therapy for Vietnam Veterans," pp. 195–209, in Sonnenberg, S.; Blank, A.; Talbott, J., *The Trauma of War: Stress and Recovery*, American Psychiatric Press, Inc., Washington, D.C., 1985, p. 200.

28. Lifton, op. cit.

29. Williams, Tom, "A Preferred Model for the Development of Interventions for Psychological Readjustment of Vietnam Veterans: Group Treatment," p. 41, in Williams, op. cit.

30. Harrington, op. cit.

31. Williams, op. cit.

CHAPTER THIRTEEN

1. President's Commission on Mental Health, "Mental Health of Vietnam era veterans," Volume III, pp. 1321–1328, U.S. Government Printing Office, Washington, D.C., 1978 as cited on p. 100, in Williams, C., "The Veteran System with a Focus on Women Partners: Theoretical Considerations, Problems, and Treatment Strategies," pp. 73–124, in *Post Traumatic Stress Disorders of the Vietnam Veteran*, edited by Williams, T., Disabled American Veterans, Cincinnati, Ohio, 1980.

2. Kulka, Richard, A., et al., *Contractual Report of Findings from the National Vietnam Veterans Readjustment Study*, Research Triangle Institute, Research Triangle Park, North Carolina, 1988; Center for Policy Research, "The adjustment of Vietnam era veterans to civilian life," New York, 1979, as cited in Williams, C., op. cit., p. 100.

3. Williams, C., op. cit., p. 100.

4. Rawlings, Edna I. and Carter, Dianne K., "Divorced Women," pp. 27–28, in *Counseling Women III, The Counseling Psychologist*, vol. 8, no. 1, 1979; Williams, Elizabeth F., *Notes of a Feminist Therapist*, Praeger Publishers, NY, 1976; Miller, Jean Baker, *Towards a New Psychology of Women*, Boston, Beacon, 1976.

5. Williams, E., op. cit., p. ix–x.

6. Savina, Lydia, *Help for the Battered Woman*, Bridge Publishers, South Plainfield, NJ, 1987; Walker, Lenore, *The Battered Woman*, Harper and Row, New York, 1970.

7. Idem.

8. Schechter, Susan, "The Future of the Battered Woman's Movement," p. 22, *Aegis*, Summer/Autumn, 1980, pp. 20–25.

9. "Post-Traumatic Stress Disorder: Implications for Treatment," pp. 19–34 in *Post Traumatic Stress Disorders: A Handbook for Clinicians*, edited by T. Williams, ed., Disabled American Veterans, Cincinnati, Ohio, 45214, 1987, p. 23.

10. Newman, op. cit.

11. *Everything You Always Wanted to Know About Child Abuse and Neglect*, National Center on Child Abuse and Neglect (NCCAN), Department of Health and Human Services, PO Box 1182, Washington, D.C. 1984; Helfer, Ray and Kempe, C. Henry, *Child Abuse and Neglect: The Family and the Community*, Ballinger Publishing Company, Cambridge, MA, 1976; Martin, H. and Kempe, C. Henry, *The Abused Child: A Multidisciplinary Approach to Developmental Issues and Treatment*, Ballinger Publishing Company, Cambridge, MA, 1976; Armstrong, Louise, *Kiss Daddy Goodnight*, Pocket Books, New York, NY, 1978; Rubinelli, Jackie, "Incest: It's Time We Face Reality," *Journal of Psychiatric Nursing and Mental Health Services*, April 1980, Vol. 18: No. 4, pp. 17–18; Cormier, Bruno, et al., "Psychodynamics of father-daughter incest," *Canadian Psychiatric Association Journal*, Vol. 7, No. 5, pp. 203–217, October 1962; Weinberg, S., *Incest Behavior*, Citadel Press, New York, 1963; Savina, op. cit.

12. Idem.

13. Courtois, Christine, *Healing the Incest Wound*, W W. Norton & Co., New York, NY, 1988.

14. Williams, Candice, "The Veteran System with a Focus on Women Partners: Theoretical Considerations, Problems, and Strategies," p. 96, in *Post-traumatic Stress Disorders: A Handbook for Clinicians*, Williams, T., Editor, Disabled American Veterans, Cincinnati, Ohio, 1980, pp. 73–124.

EPILOGUE

1. Richburg, Keith B., "Vietnam is pressing ahead with informal US exchanges," *The Washington Post*, Feb. 11, 1988, p. A54; Downs, F., "Vietnam: My Enemy, My Brother," *The Washington Post*, Outlook, Jan. 31, 1988, D1-D22.

2. Resnick, J.L., "Women and Aging," *The Counseling Psychologist, Counseling Women III*, Vol. 8, No. 1, pp. 29–31.

3. Solomon, Z., Chair, "Integrity vs. Despair: Trauma, Grief, and the Older Adult," Audio Tape 73, International Society for Traumatic Stress Studies, Annual Convention, Chicago, Illinois, 1994.

4. van der Kolk, Bessel, "The compulsion to repeat the trauma," *Psychiatric Clinics of North America*, p. 397, Vol. 12:2, June, 1989, pp. 389–411.

5. van der Kolk, 1989, op. cit.

6. van der Kolk, 1989, op. cit.

Index